Transforming Communications – Studies in Cross-Media Research

Series Editors

Uwe Hasebrink
Hans Bredow Institute for Media Research
University of Hamburg
Germany

Andreas Hepp
ZeMKI, University of Bremen
Germany

We live in times that are characterised by a multiplicity of media: Traditional media like television, radio and newspapers remain important, but have all undergone fundamental change in the wake of digitalization.

New media have been emerging with an increasing speed: Internet platforms, mobile media and the many different software-based communication media we are recently confronted with as 'apps'. This process is experiencing yet another boost from the ongoing and increasingly fast sequence of technological media innovations. In our modern social world, communication processes take place across a variety of media. As a consequence, we can no longer explain the influences of media by focusing on any one single medium, its content and possible effects. In order to explain how media changes are related to transformations in culture and society we have to take into account the cross-media character of communications.

In view of this, the book series 'Transforming Communications' is dedicated to cross-media communication research. It aims to support all kinds of research that are interested in processes of communication taking place across different kinds of media and that subsequently make media's transformative potential accessible. With this profile, the series addresses a wide range of different areas of study: media production, representation and appropriation as well as media technologies and their use, all from a current as well as a a historical perspective. The series 'Transforming Communications' lends itself to different kinds of publication within a wide range of theoretical and methodological backgrounds. The idea is to stimulate academic engagement in cross-media issues by supporting the publication of rigorous scholarly work, text books, and thematically-focused volumes, whether theoretically or empirically oriented.

More information about this series at
http://www.springer.com/series/15351

Olivier Driessens · Göran Bolin
Andreas Hepp · Stig Hjarvard
Editors

Dynamics Of Mediatization

Institutional Change and Everyday Transformations in a Digital Age

palgrave
macmillan

Editors
Olivier Driessens
The Department of Sociology
University of Cambridge
Cambridge, UK

Göran Bolin
Department of Media and Communication Studies
Södertörn University
Huddinge, Sweden

Andreas Hepp
ZeMKI Centre for Media, Communication and Information Research
Universität Bremen
Bremen, Germany

Stig Hjarvard
Department of Media, Cognition, and Communication
University of Copenhagen
Copenhagen, Denmark

Transforming Communications – Studies in Cross-Media Research
ISBN 978-3-319-62982-7 ISBN 978-3-319-62983-4 (eBook)
DOI 10.1007/978-3-319-62983-4

Library of Congress Control Number: 2017947740

Cover Design by Fatima Jamadar

Printed on acid-free paper

This Palgrave Macmillan imprint is published by Springer Nature
The registered company is Springer International Publishing AG
The registered company address is: Gewerbestrasse 11, 6330 Cham, Switzerland

Preface

The idea for this book originates from recent discussions in the European Communication Research and Education Association (ECREA). The Temporary Working Group "Mediatization" was established in 2011 and became a permanent section of ECREA in 2016. It has provided a very important forum for the development of the agenda of mediatization research as well as an organizational framework for workshops and publications. This book is the latest addition to these activities. The editors of this book all served as management members of the working group and section at various points in time, and we would like to thank all of the participants and annual workshop organizers during the last years for their invaluable contribution to the advancement of the study of mediatization.

Cambridge, UK
Huddinge, Sweden
Bremen, Germany
Copenhagen, Denmark,
May 2017

Olivier Driessens
Göran Bolin
Andreas Hepp
Stig Hjarvard

Contents

Editors and Contributors

About the Editors

Olivier Driessens is Lecturer in the Sociology of Media and Culture at the University of Cambridge. His research interests include celebrity, visibility, social change and social theory. He has published in journals such as *Theory and Society*, *International Journal of Cultural Studies* and *Media, Culture and Society.*

Göran Bolin is Professor in Media and Communication Studies at Södertörn University, Stockholm, Sweden. His research focuses on the interrelations between media production and consumption in the wake of digitization. He is the author of *Value and the Media: Cultural Production and Consumption in Digital Markets* (Ashgate, 2011) and most recently *Media Generations: Experience, Identity and Mediatised Social Change* (Routledge, 2016).

Andreas Hepp is Professor of Media and Communication Studies at the ZeMKI (Centre for Media, Communication and Information Research), University of Bremen, Germany. His main research areas are media sociology, mediatization research, datafication of social practices, transnational and transcultural communication, and qualitative methods of media research. His latest book, *The Mediated Construction of Reality* (Polity Press, 2017, with Nick Couldry), is about the change of society through digital media and datafication and was awarded the Theory Prize by the German Communication Association.

Stig Hjarvard is Professor of media studies at the University of Copenhagen. His research interests include news media, media history, media sociology and mediatization theory. He is the author of *The Mediatization of Culture and Society* (Routledge, 2013) and co-editor of *The Dynamics of Mediatized Conflicts* (Peter Lang, 2015).

Contributors

Marian T. Adolf is Professor of Media Culture at Zeppelin University in Friedrichshafen, Germany. His work focuses on the sociology of media and communication, the sociology of knowledge and media culture. Recent publications include *Knowledge: Is Knowledge Power?* (Routledge, 2017, with Nico Stehr).

Magnus Andersson is associate professor in Media and Communication Studies at Lund University (Sweden). His research takes its point of departure in the relationships between mediation, everyday life, spatiality and mobility. He has published in journals such as the *European Journal of Cultural Studies*, *Crossings: Journal of Migration and Culture* and *Culture Unbound*.

Barbara Brodzińska-Mirowska is an assistant professor in the Department of Journalism and Social Communication at Nicolaus Copernicus University in Toruń (Poland). Her scientific interests are focused on political communication, professionalization of this processes in particular, political public relations, interelectoral communication and mediatization of politics. She is the author and co-author of books and articles related to party politics communication activities, professionalization of political communication and new media.

Christa Lykke Christensen is Associate Professor in Film & Media Studies at the University of Copenhagen. Her research interests include fashion and the media, lifestyle media, mediated health expertise, ageing and older people's media use, and children's television programming.

Magnus Fredriksson is Associate Professor at the University of Gothenburg. His research focuses on strategic communication in general and strategic communication in public sector organizations in particular. His work has been published in journals such as the *European Journal* *of Communication*, *International Journal of Strategic Communication*, *Organization Studies*, *Public Administration* and *Public Relations Inquiry*.

Ruth Garland received her Ph.D. from the London School of Economics in 2017 and lectures at Brunel University, London. She spent more than 25 years in public sector strategic communications, mostly at the BBC. She has published in journals such as *Public Relations Inquiry* and *Media, Culture & Society*.

Arno van der Hoeven is Assistant Professor in the Department of Media and Communication, Erasmus University Rotterdam, The Netherlands. His main research interests include popular music, cultural heritage, and local identity. Next to his teaching and research activities, Arno is chair of the board of the heritage organization DIG IT UP.

Nete Nørgaard Kristensen is Associate Professor in Media Studies at the University of Copenhagen, Denmark. Her research areas include arts, cultural and lifestyle journalism; political communication; and media, war and conflict. She has published in journals such as *Communication, Culture & Critique*; *Digital Journalism*; *Journalism: Theory, Practice & Criticism*; *Journalism Practice*; *Media, War & Conflict*; *Northern Lights* and *Nordicom Review*.

James Miller is professor of communications in the School of Cognitive Science at Hampshire College (Amherst, MA, USA). His recent research focuses on the tendency of emerging new media to be embedded in built environments, as in the internet of things. A member of the Five College Architectural Studies program, he has been a visiting professor at the MIT Media Lab.

Christian Hviid Mortensen is a media historian and curator of media heritage at the Media Museum in Odense, Denmark. His research interest sits at the intersection of media studies, popular culture, memory studies, museology and the history of technology. He has curated diverse exhibitions on video games, comic books, radio sound and reality TV. Christian sits on the editorial board of MedieKultur.

Ximena Orchard received her Ph.D. from the University of Sheffield. She worked as a journalist and is now Lecturer in Political Communication and Research Methods. Her research interests include the relationship between media and policymaking, public communication and mediatization studies.

Josef Pallas is Professor at Uppsala University (Sweden). His research focuses on the expansion, dynamics and consequences of mediatization in a context of governance of contemporary organizations. His work has been published in journals such as the *European Journal of Communication*; *International Journal of Strategic Communication*; *Media, Culture & Society*; *Organization Studies*; *Public Administration* and *Public Relations Review*.

Zrinjka Peruško is Professor in the Sociology of Media and Communication at the University of Zagreb (Croatia). Her research interests include comparative research of media systems, audience dynamics, media cultures and democratic media reform in Central and Eastern Europe. She has published in journals such as the *International Journal of Communication*; *View: Journal of European Television, History and Culture*; *East European Politics and Societies* and *Javnost—The Public*.

Tobias Pontara is Associate Professor in Musicology at the University of Gothenburg (Sweden). His research interests lie chiefly in film music, music philosophy and the cultural study of music. He has published in journals such as *Philosophical Studies*, *Nineteenth-Century Music*, *Music and the Moving Image* and the *International Review of the Aesthetics and Sociology of Music*.

Kim Christian Schrøder is Professor of Communication at the Department of Communication and Arts, Roskilde University, Denmark. His books include *Audience Transformations: Shifting Audience Positions in Late Modernity* (2014, co-edited) and *Researching Audiences* (2003, co-authored). His recent work explores ways of mapping news consumption from the perspective of methodological pluralism.

Ulrik Volgsten is professor of Musicology at Örebro University (Sweden). His research is concerned with musical communication in different media. In addition to the conceptual history of Western music (composer, work, listener), an important focus of his research has been on the role of affect attunement for the musical experience.

Łukasz Wojtkowski is Assistant Professor in the Department of Journalism and Social Communication of Nicolaus Copernicus

University in Toruń. He is the author of two books on mediatization of politics and culture and a dozen or so articles and book chapters. His research interests include mediatization of culture and society, critical theory, and digital culture.

List of Figures

List of Tables

CHAPTER 1

Introduction: Situating Dynamics of Mediatization

Olivier Driessens and Stig Hjarvard

1.1 Purpose of the Volume

This volume aims to take an important step in the further consolidation of mediatization research. Whereas previous research has provided ample evidence of how societies and cultures have changed in relation to media-communicative changes, here the focus is less on these *outcomes* of change and more on the concrete *dynamics* of change. How is mediatization actually taking place? Which dynamics can be observed that produce but, importantly, also prevent or neutralize media-related changes in social practices and institutions?

One of the first efforts to refine our understanding of mediatization processes through specific dynamics has been Schulz's (2004) article on mediatization as an analytical concept. He distinguished between extension, substitution, amalgamation and accommodation. Media allow humans to extend their communication and interaction in time and space

O. Driessens (✉)
University of Cambridge, Cambridge, UK
e-mail: od252@cam.ac.uk

S. Hjarvard
University of Copenhagen, Copenhagen, Denmark
e-mail: stig@hum.ku.dk

O. Driessens et al. (eds.), *Dynamics Of Mediatization*,
Transforming Communications – Studies in Cross-Media Research,
DOI 10.1007/978-3-319-62983-4_1

and also extend their semiotic palette of expression. Social practices may also be substituted by mediated practices, such as when online banking replaces face-to-face encounters between customers and employees in the bank around the corner. Amalgamation implies that mediated forms of interactions blend seamlessly with non-mediated forms, such as when children's play integrates narratives of popular media (e.g. *Star Wars*) into physical forms of play. Finally, accommodation denotes the reciprocal adjustments of institutional and organizational structures and norms between various social domains; political parties' accommodation to the norms and structures of the news media is an obvious case in point.

These four general dynamics provide a first and general understanding of processes of mediatization. Although they are important, they do not suffice to understand the specific ways in which media are involved in cultural and social change and how they come to condition human communication. Media-related dynamics of change are not isolated mechanisms, but socially and culturally contextualized and interactional. Therefore, a central concern of this volume is how exactly mediatization and its dynamics are related to other (meta-)processes such as commercialization, politicization or globalization and—as some authors in this volume argue—also "musicalization" (Pontara and Volgsten, Chap. 12) or even "audiencization" (Schrøder, Chap. 5). Granted, explaining the interrelationships between such meta-processes is a major task that cannot be completed in a single volume, but we trust that the different chapters in this book will encourage scholars to continue to pursue this agenda in future research. This research agenda is important to prevent attributing observed changes only or mainly to media, which would make "mediatization" a container concept of little analytical value, something several scholars (Deacon and Stanyer 2014; Lunt and Livingstone 2016) have already alluded to.

Added to our non–media-centric approach, we greatly value an open research agenda in terms of media, technologies and communications that are relevant for mediatization studies. This explains the inclusion of chapters on music (Pontara and Volgsten, Chap. 12) and the automobile (Miller, Chap. 10), for example. Also, questions on data and datafication are at the core of mediatization studies and scholars have begun to address these questions in terms of "deep mediatization" (Couldry and Hepp 2017). Several chapters in this volume also speak to this topic. As such, we argue that scholars who are studying processes such as datafication can greatly benefit from a mediatization framework. It is vital to understand these processes from a long-term perspective and to acknowledge their interrelationships with media-related changes that pre-date the advent of networked communication and digital data.

This is also why we want to be very explicit about our reasons for studying institutional change and everyday transformations *in a digital age*, as the title of this volume indicates. To be clear, this is not to brush off the dust of a sub-discipline that was born before the digital became a hot research topic. The digital age is included as a signifier of the temporal context of our writing and analysis. This means that this volume and its chapters acknowledge and analyse the (sometimes fundamental) role of digital media and data in social change. Here, we must stress that our focus is not on the mere increased availability of digital data or the large-scale use of digital media and platforms, but crucially on the *social and cultural changes* that the digital engenders in our societies, institutions, practices and life worlds. This is also what distinguishes mediatization studies from other (sub)disciplines. The consequences of digitization, not the technical process of digitization itself, are important because "the digital" allows for new and intensified forms of integration of media into culture and society.

Equally so, situating our work in the digital age does not imply that the digital is taken as the single or dominant force of social change. This would be overly simplistic "epochalist thinking" (Savage 2009). A premise of the chapters in this volume is the continued relevance of "pre-digital" media and communications. Some chapters then look at these forms of media and communication in interrelation with the digital; others do so less or not at all. This combined approach that integrates dynamics related to different kinds of media, technologies, platforms and modes of communication is most fruitful for presenting a holistic analysis of media-related social change.

1.2 Organization of the Volume

How this translates into the specific work included in this volume will be explained in the next paragraphs. Overall, the chapters have been structured in three parts: the first part presents chapters that reflect on mediatization research and theories, the second part includes chapters that focus on dynamics of mediatization in politics and organizations, and the third part focuses on dynamics in everyday life and culture. Rather than summarizing the chapters in a chronological order now, we have chosen to organize our presentation of the volume by situating the chapters on a vertical and horizontal axis. This improves our ability to draw out links between the chapters and to explain where they can be situated on the research agenda of mediatization studies. The vertical axis includes dimensions such as the level of analysis, from macro to micro, or top-down versus bottom-up dynamics. The horizontal axis orients mediatization research in terms of the field(s) of analysis, the geographical location or the theoretical approach.

1.2.1 Vertical Axis

The volume combines a considerable number of chapters that present a wider reflection and meta-narrative on mediatization studies with chapters that conduct empirical analyses of particular areas. On the one hand, the reflexive pieces either focus on mediatization studies as a sub-discipline or zoom in to present the state of affairs and future directions of a specific field of analysis. An example of the former is Marian Adolf's chapter (Chap. 2) in which he disentangles the theoretical approaches within mediatization studies and connects these with related theories such as medium theory. Magnus Andersson's chapter "Unfolding mediatization" (Chap. 3) argues along similar lines and aims to stipulate possibilities for future mediatization research. Together, these chapters also address Ekström et al.'s (2016) call to mediatization scholars to reconnect with previous theories of media-related social change—a journey that Stefanie Averbeck-Lietz (2014) has also embarked on. An example of reflections on the state of affairs of particular areas is Barbara Brodzińska-Mirowska and Lukasz Wojtkowski's chapter on the mediatization of politics (Chap. 7). As a way to integrate various dimensions of media's influence on politics, they suggest a multi-dimensional model that embraces three essential levels: macro, meso and micro.

On the other hand, next to the more reflexive contributions, several chapters choose a grounded approach to advance empirical mediatization research. Ruth Garland, for example, draws on extensive interview data with press officers working for the British government, to understand the dynamics between accepting and resisting media influences in their institutions and practices (Chap. 8). Also based on interview data, with both politicians and journalists, Ximena Orchard studies the conception of media autonomy in Chile (Chap. 9). A final example is Nete Nørgaard Kristensen and Christa Lykke Christensen's qualitative study of Danish fashion blogs that demonstrates how mediatization can be linked with personalization and individualization (Chap. 11).

Another dimension of the vertical axis is the level at which the studies can be situated. A few chapters focus particularly on the societal level. A foremost example here is Zrinjka Peruško's chapter, which aims to marry mediatization theory with media systems analysis to explain the contextual specificity of social change (Chap. 4). Also, the contribution on musicalization as a process next to (and in interrelation with) mediatization by Tobias Pontara and Ulrik Volgsten (Chap. 12) can be categorized as a macro-level analysis. Other chapters focus more on the organizational level. Garland's and Orchard's above-mentioned chapters on politics are cases of this, but also the study by Magnus Frederiksson and Josef Pallas on the way that organizations translate media formats and logics into everyday practices can be situated here (Chap. 6). Finally, a few chapters point their analytical lens primarily at the micro level. The aforementioned chapter on fashion blogs studies Danish bloggers (Chap. 11), whereas Kim Christian Schrøder (Chap. 5) aims to bring audiences more prominently into the equation of mediatization studies. This argument is in some ways similar to Witschge's (2014) plea to include audiences next to politicians and journalists in analyses on the mediatization of politics.

Interestingly, Schrøder presents his piece on the role of audiences and their logics in media-related social change also as a call for the wider recognition of bottom-up dynamics in mediatization studies. Brodzińska-Mirowska and Wojtkowski, who were mentioned above already, also identify this as one particular way forward for studies on the mediatization of politics. In other words, agency and social action need to be brought more into the limelight, such as through the study of particular agents' social and media-related practices (e.g. Driessens et al. 2010; Lövheim 2011).

1.2.2 Horizontal Axis

Several references to chapters on the mediatization of politics have already been mentioned and together with the mediatization of religion (Hjarvard 2016; Knoblauch 2014; Lövheim 2011) these have easily been the most popular fields of analysis for mediatization scholars. Therefore, we are pleased that several chapters in this volume examine areas that have previously gained much less or even hardly any attention. The chapters on fashion, music and (space and) the automobile have been referred to already, but there are also important contributions on museums and cultural heritage. In the first of these, Christian Hviid (Chap. 13) points out that the intertwining of media and museums allows for new ways of engaging with history and memory. Arno van der Hoeven (Chap. 14) demonstrates how mediatization may accentuate already-existing trends towards inclusiveness and participation in articulating urban cultural heritage allowing local users to actively contribute to the construction of cultural heritage.

Another dimension on the horizontal axis is the spatial context of the studies and its authors. Although traditionally mediatization studies has been dominated by Nordic and German scholars, followed by scholars in the UK, for several years we have been able to observe a wider engagement with this body of work around the world. This is also reflected in this volume, which has contributions from Poland (Brodzińska-Mirowska and Wojtkowski), Croatia (Peruško), the US (Miller) and Chile (Orchard). Given recent conferences on mediatization in Latin America and Asia, there are hopeful signs that eventually we might de-Westernize mediatization studies and have a global conversation on social change related to media and communicative change.

Next, we conceive of this volume as yet another step in the further rapprochement of the different strands within mediatization research (see also Couldry and Hepp 2013). These are often labelled the institutionalist perspective, the socio-cultural perspective and the materialist perspective (Lundby 2014; Finnemann 2011). Each of these perspectives involves an emphasis on specific levels of analysis (macro, meso or micro), a particular understanding of the relationship between structure and agency, or different views on the temporality of change. We argue that, notwithstanding some insurmountable differences, what these different perspectives have in common is much greater than what divides them. To some extent, we can think of the three perspectives more as a reflection of the different origins of various researchers, of their intellectual trajectory so to speak. Therefore, we should appreciate the strengths and complementarity of the different approaches while continuing to work on their improvements, as has also been suggested in Chap. 2 by Adolf and Chap. 3 by Andersson. The complementarity and fluidity of approaches are also reflected in this volume. Some articles that focus on organizations blend the institutionalist with the socio-cultural perspective (e.g. Chap. 6 by Fredriksson and Pallas and Chap. 5 by Kim Schrøder), whereas chapters on everyday life (the natural territory of the socio-cultural perspective) also strongly focus on the role of institutions, such as museums and archival bodies (Hviid, Chap. 13; van der Hoeven, Chap. 14), or study changes of institutions (such as fashion) through some agents' actions (Nørgaard Kristensen and Lykke Christensen, Chap. 11).

To conclude, the ambition of mediatization research is to build a comprehensive and holistic understanding of the role of media in cultural and social change. This comprises not only different levels of analysis (macro, meso and micro) and structural and agency perspectives but also a contextualized and nuanced understanding of media-related change. Crucially, this means acknowledgement of the mutual interdependence of media and societies, appreciation of the contextual differences of how mediatization can potentially be realized—in terms of geography and social fields, for example—and attention not only for these outcomes of change but also for its dynamics and underlying causes and how these can be interacting. Starting from these premises, this volume has the ambition to contribute especially to a better understanding of the latter and should be seen as a call not only for media scholars but also for other social scientists to continue the study of media-related social change in all its complexity.

References

Averbeck-Lietz, Stefanie. 2014. Understanding mediatization in "First modernity": Sociological classics and their perspectives on mediated and mediatized societies. In *Mediatization of communication: Handbook of communication science*, ed. Knut Lundby, 109–130. Boston: de Gruyter Mouton.

Couldry, Nick, and Andreas Hepp. 2013. Conceptualizing mediatization: Contexts, traditions, arguments. *Communication Theory* 23 (3): 191–202.

Couldry, Nick, and Andreas Hepp. 2017. *The mediated construction of reality*. Cambridge: Polity.

Deacon, David, and James Stanyer. 2014. Mediatization: Key concept or conceptual bandwagon? *Media, Culture and Society* 36 (7): 1032–1044.

Driessens, Olivier, Karin Raeymaeckers, Hans Verstraeten, and Sarah Vandenbussche. 2010. Personalization according to politicians: A practice theoretical analysis of mediatization. *Communications* 35 (3): 309–326.

Ekström, Mats, Johan Fornäs, André Jansson, and Anne Jerslev. 2016. Three tasks for mediatization research: Contributions to an open agenda. *Media, Culture and Society* 38 (7): 1090–1108.

Finnemann, Niels O. 2011. Mediatization theory and digital media. *Communications: The European Journal of Communication Research* 36 (1): 67–89.
Hjarvard, Stig. 2016. Mediatization and the changing authority of religion. *Media, Culture and Society* 38 (1): 8–17.
Knoblauch, Hubert. 2014. Benedict in Berlin: The mediatization of religion. In *Mediatized worlds: Culture and society in a media age*, ed. Andreas Hepp, and Friedrich Krotz, 143–158. Basingstoke: Palgrave.
Lövheim, Mia. 2011. Mediatisation of religion: A critical appraisal. *Culture and Religion* 12 (2): 153–166.
Lundby, Knut. 2014. Mediatization of communication. In *Mediatization of communication*, ed. Knut Lundby, 3–35. Berlin: de Gruyter.
Lunt, Peter, and Sonia Livingstone. 2016. Is 'mediatization' the new paradigm for our field? A commentary on Deacon and Stanyer (2014, 2015) and Hepp, Hjarvard and Lundby (2015). *Media, Culture and Society* 38 (3): 462–470.
Savage, Mike. 2009. Against epochalism: An analysis of conceptions of change in British sociology. *Cultural Sociology* 3 (2): 217–238.
Schulz, Winfried. 2004. Reconstructing mediatization as an analytical concept. *European Journal of Communication* 19 (1): 87–101.
Witschge, Tamara. 2014. Passive accomplice or active disruptor: The role of audiences in the mediatization of politics. *Journalism Practice* 8 (3): 342–356.

PART I

Rethinking the Dynamics of Mediatization

CHAPTER 2

The Identity of Mediatization: Theorizing a Dynamic Field

Marian T. Adolf

2.1 Introduction

Mediatization research arguably has become one of the most vibrant fields of international media and communication research. Drawing on a wide range of theoretical resources and phenomenal domains, it attracts scholars from a variety of scholarly backgrounds and disciplinary traditions. In the course of its development, we witness mounting debates over orientations and concepts and an increase in self-reflection about theoretical foundations and analytical perspectives. Against this background, this contribution seeks to discuss the self-understanding of mediatization studies as it navigates between congruity and disparity. Based on a review of mediatization literature and related fields such as media sociology as well as a discussion of the criticisms that have been brought to its doorstep, I analyse the dynamics of mediatization with regard to the field's quest for conceptual and theoretical identity.

I begin by (2.2) assembling a number of prevalent self-descriptions of mediatization as pertaining to the dynamics of media and social change

M.T. Adolf (✉)
Zeppelin University, Friedrichshafen, Germany
e-mail: marian.adolf@zu.de

O. Driessens et al. (eds.), *Dynamics Of Mediatization*,
Transforming Communications – Studies in Cross-Media Research,
DOI 10.1007/978-3-319-62983-4_2

and discuss earlier attempts at mapping and defining the scope, aims and approaches to mediatization. The following section (2.3) argues that subordinate social-theoretical differences are used in categorizing mediatization approaches that are rather indicative of programmatic struggles over distinction instead of substantial differences. Instead, I suggest that much graver issues lie with (2.4) divergent definitions of the media which spawn (2.5) unresolved discrepancies on an epistemological level. A suggestion for a more (2.6) differentiated approach to understanding the media is made before I (2.7) conclude by proposing an alternative way to map and systematize the burgeoning field of mediatization research.

2.2 Mediatization: Concepts, Critique and Debates

The least common denominator of mediatization research might be found in Nick Couldry and Andreas Hepp's assertion that mediatization "does not refer to a single theory but to a more general approach within media and communications research" (Couldry and Hepp 2013: 197). It provides media and communication scholars with a concept for "research on the wider 'consequences' of mediated communications on our present cultures and societies" which redirects research "away from models of theorizing influence as an 'effect' of media texts to a more extensive understanding of 'mediatization' as a way of capturing the wider consequences of media's embedding in everyday life" (Couldry and Hepp 2013: 195).

As such, mediatization as a term is indicative both of a reorientation of the field of media and communication studies (prompting some to fear a looming paradigm shift; see Meyen 2014: 468f.) as well as of an overall increase in the importance of the role of the media for contemporary societies. There is a kinship with other attempts to capture the rise to societal prominence of the media and mediated communication, such as "Media Culture" (Adolf 2012; Kellner 1995), "Media Society" (Saxer 2012) or "Media Life" (Deuze 2014), to name just a few. Mediatization reflects the increasing interest in explicating the interdependence of media change and social change and represents the latest attempt of communication research to investigate the larger, socio-structural as well as socio-cultural consequences of the development of societal communication in conjunction with the techno-material characteristics (affordances) of the media. Still, inaugurating mediatization as a "category to describe change" (Couldry and Hepp 2013: 197) or an "observational platform for cultural and social change" (Gentzel 2015: 182) sets a wide scope indeed. No wonder that we find a great variety of questions, approaches and research problems subsumed under the same designation.

This in turn has initiated a number of attempts to produce a "map" of mediatization research efforts. Some time ago, Friedrich Krotz (2009: 29) separated a "functionalist" from a "cultural or social perspective". In 2013, Couldry and Hepp (2013: 196) had moved on to distinguish an "institutionalist" from a "social-constructivist" tradition. And in their reply to Deacon and Stanyer (2014), Hepp et al. (2015) differentiate between an "institutional", a "cultural" and a "material" perspective (see also Lundby 2014b): The *institutional approach* looks at "transforming patterns between various institutions in society, the media themselves becoming a semi-independent institution" (Hepp et al. 2015: 6). The *cultural approach* "is concerned with the inner workings of the communication processes of all types of media" (2015: 6), or in the words of Krotz "how people construct the social and cultural world" (Krotz 2009: 24f.). And Lundby (2014b: 11) describes the *material concept* as a "perspective that underlines that media are always materialized".

Beside this recurring sub-division of perspectives, there are other attempts to order the field: Ampuja et al. (2014) have suggested a secondary classification that differentiates a "strong form" of mediatization ascribed to researchers such as David Altheide, Stig Hjarvard, Jesper Strömbäck, Winfried Schulz and others that pursue an institutionalist approach or hail from the field of political communication and a "weak form" of mediatization which subsumes proponents that have been known to criticize these "institutionalists" as too media-centric (e.g. Andreas Hepp, Friedrich Krotz or Nick Couldry). Alternatively, Marcinkowski and Steiner (2009: 21) introduce a "push-and-pull model" of medialization, which situates the specific preconditions of mediatization within "mediatized systems" rather than with the media as such. And Klaus Bruhn Jensen (2013) has argued that the most important difference in contemporary mediatization research is whether the term is used to denote a "sensitizing" or "definitive" concept (in the sense of Blumer 1954) for exploring the media's societal significance.

This development has prompted "calls to order" from both within and outside the field of mediatization research: Winfried Schulz, whose four-dimension matrix is one of the most commonly cited models of mediatization processes (Schulz 2004), recently posed the tongue-in-cheek question that if mediatization was the answer, “What was the question again?” (Schulz 2013). And political scientists Deacon and Stanyer’s (2014: 8f.) criticism sparked a somewhat heated debate in *Media, Culture & Society* about the usefulness of the mediatization concept, which they see as a “universal concept of no difference”; and they conclude: “In its most common application, the term is more a calling card than a concept” (2015: 656).

Such critiques seem expectable given mediatization’s conceptual multiplicity and broad empirical application (see, for example, the contributions in Krotz and Hepp 2012). The many approaches and nuances certainly raise the question to *what* these different perspectivations offer alternative approaches *to*—that is, what exactly mediatization as a research concept tries to capture and analyse. It is regularly used ambiguously, referring to the *state* of being “mediatized” or to the *process* of mediatization or both. Also, the object(s) as well as the mechanism(s) of mediatization often are mentioned only in passing. Suggestions as to the *explanandum* of mediatization research include “communication”, “communicative practices”, “constructions of reality”, “modernity”, “society and culture” and (mediatized) “worlds”. This list could be extended (see Lundby 2014c). Further ambiguity ensues with regard to diverging timelines mediatization is concerned with (Lundby 2014b, Livingstone and Lunt 2014): Whereas Friedrich Krotz devises mediatization as a historical *meta-process* akin to individualization or globalization, some see it as a more recent phenomenon and yet others apply their analysis predominantly to phenomena of the digital transformation in the wake of internet-based platforms.[1]

These debates are as noteworthy for a number of reasons: Most importantly, they represent the attempt of coming to terms with the ground rules of a common research endeavour based on shared perceptions of media and social change. As such, they provide the opportunity to observe a research field “in the making” and to track decisive processes of defining, delimiting and prioritizing relevant premises and questions. Pertaining to the subject of mediatization research more directly, the variety of, and disputes over, concepts are also a struggle over the identity of mediatization: how do the various perspectives relate to each other, how wide may mediatization be defined, where do we draw the line, and who gets to decide? How may the diversity of perspectives within such a young field be explained, and what substantiates the differences? And more practically: what consequences do possible choices on a conceptual plane imply for empirical research efforts? Self-descriptions of any academic research field tend to become implicit and subsequently truncate what is possible and legitimate within an intellectual endeavour. Generally, the importance of the theoretical setup of any research effort is of utmost significance: one's choice of theory—or what Jensen (2013) calls, more precisely, conceptions—prefigures what might be found: "The overarching explanatory approaches identify relevant parameters and constitute the terminological space for formulating useful research questions as well as the design of fertile research programs" (Carrier 2006: 56–57). That is why the debate over the *identity* of mediatization research matters.

Addressing the state of affairs, Knut Lundby, in his introduction to the massive volume on *Mediatization of Communication* (2014b), summarizes the discussion over appropriate notions of mediatization within a matrix that compares conceptual differences by looking at three contentious aspects: *time*, *technology* and *theoretical foundation*. When does mediatization as a process set in? What role does the materiality of media play in these accounts of social and cultural change? And which theoretical grounding is used in order to conceptualize the process? Using Lundby's matrix as a guide, I subsequently discuss what I perceive as the two most fundamental problems of theorizing mediatization. *Time*, *technology* and *theory* may vary not only because of carefully considered choices on a theoretical plane, but because of issues rarely explicated. One is situated on a social-theoretical level and concerned with the proper analytical foundation of the endeavour to research mediatization processes (Sect. 2.3). The other is located on what might be designated as a medium-theoretical level: this is the site of more or less implicit disputes about what constitutes a medium or the media (Sect. 2.4).

2.3 The Tale of the Two Traditions: Institutionalist Versus Constructivist Perspectives

I first turn to the most frequent and prominent differentiation: the one between (1) an "institutionalist" and (2) a "social-constructivist" variant of mediatization research. Couldry and Hepp (2013: 196) describe the *institutional approach* as follows:

> Coming mainly from journalism studies and political communication, the institutionalist tradition understood media more or less as an independent social institution with its own sets of rules [...]. Mediatization here refers to the adaptation of different social fields or systems (for example, politics or religion) to these institutionalized rules. The latter are mainly described as a 'media logic' (Altheide and Snow 1979): that is, in the widest sense of the word, institutionalized formats and forms of staging.

Contrasting this variant (which in the German language debate is often associated with the term *Medialisierung*), they go on to describe what they denote as a *social-constructivist* approach, which

> highlights the role of various media as part of the process of the communicative construction of social and cultural reality (Berger and Luckmann 1991 [1966]). [...] The term 'mediatization' here is designed to capture both how the communicative construction of reality is manifested within certain media processes and how, in turn, specific features of certain media have a contextualized 'consequence' for the overall process whereby sociocultural reality is constructed in and through communication (Couldry and Hepp 2013: 196).

There are at least two points of contention with this differentiation. First, while all typologies rely on a certain degree of generalization, the categories employed here are all too imprecise. What is bundled together are approaches that are inherently heterogeneous, insinuating congruence where there is none to be found. Second, the distinction used in denoting the two traditions inflates the factual differences between the so-called "institutionalist" and "constructivist" accounts. In fact, it might be argued that the differentiation is mostly hinged on the controversial use of the term *logic*, which dates back to pioneering work by David L. Altheide and Robert Snow (1979).

By focusing too narrowly on a critique of the allegedly static term "logic", this distinction covers over the fact that in Altheide's and other "institutional" approaches too, the central claim is that the media interfere with the way social reality is created by way of communication. To quote Altheide and Snow, analysing media logic is about its "role [...] in the construction and legitimation of social order" (1979: 245). Altheide and Snow (1979) certainly never meant to devise "media logic" as a deterministic concept. On the contrary, the focus of their analysis rests on journalistic practices and routines and is grounded in an empirical observation of these patterns of the production of news. Media logic refers to a *social* logic that can be shown to prevail in media production in the field of "mass communication". "Our aim was to set forth the parts of a 'logic in use' as a kind of 'socio-logic' that was reflexive of the communication order, including changing and emergent technologies, and the ways in which social life—through social interaction and routines—was being transformed. Our first published statement, *Media Logic*, focused on interaction, routines, and social institutions".[2]

If you tweak the original metaphor of "logic" just slightly and substitute for it more traditional terms such as "habitual practices", "cultural patterns", "institutional rules", "systems rationality", or even "moulding force", then the critique of the allegedly monolithic concept seems less compelling. Here, the semantics invoked hide more than they reveal, since all mediatization approaches necessarily rely on concepts that capture specific, repetitive patterns of mediated social action in order to delineate that which unites certain recurring practices. After all, we are dealing with supra-individual occurrences (communication) and thus with the question of how to explain intersubjective co-orientation that is manifested in observable patterns. As Berger and Luckmann in their classic coining of the term *institution* state: "The typifications of habitualized actions that constitute institutions are always shared ones. [...] Institutionalization occurs whenever there is a reciprocal typification of habitualized actions by types of actors" (Berger and Luckmann (1991 [1966]: 72).

Since what is an institution if not a set of social roles and procedures that, often highly professionalized, outputs social facts that appear to be "natural" rather than of human creation? In other words, if the dependent variable is "social reality", then the dominant "media logic" of a medium (or a communication genre, or a media system) plays an active role in establishing what is supposed to be factual and important and to be interpreted by the audience (in certain ways and not others), *just as much* as in "social constructivist" or "culturalist" approaches. *Any* kind of social constructivism is ultimately based on the premise that social reality is the product of social practices and meanings that become consequential and orient further social action. It is exactly this moment of "co-orientation"—and how it is conceptualized—that all constructivist approaches try to capture, as such explanations let us see through the apparent "normalcy" of everyday social reality and understand how and under which circumstances it is actively created.

The assertion that the media play an important part in the production of such a commonly shared reality through largely standardized formats, professional roles, story arcs, narrative styles, and so on thus cannot be what *qualitatively* demarcates the different viewpoints. If anything, the distinction between "institutionalist" and "constructivist" accounts seems to run along the lines of the classic micro/macro divide, as the institutional logic observes processes on the level of communication systems, and the social-constructivist perspective is often focused on everyday mediated interaction and the appropriation of media technologies. But even this distinction does not follow cogently from the concepts themselves (the studies of news production by Altheide and Snow being a case in point). Both macro as well as micro perspectives ultimately may rest on a constructivist premise.

While I suspect that the root of this flawed dichotomy is due to the respective focus along the old/new media divide that (also) runs through mediatization research, even here it is not persuasive. Neither does the institutional perspective depict the power of mass communication as a hermetic, determining logic (as is sometimes claimed), nor is individual media use completely unaffected by institutional influences in, for example, developing media repertoires. And while the institutional variant ultimately asks about the consequences that flow from the large media organizations, an appropriate account of people's everyday communicative practices must also reckon with the "moulding forces" inherent in the "new" technologies and platforms used in symbolic interaction with others. Today, the analysis of the traditional media's (institutional) power in selecting and presenting ("formatting") needs to be complemented by an examination of the "viral" properties of net-based communication. The integrative role of popular television programs, for example, is complemented by the aggregating function of popular on-demand streaming services, YouTube channels and social network sites. Thus, a critique of the standardization of mass media formats must be supplemented by a critical assessment of the dispositive affordances and typical uses of net-based media platforms, as depicted by van Dijck and Poell (2013), who even adopt the term "logic" to digital media and investigate the properties of a "social media logic".

This is not to say that there are no differences between these approaches, but it might indeed be argued that—in relation to the bigger picture within the field of communication and even of social science as a whole—they have more in common than separates them: they might be traced along the same conceptual continuum rather than positioned as antagonistic perspectives. We are dealing here with gradual differences or foci of what is fundamentally the same research problem. A differentiation that is hinged merely on the scale or scope of particular approaches is surely not the last resort for a systematic conceptualization of mediatization research. It might be argued that the time has come to transcend this overstated divide, while acknowledging that the debate was crucial for developing a more nuanced account of mediatization by elaborating on the initial differences of the "strong" and the "weak" program of mediatization. The critique of the concept of a "media logic" served as a midwife for a more comprehensive theoretical discussion (see, for example, Jensen 2013; Lundby 2014a).

2.4 Media Concepts in Mediatization Research

While there is no shortage of arguments about how to conceptualize the connection between societal communication and social and cultural change, there is precious little debate over what exactly is meant by "media" in mediatization theory. Just as I have argued that the social-theoretical differences in mediatization research seem unfit for a categorical differentiation of approaches, I maintain that media-theoretical differences have so far been smoothed over. Whereas Livingstone and Lunt (2014: 708) express their vexation over "the lack of clarity over timescales [...] for a theory defined by its historical vision", the same holds true, and probably even more so, for the lack of clarity regarding the term that gives mediatization its name.

A number of problems are attached to the term medium for and within mediatization research. There is, first, the widely observable fact that different strands of mediatization research focus on different kinds of media. Most notably, whereas some focus on mobile, networked, digital media, often in the context of everyday communication, others are preoccupied with the broadcasting media, their transformation and their relationship with other institutional fields or social subsystems. The challenge with this divergence lies not so much with what Deacon and Stanyer (2014: 3) identify as the differences between "big" media's "centripetal power" and the "small" media's "centrifugal presence". More fundamentally, the discourse on mediatization tends to lump together various conceptualizations of mediated communication into one neat category and call it "the media", which is the more fundamental problem for the purpose of this discussion. As Ampuja et al. (2014: 119) correctly note, "what is meant by "media" in the mediatization discourses [...] is far from clear".

Mediatization research inherited this shortcoming from academic (mass) communication research that mostly takes the concept of "medium" and the "media" for granted. This blind spot of communications could be ignored as long as its material research object(s) showed little variation for the greater part of the second half of the twentieth century—which is the very era in which the boundaries of media and communication studies we still grapple with today were established. This draws our attention to the following observations: first, that the most common usage of the term *media* in our fields is literally synonymous with the term *mass communication* and that, second, this confounding of terms was practically inconsequential—aside from more theoretically inclined debates at the fringes of the field—as long as mass communication and public communication were virtually the same thing.

Against the background of the rapid transformation of our media environment, the increase in communicative networks by virtue of new media technologies and the diversification of media use (production, audiences and repertoires), such an approach is no longer tenable. Although today no one would contend that digital media and communication drive a great number of transformational processes within societal communication, we still suffer from the fallout of *under-theorizing* the media. The new situation creates various conceptual problems that, so it seems, we often try to solve on the *social theoretical level* (discussed above) instead of where they really originate, namely from unclear and often conflicting understandings of "the media".

One of the few instances where this decisive question for mediatization research is raised can be found in Ampuja et al. (2014: 119) critical discussion of "strong" and "weak" forms of mediatization:

> It seems that in its current use, the concept of media functions as a 'meta-concept' or, to be more precise, a conceptual displacement for means of communication and the communicative relations that structure it. It thus allows 'communication' to return to its previous wider meaning, while it isolates and valorizes the particular instrumentalist sense that had been ascribed to communication in the form of a regulated system of transmission. In fact, there can be no communication without corresponding

> 'media' that constitute its 'material or social form', just as there can be no society or culture without communication. Thus, when investigated rigorously and coherently, 'media' turns out to be a concept historically just as broad as that of communication.

In order to speak of "*media*-tization" in a coherent conceptual fashion, we have to increase our efforts in theorizing and delimiting the breadth of the term. In other words, the problem is not so much how to "think *beyond* the media" (Lundby 2014b: 9, my emphasis) but to spend more time thinking *about* the media.

2.5 Hidden Epistemologies: The Media as a Social and Material Entity

For the purpose of the following discussion, I return to Knut Lundby's differentiation of cultural, material and institutional approaches to mediatization and the associated "issues of contention" of *time*, *technology* and *theory* (Lundby 2014b: 5). Although this matrix serves as a heuristic tool to describe the different perspectives fleshed out in the literature, it does not fully uncover their consequential implications.

There is, first, the fact that the analytical differentiations listed in the matrix turn out to be interdependent. The dimension of "time" is really a consequence of choices made on the level of "theory" that presume a certain "technology" (i.e. materiality of the media). For example, research on the economic crisis of journalism in the wake of digitization will put you firmly within a particular time frame, as will an inquiry into the iconic properties of early script as a medium of legal rule. How one *theorizes* mediatization is thus dependent on reciprocal assumptions on the level of time and technology, as time precludes decisions of available technologies, and vice versa. If this is indeed the case, then the matrix mainly reflects the progression over time of technologies that fall under a theory's implicit assumption of what is to be defined as a "medium". What emerges as the key variable behind this differentiation is the particular understanding of the *nature* of a medium, and what counts as one.

Against this background, second, what features as a *medium* or *the media* becomes the primordial choice of any inquiry into mediatization: "Potentially, 'media' can include a range of practices and institutions not limited to the transmission of 'information', 'meanings' or 'codes'; in other words, it can include such generalities as language (conceived of as a medium for creating human community), writing or even money (conceived of as the concrete medium for establishing a relationship of exchange of values)" (Ampuja et al. 2014: 119).

Consider the following, random examples of how the theoretical designation of *medium/media* invariably sets the stage on which the inquiry proceeds: If (1), as John B. Thompson (1995: 18f.) asserts, all *communication* is dependent on media and thus the vocal cord assumes the status of a (material) medium, then mediatization becomes a process of the *longue durée* dating back to the phylogenetic development of the speech apparatus. Given such a comprehensive media concept, all human communication is by definition modelled as materially and physically mediated, the "technical medium [representing] the material substratum of symbolic forms [...]" (Thompson 1995: 18). Or consider (2) Mikko Lehtonen's (2015) position that sees all human *experience* as always already mediated by our bodies and faces, by language and speech, as people's minds, their cognition and affects are never immediately accessible to others. Even the ideal-typical, dyadic face-to-face encounter that communication scholars (as well as social theorists) often take as the point of departure for theorizing mediated modes of communication is, from this point of view, not an instance of *unmediated* communication. Such a viewpoint entails that if mediatization were to have analytical usage there would have to be a discernible reason to assume mediation as a defining process in the relation between an individual and his or her natural and social environment. Since the term mediatization implies that there is a categorical difference between "reality" and "the media", Lehtonen more or less refutes the notion. Deploying such a concept of the media, he has no choice but to dismiss the assumption that mediated interaction[3] might be differentiated according to measures of immediacy at all.

Whether one agrees with these propositions or not, it becomes clear that the various conceptualizations of mediatization are always hinged on the place a theory affords to the media. Most importantly, there is a rift that divides a *social* (media as *means* of communicative action) from a *material* (media as "mediality") tradition of theorizing the media which seems much more decisive than the conceptual increments that separate various degrees of the *aggregation of social action* outlined above (Sect. 2.4). One might sketch the extreme positions within this implicit "media in mediatization" issue between a primarily social understanding—in which the media disappear behind their organizational, institutional or practical *usage* on one end of the spectrum—and another extreme which posits that "the fact that media are seen as a priori of our experience of the world [...] elevates media to an unavoidable condition of the possibility of perception, communication, and cognition" (Krämer 2015: 30).

What these divergent conceptualizations boil down to is a paradigmatic choice of what comes first: *the medium* or the *act of communication*. Lundby (2009: 117) is clearly on the *social* side of the divide when he insists that "Mediatization research should put emphasis on how social and communicative forms are developed when media are taken into use in social interaction". In the same anthology, the *material* perspective is most prominently displayed in Friesen and Hug's assertion that whenever we avail ourselves of a medium, the medium ultimately takes over as "mediatic forms" subsequently determine "what is possible and impossible in human communication, expression and social organization" (Friesen and Hug 2009: 68). In this perspective, the medium is primary, preceding all acts of communication. Owing to their postulatory character, such statements are really premises, situated at the very foundation of a theoretical position—what Foucault would call "episteme" (1994 [1966])—prompting me to label these differences "epistemological" as they are not negotiable on a theoretical level. A typical indication that a debate has reached these limits is usually found in the frequent accusation that one's research is bordering on *technological* or *social determinism*, respectively. Importantly, these differences go beyond the integrative and stabilizing properties that a discipline's methodology typically provides, which reflects the heterogeneous backgrounds of the current mediatization community. As long as the term medium/media is unable to shed its fate as a "blind-spot" and as long as there is a lack of conceptual debate about their nature, it will continue to cause "fault lines" on other analytical dimensions.

In summary, one can identify at least three basic perceptions of mediatization that may appear similar at first glance but really are based on quite different premises, thus suggesting different identities of the field.

Social-Instrumental Notion of the Media as Communication

First, mediatization may refer to the extension of human communicative action by ever more functional means of communication. The name of these means is "the media", and their definitional status depends on an instrumental notion of what they *do*. As Knut Lundby puts it (2014b: 8), "The media [...] *act as agents* of cultural and social change" (my emphasis, M.A.). From this perspective, communication takes precedence over the media, whose character as material technology is usually side-lined by an emphasis on the importance of human agency or institutional practice. In this case, mediatization might really turn out to be an unfortunate choice of words since it is not "the media" that drive the changes subsumed under mediatization but the societal shifts behind it. What moves to the centre of the discussion is the "communicatization" of human sociality, which is an intriguing observation in itself.[4]

Modern-Institutional Notion of the Media as Cultural Producers

Second, mediatization is used to put an emphasis on people's increasingly "mediated" access to reality or their social and natural environment, implying the growing historical importance of the media which become the main interfaces of human experience and knowledge. This development endows the media with a critical societal function and renders them ever more powerful. Such approaches frequently exhibit a structural bias for mass communication (i.e. organized, professionalized and typified forms of mediated communication). This follows from the fact that what motivates such inquiries is the question how this kind of "access" to the world is shaped by the media and their institutions: the rationality of selecting, producing and distributing messages and procuring attention in a highly organized setting (cf. Franck's *Economy of Attention* 1999).[5] In this reasoning, the mediatization process is usually tied to the genealogy of media-technological innovation and the institutionalization of a media system (expansion, commercialization, etc.), thus native to *modern* social formations and often used diagnostically to make sense of accelerated social change (a media-centred perspective on the media as *drivers* of social processes).

Philosophical Notion of the Media

And, third, mediatization may take the form of another perspective on the unavoidable and involuntary "mediated-ness" of any human relation with reality representing an old philosophical topic in a new, contemporary guise, namely that "real" (i.e. unmediated) reality is unavailable to human knowing, and that thus all the perceptions of the mind may never be corroborated against the untarnished factuality of what exists. Here, mediatization cannot be divorced from the question of how human beings are positioned vis-à-vis reality: how do we have access to our natural and social environment, what is the relationship between what we perceive and the true nature of the world? In this view, it is a false premise to differentiate between "what is represented" and its "representations", as the objects of our natural and social environment are always available only as representations. In their contemporary deployment (e.g. in Media Philosophy), such approaches usually highlight the "mediality" of forms of mediation which subsequently impact upon the modalities of communication and beyond, as there "there can be nothing 'outside' of media" (Krämer 2015: 30).

Though surely incomplete, this breakdown of the various epistemological undercurrents that enter mediatization discourse by way of respective media concepts draws our attention to the importance of a more thorough theorization of the term. It is the differences that Knut Lundby subsumes under the category of *technology*—which might better be termed *materiality* of *a medium/the media*—that are the most problematic. Within the current discussion of structuring the field, they are the most consequential yet neglected preferences. It becomes increasingly obvious that different understandings of the media will inevitably reflect upon how we conceptualize the process of mediation, and—as I have tried to show—ultimately on the concept of mediatization itself. I thus agree with Niels Ole Finnemann (2011: 78) who concludes his analysis of exemplary notions of mediatization theory as follows: "Perhaps media studies should finally provide itself with a conceptual framework covering all media". In the next section, I will attend to this appeal.

2.6 Towards an Integrative Concept of the Media

I have suggested adopting Siegfried Schmidt's four-dimensional model (2000), which casts a medium as the specific relation of its semiotic, technological *and* institutional properties that flow into a concrete media text or product. When we use the term media, all of these dimensions are invoked albeit with varying emphases. Still, all of them need to be considered as they play a specific role in the processes that we subsume under the mediatization concept[6]:

On a (1) semiotic or symbolic dimension, the choice of certain means of communication (verbal and graphic codes, meaningful objects, i.e. significant symbols) already implies both a certain *materiality* as well as a particular *context* of knowledge (cf. Thompson 1995: 22). It is here, where meaning is encoded by using particular "communication instruments".[7] I may carefully choose an emoticon to convey "more than words can say" or I may whistle the tune of *The Good, the Bad and the Ugly* to subtly express my state of mind. I may carve in stone what I think must outlast time itself or I may carefully type my thoughts into a computer using script to convey my ideas. Such choices, voluntary or not, are always already and inescapably embedded in cultural contexts (first and foremost: a concrete language), social conventions, and socially situated knowledge (cf. Hug 2013; Adolf and Stehr 2017). Thus, they will always impact upon both the message as well as the wider communication process.

The second dimension comprises (2) the corresponding material technologies ("technical implements") used in, invented for, or adapted to communication processes. These technical means enable communication to take concrete material shape, and extend it beyond the confines of co-presence and co-temporality, while also imposing their dispositive character as well as required competencies (cultural techniques) upon the message and the process. Importantly, diffusion requires infrastructures whose creation, operation and maintenance are beyond any single individual to accomplish. Technological innovation, economic capital and political regulation meet in the process of implementing, for example, broadcasting networks as public or private services (or both) or standard protocols for data transmission.

Which is why (3) media not only are technological entities but also depend on socio-systemic institutionalization, including a host of interconnected organizations. Any instance of the implementation of media as infrastructures is imaginable only as a collective effort, of expertise in a whole number of social and knowledge fields. Supra-individual structures of communication need supra-individual organization: the building of the new telegraph line, the standardization of wireless frequencies, the legal framework for broadcasting agencies as well as their funding schemes and so on are imaginable only in social formations that are highly organized and based on a complex division of labour (resources).

Finally, (4) the fourth dimension consists of the messages and content, interactions, transmissions and exchanges that are based on the above preconditions and their specific combination. Broadcasts, programs, newspapers, as well as telephone calls, instant messages or tweets do not emerge out of thin air but originate from socially situated individual and collective actors, from cognitions, feelings and ideas, vested interests, professional ethics, artistic expressions and practical routines. They follow certain conventions, make up distinct genres, and tend to create specific settings of their reception. Importantly, these resulting communicative acts cannot be divorced from their formation: The output of the combination of semiotic instrument, media technology and social institutionalization is not arbitrary but is dependent on the selections on these preceding levels.

Mediatizing factors may be traced not only to the totality of a medium, the media or a media system but to any one of these dimensions: the nature of the symbolic means, the material formatting of the technology, the organizational rationality that accrues into institutional patterns as well as traditional genres or unique messages are all, at one and the same time, origins as well as targets of mediatization. Such a differentiated media-model not only may inform a more comprehensive discussion about mediatization research's understanding of the media but is also sufficiently inclusive to encompass both broadcast as well as digital media and corresponding modes of communication; it also transcends the assumed contradiction between individualist and institutionalist accounts of mediatization. And it compels us to pursue a more comprehensive conceptual frame for researching mediated communication, as I will argue in the concluding section.

2.7 Conclusion: Communication, Media and Sociality

In summary, the idea of mediatization rests on observations that seem trivial only at first glance, namely that the media are a consequential social force by virtue of their mere existence (Schulz 2013: 61) and that their role and relevance always lie in conjunction and intertwinement with other social and cultural processes. These realizations translate into two exigencies that together constitute the *identity* of mediatization research, regardless of a study's disciplinary origin or the terminology it might use.

First, to use the words of John B. Thompson, we "can understand the social impact of the development of new networks of communication and information flow only if we put aside the intuitively plausible idea that communication media serve to transmit information and symbolic content to individuals whose *relations to others remain fundamentally unchanged*" (Thompson 1995: 4, my emphasis). *Second*, in order to heed the embeddedness of all acts of communication, we can no longer afford to theorize media and communication separately and as divorced from their context. In other words, if the way we relate to our social and natural environment and how we conceive of the world, each other and even ourselves are so deeply entangled with communication and mediation, then the "history of society" could be written as a "history of the media" (Schmidt 2003: 137).

Given the scope of this research endeavour, it is no wonder that mediatization research exhibits such a wide array of foci and conceptual variation along the categories *time*, *theory* and *technology*. Still, if I am correct in concluding that current mediatization theories are often implicitly premised on their emphases regarding time and technology and that these two variables ultimately may not be detachable, then a somewhat different order of the field may be depicted: We might find that these various conceptualizations, while providing important insights into mediatization as a social and cultural process, may be better organized along a different continuum:

1. From within a more *anthropological understanding*, the media (or constitutive processes thereof; see the respective dimensions of a *medium* above) have *always* played an important part in our individual and collective development as communication is the basic operation of all human sociality and cooperation and thus a vital aspect of our cultural genealogy and form of social organization. It is "the mechanism through which human relations exist and develop—all the symbols of the mind, together with the means of conveying them through space and preserving them in time" (Cooley 1909: 61). Thus, the evolution of human sociality is tied from the beginning to incremental increases in the functionality and sophistication of the instruments and technologies of communication (i.e. the media). If, as John Dewey (1916: 5, emphases in original) already pointed out a hundred years ago, "society not only continues to exist *by* transmission, *by* communication, but it may fairly be said to exist *in* transmission, *in* communication" and thus there "is more than a verbal tie between the words common, community and communication", then indeed human history may legitimately be written as the history of the media, as Schmidt claims.[8]

2. While the continuity of this anthropological development truly constitutes a meta-process (in the sense of Friedrich Krotz), we might put a particular emphasis on the role of mediated communication in the modern age of complex social organization (i.e. *modern society*). Such a contemporary, more sociological approach does not contradict observations on an anthropological level but rather is focused on the temporal acceleration, phenomenological multiplication and social intensification of mediatization as we move towards the present. Again, we find a witness in Charles Horton Cooley, who realized a long time ago that when "we come to the modern era, especially, we can understand nothing rightly unless we perceive the manner in which the revolution in communication has made a new world for us" (Cooley 1909: 65). No wonder that studying such processes within *complex social formations* (such as modern society) also leads to much more varied conceptualizations of mediatization itself. Importantly, such diagnoses of current social and cultural changes imply *reflexive* approaches, adding yet another layer to mediatization research: we study our own (personal, academic, societal) *mediatedness* (i.e. the fact of how much we rely on the media today) inevitably from *within* a state of mediatization. In modern social formations, society *itself* is accessible only in and through the media, a point famously promoted to sociological prominence by Niklas Luhmann (2000). And given the digital transformation we witness today, society continues to grow even more dependent on media, who play an ever greater role *both* as cultural resources (i.e. producers of meaning) *and* as means of communicative action (techno-material means shaping communicative practices).

Whatever our particular approaches might look like, mediatization urges us to research the question of the societal and cultural role and consequences of the media. It puts a terminological bracket around the many and manifold attempts to create a comprehensive social theory of the media. As such, its main benefit may be found in the way it continues to modify and advance the questions and perspectives of our research decisively. Not only has it allowed us to overcome traditional disciplinary demarcations by providing a common trajectory and sense of relevance, but it lets us rediscover and synthesize earlier attempts at theorizing the media as social and cultural forces. As such, mediatization has helped to channel previously isolated scholarly studies and communities into a more coherent picture of what is going on with our societies: that the media have become a decisive force and a defining aspect of contemporary life and that, only upon this realization, we find that this has really always been the case.

Notes

1. Livingstone and Lunt (2014: 705) have introduced a similar differentiation, naming these timelines the "*longue durée* of cultural evolution", "institutionalized forces of high modernity" and "the socio-technological transformations of recent decades".
2. Personal correspondence (13 Nov. 2009).
3. Here, he uses John B. Thompson's three modes of communication—"face-to-face interaction", "mediated interaction" and "mediated quasi-interaction" (Thompson 1995: 82f.)—as prototypical for a mediatization perspective.
4. Knoblauch has suggested that "the waning force of tradition and shared knowledge (about a common life world, M.A.) can only compensated through communicative traditions" (1996: 18, my translation), necessitating an enormous and continuous increase in communication in modern social formations.
5. Such analyses are often informed by research into the ways professional communication impacts upon the (re)production of occurrences and events (sensationalism, scandalization and personalization, i.e. the habitualized reduction of topical complexity to storylines that lend themselves to easy narration, a structural bias towards mass popularity, etc.).
6. I have made this point before in a similar context, but it bears repeating (see Adolf 2013 [2011]).
7. Importantly, especially in the light of the discussion above, Schmidt emphasizes that such "communication instruments" are not media themselves, effectively excluding speech and script from the category of which they are only a constitutive part. See the recently translated *Histories & Discourses* (Schmidt 2016) for his extended argument.
8. And, indeed, media studies and mediatization discourse have recently seen valuable contributions from the historical community (see, for example, Bösch 2015) as it discovered the media as a central research object.

Acknowledgements This contribution draws on a number of presentations held throughout 2014–15 in Siegen, Stockholm, Friedrichshafen and Copenhagen on questions regarding the epistemological foundations of mediatization research.

I wish to thank the participants of these discussions, in particular Stig Hjarvard, Friedrich Krotz, Wolfgang Reißmann and Peter Gentzel. Also, I need to acknowledge the helpful comments by an anonymous reviewer as well as by the editors of this volume.

References

Adolf, Marian. 2012. Media culture. In *The Wiley-Blackwell encyclopedia of globalization*, ed. George Ritzer. Oxford: Wiley-Blackwell. doi:10.1002/9780470670590.wbeog375.

Adolf, Marian. 2013 [2011]. Clarifying mediatization: Sorting through a current debate. *Empedocles. European Journal of the Philosophy of Communication* 3 (2): 153–175.

Adolf, Marian, and Nico Stehr. 2017. *Knowledge*. Second, revised and extended edition. London: Routledge.

Altheide, David L., and Robert Snow. 1979. *Media logic*. Beverly Hills: Sage.

Ampuja, Marko, Juha Koivisto, and Esa Väliverronen. 2014. Strong and weak forms of mediatization theory: A critical review. Special issue, *Nordicom Review 35*: 111–123.

Berger, Peter L., and Thomas Luckmann. 1991 [1966]. *The social construction of reality: A treatise in the sociology of knowledge*. London: Penguin.

Blumer, Herbert. 1954. What's wrong with social theory? *American Sociological Review* 19 (1): 3–10.

Bösch, Frank. 2015. *Media and historical change: Germany in international perspective, 1400–2000*. Oxford: Berghahn Books.

Carrier, Martin. 2006. *Wissenschaftstheorie*. Hamburg: Junius.

Cooley, Charles H. 1909. *Social organization*. New York: Charles Scribner's Sons.

Couldry, Nick, and Andreas Hepp. 2013. Conceptualizing mediatization: Contexts, traditions, arguments. *Communication Theory* 23: 191–202. doi:10.1111/comt.12019.

Deacon, David, and James Stanyer. 2014. Mediatization: Key concept or conceptual s? *Media, Culture and Society* 36 (7): 1032–1044.

Deacon, David, James Stanyer, et al. 2015. Mediatization of or mediatization and: A response to Hepp et al. *Media, Culture & Society* 37 (4): 655–657.

Deuze, Mark. 2014. *Media Life*. Cambridge: Polity Press.

Dewey, John. 1916. *Democracy and education*. New York: Macmillan.

Finnemann, Niels O. 2011. Mediatization theory and digital media. *Communications* 36: 67–89.

Foucault, Michel. 1994 [1966]. *The order of things: An archaeology of human sciences*. New York: Vintage.

Franck, Georg. 1999. The economy of attention. *Telepolis*, Dec 7. www.heise.de/tp/artikel/5/5567/1.html. Accessed 21 Apr 2017.

Friesen, Norm, and Theo Hug. 2009. The mediatic turn: Exploring concepts for media pedagogy. In *Mediatization: Concept, changes, consequences*, ed. Knut Lundby, 63–83. Frankfurt am Main: Peter Lang.

Gentzel, Peter. 2015. *Praxistheorie und Mediatisierung*. Wiesbaden: Springer VS.

Hepp, Andreas, Stig Hjarvard, and Knut Lundby. 2015. Mediatization: Theorizing the interplay between media, culture and society. *Media, Culture and Society* 37 (2): 1–11.

Hug, Theo. 2013. On the medialization of knowledge in the digital age. *International Journal of Humanities and Social Science* 3 (11). http://ijhssnet.com/journals/Vol_3_No_11_June_2013/3.pdf. Accessed: 21 Apr 2017.

Jensen, Klaus B. 2013. Definitive and sensitizing conceptualizations of mediatization. *Communication Theory* 23: 203–222.

Kellner, Douglas. 1995. *Media culture: Cultural studies, identity, and politics between the modern and the postmodern*. New York: Routledge.

Knoblauch, Hubert. 1996. *Kommunikative Lebenswelten. Zur Ethnographie einer geschwätzigen Gesellschaft*. UVK: Konstanz.

Krämer, Sybille. 2015. *Medium, messenger, transmission. An approach to media philosophy*. Amsterdam: Amsterdam University Press.

Krotz, Friedrich. 2009. Mediatization: A concept with which to grasp media and societal change. In *Mediatization: Concept, changes, consequences*, ed. Knut Lundby, 21–40. New York: Peter Lang.

Krotz, Friedrich, and Andreas Hepp. 2012. *Mediatisierte Welten: Beschreibungsansätze und Forschungsfelder*. Wiesbaden: Springer VS Verlag.

Lehtonen, Mikko. 2015. Mediatisation and human practice. Beyond 'Immediacy' and 'Mediation'. Presentation manuscript keynote lecture at the international research workshop Mediatisation of Culture and Everyday Life, April 23–24, Stockholm.

Livingstone, Sonia, and Peter Lunt. 2014. Mediatization: An emerging paradigm for media and communication studies. In *Mediatization of communication: Handbooks of communication science* (21), ed. Knut Lundby, 703–724. Berlin: De Gruyter Mouton.

Luhmann, Niklas. 2000. *The reality of the mass media*, trans. K. Cross. Stanford: Stanford University Press.

Lundby, Knut. 2009. Media logic: Looking for social interaction. In *Mediatization. Concepts, changes, consequences*, ed. Knut Lundby, 101–119. New York: Peter Lang.

Lundby, Knut. 2014a. *Mediatization of communication*. Berlin: de Gruyter.

Lundby, Knut. 2014b. Mediatization of communication (introduction). In *Mediatization of communication*, ed. Knut Lundby, 3–35. Berlin: de Gruyter.

Lundby, Knut. 2014c. A pattern in social theories of change within mediatization research. Presentation manuscript for the ECREA-TWG Mediatization, ECREA Conference "Communication for Empowerment", November 12–15, Lisbon.

Marcinkowski, Frank, and Adrian Steiner. 2009. Was heißt Medialisierung? Autonomiebeschränkung oder Ermöglichung von Politik durch Massenmedien? National Centre of Competence in Research (NCCR) Challenges to democracy in the 21st Century. Working Paper No. 29. Online: www.nccr-democracy.uzh.ch.

Meyen, Michael. 2014. Review of Friedrich Krotz et al. "Mediatisierung sozialer Welten". *Publizistik* 59 (4): 468–469.

Saxer, Ulrich. 2012. *Mediengesellschaft: Eine kommunikationssoziologische Perspektive*. Wiesbaden: Springer VS.

Schmidt, Siegfried J. 2000. *Kalte Faszination*. Frankfurt am Main: Suhrkamp.

Schmidt, Siegfried J. 2003. Medienentwicklung und gesellschaftlicher Wandel. In *Medienentwicklung und gesellschaftlicher Wandel*, ed. Markus Behmer, Friedrich Krotz, Rudolf Stöber, and Carsten Winter, 135–150. Wiesbaden: VS-Verlag.

Schmidt, Siegfried J. 2016. *Histories & discourses: Rewriting constructivism*. London: Andrews.

Schulz, Winfried. 2004. Reconstructing mediatization as an analytical concept. *European Journal of Communication* 19 (1): 87–101.

Schulz, Winfried. 2013. Medialisierung—Was war noch gleich die Frage? In *Realismus als Beruf. Beiträge zum Verhältnis von Medien und Wirklichkeit*, ed. Nikolaus Jackob, Marcus Maurer, Simone C. Ehmig, Stefan Geiß, and Gregor Daschmann, 49–66. Wiesbaden: Springer VS.

Thompson, John B. 1995. *The media and modernity*. Cambridge: Polity.

van Dijck, José, and Thomas Poell. 2013. Understanding social media logic. *Media and Communication* 1 (1): 2–14. doi:10.12924/mac2013.01010002.

CHAPTER 3

Mediatization from Below

Magnus Andersson

3.1 Introduction

In my view, one of the most illustrative examples of mediatization is today's tourism and the ways it is marked by media representations and media technologies of different kinds (compare Jansson 2007a; Polson 2016). For example, as tourists, we might get travel inspiration from glossy magazines, newspaper supplements and/or social media. Travel guides and travel planning apps help us to organize the trip and we might publish the plans on Facebook (and thereby inform our social network of how exciting our lives are). At the resort, we may find our way around and feel at home, geographically and socially, thanks to Google Maps and TripAdvisor, while keeping friends, family, acquaintances and colleagues updated about weather and daily activities. Arriving home, we might get a nice—personalized—virtual photo album generated by Google Photo.

For many of us in the Western world, media representations, technologies, practices and algorithms have altered the notion of tourism, its conduct, practices and signification. Other domains (e.g. work and home) have been transformed in corresponding ways (cf. Gregg 2011).

M. Andersson (✉)
Lund University, Lund, Sweden
e-mail: magnus.andersson@kom.lu.se

O. Driessens et al. (eds.), *Dynamics Of Mediatization*,
Transforming Communications – Studies in Cross-Media Research,
DOI 10.1007/978-3-319-62983-4_3

Such media-related transformations of confined social phenomena illustrate how "social processes in a broad variety of domains and at different levels become inseparable from and dependent on technological processes and resources of mediation", as Jansson (2013: 281) describes mediatization.

The strength of the concept of mediatization is that it enables concrete descriptions of rather vague and subtle media-related transformations in certain, demarcated settings, as illustrated above. Mediatization research is justified by the complexity of today's media-saturated society where questions are raised which cannot be reduced to aspects of production, representation and usage (i.e. the traditional approaches of media and communication studies) (cf. Livingstone 2009; Hepp et al. 2015: 321). Contextual approaches—built upon non-linearity and where communication and mediation are seen as circulation and exchange—can be rewarding in that respect (Silverstone 1999; Boyer 2012). Mediatization from below, the approach favoured here, is based on thorough analyses and thick descriptions of social settings at a *micro* level—contexts which are marked by endless numbers of varied mediations (cf. Hepp and Krotz 2014). This is something other than mediatization research as a *macro*-oriented "second-order investigation" (Livingstone and Lunt 2014: 720) trying to grasp "a high-level societal meta-process concerned with the historical adjustment to or appropriation of media logics by institutions and cultural practices" (Lunt and Livingstone 2016: 466). It is also different from an institutional approach at a *meso* level, considering societal institutions as the key to understand mediatization of culture and society (Hjarvard 2013; 2014a; 2014b). Though different, these approaches do not have to be inconsistent. In each specific way, they contribute to the meta-theoretical framework—as long as this is kept dynamic.

Mediatization research is a growing body of research and as such represents a wide range of foci. As with all emergent and successful traditions, there are vivid discussions on directions, approaches and epistemologies. Scholars focusing on (political) effects and functions of the mass media (Strömbäck and Esser 2009; Kunelius and Reunanen 2012; Asp 2014) coexist with scholars interested in the constitution of everyday lifeworlds (Hartmann 2009; Jansson 2013; Deuze 2014; Madianou 2014). Hence, the debates between functionalism and cultural studies, which once had a huge imprint on media and communication studies as a discipline, now may be unfolded within the same area of research.

This diversity has led Andreas Hepp, in different constellations, to talk about mediatization research as constituted of two traditions: an institutional traditional focusing how institutions are affected by media institutions (see Hjarvard 2013) and a social-constructionist tradition with interest in how the media contribute to the constitution of the daily social world (Hepp 2013a; Couldry and Hepp 2013; Hepp and Krotz 2014).[1] Arguing that these two traditions are rooted in functionalism vis-à-vis cultural theory is to simplify. While scholars of mediatization of politics discuss functions of the media and refer to system theory (Kunelius and Reunanen 2012; Meyen et al. 2014), Hjarvard (2013), the main proponent and developer of an institutional perspective, leans more towards structuration than system theory.[2]

Owing to the manifold foci (at different levels), theoretical underpinnings and epistemologies, mediatization research may appear to be unclear. In addition, the theoretical density of some approaches (see, for example, Jansson 2013; Hepp and Hasebrink 2014) may lend the concept of mediatization a rather abstract character. In addition, it is not always clear in mediatization research how the studied thing/field/practice/institution is influenced by media institutions/representations/technologies/practices. My concern in this text is not to simplify but to clarify mediatization, putting an explicit stress on "from below". For that reason, I will discuss two aspects: the first one is the fuzzy use of the concept of media since "the media", whatever they signify, are crucial when discussing a process where phenomena are said to be influenced, shaped or moulded by the media (Hjarvard 2013; Hepp 2013b). Second, I will discuss approaches and how the dynamics of mediatization can be grasped. My starting point and main interest is the social-constructionistic tradition and its ground in symbolic interactionism where people perpetually interpret and thereby create the world in interaction with one another. In order to provide a theoretical contextualization, the institutional perspective will also be discussed to some extent.

3.2 The Concept of Media

Although there are several definitions of mediatization, most of them come down to *increased dependence of the media in various fields and contexts* (see Jansson 2013; Hepp 2013b: 31–38; Hjarvard 2013: 19). What "the media" means in that sentence is, however, another matter. There are examples of elaborations and substantial discussions of the concept of media within mediatization research (see Hepp 2012: 21; Krotz 2014: 79). Generally, however, the scholarly habitual use of the term is non-specified and comprises a range of meanings: communication technologies, mass media institutions, media companies, journalism, news organizations, media representations, cultural forms or media practices. Some scholars use an indefinite media concept very deliberately. Couldry, for example, motivates his use of a non-specific "the media" with "that many common-sense assumptions about the media's authority operate with a sense of 'the media' which *is* highly non-specific" (2000: 6, *italics in original*). Hence, the non-specific media might be justified by the public discourse (which I will come back to later). Nevertheless, there are many examples of less deliberately scholarly use of a non-specified concept of the media. The problem seems to be of a double nature. On the one hand, media are sometimes defined as "communication technologies" (see Lundby 2014: 8), which is a very wide and inclusive definition. On the other hand, in practice, "the media" are often reduced to institutional or journalistic mass media, plus institutional digital media. The neglect of "communication technologies" such as books, postcards, blackboards and posters may be regarded as a legacy of the social scientific and functionalistic origin of large parts of media and communication studies.[3] American communication research from the 1930–1940s on public opinion, political communication, media functions, propaganda and masses (e.g. Lasswell 1948) has long shaped the development of media and communication studies.

An ambiguous concept of media weakens the mediatization framework and complicates communication between different traditions within the field. For example, it can be argued that "In late-modern societies, media have become co-constitutive for the articulation of various social fields in their present form" (Hepp et al. 2015: 321). Yet it is problematic to use education as an exemple (ibid). A historical glance at the classroom reveals that school always has been marked and moulded by "communication technologies". It used to be books, blackboards and posters. Today, it is tablets, PowerPoint and Wikipedia (cf. Breiter 2014).

There seems to be a pattern where the two traditions of mediatization research stress different aspects of the wide concept of media. In an institutional tradition, "the media" tends to be a shorthand for journalism, mass media institutions or news organization (see, for example,

Strömbäck and Esser 2009; Ihlen and Pallas 2014), whereas the social-constructionist tradition often refers to media technologies and communication media when using the media (Hepp 2013b). As Gitelman puts it:

> Naturalizing, essentializing or ceding agency to media is something that happens at a lexical level every time anyone says 'the media' in English, as if media were a unified natural entity, like the wind. (Gitelman 2006: 2)

Hence, the risk with "the media" without specification is that one ascribes agency to the media and thereby neglects producers, investors, designers, peers and their role in the production of meaning (Gitelman 2006: 9). This argument is very relevant for mediatization research, which has a strong focus on social change and transformation. The media—regardless of whether one means institutions, representations or technologies—play vital parts in many processes, but the question is which aspects of the media are decisive. The socially varied outcome in different contexts tells us that this is not a media logic or media determinism. Instead, the social has to be included in the analysis. This justifies a phenomenological or symbolic interactionist perspective since "[a] network or an institution does not function automatically because of some inner dynamics [...]; it functions because people at different points do something" (Blumer 1969: 19).

To reiterate, in relation to the concept of media, two things are particularly important in relation to the dynamics of mediatization. The first thing is an *elaborated* definition of the media—elaborated since the discussion stretches beyond the concept of media and includes a foundational view on communication (Hepp 2012: 18–22). Second, to clarify and concretize mediatization as a concept and as an approach, one should strive for specificity, referring to which aspects of the media and which dimension of mediations are at play. Such specificity requires the elaborated definition from the first point.

In order to elaborate the notion of media within mediatization research, it is relevant to consider mediatization in relation to the dominant modes of thinking in media and communications, the perspectives that Carey (1989) discusses as transmission and ritual and that Silverstone describes as "influence and effects" verses "ritual and reflexivity" (2005: 190). My main interest is in the social-constructionist tradition and its strong links to a ritual view of communication since that is the foundation of an approach where mediatization is grasped from below. The institutional perspective and its much weaker link to transmission will be discussed as well, most of all as a contrast.

When Carey (1989: 18) explains a ritual view on communication, he stresses that sharing of meaning is something other than imparting attention. Here, a medium is seen "like a Balinese cockfight, a Dickens novel, an Elizabethan drama, a student rally, it is a presentation of reality that gives life an overall form, order, and tone" (Carey 1989: 21). What is stressed in communication-as-ritual is sharing, non-linearity, contextualization, dialectics, sociality and (in a certain sense) imagination. These themes, quite typical of cultural approaches within media studies, are often present in social-constructionist mediatization research (see, for example, Jansson 2007a; Hartmann 2009; Hepp 2013b; Fornäs 2014; Madianou 2014). As a consequence, the media are harder to delineate. The recognition of symbolic content as well as material technologies (cf. Silverstone 1994) is a first step, but not the last. A ritual view of media and communication also implies that the social is an essential part of media and mediation; "the media have to be explained as social just as they are required to be part of the explanation of the social" (Silverstone 2005: 203).[4] This implies a perspective that considers mediated communication not primarily as a "production–reception polarity" but first and foremost as "circulation and exchange" (Boyer 2012: 387). This social extension of the media is implicitly expressed in mediatization research through its anchorage in symbolic interactionism and its parallel repudiation of technological determinism (Krotz 2008: 23; Hepp 2013a).

While transmission or dissemination is never mentioned when Hjarvard (2013) outlines the foundation of an institutional perspective, the scholars of mediatization of politics stand out in the way they stress mediatization as effects (Meyen et al. 2014; Strömbäck and Esser 2014: 384), which is an explicit expression of a transmission perspective. Also, Kunelius expresses a foundation in a transmission view when stating that a "key question in thinking about mediatization refers to the way media's habits and routines of representation shape our relationship to reality" (2014: 70). Moreover, the general focus on attention and media exposure within the institutional tradition implicitly indicates a basis in a linear model of communication, which has distinct (central) producers and (more peripheral) audiences. This tendency is also salient when digital media are considered (Enli and Skogerbø 2013; Haßler et al. 2014).

I want to underscore that I am not arguing against studies that are based on communication as transmission and are focusing media attention. They are justified by an "economy of signs and space" (Lash and Urry 1994), where attention is the currency for politicians, cities, celebrities, churches, sport clubs and various associations. Nevertheless, the view on communication illustrates the sharp theoretical differences within mediatization research.

3.3 Elaborating the Media

Having established the explicit link between a social-constructionist tradition and a ritual view on communication, I am going to elaborate the concept of media in order to clarify which aspects of the media and mediation are moulding social contexts and phenomena (see Hepp 2012). In 1986, in the introduction of his book *Family Television*, David Morley wrote "In short, my focus of interest has thus shifted from the analysis of the pattern of differential audience 'readings' of particular programme materials, to the analysis of the domestic viewing context itself" (Morley 1986: 14). This could be seen as the start of a contextual and media ethnographic turn within audience studies. It did not challenge the definition of the media explicitly, yet the changed focus from texts to contexts—and thereby rituals—was an important step to consider the social as a necessary dimension of the mediation (see Gray 1992; Silverstone and Hirsch 1992).[5] With this "contextual turn" as the point of departure (Jansson 2007b: 192), there have been several examples of traditions, which in different ways have stretched the concept of media, as well as the perspective on mediation, in different directions. Bringing these elaborations together entails a more nuanced understanding of the media.

The concept of media may be seen as multi-layered, a view elaborated by domestication research. This originally British tradition started as a critique against the functionalism of diffusion of innovation research and focused on how media and technologies were familiarized and finally become second nature in people's lifeworlds (Berker et al. 2006). The central principle of the tradition, expressed by Roger Silverstone, is the necessity to consider the media as both symbolic and material objects; they lodge a double meaning, which has to be doubly articulated.[6] He uses television as an example:

> Through its double articulation into culture its significance is extended beyond its status 'simply' as object or medium, for in its status as a medium, and through the provision of information and entertainment, television provides the basis for an 'education', a competence, in all aspects of contemporary culture. (Silverstone 1994: 123)

Hartmann later elaborated, stretched and developed the tradition in different empirical and theoretical directions (2006, 2009, 2014). She reflects over, among other things, imagination as an aspect of the media and as a potential link between domestication and mediatization (Hartmann 2009: 234–237). The imagination is here understood as discourse: "the whole discursive construction around (new) media, their potential societal consequences, the utopian and dystopian debates, etc." (2009: 235). Looking through a domestication framework, one could argue that people in their everyday lives have to appropriate and make sense of, first, a material object (technology); second, a medium mediating symbolic content; and, third, discourses about these material objects and mediating media. An important aspect of this, as Hartmann stresses, is that there is a parallel process of, on the one hand, more media to consume and, on the other hand, more consumption at media display (2009: 236). In other words, media texts of different kinds tell us how we should relate to media of different kinds.

Hartmann's twisting and turning of the concepts of media and mediation illuminates the complexity and therefore is fruitful in this discussion. As mentioned earlier, the discursive aspect of mediation is also in focus in Couldry's work. For him, media power is derived because "we believe in the authority of media discourse in countless local contexts, because we believe that most others believe the same, and because we act on the basis of these beliefs on countless specific occasions" (2000: 5). Such reasoning moves beyond linear communication models where produced texts are "decoded" by the audience. Also, Silverstone (2005) touches on the discursive level when he elaborates on the media within the discussion on mediation. For him, the unclear boundaries of media are a consequence of the deep integration of the media in the rituals of everyday life.

> The analysis of mediation [...] requires us to understand how the processes of mediated communication shape both society and culture, as well as the relationships that participants, both individual and institutional, have

> to their environment and to each other. At the same time such analysis requires a consideration of how social and cultural activity in turn mediates the mediations, as institutions and technologies as well as the meanings that are delivered by them are appropriated through reception and consumption. Mediation, in this double sense, is both literal and metaphorical. *The boundaries around media technologies may be visible when we look at the machine or gaze at the screen, but they have become entirely blurred in practice, in use and in fantasy, and as they become incorporated into, or unsettle, the rituals of everyday life.* (Silverstone 2005: 203, *my italics*)

The citation underscores that the media constitute the environment in which media practices are conducted. Furthermore, in the context of daily toil, the distinction between mediation and media technology is difficult to sustain.

A different, though related, elaboration of the media, mediation and communication is conducted within communication geography through a problematization of the spatial boundaries of the contexts (Jansson 2007b: 192). Stressing spaces rather than contexts, Jansson discusses the dialectics between space and communication through the concept texture (2007b), which could be seen as the "communicative fabric of space" (Jansson 2013). This spatialization enables new ways of thinking regarding mediation. An expression of that is when Tacchi, considering a media ethnographical study, discusses a domestic radio texture as a social soundscape "within which people move around and live their daily lives" (1998: 26). This spatialization of the media is also present in Madianou and Miller's media ethnographical studies (2013), where they coin the concept polymedia, which, among other things, means a "communicative environment". The relevance of considering the spatial dimension of the media stems from space (and distance) as an essential part of communication (Carey 1989) and from the idea that a great share of the dynamics of mediatization is of a spatial character. For example, the mediatized home is, among other things, a home with blurred boundaries (Andersson 2006).

So far, I have argued that the social is an essential aspect of the media and that domestication research and communication geography, as media ethnographical approaches, contribute to a widening of the notion of media. Furthermore, "the media" as intermediate means of communication—representing imparting as well as sharing (Williams 1983: 73)—are articulations of different layers: technology, symbolic content and discourse. All of these layers are not equally important in all processes of mediatization, but awareness of them hinders us from drawing premature conclusions about media influences—without considering which layers of the media are entangled. These elaborating manoeuvres are thereby paving the way for grasping the dynamics of mediatization.

Pushing the notion of media in a social direction is in line with arguments within media history, where the delineation of the media is a central and significant issue. The media, as Marvin notes, "have no natural edges. They are constructed as complexes of habits, beliefs and procedures embedded in elaborate cultural codes of communication" (1988: 8). In a similar but more elaborated way, Gitelman defines the media as

> socially realized structures of communication, where structures include both technological forms and their associated protocols, and where communication is a cultural practice, a ritualized collocation of different people on the same mental map, sharing or engaged with popular ontologies of representation. (2006: 7)

With "associated protocols", Gitelman means "a huge variety of social, economic and material relationship" (2006: 7). If one follows Gitelman's argument, it means that a medium such as Facebook includes everything from hardware and software and commercially based algorithms to people's biographical self presentations and their tacit agreement of appropriate behaviour on Facebook.

It may seem like an awkward and clumsy definition. Nevertheless, this is in line with media as an articulation of several aspects. Inspired by Canadian and German medium theory as well as cultural studies and Geertzian anthropology, Gitelman strives for as open and inclusive a definition as possible. To make the definition work in empirical contexts, she stresses the importance of specifying in order not to essentialize and ascribe agency to the media (2006: 8). Following Gitelman's advice means that rather than discuss the character of social media in general, it makes more sense to discuss, say, "social media in a Scandinavian urban middle class context in the 2010s".

This leads to the conclusion of this exposé of the concept of the media. The mediatization research is well theorized in many ways but is under-theorized when it comes to the concept of the media (cf. Ampuja et al. 2014: 119; Kunelius 2014: 80). If one is going to grasp the dynamics of mediatization, there are two important things to keep in mind. First, one should strive for an elaborated definition of the media since that would enable further theoretical elaboration of mediatization. As has been shown above, the media cannot be reduced to anonymous technologies for conveying information. The media are articulated from social, spatial, technological, symbolic and discursive aspects and are continuously involved in dialectic and non-linear relationships everywhere around us. Second, with such a multi-faceted media concept—which is in no way unique for the contemporary era, as Marvin and Gitelman remind us—one should strive for specification in order to grasp which aspects are particularly salient in the studied mediatization process. Hence, specifying is more important than agreement on how to define the media.

3.4 Approaching Mediatization

In order to grasp the nuanced dynamics of mediatization, I take as the point of departure the detailed, multi-faceted and specified concept of media argued for above and advocate a contextual approach where mediatization is considered from below. Media anthropology, with its thick descriptions and detailed analyses of confined worlds, is here a relevant source of inspiration (Hirsch 1998). The outlined ethnographical strategy is partly in contradiction to other scholars' argument concerning mediatization as a meta-framework on the same level as, for example, globalization (Krotz 2008; Hepp 2013b). However, in this respect, it is important to notice that globalization research concerns not only global structures and flows but also studies of "microglobalization" and "globalized lifeworlds" (Dürrschmidt 2000). As has been argued, the social practices of everyday local life are the origin of meta-processes such as globalization (Tomlinson 1999: 10; Beck 2002: 23).

The heterogeneous backgrounds of mediatization researchers mean that there are a variety of views on what mediatization research is, what ought to be studied and how. There is a tendency for the research, at least if we judge from some recent anthologies, to be dominated by elaborated theoretical frameworks, which sometimes are accompanied by smaller case studies (see Lundby 2009, 2014; Hepp and Krotz 2014). The drawback with a "grand narrative", as Cronqvist and colleagues discuss in relation to mediatization (2014: 18–20), is that it might lead to deductive top-down approaches, associated with the risk of presupposing "what needs to be demonstrated" (Silverstone 2007: 5). In other words, empirical analyses might become illustrations of theories already set. I believe in a more open and abductive approach, where empirical case studies focusing on the subtle social mechanisms of mediatization may mould the theoretical framework. Applied rightly, such a strategy also enables us to grasp fine-tuned social differences. For example, how different are mediatization processes for different types of tourism; for tourists and travellers? Or what does the mediatized home look like in different socio-cultural contexts? A bottom-up approach is not uncommon within a social-constructionist tradition (Hepp and Krotz 2014). Yet the present approach is consciously constructed not to start off in any dense and complex theoretical frameworks (see Hepp and Hasebrink 2014), since they might confine the analytical openness.

Furthermore, the approach of mediatization from below is positioned against an institutional tradition. Social interaction as well as the meaning of media in the context of everyday life are acknowledged also in this tradition (Hjarvard 2014a: 202), although in order to avoid "the myriad of variations of situated interaction" (2014a: 204), Hjarvard argues that the social interactions should be framed by societal institutions, like family politics and work. In another context, Hjarvard states that there is "a limited set of institutions in society" (2014b: 136). I see problems with making institutions, like family or work, the starting point for an analysis of the mediatized social world. First, owing to the myriad family constellations (or work conditions) and associated media-related practices, the institution represents an analytical level which is too general and risks reducing all social variety within the field. In addition, when a limited number of firmly established institutions are the point of departure, there is a risk one misses things that happen beyond them. For example, there might be new forms of living together (in relation to family), new forms of local engagement (in relation to politics), and increased existential reflections in everyday life (in relation to religion/existentialism)—which all are phenomena with possible relation to aspects of the media. A bottom-up approach, anchored in social worlds, provides better conditions for grasping these kinds of social changes.

There are several aspects to take into consideration when outlining an approach for grasping the dynamics of mediatization from below. In the following paragraphs, I will point out four central aspects: historical awareness, quantitative verses qualitative aspects, non–media-centric studies, and double theorization.

Whether one approaches mediatization on a macro or micro level, it is about dynamics, transformation, change, alteration or transition of social phenomena, institutions or society. Implicitly, mediatization implies comparative studies, juxtaposing "a before" and "an after". However, as media historians argue, one should be aware of not making the past the non-mediatized frame of reference (Cronqvist et al. 2014). The tourist example in the introduction of this text illustrates this. The mediatization of today's tourism does not imply that the media and tourism were separate phenomena in earlier eras. Tourism and discourses of tourism have always been interdependent (Urry 1990). The essence of the argument is instead that the media and mediation mark tourism differently today, probably in a more intense way, than in other eras. This is a parallel to Doreen Massey's argument that one should understand globalization not as something new in the end of the twentieth century but as an *intensification* of the connectivity between centres and peripheries. Colonialism is a crude reminder that there have been previous connections (Massey 1995: 52).

Another question concerns whether mediatization refers to quantitative or qualitative aspects—or both. Hepp and Krotz, for example, argue for quantitative *and* qualitative aspects of mediatization (2014: 5). Whereas the qualitative aspects are related to the specificity of different media, they argue that in quantitative terms mediatization relates to "the increasing temporal, spatial and social spread of media communication" (2014: 5). The increased presence of media in varied social contexts is of course an important condition of mediatization. Nevertheless, I think the quantitative aspect is problematic in this context and this is for two reasons. First, there is a risk of media determinism, that one presumes that increased access to media changes lifeworlds. However, from audience studies, we know that the presence of media does not say anything about the use of media. Second, if changed signification of social phenomena is what mediatization is about, it is questionable whether quantity has more than an indirect part of it. Mediatization of politics does not refer to the fact that politics are frequently mediated in news media, to take an example from the institutional tradition. Rather, it refers to how these many mediations (actual or potential ones) shape the behaviour of political actors. Hence, in this example, the mass media contribute to a change of the notion of politics, its content and conduct. Another example: there is a tendency that the mediatized home is linked to increasing amount of media technology in homes, or the great amount of domestic media usage (Peil and Röser 2014). Instead, I would argue that the mediatized home is about transformed notion(s) of home: how its content and conduct are marked and modified by media practices, media representations and media technologies. A concrete example of a research question here would be how hashtags (and the practices behind them) such as #home, #athome, #homesweethome and #homedecor (together accounting for more than 75 million posts on Instagram in August 2016) affect the notion of home.

The next question is what to study with a qualitative approach. As many have discussed, mediatization research requires a broader perspective, relating to other traditions, perspectives and even disciplines (Hjarvard 2012). As Hepp and colleagues express it, "by focusing on 'mediatization', we must ask much more fundamentally: how are media and communications related with certain sociocultural forms and their transformation(s)? Which interrelations do we find? What consequences can we observe during these transformational processes?" (2015: 321). In other words, a narrow focus on media texts or mediation or both is problematic when studying mediatization; one cannot grasp the increased dependence of media institutions or communication technologies and the altered signification of institutions like sports, politics or fashion by the study of various media representations or media institutions. The point of departure has to be the phenomena per se; to reveal the transformed notion of these phenomena, one needs first-hand contextual observations of them in their entireties. Thus, mediatization research has to be part of what Morley calls *non-media-centric media studies* (2007: 200; compare Hepp 2013b: 132–136). This term summarizes the contextualizing approaches, which also Moores (2005: 1–4; 2012), Silverstone (2007: 5) and Pink and Leder Mackley (2013) favour. The basic idea is that the best prerequisite for grasping the taken-for-granted meaning of media in everyday life—that is, the nuanced layers of the mediatization—is to focus on everyday life rather than media.

Hence, the social phenomenon or sphere of interest should be the starting point. Yet in order to conduct ethnographical thick descriptions of the social phenomenon, it has to be confined. Hepp's (2013b: 77–78) discussion of Benita Luckman's "small lifeworlds" is a pertinent reference in this context. Such confined contexts of the social world are very relevant objects of study in order to disclose the underlying social mechanisms and thereby keep the analysis transparent. Furthermore, the study of confined social contexts is in line with Krotz' argument that symbolic interactionism constitutes an excellent starting point for mediatization research. Symbolic interactionism stresses the social as an essential aspect of everything, as something that creates, affirms and transforms objects in people's world (Blumer 1969: 12). To understand mediatization of confined social phenomena, we have to understand not only actions and practices of the involved participants but also the underlying reflections, interpretations and meanings and how they derive from social interaction. As Blumer puts it, "social interaction is a process that *forms* human conduct instead of being merely a means or a setting for the expression or release of human conduct" (1969: 8, *italics in original*).

There is an additional aspect of the social phenomena one is going to study. Since these phenomena are as complex and multi-faceted as the media, the studied phenomenon should be as theoretically elaborated as the notion of media, discussed above. Consequently, one has to conduct what could be called a ***double theorization***. For example, to study the mediatization of home, we have to recognize that the home is a social construction constituted of material, practical and discursive aspects (Blunt and Dowling 2006: 1–3), not a static container for living. A double theorization like this enables us to deconstruct the mediatized home and reveal which domestic aspects interplay with which aspects of the multi-layered media.

3.5 Conclusion

Owing to the manifold applications and shifting underpinning epistemologies, mediatization research might appear to be unclear. Owing to some dense and complex theoretical frameworks, it might appear to be abstract. Theoretical concepts should not be simplified, but they may very well be clarified and unfolded. It can be achieved if the process of theorization is transparent, if arguments trickle up from concrete and intermediate levels to abstract ones. In this article, I have argued that specifying what one means by "media" is one way to clarify mediatization research. However, such a specification must be preceded by an elaboration of the notion of media and a recognition that the media as intermediate means of communication are articulations of different layers: technology, symbolic content and discourse. Furthermore, I have discussed a bottom-up approach with ethnographical thick descriptions of clearly delineated contexts or phenomena, guided by contextualization and a focus on social aspects beyond media representations and media technologies. The deep anchorage in the social world is favourable when it comes to grasping the dynamics of mediatization.

This means that I do not see mediatization research as a second-order investigation, as Livingstone and Lunt (2014: 720f.) suggest. Nor do I consider mediatization theory as "part of a broader a paradigm shift within media and communication research" (Hepp et al. 2015: 321). The epistemological backgrounds and the different view on communication among mediatization scholars are too diverse to represent a unified paradigm or even a homogeneous perspective. Yet I do want to stress that the outlined approach does not contradict institutional or meta-theoretical approaches to mediatization; it is an additional contribution to an already broad repertoire of mediatization research.

A final important aspect concerns the relation of mediatization traditions to other traditions within media and communication studies. A risk with considering mediatization as a concept of a meta level is that other concepts or perspectives (or both) within social and cultural theory in general and media and communication studies in particular are seen as subordinated. In that sense, it is better to consider mediatization as equal to other perspectives. There are, for instance, several examples of very relevant research frameworks where mediatization is fruitfully combined with other approaches. I am thinking especially of Hartmann's (2009, 2014) theoretical elaborations on the relationship between domestication and mediatization, Jansson's (2007a, 2013) recurrent framework of mediatization and communication geography, and lastly Madianou and Miller's coining of the concept of polymedia, which theoretically draws from mediatization (and mediation) and media ethnography (2012, 2013; compare Madianou 2014). The strength of these studies is that they conduct double theorization and let mediatization be part of a mutually reinforcing relationship with another theoretical tradition.

Notes

1. I am aware that other, threefold, categorizations have been discussed (Lundby 2014; Bolin 2014). Yet I will stick to this twofold one since I think it better clarifies the underlying theoretical differences.
2. Still, there are some parallels between viewing society as a set of institutions (Hjarvard 2014b: 136) and as a set of systems (Luhmann 2013).
3. See Jülich et al. (2008: 12–17) for a critique of the narrow concept of media within media and communication studies. Worthy of notice is Krotz

(2014), one of the few who exemplify mediatization with the book as medium—the book in the twelfth century, to be precise.
4. The stress on the social as an essential dimension of the media is the reason why I am not going to discuss medium theory and its extensive concept of the media in this article.
5. In addition, these studies constitute an interesting background to the contemporary focus on practice theory and non-representational theory within social and cultural theory (see Nansen et al. 2011).
6. Hartmann discusses the possibility of even a triple articulation (2006).

Acknowledgements Many thanks to my colleague Marie Cronqvist, the editors of this volume and an anonymous reviewer for their constructive criticism of an earlier draft of this article.

References

Ampuja, Marko, Juha Koivisto, and Elsa Väliverronen. 2014. Strong and weak forms of mediatization theory: A critical review. *Nordicom Review* 35: 111–123.

Andersson, Magnus. 2006. The flexible home. In *Geographies of communication: The spatial turn in media studies*, ed. Jesper Falkheimer, and André Jansson, 171–188. Göteborg: Nordicom.

Asp, Kent. 2014. Mediatization: Rethinking the question of media power. In *Mediatization of communication*, ed. Knut Lundby, 349–373. Berlin: De Gruyter.

Beck, Ulrich. 2002. The cosmopolitan society and its enemies. *Theory, Culture & Society* 19 (1–2): 17–44.

Berker, Thomas, Maren Hartmann, Yves Punie, and Katie J. Ward. 2006. *Domestication of media and technology*. Maidenhead: Open University Press.

Blumer, Herbert. 1969. *Symbolic interactionism: Perspective and method.* Berkeley: University of California Press.

Blunt, Alison, and Robyn Dowling. 2006. *Home*. London: Routledge.

Bolin, Göran. 2014. Institution, technology, world: Relationships between the media, culture and society. In *Mediatization of communication*, ed. Knut Lundby, 175–197. Berlin: De Gruyter.

Boyer, Dominic. 2012. From media anthropology to the anthropology of mediation. In *Mediatization of communication*, ed. Richard Fardon, Oliva Harris, Trevor H.J. Marchand, Cris Shore, Veronica Strang, Richard Wilson, and Mark Nuttall, 383–392. London: Sage.

Breiter, Andreas. 2014. Schools as mediatized worlds from a cross-cultural perspective. In *Mediatized worlds: Culture and society in a media age*, ed. Andreas Hepp, and Friedrich Krotz, 288–303. Basingstoke: Palgrave Macmillan.

Carey, James. 1989. *Communication as culture: Essays on media and society*. New York: Routledge.

Couldry, Nick. 2000. *The place of media power: Pilgrims and witnesses of the media age*. London: Routledge.

Couldry, Nick, and Andreas Hepp. 2013. Conceptualizing mediatization: Contexts, traditions, arguments. *Communication Theory* 23 (3): 191–202.

Cronqvist, Marie, Patrik Lundell, and Pelle Snickars. 2014. Inledning. In *Återkopplingar*, ed. Marie Cronqvist, Patrik Lundell, and Pelle Snickars, 9–28. Lund: Mediehistoriskt arkiv, Lunds universitet.

Deuze, Mark. 2014. Media life and the mediatization of the lifeworld. In *Mediatized worlds: Culture and society in a media age*, ed. Andreas Hepp, and Friedrich Krotz, 207–220. Basingstoke: Palgrave Macmillan.

Dürrschmidt, Jörg. 2000. *Everyday lives in the global city: The delinking of locale and milieu*. London: Routledge.

Enli, Gunn, and Eli Skogerbø. 2013. Personalized campaigns in party-centred politics: Twitter and Facebook as arenas for political communication. *Information, Communication & Society* 16 (5): 757–774.

Fornäs, Johan. 2014. Culturalizing mediatization. In *Mediatized worlds: Culture and society in a media age*, ed. Andreas Hepp, and Friedrich Krotz, 38–53. Basingstoke: Palgrave Macmillan.

Gitelman, Lisa. 2006. *Always already new: Media, history, and the data of culture*. Cambridge MA: The MIT Press.

Gray, Ann. 1992. *Video playtime: The gendering of a leisure technology*. London: Routledge.

Gregg, Melissa. 2011. *Work's intimacy*. Cambridge: Polity Press.

Hartmann, Maren. 2006. The triple articulation of ICTs. Media as technological objects, symbolic environments and individual texts. In *Domestication of media and technology*, ed. Thomas Berker, Maren Hartmann, Yves Punie, and Katie J. Ward, 80–102. Maidenhead: Open University Press.

Hartmann, Maren. 2009. Everyday: Domestication of mediatization or mediatized domestication? In *Mediatization: Concept, changes, consequences*, ed. Knut Lundby, 225–242. New York: Peter Lang.

Hartmann, Maren. 2014. Home is where the heart is? Ontological security and the mediatization of homelessness. In *Mediatization of communication*, ed. Knut Lundby, 641–660. Berlin: De Gruyter.

Haßler, Jörg, Marcus Maurer, and Corinna Oschatz. 2014. Media logic and political logic online and offline: The case of climate change communication. *Journalism Practice* 8 (3): 326–341.

Hepp, Andreas. 2012. Mediatization and the 'molding force' of the media. *Communications* 37 (1): 1–25.

Hepp, Andreas. 2013a. The communicative figurations of mediatized worlds: Mediatization research in times of the 'mediation of everything'. *European Journal of Communication* 28 (6): 615–629.

Hepp, Andreas. 2013b. *Cultures of mediatization*. Cambridge: Polity Press.

Hepp, Andreas, and Uwe Hasebrink. 2014. Human interaction and communicative figurations: The transformation of mediatized cultures and societies. In *Mediatization of communication*, ed. Knut Lundby, 249–272. Berlin: De Gruyter.

Hepp, Andreas, and Friedrich Krotz. 2014. Mediatized worlds—Understanding everyday mediatization. In *Mediatized worlds: Culture and society in a media age*, ed. Andreas Hepp, and Friedrich Krotz, 1–15. Basingstoke: Palgrave Macmillan.

Hepp, Andreas, Stig Hjarvard, and Knut Lundby. 2015. Mediatization: Theorizing the interplay between media, culture and society. *Media, Culture and Society* 37 (2): 314–324.

Hirsch, Eric. 1998. Bound and unbound entities: Reflections on the ethnographic perspectives of anthropology vis-à-vis media and cultural studies. In *Ritual, performance, media*, ed. Felicia Hughes-Freeland, 208–228. London: Routledge.

Hjarvard, Stig. 2012. Doing the right thing: Media and communication studies in a mediatized world. *Nordicom Review* 33 (1): 27–34.

Hjarvard, Stig. 2013. *The mediatization of culture and society*. London: Routledge.

Hjarvard, Stig. 2014a. Mediatization and cultural and social change: An institutional perspective. In *Mediatization of communication*, ed. Knut Lundby, 199–226. Berlin: De Gruyter.

Hjarvard, Stig. 2014b. From mediation to mediatization: The institutionalization of new media. In *Mediatized worlds: Culture and society in a media age*, ed. Andreas Hepp, and Friedrich Krotz, 123–139. Basingstoke: Palgrave Macmillan.

Ihlen, Øivind, and Josef Pallas. 2014. Mediatization of corporations. In *Mediatization of communication*, ed. Knut Lundby, 423–441. Berlin: De Gruyter.

Jansson, André. 2007a. A sense of tourism: New media and the dialectic of encapsulation/decapsulation. *Tourist Studies* 7 (1): 5–24.

Jansson, André. 2007b. Texture: A key concept for communication geography. *European Journal of Cultural Studies* 10 (2): 185–202.

Jansson, André. 2013. Mediatization and social space: Reconstructing mediatization for the transmedia age. *Communication Theory* 23 (3): 279–296.

Jülich, Solveig, Patrik Lundell, and Pelle Snickars. 2008. Mediernas kulturhistoria: En inledning. In *Mediernas kulturhistoria*, ed. Solveig Jülich, Patrik Lundell, and Pelle Snickars, 9–29. Stockholm: Statens ljud- och bildarkiv, Mediehistoriskt arkiv 8.

Krotz, Friedrich. 2008. Media connectivity: Concepts, conditions and consequences. In *Connectivity, networks and flows: Conceptualizing contemporary communications*, ed. Andreas Hepp, Friedrich Krotz, Shaun Moores, and Carsten Winter, 13–33. Cresskill NJ: Hampton Press.

Krotz, Friedrich. 2014. Media, mediatization and mediatized worlds: A discussion of the basic concepts. In *Mediatized worlds: Culture and society in a media age*, ed. Andreas Hepp, and Friedrich Krotz, 72–87. Basingstoke: Palgrave Macmillan.

Kunelius, Risto. 2014. Climate change challenges: An agenda for de-centered mediatization research. In *Mediatization of communication*, ed. Knut Lundby, 63–86. Berlin: De Gruyter.

Kunelius, Risto, and Esa Reunanen. 2012. The medium of the media: Journalism, politics, and the theory of 'mediatisation'. *Javnost* 19 (4): 5–24.

Lash, Scott, and John Urry. 1994. *Economies of signs and space*. London: Sage.

Lasswell, Harold D. 1948. The structure and function of communication in society. In *The communication of ideas*, ed. Lyman Bryson, 32–51. New York: Harper & Brothers.

Livingstone, Sonia. 2009. On the mediation of everything: ICA presidential address 2008. *Journal of Communication* 59: 1–18.

Livingstone, Sonia, and Peter Lunt. 2014. Mediatization: An emerging paradigm for media and communication research? In *Mediatization of communication*, ed. Knut Lundby, 703–724. Berlin: De Gruyter.

Luhmann, Niklas. 2013. *Introduction to system theory*. Cambridge: Polity Press.

Lundby, Knut. 2009. Media Logic: Looking for Social Interaction. In *Mediatization: Concept, changes, consequences*, ed. Knut Lundby, 101–119. New York: Peter Lang.

Lundby, Knut. 2014. Introduction: Mediatization of communication. In *Mediatization of communication*, ed. Knut Lundby, 3–38. Berlin: De Gruyter.

Lunt, Peter, and Sonia Livingstone. 2016. Is 'mediatization' the new paradigm for our field? A commentary on Deacon and Stayer (2014, 2015) and Hepp, Hjarvard and Lundby (2015). *Media, Culture and Society* 38 (3): 462–470.

Madianou, Mirca. 2014. Polymedia communication and mediatized migration: An ethnographic approach. In *Mediatization of communication*, ed. Knut Lundby, 323–348. Berlin: De Gruyter.

Madianou, Mirca, and Daniel Miller. 2012. *Migration and new media: Transnational families and polymedia*. London: Routledge.

Madianou, Mirca, and Daniel Miller. 2013. Polymedia: Towards a new theory of digital media in interpersonal communication. *International Journal of Cultural Studies* 16 (2): 169–187.

Marvin, Carolyn. 1988. *When old technologies were new: Thinking about communication in the late nineteenth century.* Oxford: Oxford University Press.

Massey, Doreen. 1995. The conceptualization of place. In *A place in the world?*, ed. Doreen Massey, and Pat Jess, 45–77. Oxford: Oxford University Press.

Meyen, Michael, Marcus Tieroff, and Steffi Strenger. 2014. Mass media logic and the mediatization of politics: A theoretical framework. *Journalism Studies* 15 (3): 271–288.

Moores, Shaun. 2005. *Media/theory: Thinking about media and communication.* London: Routledge.

Moores, Shaun. 2012. *Media, Place and Mobility.* Basingstoke: Palgrave Macmillan.

Morley, David. 1986. *Family television: Cultural power and domestic leisure.* London: Routledge.

Morley, David. 2007. *Media, modernity and technology: The geography of the new.* London: Routledge.

Nansen, Bjorn, Michael Arnold, Martin Gibbs, and Hilary Davis. 2011. Dwelling with media stuff: Latencies and logics of materiality in four Australian homes. *Environment and Planning D: Society and Space* 29: 693–715.

Peil, Corinna, and Jutta Röser. 2014. The meaning of home in the context of digitization, mobilization and mediatization. In *Mediatized worlds: Culture and society in a media age*, ed. Andreas Hepp, and Friedrich Krotz, 233–249. Basingstoke: Palgrave Macmillan.

Pink, Sarah, and Kerstin Leder Mackley. 2013. Saturated and situated: Expanding the meaning of media in the routines of everyday life. *Media, Culture and Society* 35 (6): 677–691.

Polson, Erica. 2016. Negotiating independent mobility: Single female expats in Bangalore. *European Journal of Cultural Studies*, Online First.

Silverstone, Roger. 1994. *Television and everyday life.* London: Routledge.

Silverstone, Roger. 1999. *Why study the media?*. London: Sage.

Silverstone, Roger. 2005. The sociology of mediation and communication. In *The Sage handbook of sociology*, ed. Craig Calhoun, Chris Rojek, and Bryan Turner, 188–207. London: Sage.

Silverstone, Roger. 2007. *Media and morality: On the rise of the Mediapolis.* Cambridge: Polity.

Silverstone, Roger, and Eric Hirsch. 1992. *Consuming technologies: Media and information in domestic spaces.* London: Routledge.

Strömbäck, Jesper, and Frank Esser. 2009. Shaping politics: Mediatization and media interventionism. In *Mediatization: Concept, changes, consequences*, ed. Knut Lundby, 205–223. New York: Peter Lang.

Strömbäck, Jesper, and Frank Esser. 2014. Mediatization of politics: Transforming democracies and reshaping politics. In *Mediatization of communication*, ed. Knut Lundby, 375–404. Berlin: De Gruyter.
Tacchi, Jo. 1998. Radio texture: Between self and others. In *Material cultures: Why some things matter*, ed. Daniel Miller, 39–60. London: UCL Press.
Tomlinson, John. 1999. *Globalization and culture*. Cambridge: Polity Press.
Urry, John. 1990. *The tourist gaze: Leisure and travel in contemporary societies*. London: Sage.
Williams, Raymond. 1983. *Keywords*. London: Fontana Press.

CHAPTER 4

Mediatization: From Structure to Agency (and Back Again)

Zrinjka Peruško

4.1 Introduction

Mediatization is a non-linear (Esser 2013; Couldry 2014; Hjarvard 2013) and contextually sensitive process; conditions of structures and cultures influence its shape. In addition to (expected) variations in relation to macro contextual conditions, mediatization takes place in media-related social practice/interaction at different levels of society (Couldry 2012; Krotz 2009, 2014; Hjarvard 2008, 2014; Hepp and Hasebrink 2014). From this, it follows that only a comprehensive social theory addressing the variations both at the structural level and at the level of social practice can fully explain it. Following from these premises, this chapter has two related theoretical aims.

First, it attempts to expand on the mediatization-as-structuration thesis (Hjarvard 2014a) by relating the media system as structure to media use as agency. Related to this is the proposal for a multi-level mixed methods research program as especially appropriate for empirically investigating mediatization as a multi-level and multi-dimensional social process. A

Z. Peruško (✉)
University of Zagreb, Zagreb, Croatia
e-mail: zperusko@fpzg.hr

O. Driessens et al. (eds.), *Dynamics Of Mediatization*,
Transforming Communications – Studies in Cross-Media Research,
DOI 10.1007/978-3-319-62983-4_4

set of empirical studies that relate the structural and the action/practice level—media systems/landscapes and media use (including both reception, sharing/distribution and production by the audiences)—will be reviewed in order to provide an example of the structuration approach in mediatization research. Directions of further empirical study of the structuration process will be sketched with the aim of increasing the attention to agency within the institutional approach to mediatization.

Second, focusing on the structural level, this chapter endeavours to show differences in the state of mediatization of media systems as structural macro conditions of mediatized practice. This will be explored by placing media systems research in a broader context of mediatization. As a contribution to de-Westernizing mediatization, both Western and Eastern Europe are addressed in the discussion of mediatization in empirical terms. Despite recent attempts to expand the approach in geographical terms, there is still insufficient empirical evidence that the process/outcome of mediatization even exists outside of the "rich countries" (Couldry and Hepp 2017). This chapter aims to contribute to filling in some blanks in this regard.

The chapter unfolds as follows. First, the structuration approach to mediatization is reconsidered in relation to its empirical usefulness, and a mixed methods research strategy is proposed as the most promising (as the main use of theory is to aid in our understanding of the empirical world, the mediatization approach will advance only as fast as we are able to conceptualize, operationalize and measure/describe/understand mediatization in its different variations). Next, the focus is placed on the structural level with a discussion of dimensions describing contemporary media systems in relation to indicators that describe mediatization. The discussion of mediatization at the macro level proceeds with empirical examples of European country clusters/media systems and their different levels of mediatization. The third step brings back the level of media practice (theorized as agency in terms of the structuration approach, Giddens 1984) as varied aspects of media use which is related to the mediatized structural contexts.

4.2 A Mixed Methods Approach for Empirical Investigation of Mediatization

Research still seems to be divided by specific understandings of mediatization in the three approaches. The institutional approach to mediatization is most often linked to (post)positivist epistemologies and quantitative designs focusing on the institutional macro or meso levels, constructivist approaches are usually linked to interpretivist or critical epistemologies and qualitative designs and focus predominantly on practice or the micro levels, while the materialist/technological approaches put the spotlight on the way technology's affordances play a role. (For overviews of the approaches, see Lundby 2009, 2014a, 2014b; Livingstone and Lunt 2014; Bolin 2014.) But, as recent work is increasingly noting, the process of mediatization spans the macro, meso and micro levels—changes in institutions provide different contexts for media- and communication-related action for individuals, and changes in individual (or group) practices in time shape changes in the institutions.

There are several sociological theories that are good candidates for integrating the macro and the micro levels (or the field of structures with the field of actions) that in one way or another have already been addressed within mediatization research—Giddens's structuration theory (Hjarvard 2014a), Bourdieu's field theory (Couldry 2014; Bolin 2017), Habermas's theory of communicative action (Bolin 2010)—although they have yet to see an empirical application. (Benson's 2014 empirical application of field theory in a study of immigration news in France and the US in a multi-method comparative research design is an exception but is on the outside of the mediatization conversation.)

If mediatization is a multi-level social process at the micro, meso and macro levels of society with variable manifestations in different social fields (Hjarvard 2014a; Jansson 2002; Livingstone 2009; Strömbäck 2008), then these multiple levels can be empirically approached only in a mixed-method design including both quantitative and qualitative research strategies. Mixed methods research linking levels of individual agency (micro level, although agency can be at any level depending on the character of the actors) with the macro-level structures has been used in conjecture with Bourdieu's reflexive sociology in the study of information systems (Fries 2009) and news (Benson 2014). Although Giddens's structuration theory is found "too lacking in specification to actively guide research" (Poole 2009: 583), the inspiration of the structuration thesis has often (Jones and Karsten 2008) been used as the backdrop in mixed methods research of information systems where the functional analysis is used to study structures, and "interpretive studies are needed to illuminate the constitution of the system" (Poole 2009: 584). Bolin (2017) recently presented a cross-generational and cross-cultural analysis of mediatization and media use which uses on Bourdieu's field theory and highlighted exactly the structure/agency relationship. The contribution of field theory to understanding agency as constitutive of the media field has so far placed more attention on journalists as actors (Bourdieu 2005; Benson and Neveu 2005).

Many empirical studies of mediatization have been undertaken in recent years, primarily in relation to mediatization of politics, religion, family, childhood play, migration, culture and sport (Scannell 2016; Hjarvard and Petersen 2013; Hepp et al. 2010; Lundby 2014a). Only a few attempts at comparative cross-national or longitudinal research exist, predominantly in respect to the spatial or temporal variations in the mediatization of politics in Western European contexts (Magin 2015; Udris and Lucht 2014; Umbricht and Esser 2013). Bolin's (2017) cross-temporal and cross-cultural analysis of media generations in a comparative perspective of Sweden and Estonia is a rare exception.

This chapter argues for a comparative cross-country multi-level structuration approach as an empirical research agenda of mediatization following Stig Hjarvard's (2014a: 124) structuration approach to mediatization where "the duality of structure and agency and … long-term institutionalization of media-influenced patterns of social interaction [are] at the heart of the theory of mediatization". In the following section, the structural level of media landscape will be further defined in relation to mediatization.

4.3 Structure

Many changes associated with mediatization are seen to originate with the mass media (i.e. in the television era) (Schulz 2004; Strömbäck 2008). Others find evidence of mediatization-related changes since the times of the first communication technologies (Krotz 2009). Couldry and Hepp (2017) identify three *waves* of mediatization—mechanization, electrification and digitalization (including datafication) as the last wave of deep mediatization (2017: 34). The notion of *regimes* of mediatization is developed by Hjarvard (2014b: 204) to picture changes in the relationships of power between institutions in the media field.

In this chapter, mediatization is investigated in the current wave of digitalization in deep mediatization, when the process of media-related change is not linked to any singular media but to the entire media environment or ensemble (Couldry 2012; Finnemann 2014). There are several competing terms for this: media system, media landscape, communication ecology, or media manifold (Couldry and Hepp 2017).

Bolin (2017) uses the concept of "objective" media landscapes to describe the structural level as opposed to "subjective" media landscapes, which are composed of individually selected media and content.

As Friedrich Krotz (2014: 148f.) has emphasized, analysis of mediatization needs to start with the analysis of the changes in the media system. Seen as structural conditions of mediatization (Strömbäck 2008; Hepp et al. 2010; Hjarvard 2008; Krotz 2009; Schrott 2009), *media systems* (used here as a descriptive term and not as a theoretical proposition) have not been sufficiently analysed (Deacon and Stanyer 2014; Livingstone and Lunt 2014; Magin 2015). Within the institutional perspective, mediatization is seen "as an inter-institutional process in which particular practices of mediations ... are influenced by several institutional structures" (Hjarvard 2014b: 203). The attention to the transformations in the wider media ecology is highlighted in the technological mediatization perspective (Livingstone and Lunt 2014; Finnemann 2014; Deuze 2011), whereas the cultural constructivist perspective sees the surrounding media landscape as "material and mental environment" (Nowak 1996, cited in Bolin 2014: 188). In none of these contexts is media system further conceptualized or defined.

The predominant understanding of media systems today is focused on the relationship of news media and politics (Hallin and Mancini 2004). The prevailing model by Hallin and Mancini (2004) defines media systems with five main dimensions/variables: (1) the political system, (2) the media market, (3) the degree of the autonomy and professionalization of journalism, (4) political parallelism and (5) the role of the state. Three models of media systems in Western Europe and North America were constructed on the basis of case studies and research evidence: the liberal model is best represented by the US (although the UK and Ireland are also included), the democratic corporatist model includes the Northern and Central European countries, including Germany, and the polarized pluralist model includes the Mediterranean part of Europe, including Italy and Greece. Comparative empirical operationalization of the model in Eastern and Western European countries (Peruško et al. 2013; Peruško 2016) and Western Europe and North America (Brüggemann et al. 2014) has used current aggregated cross-country data but has not expanded on the definition of a media system in relation to the ongoing developments in the media. In his description of "hybrid media logics" and "hybrid" media systems, which can be seen to pertain to the digital phase of deep mediatization, Chadwick includes technologies as well as "genres, norms, behaviors, and organizational forms" (2013: 4) but without considering the broader institutional and political makeup of the legacy and digital media or the broadening of the concept of media system beyond political journalism.

In this chapter, we are concerned with the conceptualization, definition, operationalization and empirical testing of media systems as the macro condition of mediatization. The key question is how are differences at the level of common institutional structures linked to the degree to which a media system is mediatized? Put differently, we are looking to make a systematic representation of what constitutes mediatization at the structural level of media landscape.

What dimensions reflect the most important characteristics of media systems in high modernity/deep mediatization? Building on the accepted notion that a media system is not only a grouping of media or media-related practices but that institutions (in previous research predominantly political institutions) play an important role (Blumler and Gurevitch 1995; Hallin and Mancini 2004), a model of digital mediascape was developed (Peruško et al. 2015). While describing the most important characteristics of media systems in high modernity, the model also accounts for the critique of the dominant model of Hallin and Mancini (2004): a predominant focus on journalism and legacy media of press and television to the detriment of "new" media (at the time of the writing of their book deep mediatization was just starting), insuficient attention to the change in the status of the state in the network age, and no place for media culture and global media developments (Hardy 2012). Four dimensions of digital mediascapes have been proposed to account for the changes in purpose and scope of contemporary media systems: (1) the dimension of institutional inclusiveness, (2) the dimension of globalization, (3) the dimension of digitized media market, and (4) the dimension of media culture (Peruško et al. 2015, 2016). Here, they will be reviewed in relation to their contribution to describing the system level of mediatization.

4.3.1 *The Empirical Studies: How Media Systems Were Measured and Constructed and Related to Audience Practice*

A series of empirical studies worked with these dimensions from a structuration perspective in looking for the relationship of the structural level of media system and media-related practice—media use (Peruško et al. 2015; Peruško and Vozab 2015; Aroldi et al. 2015) and journalistic practice (Peruško et al. 2016)—giving us an opportunity to review the results in terms of the role of the structural level of mediatization in media-related practices. Before we proceed, a brief account of the conceptualization and measurement of the four dimensions and the description of research design and procedures is provided.

The institutional dimension was originally operationalized as the quality of democracy and social and economic inclusiveness and measured with the Economist Intelligence Unit (EIU) Democracy Index and United Nations Development Programme (UNDP) Human Development Index (HDI), respectively (Peruško et al. 2015). The dimension was later expanded to include additional variables on the type of regime (also based on the EIU Democracy Index) and freedom of expression, operationalized by averaging the Reporters Without Borders and Freedom House Freedom of Expression Indexes (Peruško et al. 2016). Media market was operationalized with newspaper circulation (per capita), TV audience concentration (C 3), broadband internet (fixed (wired) broadband subscriptions per 100 inhabitants), social media penetration (percentage of population using social media), fixed telephone change 2003–2013, and smartphone penetration (percentage of population owning a smartphone). In the 2016 study, the dimension was extended with the market position of public television (rank in the first three audience preferences). The dimension of media culture was measured with per-capita import and export of media culture and included newspapers, journals and periodicals, cinematographic films, video games and consoles and recorded media (CDs, DVDs, gramophone records etc.) (Peruško et al. 2016). The aggregate statistics were obtained from published data by international institutions and associations: the European Audiovisual Observatory, ITU, WAN-IFRA, EUROSTAT and UNCTAD (Peruško et al. 2015, 2016). Globalization was operationalized with the KOF Index of Globalization, which measures the concept on three dimensions: "economic globalization, characterized as long-distance flows of goods, capital and services as well as information and perceptions that accompany market exchanges; political globalization, characterized by a diffusion of government policies; and social globalization, expressed as the spread of ideas, information, images and people" (Dreher 2006: 1092).

Variables were linked with standardized values as described above, and hierarchical cluster analysis was performed twice to group countries into media systems (Ward's method with Euclidean distance was used as a measure of similarity, and the elbow method was used in identifying the number of groups; variables were standardized as z-scores). In the first study, 23 Eastern and Western European countries were analysed (Peruško et al. 2015: Table 4.1, 349; values in Table 4.2, 351). The second cluster analysis with the use of the extended model was performed on 33 Eastern and Western European countries (Peruško et al. 2016). The country groupings will be presented below together with the characteristics of the digitized media systems related to mediatization, which are developed in the next section.

After the cluster analyses of media systems, regression analysis was performed on audience data, in some of the studies after factor analysis. The audience data were collected in 2013 with the same questionnaire on representative national samples of online audiences in nine participating countries (N = 10,742) in a cross-European project (Jensen and Helles 2015).

Three studies which are used as examples in this chapter were performed on the same data set of audiences and media systems to account for differences or similarities in media-related practices: in terms of preference of the type of media (Peruško et al. 2015), audiences' online engagement practices (Peruško and Vozab 2015) and spaces of media use (Aroldi et al. 2015). Audience studies were performed in only nine countries: Belgium, Croatia, Denmark, Germany, Hungary, Israel, Italy, Poland and Portugal (comparative project is described in Jensen and Helles 2015). Since these countries cluster in the same media systems in the original and the expanded model, regression analysis of macro-level influences on media use will be interpreted with both media system clusters. Audience practices constitute agency in respect to the structuration approach.

The four dimensions of digital media systems will now be engaged in the mediatization perspective and related to criteria for evaluating mediatization empirically at the media systems level.

4.3.2 *Inclusive Institutions Dimension*

Hjarvard finds that "mediatization is, obviously, dependent on the proliferation of various media forms, but the transformative process of mediatization is a result of various institutions' changing access to and varying control over these vital resources" (2014b: 204). The type of political

Table 4.1 Bivariate correlation between all digitized media landscape variables

	1	*2*	*3*	*4*	*5*	*6*	*7*	*8*	*9*	*10*	*11*	*12*	*13*	*14*
Democracy	1													
Social & economic equality	0.82**	1												
Political regime	0.71**	0.34*	1											
Media freedom	0.91**	0.79**	0.69**	1										
Newspaper circulation	0.68**	0.64**	0.21	0.55**	1									
TV audience	0.23	0.04	0.17	0.21	0.27	1								
Market position of public television	0.46**	0.58**	–0.01	0.4*	0.47**	0.13	1							
Internet	0.74**	0.82**	0.32	0.67**	0.67**	0.05	0.51**	1						
Social media	0.5**	0.35*	0.21	0.33	0.51**	0.5**	0.37*	0.45**	1					
Telephone change	0.47**	0.43*	0.17	0.42*	0.55**	0.17	0.15	0.31	0.27	1				
Smartphone	0.51**	0.59**	-0.03	0.29	0.64**	-0.04	0.61**	0.57**	0.49**	0.44**	1			
Cultural import	0.51**	0.62**	0.19	0.54**	0.45**	-0.12	0.44*	0.61**	0.3	0.25	.54**	1		
Cultural export	0.29	0.39*	0.13	0.38*	0.2	-0.15	0.26	0.4*	0.13	0.09	0.31	.88**	1	
Globalization	0.57**	0.71**	0.32	0.67**	0.28	-0.06	0.33	.47**	0.1	0.31	0.27	.6**	.4*	1

Note *p ≤ .05; **p ≤ .01
Source Peruško et al. 2016

Table 4.2 Digitization of European media landscapes in deep mediatization

Media landscape	*Countries**	*System characteristics*	*Mediatization*
Inclusive	Austria, ***Denmark***, Finland, Iceland, Netherlands, Sweden	Highest political inclusiveness, highest social inclusiveness, highest globalization, highly developed digital media market, highest imports & exports in cultural industry sector and moderate TV concentration	Most pronounced structural mediatization indicators, except TV audience fragmentation; Internet and radio used in more places than in most other types (except Israel); most varied media use in common domestic places (with Convergent media system)
Convergent	***Belgium***, Estonia, France, ***Germany***, Ireland, ***Italy***, Malta, Slovenia, Spain, United Kingdom	High social and high political inclusiveness, highest globalization, higher to moderately developed digital media market, low TV concentration, and developed and open cultural industry sector	High to moderate structural mediatization indicators, Most active online audiences in public connection/civic participation
Peripheral	Bulgaria, ***Croatia***, Cyprus, Czech, FYRM, Greece, ***Hungary***, Latvia, ***Poland***, ***Portugal***, Romania, Serbia Slovakia	Lower political and social inclusiveness, lower globalization, less developed digital media market and not significant cultural industry sector, higher TV concentration	Less advanced structural mediatization indicators More than average ubiquitous media use, on-line news use, points towards mediatization of practices (agency over structure)
Non-inclusive	Russian Federation, Turkey	Lowest political, social and economic development, lowest globalization, low Internet, but medium smartphone penetration, most fragmented TV audiences, lower position of public television, lowest import and export of culture	The lowest scores on all mediatization indicators except audience fragmentation; only moderate smartphone diffusion might speak to practices of mediatization.

(continued)

Table 4.2 (continued)

Media landscape	*Countries**	*System characteristics*	*Mediatization*
Israel	*Israel*	Lower political and higher social inclusiveness, lower globalization, moderately developed digital media market (but highest social media diffusion), less open creative economy and highest TV concentration	Less advanced structural mediatization indicators, except social media penetration (linked to higher HDI) Most ubiquitous media users, points to mediatization of practice

Adapted from Peruško et al. 2015, 2016

* In bold are countries included in the comparative audience study (Jensen and Helles 2015)

Two countries changed clusters between the first and second study: Austria clustered in the Convergent system in the 2015 study, and Slovenia in the Peripheral system regime is one of the key points in the Hallin and Mancini (2004) model of media systems, and the names of the three types are derived from the predominant characteristics of their political field. In choosing to move beyond journalism in constructing a new media system model, the institutional field needs to be seen in a broader perspective. Mediatization has also been identified with the advent of autonomous media institution (Hjarvard 2008; Strömbäck 2008).[1] The concept of inclusive institutions developed by Acemoğlu and Robinson (2012) illuminates this point. Inclusive institutions—as found in democracies—promote free expression and free invention as well as ensure the necessary freedom for the "creative disruption" that is a basis for technical and social innovation and economic progress (Acemoğlu and Robinson 2012). While the processes that drive mediatization have not so far been systematically analysed, most authors who date mediatization with high modernity and later expect commercialization to play a part in increased mediatization (Strömbäck 2008; Udris and Lucht 2014).

In addition to the usual strong relationship between the HDI, democracy, globalization (Norris and Inglehart 2009) and media freedom, the correlation analysis performed on the digital mediascape model found strong or moderate correlations between democracy and several variables describing the digitized media market—internet diffusion, newspaper circulation, smartphone and social media penetration as well as the strong position of PSB (Table 4.1). Additionally, HDI is strongly related to newspaper circulation and internet diffusion.

This would suggest that those media systems with higher inclusiveness in both the political and the socio-economic field are more mediatized.

4.3.3 Globalization

Globalization has long been associated with contemporary developments of media and communication technologies, which are seen as its drivers. Manuel Castells (1996) and Arjun Appadurai (2000 [1990]) are the most well known among social theorists who investigate this relationship (Ampuja 2012). While important critiques of the media system approach come from those who challenge the primacy of the nation state as an analytical unit (the methodological nationalism critique of Ulrich Beck), the importance of the national media system remains as the place of media use and regulation—Flew and Waisbord (2015) show in cross-country comparisons of the internet that states maintain legal control of the boundaries also in the digitized media system. Without a doubt, contemporary media systems are affected, and can be differentiated, by their participation in the global flows.

Globalization of media markets is expected to promote the convergence of media systems (Hallin and Mancini 2004; Voltmer 2012 quoted in Flew and Waisbord 2015: 626). Globalization as a process is seen to be connected to mediatization (Hepp et al. 2010) where globalization is expected to support the spread of mediatization and centrifugal, fragmenting forces in media consumption (Hjarvard 2008). Correlation analysis performed on the digital mediascape model shows significant and moderate relations between the degree of globalization and that of internet diffusion (Table 4.1). Higher globalization then can be considered an indicator of higher mediatization. Higher degree of globalization would also be expected to be linked with higher audience fragmentation. (In television, this would show as lower television channel concentration in terms of audience size in a multi-channel environment.)

4.3.4 Digital Media Market

The dimension of technology is where the change is most readily visible in the digitized media system, and technology has been underlined as an area that should figure more prominently in mediatization research (Finnemann 2014). Increase in mediatization is very much linked to media innovations in the digital age and the increase of media and media channels.

Media system is composed of a comprehensive media matrix, a set of available media together with their different institutionalizations and usages which vary across media systems according to political, economic and cultural contexts (Finnemann 2014: 299). Emerging media systems in the digital age are affected by the changes in media technologies, institutions and practices: digitization, mobility, media abundance, network architecture and mass self-communication and a hybridization of old and new media logics in media institutions and formats (Castells 2009; Couldry 2012; Chadwick 2013). Fortunati (2005) describes it as the mediatization of the internet and the internetization of the mass media. From flow (Williams 2003 [1974]) to torrent flow (Gittlin), from television galaxy (McLuhan, Castells) to network flow (Castells 1996), the cross-media environment (Hasebrink and Domeyer 2012) of today is a result of converging social forces, including technological developments, policy decisions, interconnectedness of people and countries, institutions and new social practices.

The spread of different media (in terms of their penetration or use) thus can be used to gauge the degree of mediatization. In relation to the present-day digitized media landscapes, it is expected that higher penetration of digitized media is related to higher mediatization, and the broader the multi-media matrix, the higher the mediatization.

Bivariate correlation confirmed that the spread of broadband is related to openness of the creative economy as well as to social media and smartphone penetration (Table 4.1).

4.3.5 *Media Culture*

Media systems are more than containers of news; they should also be seen as systems of cultural production and consumption and in terms of cultural flows in increasingly globalized mediascapes (Appadurai 2000 [1990]; Esser 2013; Peruško and Čuvalo 2014). Although the focus on political institutions and the news media-politics dynamic makes sense in relation to political communication or mediatization of politics, a broader view is necessary to show a more comprehensive interplay between media, culture and society in terms of mediatization. Entertainment, and not news, is the largest business in both the legacy and digital media. Rantanen (2013) also argues against methodological structuralism that naturalized the political in media system research to the detriment of new media cultures.

Mediatization is expected to expand the realm of media culture (Jansson 2002, in Hjarvard 2008: 108), so the size of the sector of media culture, or the export and import of cultural goods, can be used as an outcome indicator of the degree of mediatization. Even if the media is a global business, a great majority of large media corporations are "national corporations with international operations" (Flew and Waisbord 2015: 627), so it makes sense to take account of the cultural production and exchange as one of the media system dimensions. In this respect, mediatization is seen as driving the increase in the media culture sector, not the other way around.

4.3.6 *Mediatization in European Media Landscapes*

Considering these conceptualizations of drivers of mediatization at the level of digital media systems, we can distil a set of propositions as indicators of mediatization at the structural level. In evaluating the variations across European digitized media landscapes in terms of the presence or degree of mediatization, we could be guided by the following set of premises. Higher degree of mediatization is in times of deep mediatization positively related to the following:

1. the higher spread of all the media, and especially the digital media, which is also linked to a higher commercialization of the overall media market,
2. the larger sector of creative industries or media culture,
3. higher globalization,
4. higher audience fragmentation, and
5. more inclusive political and social institutions.

Obviously, no absolute measures of the degree of mediatization can be attached to these dimensions, but the proportionate levels of mediatization need to be "calibrated" on the basis of comparative analysis. It is expected that the levels of mediatization will be dynamic, both internally (i.e. within one media system) as well as in comparison between media systems; since mediatization is a multi-causal affair, different development in assorted dimensions over time in various media systems may influence mediatization in varied ways.

Based on the variations in variables constructing the dimensions presented above, five main clusters/types of digitized media landscapes were identified in the two empirical studies (Peruško et al. 2015, 2016): the *inclusive media landscape*, the *convergent mainstream media landscape*, the *peripheral media landscape*, the *non-inclusive media landscape*, and Israel which clustered separately (Table 4.2).

The most mediatized *inclusive* cluster—composed of countries that are part of the democratic-corporatist model (Hallin and Mancini 2004): Denmark, Sweden, Finland, Iceland, Austria and The Netherlands—shows the highest values in political and social inclusiveness and in the diffusion of digital media. It also shows highest globalization values and the highest exports and imports of the cultural industry. Moderate levels of TV concentration, hence a lesser fragmentation of audiences, go hand in hand with the highest position of PSB in television viewership. The highest institutional inclusiveness in this cluster with the largest spread of digital media supports the argument that inclusive institutions allow for the most disruptive technological development that is necessary for economic development. New media landscape in the Inclusive countries is characterized by high diffusion of digital technology. Regulatory changes—increased liberalization—and concentration of ownership bringing about also market changes, with increased position of transnational media organizations: for instance, Netflix has a larger audience share in the Nordic countries that in the rest of Europe (Schwarz 2016). Despite increased commercialization and tabloidization in some countries (Finland) and a decline of the importance of political press, PSB still holds the highest position in Europe (Herkman 2012: 376). The inclusive cluster exhibits the highest values in all of the proposed indicators of mediatization, except regarding audience fragmentation (therefore, the relationship of mediatization and audience fragmentation should be further examined).

The *convergent* cluster is composed of European old democracies that take part in all three of the Hallin and Mancini (2004) models: France, Italy and Spain from the Mediterranean model, Germany and Belgium from the democratic corporatist model, and Ireland and the UK from the liberal model, Malta, plus post-socialist Slovenia and Estonia. The convergent European digitized media system shows the second largest creative economy sectors per capita, high democracy and human development values, higher-than-average globalization indicators with the expected lower concentration of television audiences, signalling a more fragmented television audience, but only a moderately to highly developed digitized media market. This gives the convergent cluster the second place in relation to degree of mediatization in Europe. By comprising two countries from new European Union (EU) member states in Central and Eastern Europe (CEE), this cluster gives further argument for the thesis of media systems convergence. The drivers of convergence need to be further investigated, as most CEE countries cluster expectedly in the next cluster.

The *peripheral* cluster is composed of peripheral European countries of the south and east, including countries from the Hallin and Mancini (2004) Mediterranean model: Greece and Portugal, post-socialist EU members Bulgaria, Croatia, Czech Republic, Hungary, Latvia, Poland, Romania, Slovakia as well as Cyprus, Former Yugoslav Republic of Macedonia, and Serbia. This cluster is characterized by lower-than-average values for political and social inclusiveness, lower spread of digital media, lower globalization, less open creative economy, and higher TV concentration. In this case, smaller television audience fragmentation is not due to strong PSB but to the less developed new technological and institutional affordances, linked to weak markets. This digitized mediascape is characterized by lower mediatization values in all the indicators, in comparison with the previous two types of media landscapes. It includes a group of countries on the east and south of Europe that are lagging in structural conditions which promote mediatization, both at the institutional and the technological level.

The Israeli media system clustered separately in the first analysis (Israel was not included in the second round), showing a divergence in main characteristics from the previous three media systems. It is characterized by higher social inclusiveness and social media diffusion accompanied with highest television audience concentration in a moderately developed media market. It scores lower on political inclusiveness, globalization and openness of creative economy (Peruško et al. 2015). These contradictory findings are an invitation to further investigation as well.

The *non-inclusive digitized media landscape* (Peruško et al. 2016) is composed of Turkey and the Russian Federation, both of which have low scores of institutional inclusiveness (Turkey is classified as a hybrid regime, and Russia as an authoritarian regime) and freedom of expression as well as low HDI. Additionally, they share the lowest globalization scores and have low internet diffusion but at the same time the most fragmented television audience market. They also share medium values of smartphone diffusion. Unfortunately, these countries were not included in the comparative audience study, but the aggregate data on the digital media market provide some pointers. It is obvious from all of the examples that television audience fragmentation is not linked with high internet diffusion or high globalization in all media systems.

4.4 Agency

In his review of mediatization research in relation to theories of social change, Lundby (2014b) finds that all three approaches to mediatization engage with the relation between structure and agency: the institutional approaches favour the structural level in the institutional logic, the constructivist approaches favour agency in the micro-level process of symbolic interaction as the vehicle for the social construction of reality, and the material approaches—which are also stronger on the material conditions (i.e. structures)—favour technological affordances as vehicles of change. The proposal in this chapter is to enhance the attention to the aspect of agency within the institutional perspective by integrating multi-level and multi-method research designs with quantitative and qualitative research strategies which would be capable of accounting for not only the structural-level and aggregate individual-level variations but also the meanings and *raison* associated with communication and other media-related social practice. In defining grounds for a mixed methods research strategy, Creswell and Plano Clark (2011) acknowledge that certain theoretical perspectives require both quantitative and qualitative data—this is especially highlighted in approaches that relate structure and agency (their example is Bourdieu's field theory). In this proposal pertaining to mediatization research, two more of the listed reasons apply: one data source is not enough—to understand mediatization we need to examine both the institutional and the level of practice, and there is a need to explain initial results—qualitative studies need to complement quantitative results to add meaning and insight to the process of (mediated) social construction.

In the following section, some examples of surveyed media practices in the analysed media system will be presented as illustrations of practice in mediatization as structuration. No claim is made about a return causal relationship between the audience behaviours/practices studied here and the change in the type of media system; in the regression analyses performed in the example studies, a lot of variance was left unexplained, suggesting that there are additional variables at play. The patterns of audience practices in different digitized media systems need to be complemented by qualitative studies looking at the self-reflexive aspects of these practices as *praxis*. Even then, the change to the structures will be evident only in the future—the direction of which we might only guess.

Three empirical studies linking the macro-institutional level of media system and media-related practices of citizens/audiences/consumers are re-examined below in view of the mediatization process and the empirically grounded variations in mediatization in four European digitized media landscapes. All studies show the prevailing influence of the structural institutional level on user practice ("strategy follows structure"; Benson 2014). While individual variables of gender, age, education and income expectedly explain some of the variance, the structural context of the media system where the practices took place explains additional variance. Audience studies were performed in only some of the countries included in the media system analysis: Denmark is the only country in the *inclusive* media system; Belgium, Germany and Italy in the *convergent* media system; Croatia, Hungary, Poland and Portugal in the *peripheral* media system; and Israel. Audience studies were not conducted for the countries in the *non-inclusive* system.

The largest (in terms of the percentage of explained variance) impact of the institutional context in respect of the use of legacy or online media was found in relation to reading habits in the digital media, especially for reading newspapers on internet news sites (Peruško et al. 2015: 356). The *inclusive system* exhibits the greatest diffusion of digitized media and the highest institutional inclusiveness but the lowest use of news on the internet; audiences in the *peripheral* digitized mediascape exhibit the highest scores in this variable. This is an unexpected finding if we expect higher structural-level mediatization to transpose to higher level of practices; this finding would suggest that we are not dealing with a linear relationship.

Regarding patterns of digital engagement, European audiences were found to diverge along the information and entertainment practices, or public (Couldry et al. 2007) versus private connection. The public connection activities like writing entries at debate sites and blogs, writing and reading e-mails, getting news, reading entries at debate sites and blogs, using websites concerning interests or hobbies, and online shopping and banking are more likely in the *convergent* digitized mediascape (Peruško and Vozab 2015). Playing computer games online, using social network sites, downloading music, film or podcasts and using chat programs all clustered in the private and social connection practices. Audiences in the *peripheral* cluster spend more time on social networks and reading news but less on practices of higher engagement like writing blogs and engaging in online debates, where the *convergent* audiences are in the lead.

Online audiences in all of the studied European countries are also structured according to the versatility of their online repertoires and cluster into three groups; *passive* users are the least versatile (mostly e-mails and online news), and the most versatile are the smallest group of *active/versatile* users who are more likely to be found in the *peripheral* digitized media landscape. *Social networkers*, who differ from the *passive* cluster only by their use of social networks, are more likely to be from Denmark (Peruško and Vozab 2015).

Regarding micro/meso spaces of media use (Vittadini et al. 2015), Israel was found to have the most diverse media mix in domestic private spaces as well as in public institutional spaces of work and school and the public interpersonal sharing places, whereas the *inclusive* and *convergent* media system clusters show most varied media use in the common domestic spaces. The internet is used in the largest number of micro/meso places in Israel, followed by the *inclusive* media system. Newspapers are also consumed in the largest number and type of places in Israel. Television spatial spread is very similar, whereas radio is used in most analysed spaces in the *peripheral* digitized media system (Aroldi et al. 2015). Two types of users are particularly interesting in view of mediatization: the *flexible* user slightly prefers the public spaces of the home but uses media a lot also in private and shared public spaces. This type is more likely in the *peripheral* media system. The *ubiquitous* user who equally uses different media in all private and public spaces is more likely in Israel and the *peripheral* digitized mediascape (Aroldi et al. 2015). Of course, we have no yardstick against which to measure whether one practice or another is more or less mediatized. As mediatization is seen as the degree of change in social practice related to media and communication, a larger number of spaces of media use would suggest an opportunity for more social practices to experience mediatization.

4.5 And Back Again

This chapter aimed to expand on the structuration approach to mediatization by a stronger focus on the agency aspect of the process in terms of media use and in relation to the media system at the structural institutional level. A multi-level approach was able to show influences of the structural level on variation of media practices (Peruško et al. 2015; Peruško and Vozab 2015; Aroldi et al. 2015). A mixed methods research strategy combining quantitative and qualitative research was suggested as the way to move mediatization research forward in terms of the possibility of explaining the mediatization process which is at the same time entrenched in both structure and practice in different social areas.

The chapter developed an empirical analysis of the similarities and differences of mediatization in media systems at the structural level. Five main dimensions that affect mediatization at the macro level were proposed and examined in relation to media landscapes of 33 countries. Higher degrees of mediatization were associated with (1) higher spread of all the media (especially the digital media), linked to a higher commercialization of the media market; (2) larger and more active sector of creative industries or media culture; (3) higher globalization; (4) higher audience fragmentation; and (5) more inclusive political and social institutions.

Media system–related changes that feed the last phase of deep mediatization were systematically and cross-culturally mapped by portraying the structural institutional configurations that characterize mediatization in Europe at the beginning of the twenty-first century. Five media landscapes with varied levels of mediatization—including *inclusive*, *convergent*, *peripheral* and *non-inclusive*—were found. Israel was also included in the analysis but clustered separately. (This obviously points to the need for including more countries in the analysis to observe other patterns of variation.) Three of the clusters include post-socialist CEE countries, which for the first time are systematically viewed from a mediatization perspective. These groupings of digitized media landscapes are historically and culturally specific and represent the shape of things in the present time according to the employed model of digital media landscapes; no claim is made of the exhaustiveness of the model. Also, present structures are the result of multi-causal historical processes. (For an example of historical institutionalism for empirical analysis of media systems, see Peruško 2016.) Hopefully this first analysis of structural media system mediatization will be extended in breadth and depth in future research.

The comparative cross-cultural analysis of media systems was accompanied with the analysis of practices of media use as agency, which allows some tentative inferences regarding audience practices in relation to degrees of mediatization at the structural level. While in all of the studies the macro level showed statistically significant influences on audience practices, the influence is more significant/stronger in relation to online activities related to civic practices (i.e. news reading and writing blogs, commenting and sharing, as opposed to only entertainment practices), in relation to internet-related media use more than in legacy media practices. There appear two types of media users in relation to where they use media that might be significant to mediatization: the flexible and the ubiquitous types, who use diverse media in different public and private spaces and thus presumably also for a greater number of social purposes. As a broader spread of the spatial use of media is an indicator of mediatization, as well as the increased number of social practices affected or created by the media (Schulz 2004), this is a potentially important finding.

Some practices that we would expect with deep mediatization are found in less developed structural contexts (i.e. the ubiquitous media user is more likely in Israel and the peripheral media system); the active users with the most versatile media repertoire are found in the peripheral media landscape, although participation in more active public connection practices like blogging and discussing online is most prevalent in the convergent mainstream media landscape. This speaks to the importance of the inclusive democratic institutional tradition and the habits of participation, more developed in old democracies, but also contradicts our expectation that the most mediatized structure (the inclusive media system) will have the most diverse media-related practices. Here again, we have perhaps more questions than answers, but the type of question we need to ask about types of audience practice and their meanings and consequences has been refined. The multi-level design should be complemented by interpretive studies aimed at explanations and meanings of these structuring practices. Audience practice emerges as an important dimension for studying mediatization, while the findings presented here point to rich possibilities for mediatization-specific mixed methods research designs in historically specific digitized media landscapes.

Note

1. Linking of mediatization to autonomous institutions (Hjarvard 2008) in terms of their autonomy from the state would mean that there could be no mediatization in, for instance, China, because its media institutions are not autonomous in this sense even though their operation in the entertainment media (not in the news) is highly commercialized. China is an example of a country with a strong spread of communication and media technology which is linked to higher mediatization, and some evidence of audience behaviour shows amalgamation and substitution practices described by Schulz (2004).

Acknowledgments This chapter was developed within the strategic area of Mediatization of Media Systems and Public Sphere in the Context of Transition at the Centre for Media and Communication Research, Faculty of Political Science, University of Zagreb, and the research project 'Cinema and Television in Post-Transition in Spain' (CSO2012-31895) at the University Carlos III, Madrid, funded by the Ministerio de Economía y Competividad del Gobierno de España [Ministry of Economy and Competitiveness, Government of Spain].

References

Acemoğlu, Daron, and James A. Robinson. 2012. *Why nations fail: The origins of power, prosperity, and poverty*. New York: Random House.

Ampuja, Marko. 2012. Globalization theory, media-centrism and neoliberalism: A critique of recent intellectual trends. *Critical Sociology* 38 (2): 281–301. Originally published online 21 Sept 2011. doi:10.1177/0896920510398018.

Appadurai, Arjun. 2000[1990]. Disjuncture and difference in the global cultural economy. In *Readings in contemporary political sociology*, ed. Kate Nash, 100–114. Oxford UK: Blackwell.

Aroldi, Piermarco, Antonija Čuvalo, Marina Micheli, Francesca Pasquali, Zrinjka Peruško, Nicoletta Vittadini, and Dina Vozab. 2015. Spaces across Europe: Where people use media. Paper presented at the 65th ICA Annual Conference "Communication across the Life Span", May 20–25, 2015, San Juan, Puerto Rico.

Benson, Rodney. 2014. Strategy follows structure: A media sociology manifesto. In *Media sociology: A reappraisal*, ed. Silvio Waisbord, 25–45. Cambridge UK, Malden MA: Polity.

Benson, Rodney, and Erik Neveu. 2005. *Bourdieu and the journalistic field*. Cambridge UK, Malden MA: Polity Press.

Blumler, J.G., and M. Gurevitch. 1995. *The Crisis of Public Communication*. London, New York: Routledge.

Bolin, Göran. 2010. Media events, Eurovision and societal centres. In *Media events in a global age*, ed. Nick Couldry, Andreas Hepp, and Friedrich Krotz, 124–138. London, New York: Routledge.

Bolin, Göran. 2014. Institution, technology, world: Relations between the media, culture, and society. In *Mediatization of communication*, ed. Knut Lundby, 175–198. Berlin, Boston: De Gruyter Mouton.

Bolin, Göran. 2017. *Media generations. Experience, identity and mediatised social change*. London: Routledge.

Bourdieu, Pierre. 2005. The political field, the social science field, and the journalistic field. In *Bourdieu and the journalistic field*, ed. Rodney Benson, and Erik Neveu, 29–47. Cambridge UK, Malden MA: Polity Press.

Brüggemann, Michael, Sven Engesser, Florin Buchel, Edda Humprecht, and Laia Castro. 2014. Hallin and Mancini revisited: Four empirical types of Western media systems. *Journal of Communication* 64 (6): 1037–1065.

Castells, Manuel. 1996. *The rise of the networked society*. Oxford: Blackwell.

Castells, Manuel. 2009. *Communication power*. Oxford: Oxford University Press.

Chadwick, Andrew. 2013. *The hybrid media system: Politics and power*. Oxford: Oxford University Press.

Couldry, Nick. 2012. *Media, society, world: Social theory and digital media practice*. Cambridge: Polity.

Couldry, Nick. 2014. Mediatization and the future of field theory. In *Mediatization of communication*, ed. Knut Lundby, 227–245. Berlin: de Gruyter.

Couldry, Nick, and Andreas Hepp. 2017. *The mediated construction of reality*. Cambridge: Polity.

Couldry, Nick, Sonia Livingstone, and Tim Markham. 2007. *Media consumption and public engagement: Beyond the presumption of attention*. Basingstoke, New York: Palgrave Macmillan.

Creswell, John W., and Vicky L.Plano Clark. 2011. *Designing and conducting mixed methods research*. Los Angeles: Sage.

Deacon, David, and James Stanyer. 2014. Mediatization: Key concept or conceptual bandwagon? *Media, Culture and Society* 36 (7): 1032–1044.

Deuze, Mark. 2011. Media life. *Media, Culture and Society* 33 (1): 137–148.

Dreher, A. 2006. Does globalization affect growth? *Evidence from a New Index of Globalization, Applied Economics* 38 (10): 1091–1110.

Esser, Frank. 2013. Mediatization as a challenge: Media logic versus political logic. In *Democracy in the age of globalization and mediatization*, ed. Hanspeter Kriesi, Sandra Lavenex, Frank Esser, Jörg Matthes, Marc Bühlmann, and Daniel Bochsler, 155–176. Basingstoke: Palgrave Macmillan.

Finnemann, Niels O. 2014. Digitization: New trajectories of mediatization? In *Mediatization of communication*, ed. Knut Lundby, 297–321. Berlin: de Gruyter.

Flew, Terry, and Silvio Waisbord. 2015. The ongoing significance of national media systems in the context of media globalization. *Media, Culture and Society* 37 (4): 620–636. doi:10.1177/0163443714566903.

Fortunati, Leopoldina. 2005. Mediatization of the net and internetization of the mass media. *Gazette: The International Journal for Communication Studies* 67 (1): 27–44. doi:10.1177/0016549205049177.

Fries, Christopher J. 2009. Bourdieu's reflexive sociology as a theoretical basis for mixed methods research: An application to complementary and alternative medicine. *Journal of Mixed Methods Research* 3 (4): 326–348.

Giddens, Anthony. 1984. *The constitution of society*. Berkley, Los Angeles: University of California Press.

Hallin, Daniel C., and Paolo Mancini. 2004. *Comparing media systems*. Three models of media and politics. Cambridge UK: Cambridge University Press.

Hardy, Jonathan. 2012. Comparing media systems. In *The handbook of comparative communication research*. ICA Handbook Series, ed. Frank Esser, and Thomas Hanitzsch, 185–206. New York, London: Routledge.

Hasebrink, Uwe, and Hanna Domeyer. 2012. Media repertoires as patterns of behaviour and as meaningful practices: A multimethod approach to media use in converging media environments. *Participations. Journal of Audience and Reception Studies* 9 (2): 757–779.

Hepp, Andreas, and Uwe Hasebrink. 2014. Human interaction and communicative figurations: The transformation of mediatized cultures and societies. In *Mediatization of communication*, ed. Knut Lundby, 249–271. Berlin: de Gruyter.

Hepp, Andreas, Stig Hjarvard, and Knut Lundby. 2010. Mediatization: Empirical perspectives: An introduction to a special issue. *Communications* 35: 223–228. doi:10.1515/COMM.2010.012.

Herkman, Juha. 2012. Convergence or intermediality? Finnish political communication in the New Media Age. *Convergence: The International Journal of Research into New Media Technologies* 18 (4): 369–384.

Hjarvard, Stig. 2008. The mediatization of society: A theory of the media as agents of social and cultural change. *Nordicom Review* 29 (2): 105–34.

Hjarvard, Stig. 2013. *The mediatization of culture and society.* New York: Routledge.

Hjarvard, Stig. 2014a. From mediation to mediatization: The institutionalization of new media. In *Mediatized worlds. Culture and society in a media age*, ed. Andreas Hepp, and Friedrich Krotz, 123–142. Basingstoke, New York: Palgrave Macmillan.

Hjarvard, Stig. 2014b. Mediatization and cultural and social change: An institutional perspective. In *Mediatization of communication*, ed. Knut Lundby, 199–226. Berlin: de Gruyter.

Hjarvard, Stig, and Line N. Petersen. 2013. Mediatization and cultural change. Special issue of MedieKultur. *Journal of media and communication research* 54: 1–7.

Jansson, André. 2002. The mediatization of consumption: Towards an analytical framework of image culture. *Journal of Consumer Culture* 2: 5. doi:10.1177/146954050200200101.

Jensen, Klaus Bruhn, and Rasmus Helles. 2015. Audiences across media: A comparative agenda for future research on media audiences. Introduction. *International Journal of Communication.* 9: 291–298.

Jones, Matthew R., and Helena Karsten. 2008. Giddens's structuration theory and information systems research. *MIS Quarterly* 32 (1): 127–157.

Krotz, Friedrich. 2009. Mediatization: A concept with which to grasp media and societal change. In *Mediatization: Concepts, changes, consequences*, ed. Knut Lundby, 19–38. New York: Peter Lang.

Krotz, Friedrich. 2014. Mediatization as a mover in modernity: Social and cultural change in the context of media change. In *Mediatization of communication. Handbooks in Communication Science*, ed. Knut Lundby, 131–162. Berlin, Boston: De Gruyter Mouton.

Livingstone, S. 2009. On the mediation of everything. *Journal of Communication* 59 (1): 1–18.

Livingstone, Sonia, and Peter Lunt. 2014. Mediatization: An emerging paradigm for media and communication research? In *Mediatization of communication. Handbooks in communication science,* ed. Knut Lundby, 703–724. Berlin, Boston: De Gruyter Mouton.

Lundby, Knut. 2009. *Mediatization: Concepts, changes, consequences.* New York: Peter Lang.

Lundby, Knut. 2014a. Introduction. Mediatization of communication. In *Mediatization of communication. Handbooks in communication science*, ed. Knut Lundby, 3–38. Berlin, Boston: De Gruyter Mouton.

Lundby, Knut. 2014b. A pattern in social theories of change within mediatization research. Paper for the panel in the TWG on Mediatization, ECREA Conference Lisboa Nov 2014 13.10.2014.

Magin, Melanie. 2015. Shades of mediatization: Components of media logic in German and Austrian elite newspapers (1949–2009). *The International Journal of Press/Politics* 20 (4): 415–437. doi:10.1177/1940161215595944.

Norris, P., and R. Inglehart. 2009. *Cosmopolitan communications. Cultural diversity in a globalized World*. New York, NY: Cambridge University Press.

Peruško, Z. 2013. Rediscovering the Mediterranean characteristics of the Croatian media system. *East European Politics and Societies* 27 (4): 709–726. doi:10.1177/0888325413494770.

Peruško, Zrinjka. 2016. Historical institutionalist approach in comparative media systems research: The case of Post-Yugoslavia. *Javnost—The Public* 2. doi:10.1080/13183222.2016.1210461.

Peruško, Zrinjka, Dina Vozab, and Antonija Čuvalo. 2013. Audiences as a source of agency in media systems: Post-socialist Europe in comparative perspective. *Medialni Studia (Media Studies)* 2: 137–154.

Peruško, Zrinjka, and Antonija Čuvalo. 2014. Comparing socialist and post-socialist television culture. Fifty years of television in Croatia. *View—Journal of European Television, History and Culture* 3 (5): 131–150. http://www.viewjournal.eu/index.php/view/article/view/96/109. Accessed 22 Apr 2017.

Peruško, Zrinjka, and Dina Vozab. 2015. Mediatization of political engagement in digital mediascapes: Comparing European online audiences. Paper presented at the ECREA Communication and Democracy Section Conference: "Political Agency in the Digital Age", Oct 9–10, 2015, Copenhagen.

Peruško, Zrinjka, Dina Vozab, and Antonija Čuvalo. 2015. Digital mediascapes, institutional frameworks, and audience practices across Europe. *International Journal of Communication* 9: 342–364.

Peruško, Z., Vozab, D., Čuvalo, A. 2016. Mediatization of journalism: Comparing European digital mediascapes. Paper presented at the 6th European Communication Research and Education Conference (ECREA), Nov 9–12, Prague.

Poole, Marshall S. 2009. Response to Jones and Karsten, "Giddens's structuration theory and information systems research". *MIS Quarterly* 33 (3): 583–587.

Rantanen, Terhi. 2013. A critique of the systems approaches in comparative media research: A Central and Eastern European perspective. *Global Media and Communication* 9 (3): 257–277. doi:10.1177/1742766513504175.

Scannell, Paddy. 2016. Media and religion. Editor's introduction to the special issue. *Media, Culture and Society* 38 (1): 3–7. doi:10.1177/0163443715615410.

Schrott, Andrea. 2009. Dimensions: Catch-all labels or technical terms. In *Mediatization: Concept, changes, consequences*, ed. Knut Lundby, 41–62. New York: Peter Lang.

Schulz, Winfried. 2004. Reconstructing mediatization as an analytical concept. *European Journal of Communication* 19 (1): 87–101.

Schulz, Winfried. 2014. Mediatization and new media. In *Mediatization of politics: Understanding the transformation of Western democracies*, ed. Frank Esser, and Jesper Strömbäck, 57–73. Basingstoke: Palgrave.

Schwarz, Jonah Andersson. 2016. Public service broadcasting and data-driven personalization: A view from Sweden. *Television and New Media* 17 (2): 124–141.

Strömbäck, Jesper. 2008. Four phases of mediatization: An analysis of the mediatization of politics. *Press/Politics* 13 (3): 228–246. doi:10.1177/1940161208319097.

Udris, Linards, and Jens Lucht. 2014. Mediatization at the structural level: Independence from politics, dependence on the market. In *Mediatization of politics: Understanding the transformation of Western democracies*, ed. Frank Esser, and Jesper Strömbäck, 114–136. Basingstoke: Palgrave.

Umbricht, Andrea, and Frank Esser. 2013. Changing political news? Long-term trends in American, British, French, Italian, German, and Swiss press reporting. Working paper 57, National Centre for Competence in Research (NCCR), Challenges to Democracy in the 21st Century. 32 p.

Vittadini, Nicoletta, Marina Micheli, Francesca Pasquali, and Piermarco Aroldi. 2015. Spaces across Europe: Where people use media. *International Journal of Communication* 9: 412–434.

Williams, Raymond. 2003[1974]. *Televisio: Technology and cultural form.* London, New York: Routledge.

CHAPTER 5

Towards the "Audiencization" of Mediatization Research? Audience Dynamics as Co-Constitutive of Mediatization Processes

Kim Christian Schrøder

5.1 Introduction

As one looks over the landscapes of news media one and a half decades into the twenty-first century, it is hard not to be overwhelmed by a sense of communicative vertigo. Everything seems to be up in the air, which has led some observers to ask whether the news media as we know them are headed for an ominous twilight or emerging from the dark into a bright dawn (Picard 2014).

Already before the appearance of the internet, the reading audiences were deserting newspapers, and observers were concerned about the tabloidization of the quality press as well as of public service news

K.C. Schrøder (✉)
Roskilde University, Roskilde, Denmark
e-mail: kimsc@ruc.dk

O. Driessens et al. (eds.), *Dynamics Of Mediatization*,
Transforming Communications – Studies in Cross-Media Research,
DOI 10.1007/978-3-319-62983-4_5

media, as these news media sought to appeal to readers and viewers in more engaging ways or, as some would have it, to impoverish the public debate by pandering to the lowest common denominator (Esser 1999; Langer 2003). As newspapers went online, offering their journalistic content to audiences for free (alongside the rise of down-market free newspapers across urban settings worldwide), audiences/readers started to defect from printed newspaper subscriptions and newsstand purchases, with potentially dire implications for the news industry's advertising-based business models.

More recently, when the revolutionizing phenomenon of social media expanded from its origins as a participatory vehicle of personal networking to become a significant source of news and civic debate (not to speak of consumer-oriented commercial promotion), it first seemed that newspapers would benefit journalistically as well as commercially as the user traffic brought to their news sites from social media like Facebook and Twitter grew exponentially. Later on, this turned out to be more of a mixed blessing, as the increased traffic was accompanied by the regime of algorithms governed partly by user and audience preferences in the form of "likes", "comments" and "shares" but also by secret or opaque preferences devised by the giant digital providers. Concomitantly, increasing proportions of the advertising revenue disappeared from the accounts of the news providers in order to instead bolster the billion-dollar surpluses of the social media empires.

These developments were accompanied by renewed democratic, commercial and domestic concerns. For the political institution, alert to the health of the public sphere, the citizens' opportunity to personalize their news and to expose themselves only to themes they were already interested in and views they agreed with appeared to some observers to forebode a society where everyone lived in "echo chambers" or "filter bubbles" [while others found little empirical evidence of such a scenario (Webster 2014)]. For the news media institution, the growing adoption by news users of ad blockers aggravated the existing threats to advertising revenue sources, as audiences tried to escape from the annoyance of attention-catching commercial messages by installing ad-blocking softwares on their computers, smartphones and tablets. In the domestic sphere, the family institution faced the multiple challenges of regulating sensible levels of digital disruption of familial routines and relations.[1]

The changes described here derive from a number of sources. Clearly, many of them originate in technological innovations, combined with content initiatives launched by news media institutions, which manifest themselves in new forms of news narration or creative transformations of traditional ones. For instance, the availability to newsmakers of small and economical technologies for visual representation has introduced a new interface of competition between broadcasters and newspapers: Long frustrated by the (public service) broadcasters' colonization of the market for online text and photo journalism (allowed and enabled by the legislation of the political system), newspapers started to boost their production of news videos for their online news sites, and for in-house niche TV channels, with the dual purpose of augmenting the audience experience and harvesting increased advertising revenue. Lisbeth Thorlacius found that eight Danish online newspapers, especially the tabloids, have doubled the number of news videos on their online front pages, from 57 videos in 2012 to 106 videos in 2014 (Thorlacius 2016). However, the force of relative audience uninterest in news videos may induce news producers to consider discontinuing such investments:

> News organizations which have thrown resources into video production may be backing the wrong horse. Across all 26 countries only a quarter (24%) of respondents say they access online news video in a given week. This represents surprisingly weak growth given the explosive growth and prominence on the supply side. [...] the main reason people give for not using more video are that they find reading news quicker and more convenient (41%) and the annoyance of pre-roll advertisements (35%) (Reuters Digital News Report 2016: 18f.).

This example of the interrelations of technological affordances, competitive relations within the news institution, modes of narration, and audience practices in the building of civic and domestic knowledge may show just a detail in the larger picture of socio-cultural development. But together with the general processes in the field of news described above, this example bears witness to momentous transformations, partly audience-driven, in the anatomy of news media landscapes. And these changes in the world of (news) media are interwoven with institutional changes in the political and cultural domains, which have to do with the ways in which the media function as resources of democratic prerequisites. Conversely, the political institution has a formative influence on the news media through the passing of media regulatory laws and the provision of media subsidy schemes.

The description thus illustrates a process of "mediatization", defined—across the divisions that exist between the different theoretical orientations within mediatization research—as "an ambitious attempt to grasp and understand the role of media and communication as part of the transforming processes of culture and society" (Lundby 2014b: 3), from the micro level of people's encounter with specific media, through the meso level of the news media institution, to the macro level of societal pillars like democracy (Lundby 2014b: 22).

The empirically anchored theoretical intervention pursued in this chapter argues that so far the formative role of audience dynamics has been underestimated and under-researched across the various strands of mediatization research. After reviewing recent authoritative research publications on mediatization, Lundby (2016: 1) concludes that "mediatization research has a more or less blind eye to the role of audiences". Especially in institutionalist mediatization research, the individual audience member is seen as a reactive agent, someone who must learn how to adapt to and cope with the forces of mediatization, rather than as someone who is also actively implicated in the constitutive complexity of mediatization (Lundby 2014b: 30). And when it comes to the serious business of distilling conceptual frameworks and models that pinpoint the essential components of mediatization as a contemporary moulding force in social change, the audience is conspicuous by its absence.

The audience as such cannot be said to not be included in constructivist mediatization theory. Here we see an intense analytical focus on people's daily life with the media, in and across the numerous "communicative figurations" they inhabit (Hasebrink and Hepp 2016). But there is little recognition of the ways in which these individual practices may aggregate into a cumulative collective force, which shapes media institutions and the media landscape as such, as well as their interrelations with other societal domains.

This chapter seeks to integrate audience practices into the DNA of mediatization research—an agenda which has recently been opened up by other scholars. For instance, Knut Lundby is engaged in a project intended to "refine the theory on mediatization of religion when it comes to the roles regular media users, i.e. people, play in the communication dynamic through their interpretations and interactions with representations in the media" (Lundby 2014a: 3). Along different lines but with the same intent, Kees Brants has taken issue particularly with the notion of "media logics", the defining feature (if any) of the institutional variety of mediatization theory, arguing that this concept "largely ignores or fails to appreciate the place and importance of considerable parts of the public as a potentially empowered, active and participating force" (Brants 2014: 9).

In broader terms, I argue that to build a theoretical and empirical audience perspective into mediatization research is one way of being "attentive to various subprocesses of mediatization, through which the complexity and internal contradictions of mediatization can be unveiled" (Ekström et al. 2016: 1095).

This may appear to be a strange project to launch at a time when audiences (so it has been argued) are largely a thing of the past (Rosen 2006). However, other scholars have argued forcefully that if audiences are liberated from the conceptual shackles of the television culture, in which audiences were seen as passive couch potatoes, audiences must be seen as a central agent of a mediatized participatory culture (Carpentier 2011).

In developing this perspective, I define the audiences of mediatization processes as those individuals or groups who are attending to or engaging with media, in their double articulation as technological devices and symbolic content, and who are acting in that capacity, or as a consequence of that attention or engagement, in a way that exerts power on players in the media landscape.

This is a definition which does not distinguish sharply between audiences as viewers, readers, listeners and spectators, and audiences as social agents, or between audiences and publics. In this respect, the definition is in agreement with the argument of Livingstone that "where once people moved in and out of their status as audiences, using media for specific purposes and then doing something else [...] in our present age of continual immersion in media, we are now continually and unavoidable audiences at the same time as being consumers, relatives, workers, and [...] citizens and publics" (Livingstone 2013: 22).[2] We could also phrase this by saying that in a digital, mediatized society, we can define the term "audience" as the people who, in their capacity as social actors, are attending to, negotiating the meaning of, and sometimes participating in the multi-modal processes initiated or carried out by institutional media (Schrøder and Gulbrandsen, in press).

Similarly, and more radically, Livingstone has suggested that "in a thoroughly mediated world, audiences and publics, along with communities, nations, markets and crowds, are composed of the same people" (Livingstone 2005: 17). This means that a manifestation of popular agency often cannot rigorously be ascribed to any one of these entities. My definition of audiences tries to overcome this impasse by considering any citizen activity that can be seen to derive from attention to or engagement with media, and that can be argued to exert a formative influence on media performance or content, as audience activity.

For instance, a "shitstorm" is a product of audiences because it comes into being as an outcome of the shitstormers being exposed to, engaging with, and participating—as audiences/public—in a specific media discourse, or limited set of media discourses, which frame typically corporate behaviour in a way that evokes indignation and discursive citizen action (see the second empirical case, below).

5.2 Towards the "Audiencization" of Mediatization Research?

Although there are many definitions of the concept of "mediatization", it has recently been argued that at this moment in time there is a certain rapprochement taking place between the rival or complementary understandings of the phenomenon, as "the contours of a shared basic understanding of the term have emerged" (Couldry and Hepp 2013: 197; see also Hepp 2013: 619). The united "inside" front formed by knights from different camps against "outside" hostile parties (such as Deacon and Stanyer 2014) also bears witness to a joint desire to defend the castle irrespective of internal differences (Hepp et al. 2015).

The spirit of rapprochement may take the form of recognizing respectfully that the different perspectives hold complementary strengths and weaknesses. For instance, siding mainly with the institutionalist tradition, calling it "the strongest case for a theory of mediatization", Livingstone and Lunt (2014: 703) find the constructivist position weaker because "it is often unclear what is being said specifically about mediatization rather than, say, about the analysis of mediation or communication or culture more widely" (Livingstone and Lunt 2014: 710). Nevertheless, they recognize that the constructivist perspective, building on the notion of "communicative figurations", "may do a better job at capturing the diverse mediations of culture across different fields" (Livingstone and Lunt 2014: 710). Therefore, rather than attempting to merge the two (and echoing Livingstone and Lunt's question "must we choose one perspective over the other?"), I suggest that it is productive to answer this question in the negative and to see the two traditions as complementary. Just as, in the struggles between quantitative and qualitative methods, it is sensible to hold that they are suited for different purposes, might we not hold that the institutionalist and constructivist perspectives can explain different aspects of the media/society nexus? This view is in accordance with the recent call by Ekström, Fornäs, Jansson and Jerslev for a more open agenda for mediatization research, as they find "the commonplace opposition between constructivist and institutionalist perspectives on mediatization counter-productive, because it tends to reproduce a dichotomized view of cultural and social life" (Ekström et al. 2016: 1098).

In such a climate of cross-fertilizing coexistence of the institutionalist and constructivist schools within mediatization theory, this chapter takes the first steps towards a discussion of the theoretical and methodological challenges arising from the need to systematically explore audience dynamics as an integral force in mediatization processes.

I argue that mediatization research, as a theoretical and empirical undertaking, is in need of"audiencization". Until now, the scholarly endeavour to develop the "mediatization" concept has lacked a systematic consideration of audience practices. This is a sin of omission that can partly be ascribed to the reluctance of audience researchers to take on the concept of mediatization, but (as already noted above) it is also the case that "audiences are more or less left out in mediatization research" (Lundby 2016: 2).

One of the foremost spokesmen of institutionalist mediatization research, Stig Hjarvard, has addressed the role of audiences in mediatization theory directly, parking the role played by audiences at a level prior to, or below, that on which mediatization analysis takes place. Discussing how mediatization research is different from previous traditions in communication research, such as effects research, uses and gratifications research, and reception research, Hjarvard (2013) argued correctly that these traditions have analysed not mediatization but "the communication circuit itself", i.e. the direct relationship between media producers, messages/texts and audiences: "The cultural and social influences of the media have accordingly been sought within the communication circuit itself, as the effect of mediated messages on audiences, or the opposite, i.e. the use of mediated messages by active audiences" (Hjarvard 2013: 2). Mediatization research is different, he argued, because it analyses the role of the media as a unified institution in its relations with other societal institutions:

> Mediatization studies move the focus of interest from the particular instances of mediated communication to the structural transformations of the media in contemporary culture and society. The influences of the media are not only to be found within the communication sequence of senders, messages, and receivers, but also in the changing relationship between the media and other cultural and social spheres. While the study of mediation pays attention to specific instances of communication situated in time and space [...], mediatization studies are concerned with the *long-term* structural change in the role of the media in culture and society, in which the media acquire greater authority to define social reality and condition patterns of social interaction. This altered understanding of the media's importance does not imply that traditional questions regarding aspects such as the effects of mediated messages on public opinion, or the purposes to which people use the media, are no longer relevant (Hjarvard 2013: 2f.).

It is, however, a question whether this argument really justifies a theoretical stance which keeps audience dynamics out of the dynamics of mediatization. It does so by allocating them to a micro-processual framework of "mediation", in which audience dynamics are played out *prior to* and separate from the moment of "mediatization", when media institutions engage other societal institutions in meso- and macro-level processes of socio-cultural change.

I would argue that when the transformative relationships between media institutions and other social institutions are played out, the media should be seen as an interwoven ensemble of technological, institutional, aesthetic and *audience* interactions. It is therefore necessary to amend the model designed by Hjarvard to encapsulate the institutional anatomy of mediatization processes.

In the model in Fig. 5.1, Hjarvard condenses institutionalist mediatization theory into a visual display of the way in which the logics of the media institution interact with the logics of other institutional domains, such as politics or education. The model shows how the logics of the media are produced by the ensemble of their technological, aesthetic and institutional domains and how the interaction of these media logics with the logics of another societal institution produces the "mediatization" of

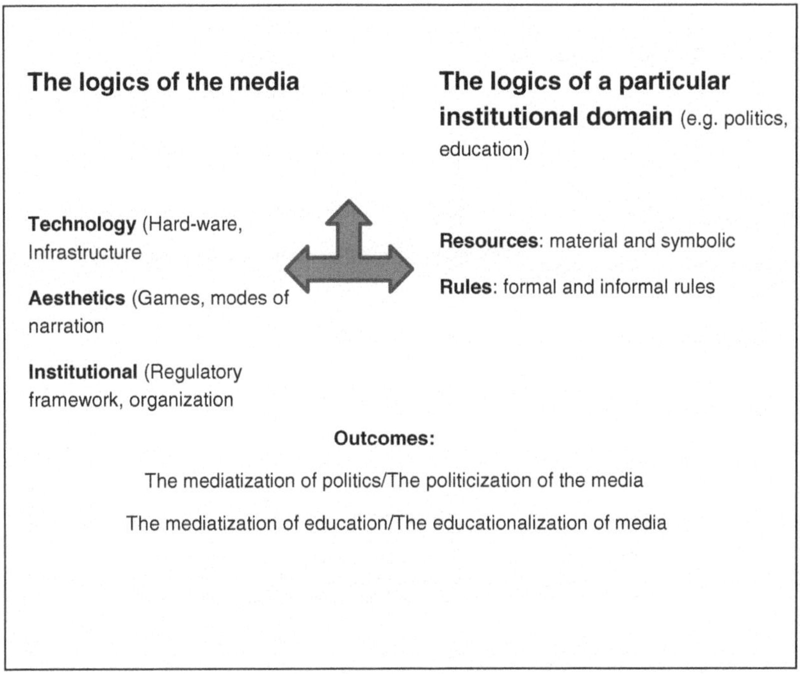

Fig. 5.1 The mutual adaptations to logics from various institutional domains Adapted from Hjarvard (2016a)

politics or education, as well as the inverse "politicization" or "educationalization" of the media, as ongoing transformative processes.

I propose that we can build a more satisfying conceptualization of mediatization if we add the element of "audience dynamics" to this model (Fig. 5.2): With news media as our example, the glimpses of transformative processes provided in the opening pages of this chapter confirm the relevance of incorporating, as Hjarvard does, the technological, aesthetic, and institutional dimensions, as well as the bi-directional relations with the political system, in the definition of mediatization. But the transformations of the news media landscape also demonstrate that audience and user dynamics play an integral role in mediatization, as reflected in the suggested amendment to Hjarvard's model. In other words, audiences play a formative role in the processes through which the media institution is a driving force in wider processes of socio-cultural change.

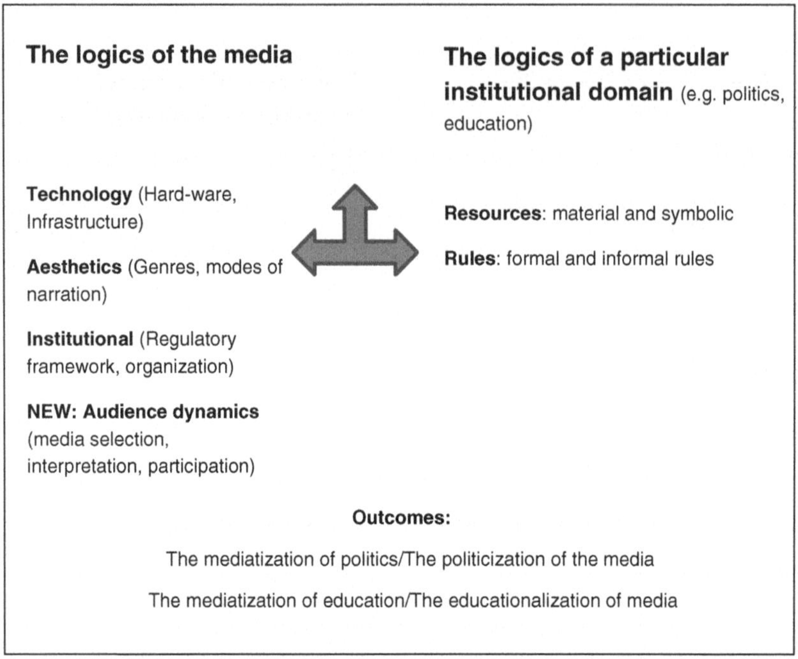

Fig. 5.2 Adding "audience dynamics" to the mutual adaptations to logics from various institutional domains Adapted from Hjarvard (2016a)

Audiences, as individuals and as an aggregate agent, are thus inherently and continuously implicated in the long-term structural developments of the media in relation to culture and society and cannot be parked at the lower level of "the communication circuit itself". The "greater authority of the media to define social reality", as Hjarvard puts it, in the form of news agendas as well as political values and attitudes is always and continuously *inscribed* with traces of the communicative circuit, in which technological and discursive affordances are negotiated through the encounter between media institutions and their practitioners on the one hand and multiple audiences in everyday life on the other.

Therefore, it can also be heuristically helpful to play with and amend another of Hjarvard's models (Fig. 5.3), which he offers as a visual display of the relationship between processes of "mediation" and "mediatization". Although this model does explain that processes of mediation

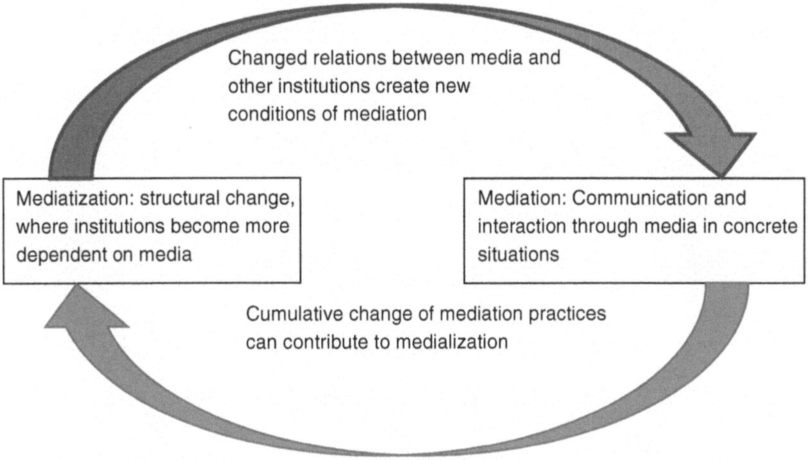

Fig. 5.3 The mutual relationship between mediatization and mediation (Hjarvard 2016b: 21)

and mediatization are interdependent, it falls short of being entirely adequate because it displays these processes visually as separate.

Although the difference may be subtle, this visual property entails conceptual implications of separateness, which we should avoid if we want to portray mediation as inscribed organically and seamlessly into mediatization. Figure 5.4 shows how mediation processes should be seen as integrated into mediatization, and the boundary between mediation and mediatization is depicted as porous.

Madianou's study of mediatized migration may illustrate the appropriateness of Fig. 5.4 for capturing the mediation/mediatization nexus. Drawing on a hybrid approach that combines constructivist mediatization theory and digital anthropology, Madianou shows how, in the contemporary condition of "polymedia", female Filipino domestic workers in the UK maintain mediated personal relationships with their children and other family members at a distance through an array of the new communication media (e-mail, smartphones, social media, webcams, mobile money, etc.), which have supplanted the letters and mailed audio/video tapes of former times. The use of new media helps these women cope with a deeply contradictory situation, in which official and everyday discourses "simultaneously brand them 'bad mothers' and

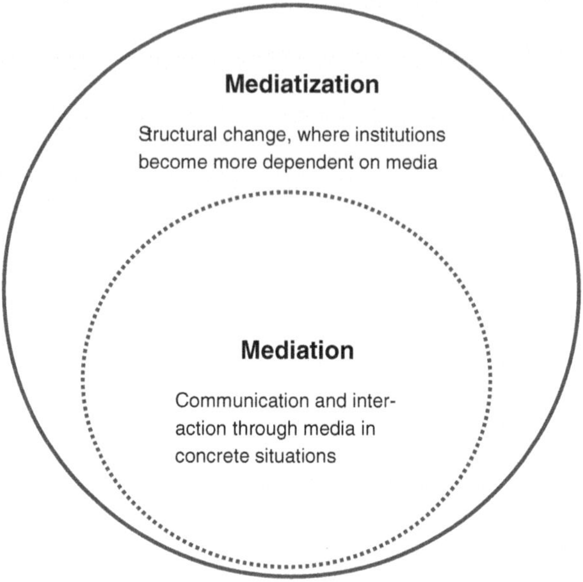

Fig. 5.4 The mutual relationship between mediatization and mediation where the latter is seamlessly inscribed inside the former

'heroes of the economy'" (Madianou 2014: 332). The universal adoption of these forms of mediated communication by the young migrant mothers means that they can alleviate some of the problems of mothering at a distance by closely monitoring the children's daily life on a daily basis. Conversely, older teenage children often experience the mothers' increased opportunities for monitoring as unwelcome surveillance.

Imperceptibly, however, out of these new patterns of mediated communication gradually grow deeper social and cultural changes. This is because the digital forms of communication help the mothers legitimate a new practice whereby—because they wish to hold onto the more fulfilling relations of gender equality in the immigrant country—what started as periods of short-term migration is "gradually turning into a long-term migration or diaspora" (Madianou 2014: 340). New practices of mediation seamlessly bring about an unexpected form of mediatization of both migration and family life. And this relationship between mediation and mediatization is not sequential, but simultaneous. We thus see how "wider structural changes are made possible through the micro-processes of mediated interactions" (Madianou 2014: 341). Figure 5.4 is superior to Fig. 5.3 in expressing how the processes of mediation and mediatization are seamlessly interwoven.

5.3 Audiences as Participants and Agents

The need to bring audiences onto a centre-stage role in mediatization theory should not be seen as merely a consequence of the "participatory turn" in media and media research. The argument in this chapter is thus different from (but related to) that advanced by Tamara Witschge (2014). Witschge asks "to what extent does audience participation in journalistic contexts challenge or confirm the institutionalist approach to mediatization theory?" (Witschge 2014: 343). In her argument, the audience has become "a *new actor* to be reckoned with within the mediatization process" (Witschge 2014: 343, emphasis added). As Witschge sees it, it is in their capacity as potential co-producers of news that audiences become important for understanding mediatization processes: "[...] how is our understanding of this process affected by the possibilities for the audience to participate as (co-)producers in the digital media sphere?" (Witschge 2014: 347).

My argument about audiences claims that even pre-participation age audiences were, and today's non-participating audiences are, co-constitutive of mediatization processes. Therefore, the need to audiencize mediatization research should be seen as something which has to do with the very nature of audiences and their integral role as agents in the communicative processes of the (mass) media.

The structural power of media audiences is largely absent in both kinds of agenda-setting mediatization literature, although the absence takes different forms in the two traditions. In the institutionalist tradition, drawing on structuration theory, it is emphasized that "media, mass media, interpersonal media, and social network media may be understood metaphorically as *social tools* by and through which agency and interaction are performed" (Hjarvard 2016a: 6). But the concrete role of audiences as agents in processes of mediatization is given scant empirical attention,[3] and as we saw above, the visual models devised to encapsulate the key dimensions of mediatization do not count audiences among the key constitutive forces. The examples given of agency often depict not audiences but the agency of so-called "institutional entrepreneurs", i.e. social actors working *within* media institutions, or in other institutional domains (politicians, teachers, etc.), who appropriate media for their institutional aims (Hjarvard 2016b: 55, 59). Also, definitions and descriptions often *mention* audiences and users. For example, in an extended example of the mediatization of sports/football, the long list of agents who help shape the structures of mediatized football includes audiences as merely those whose *experience* is transformed as a result of the interplay of football clubs, TV companies, and advertisers, not as agents whose behaviour co-produces the mediatization of football (Hjarvard 2016a: 5).

It could be argued that the audience-members-as-agents perspective comes more naturally to constructivist mediatization theory. Here, owing to its theoretical and empirical point of departure in people's "social worlds" (Krotz 2014) and in "communicative figurations" (Hepp 2014; Hasebrink and Hepp 2016), audiences are integrated as agents into the analysis, as we are urged to "begin with specific mediatized worlds", because these are "everyday manifestations of media culture" (Hepp 2013: 76). However, the power that audiences have, not just in the everyday setting but as an aggregate force in and on the media system and the wider society, is not highlighted or empirically analysed.

In the following, I shall briefly discuss three empirical examples where audience practices at the micro level of everyday, civic culture are actively and seamlessly co-shaping media institutional transformations with implications for transformations of the ways in which media function as democratic resources in the wider media culture. The examples are taken from the areas of news platform selection and repertoire-building, online audience mobilization, and media and audience discourses about politics.

These examples are not intended to offer a practical recipe, which researchers can apply in order to design a more audience-anchored kind of mediatization research. Rather, they are intended to demonstrate how an audience mind set can structure three kinds of empirical research that may shed light on processes of mediatization. Just as Hjarvard's model (Fig. 5.1) alerts researchers to three dimensions of media that should be analysed in order to understand mediatization, these three empirical examples show how a fourth, audience-oriented dimension (as visualized in Fig. 5.2) may produce a more satisfactory inventory of dimensions to build into one's research design. The precise manner in which this is done is the prerogative of the researcher designing the research.

Empirically, one could also pursue the co-shaping power of audiences and users in other research areas, such as the domestication of *media technologies* (Hutchby 2001). Media technologies come with a range of affordances for use: audiences situated in everyday life negotiate these affordances and end up "deciding" which of them to embrace. This is a general socio-cultural process of the diffusion and domestication of innovations (Haddon 2016), whose power dimension becomes more visible only when audiences turn out to embrace affordances that were not anticipated by the inventors. Among the examples are teletext, which was launched in the 1970s as a limited subtitling service but which had affordances to become the first pull-technology in the push-domain of broadcasting, with an array of complex services and contents, including short-form news reports, TV program schedules, weather forecasts, and so on. Teletext made information interactively available for TV viewers on demand (Moe and Van Den Bulck 2016) and became an important ancillary medium of television because audiences, finding that it gratified hitherto unrealized needs, started to incorporate it into their news repertoires to a point beyond critical mass, thereby transforming the news ecology at the time. To explore the flipside process of how teletext has undergone a period of "de-domestication", as this medium is heading for oblivion due to the emergence of digital and mobile information platforms, would illuminate an equally important process of audiencized mediatization.

5.4 Case 1

5.4.1 Audience News Platform Selection and Repertoire-Building as Constitutive of Mediatization

People negotiate their selection of news platforms and formats in order to build their news media repertoires in everyday life. Such repertoires can be seen as springing from an ensemble of audience logics, which crystallize at the aggregate level of the news landscape, as a co-constitutive force on the way in which the logics of the news institution encounter the logics of other societal institutions, such as the political institution (Fig. 5.1).

The process of news repertoire-building begins with the selective agency of one individual, situated in familial and other interpersonal networks, communities of work, contexts of cultural interests, and so on.

We can imagine that this individual fulfils his or her needs for information about what goes on in society—locally, nationally, globally—by selecting and using a small set of news media formats, on a variety of technological platforms (paper, radio, TV, computers, smartphones, etc.), selected from several dozen possible news formats/platforms. In a recent qualitative study, we invited the research participants to rank a total of 36 news platforms and formats according to which ones played a greater or lesser role for their feeling informed about matters great and small (Kobbernagel and Schrøder 2016).[4] Their rankings could be generalized analytically into six different news media repertoires (Fig. 5.5).

Although there are many shared features across the six repertoires, they nevertheless equip those who practice them very differently as citizens and consumers, as their properties serve very different needs for orientation, information and identity-building. For instance, practitioners of repertoire 3 appreciate the quick overview over the events of the day, whereas those who belong to repertoire 6 find the depth and background coverage of national and local dailies important. Repertoire 1 members have all but abandoned legacy media for the benefit of a variety of online news sources, including new born-online news providers and YouTube. The media mix of the repertoires also affects the market viability of the different types of news provider, as reflected in the representation of public service news providers, the private news industry, and social media in the repertoires.

These patterned repertoires represent a ground-level snapshot of the media audience dynamics that are played out across the intersecting communicative figurations in which people live their everyday lives. When they are observed from a higher altitude, through the lens of a survey of news media use, we get a different kind of pattern: another snapshot of audience dynamics, but this time one that shows the relative strength of different news platforms and formats in the marketplace or public sphere of civic resources.

Figure 5.6 shows, at the national level, how news audiences collectively mould the news landscape with respect to preferred news media. It also shows, metaphorically speaking, the shifting, audience-derived "balance of power" between different news media from 2013 to 2016—momentous transformations which in their entirety can be seen as the joint product of technological affordances, aesthetic innovations, institutional strategies, and audience dynamics (cf. Fig. 5.2). There is a considerable decline in the use of traditional TV news bulletins, which—seen

News repertoires of Danish audiences 2014 (Schrøder, 2016)

Each news repertoire is described through its five main news sources

Repertoire 1: 'Online quality omnivores'

National quality newspaper online; Born-online news site; Public service broadcaster online; YouTube; International news provider online.

Repertoire 2: 'Hybrid public service lovers'

Online public service news; National quality newspaper online; National public service TV; Public service text-TV.

Repertoire 3: '(Light) news snackers'

Tabloid newspaper online; 24-hour TV news; National public service TV; News from Facebook; News on text-TV.

Repertoire 4: 'Mainstream networkers'

National quality print newspaper; News from other social media; International TV news; National public service TV; News from Facebook.

Repertoire 5: 'The intellectual/professional networkers'

News from Facebook; Radio current affairs; Professional magazines; TV serious current affairs; News on Twitter.

Repertoire 6: 'Print addicts'

Free daily print newspaper; National print newspaper; Local weekly print newspaper; Local daily print newspaper; National public service TV.

Fig. 5.5 News repertoires of Danish audiences in 2014

from the point of view of broadcasting institutions—is compensated for by the increase in people's use of their online news services. A substantial number of people have deserted the print editions of newspapers, while their use of online newspapers has plateaued during the four years. The revolutionary change lies with the extent to which people say they get news from social media, an increase from 31 to 56%.

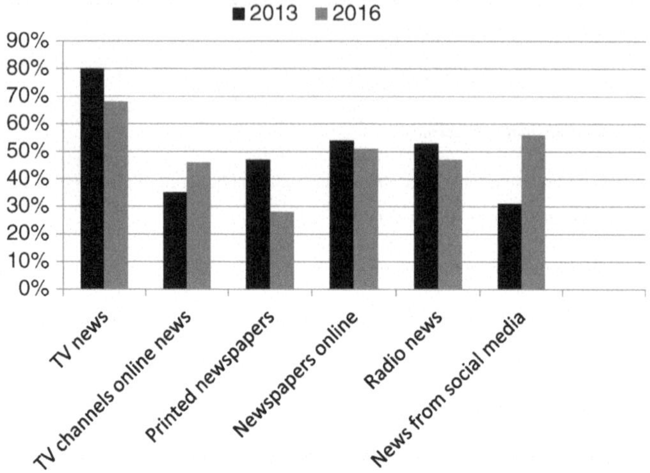

Fig. 5.6 Weekly use of news platforms, Denmark 2013–2016. *Source* Reuters Digital News Report 2013 and 2016

The wider implications of these changes of preferential patterns for the well-being of democracy are being explored in a great variety of news media research that looks into the types of content people seek on these platforms, the trust with which they consume different news outlets, the degree to which they personalize their news diet, people's inclination to participate and engage in online debates about civic matters, and many others, which cannot be pursued further here (see Reuters Digital News Reports 2013, 2016).

In light of such transformations, it makes sense, given the argument that runs through this chapter (cf. Fig. 5.2), to say that audience dynamics should be seen as an integral part of the ongoing processes of building the media logics that govern the media institutions' encounter with other societal institutions in overall processes of mediatization. We may conceptualize these audience dynamics as "audience logics".

5.4.1.1 Media Logics and Audience Logics

Elsewhere, I have suggested that at the level of the individual audience member we may understand their subjective motivations for selecting *their* constellation (or repertoire) of news platforms through the concept of *worthwhileness* (Schrøder and Steeg Larsen 2010). Here, I shall extend this concept, not just for the sake of the argument to do with 'media logics', and suggest that the dimensions of audience worthwhileness can be seen heuristically as a mechanism of audience "logic": In order for a news medium to be adopted into a person's routinized news repertoire, it must be perceived as "worthwhile" in relation to needs stemming from this person's entire context of life.

The notion of "media logics" is part of the conceptual furniture of mediatization theory. But although "logics" is a pivotal concept in institutionalist mediatization theory, it is dismissed as unhelpful in the constructivist tradition. In the constructivist camp, media power is conceptualized as the operation of influential but mellower "moulding forces" rather than as inexorable "logics" (Hepp 2013: 46).

Hjarvard has often distanced himself from a crude understanding of media logics in institutionalist mediatization theory: "The concept of logics is a metaphor and shorthand for the various modi operandi that characterize the workings of the media. [...] the notion of logics seeks to capture how these rules and resources translate into operational features in everyday practices of the media" (Hjarvard 2016a: 11). Hjarvard mentions, among such rules and resources, "established conventions among audiences and users for the usage of particular media". But as we saw above, this apparent rehabilitation of audience practices for mediatization does not mean that they are considered to belong to "the mix of overlapping logics" on a par with the "technological, aesthetic and institutional logics" as co-constitutive of mediatization (Hjarvard 2016a: 11).

However, in the previous section, I argued precisely that when analysing the dynamics of the news media landscape and its relations with the political domain, there is no contradiction in leaning on the concept of media logics and simultaneously seeing these "logics" as being interwoven with the logics emanating from news audiences.

In constructivist mediatization theory, the moulding forces of the media are seen to work alongside and through the co-creative powers of audiences and users in civil society, and a plurality of logics are at work: "It is not a simple matter of a capitalist logic of production, for example, having an impact upon the logics of use and so upon people's everyday lives. The situation is much more complex, involving the mediation of different logics, a plurality of logics" (Hepp 2013: 35).

If media logics are defined as a conceptual shorthand, "worthwhileness"-as-audience-logic can also be seen as such a conceptual shorthand for the interests, preferences, objectives and norms which guide audience members' selection and use of news media technologies, genres and brands. Without going into details here, I will point out that "worthwhileness" consists of the following seven dimensions, which jointly govern the composition of an individual's news repertoire (Schrøder and Steeg Larsen 2010). Depending on his or her lifeworld-derived inclinations and priorities, the individual will determine whether a given news platform

- is worth the *time* spent
- maintains *public connection* (Couldry et al. 2007), i.e. relations to one's networks and the wider society, through *relevant content*:
  - *democratic worthwhileness*: news content that connects the individual to political communities, the citizen identity
  - *everyday worthwhileness*: news content that connects the individual to close communities and networks and provides practical guidance for the conduct of life
- is subject to peer *normative pressures* to do with which news media are appropriate or inappropriate to use
- has *participatory* potential
- is affordable (*price*)
- has *technological appeal*
- has *situational fit*.

All of these factors enter into the individual's "worthwhilness equation", which determines which news media routinely become part of someone's news diet, ultimately with causal implications for the transformations of the entire media landscape, as depicted in Fig. 4.

These worthwhileness dimensions, which operate in people's everyday lives, can be seen as "audience logics" akin to Hjarvard's media logics: what they accomplish theoretically is to translate the audiences' "rules and resources" (ibid.) for using news media into operational components in everyday selective practices around news media. These "audience logics" serve to explain conceptually the processes whereby everyday audience agency is co-constitutive of changes in the media's provision of democratic resources and prerequisites. At the end of the day, therefore, the logics through which news media thrive or die are co-moulded by the lifeworld-derived selection and reception patterns of news audiences. It is "exactly in the conduct of everyday life that we can begin to observe mediatization processes at work" (Hartmann 2009: 225).

5.5 Case 2

5.5.1 *The Power of Online Audience Mobilization*

Media formats come with a set of conventions of use. This is the case, for instance, with live reality formats like *Dancing with the Stars*, in which there is (in the Danish adaptation) a competition between couples where one of the dancers is a professional dancer and the other is a big or small "celebrity". In a short definitional article about mediatization, Nick Couldry pointed out that the naturalized way in which we build popular cultural formats into our everyday lives testifies to the significance of mediatization processes. Using the television song contest *American Idol* as his example, he argues that our ready acceptance of the authority of such programs becomes evidence of the media's symbolic power: "The very idea that a television show is a plausible way of judging singing talent derives from the media's growing meta-capital, that is, the growing influence of media institutions over what counts as symbolic capital" (Couldry 2014: 36). The same point could be argued in relation to the normal viewing of televised dancing competitions like *Dancing with the Stars*. However, such media power is negotiable and contestable.

For *Dancing with the Stars*, the convention of viewing and participating is that four expert jury-members award points for the couples' performance on the dance floor, but at the end of an instalment it is a popular vote among the audience which decides which couple must leave the show that week. In 2013, in the Danish version, there was an audience contestation of the elitist jury, resulting in the popular vote repeatedly, week after week, saving a former national football hero (Allan Simonsen), who was an inept dancer.

The audience rebellion, caused by its non-acceptance of the format conventions, was a cross-media phenomenon initiated by the popular radio talk show *Monte Carlo*, mobilized through Facebook, coordinated by the tabloid newspaper *Ekstra Bladet*, and given additional wide publicity by multiple traditional and online news media. The TV station TV2 was deeply frustrated by this audience mobilization, which threatened the authority of the format to reward dancing talent, and one day suddenly changed the rules just a few hours before the show went on screen. All to no avail. The tabloid newspaper exploited the viral opportunities of Facebook and coordinated the vote, which again saved the couple with the footballer. Only in the semi-final did the channel finally succeed in ousting him.

In itself, this is a quite trivial incident in the history of Danish television, but it serves to show how audiences may collectively challenge the conventions of a live TV format and how this has potentially transformative implications for future vox pop-based reality programs in Denmark. Therefore, these examples (*American Idol* and *Dancing with the Stars*) show that the mediatized symbolic power of a program format is contestable given the right circumstances: The audience, *as an audience*, can withhold its acceptance and undercut the legitimacy and normativity that underlie the "normal" way in which audiences enjoy such shows: "[...] subtle forms of mutual influence are possible" (Couldry 2014: 36).

This trivial example from the area of reality television can be related to collective audience agency in innumerable other areas of the media landscape. At the time of writing, for instance, the satirical video "The Netherlands welcomes Trump in his own words" (https://www.youtube.com/watch?v=ELD2AwFN9Nc) has been liked, commented on and shared by tens of millions of people around the world. All of the individuals who did so were performing as communicative agents based in diverse kinds of cultural, political and quotidian contexts. What united them was the fact that whatever the specific motivations that drove them and whatever the concrete pleasures they derived from doing so, the starting point of their communicative agency was their common experience as members of the global audience that watched this video. The communicative agency of choosing to watch the video, and deciding to like it, share it with or comment on it to their personal social media networks can be seen as acts of giving voice in public to a political sentiment, which—however incrementally and without demonstrable effect (other than inspiring creators in a dozen other countries to produce similar satirical welcome videos)—was a contribution to the process whereby the media affect political opinion formation across diverse public spheres. Conceivably, in accordance with the age-old intentions of satire, the humorous absurdity of the claims made in this video could open the eyes of some non–die-hard Trump supporters to see the not-so-humorous absurdity of the words and deeds of the new US president.

By further extension, this kind of audience/crowd response can also turn directly against an institutional, corporate or personal target, as happens in an online firestorm, or "shitstorm" (Pfeffer et al. 2014), which thus can be seen as an example of concerted communicative agency with considerable transformative thrust.

5.6 Case 3

5.6.1 The Co-Shaping Power of Audiences on Political Discourses

The last example to support my argument about the need to acknowledge the power of media audiences for processes of mediatization goes back to a research project which illustrates the complex ways in which audiences may exercise a co-shaping discursive power over media representations of politics.

This research project compared media discourses about politics with audience discourses about politics, in a specific policy area (transport politics) (Schrøder and Phillips 2007).[5] In both sets of discourses, we identified six identical discursive repertoires,[6] five of which were related to different levels of politics (Figs. 5.7, 5.8): the parliamentary level of parties and politicians; the sub-political level of movements and activists; and the life-political level of political consumption and other everyday political practices. The five discursive repertoires identified were labelled "parliamentary democracy in action", "parliamentary democracy: politics as dirty deals", "populism: citizens against the system", "grassroots politics: growth versus environment", and "politics in daily life: negotiation of individual responsibility". In addition, we found one discursive repertoire, "meta-discourses about politics", which spanned the three political levels.

Although these discursive repertoires were the same for the media and for the audience, they held different prominence within media and audience discourses. (See the different shades of grey in Figs. 5.7 and 5.8 for the relative prominence in the sets of discourses: the darker the shading, the greater prominence.) While the positive representation of parliamentary democracy was central in the media's discourses, politics as dirty deals was more prominent in the audience discourses, in which also the personal effort to make a difference in daily life (for instance, through political consumption) played a considerable role. It was particularly interesting to observe that a prominent "populist repertoire" on politics was a shared feature of both media and audience discourses.

This raised the question of causality: some observers would see the discursive convergence of media populism and audience populism as evidence that media populism (as a possible outcome of increased tabloidization) had been transferred to the audiences, who in turn had become more populist, with implications for their voting behaviour as evidenced

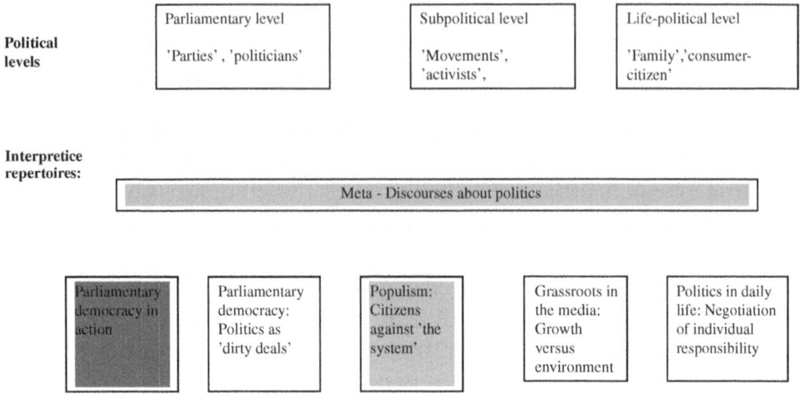

Fig. 5.7 The media's six discourses of politics. *Source* Schrøder and Phillips (2007: 907)

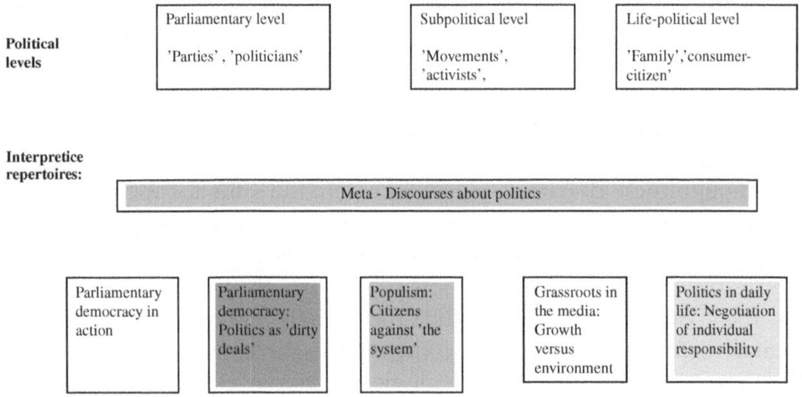

Fig. 5.8 The audiences' six discourses of politics. *Source* Schrøder and Phillips (2007: 908)

in then recent parliamentary elections. However, one could equally plausibly argue that the media were responding to populist sentiment among the voting citizens/audiences, which thus had found its way into the media discourses. The latter causal mechanism is plausible because the media are operating under a commercial competitive condition of audience orientation, which obliges them to present a picture of reality that resonates with the values of the audience groups they address—and depend on for their success or survival.

Therefore, on the one hand, in our media-saturated society, it is very hard to empirically disentangle a presumed populist sentiment among audiences from the populist media discourses to which audiences are daily exposed. But on the other hand, this *empirical* difficulty does not mean *theoretically* that we have to opt for one of these causal directions being the right one. The theoretical solution to this paradox consists in *complexifying* the way we conceptualize the notion of discursive power in a mediatized society and leaving open the possibility, as William Gamson has put it, that the power relationship between media and audience-citizens is "complex and bi-directional" (Gamson 1992).

In order to grasp such causal complexity theoretically, Schrøder and Phillips (2007) suggested that we take inspiration from Fiske and Hartley's anthropologically inspired "bardic" theory of television, extending it to include all forms of media that operate with "audience-orientation" as their fundamental condition of existence (Fiske and Hartley 1978). According to this theory of the media as society's bard, the media function under a commercial and cultural logic according to which the real originator of their messages is the audience. The attractiveness of this theory about the discursive relationship between media and their audiences lies in its accentuation of the *mutuality between media and audience discourses* in the collective construction of the culture's discursive universe.

This point corroborates the argument pursued in this chapter about the need to "audiencize" mediatization research. To reiterate a point made above, even if we accept the "greater authority of the media to define social reality" (Hjarvard 2013: 2f.), both news agendas and media discourses about politics are always *inscribed* with traces of the communicative circuit, in which public discourses are negotiated through the encounter between media institutions on the one hand and audiences in everyday life on the other.

5.7 Rethinking the Media/Audience Nexus in Mediatization Research

One of the key attractions of mediatization theory lies in its having intelligently brought aspects of media influence and power onto the research agenda (Livingstone and Lunt 2014: 706), with the "ambition of answering the difficult questions with regard to whether and how media matter and influence contemporary culture and society" (Hjarvard 2016a: 6). But in this effort, it is essential that the individual and collective agency of audiences be kept in sight and that audiences not be relegated to the role of merely adapting to and conforming with media logics.

Some proponents of mediatization theory avoid the dual pitfalls of media-centrism and audience-centrism by seeing the media as offering technological and discursive affordances that carry a thrust which is negotiated and shaped by audiences and users (Couldry 2014: 38). From a reception-analytical perspective, we may similarly conceptualize the reciprocity of media and audience power by drawing on one of the classics of audience/reception research in order to theorize the audiencization of mediatization research by connecting it metaphorically to Stuart Hall's seminal conceptual framework for reception analysis in the form of the encoding/decoding model (Hall 1973).

Heuristically, we may approach a better theoretical understanding of media/audience relations by transposing Hall's model from the textual level of hegemonic media-discursive affordances to the higher institutional level of media logics. What Hall proposed was that when faced with the hegemonic ideological force which is encoded into the media's preferred meaning, audiences can decode this preferred meaning in three different ways: through dominant, negotiated and oppositional decodings.

By analogy, and drawing on Hjarvard's notion of the "greater authority of the media", we may say that across the technological and the discursive areas, institutional media power has a "preferred thrust" (into which audience agency or even logics are already built), which out there in the wider society is met with dominant, negotiated and oppositional responses from audiences and stakeholders situated at various institutional levels, as illustrated above in the three examples drawn from empirical audience research.

In a similar vein, Adrienne Shaw has recently looked towards Stuart Hall's theory of encoding/decoding in order to build audience power into the transformative processes involving interactive media: "Interactive communication technologies require that we treat audience activity as expected and promoted by [...] texts and technologies. Because of that, we have to rethink the political implications of audience activity somewhat differently. All activity is not resistive, of course, but neither is it complicit" (Shaw 2017: 9). Relating her argument to Hutchby's coupling of the notion of technological affordances with Hall's notion of preferred readings, Shaw suggests that in the age of interactive media there are parallels between the ways we use communication technologies and read media texts, and that the concept of affordance can be metaphorically related to the encoding/decoding model in order to account for this parallel.

This could be one way of carving out a theoretical role for audience-related dynamics as a co-constitutive force in the operation of media power, or processes of mediatization. Audience practices are co-constitutive of the practices of media institutions and therefore of "media logics". Until now, this has been under-researched in mediatization research.

Notes

1. For a continuous mapping of the changing audience dynamics in the landscapes of digital and legacy news media, see for instance the annual publications of the Reuters Digital News Report, which traces the user behaviours and preferences of citizens and consumers.
2. Warner (2002) agrees that the boundary separating an "audience" from a "public" is blurred and porous. He defines an audience as a sub-category of a public, which comes into existence when the discourse that constitutes it derives from a physical event (e.g. a theatre performance) or from a media institution (e.g. television or the internet). For Warner, an audience is thus a kind of public but not all publics are audiences.
3. Among the noteworthy exceptions can be mentioned Encheva et al.'s practice-theoretical, empirically grounded study of graffiti writers' and skaters' orientation towards and use of media to display their artistic skills (Encheva et al. 2013). However, although these practices can be seen as audience practices of a communicative figuration, the study demonstrates not how the sub-cultural agents "audiencize" mainstream media but rather how their engagement with mainstream media serves to mediatize their sub-cultural practices.
4. The research participants were asked to rank their most important news media from a list of eight types of TV news and current affairs, three

types of radio news, six types of printed news, nine types of newspapers' and broadcasters' online news, five types of social media, and five types of other news media. (For a list of all 36 news platforms and formats, see Kobbernagel and Schrøder 2016.)

5. The audience role we explored in this project was that of citizen, rather than consumer, as we asked focus groups to discuss their perceptions of politics on the basis of how the media covered politics.
6. The concept of "repertoire" used here is different from the one used above in connection with users' patterned diets of news media. The discursive repertoires analysed here are defined in discursive psychology as "broadly discernible clusters of terms, descriptions and figures of speech often assembled around metaphors or vivid images" (Potter and Wetherell 1996: 89).

Acknowledgements I am grateful for the suggestions of the anonymous reviewer of this text and for my discussions with colleagues in the research group "Audience and mediated life" at Roskilde University: Jannie Møller Hartley, Fabian Holt, Anne Mølle Lindelof, David Mathieu, Susana Tosca and Norbert Wildermuth. Also, thanks to Knut Lundby for encouragement along the way.

References

Brants, Kees. 2014. Beyond media logic. Keynote address for the ECREA conference, Lisbon, 12–15 November 2014.

Carpentier, Nico. 2011. New configurations of the audience? The challenges of user-generated content for audience theory and media participation. In *The handbook of media audiences*, ed. Virginia Nightingale, 190–212. Chichester: Wiley-Blackwell.

Couldry. 2014. Mediatization: What is it? In *Media practice and everyday agency in Europe*, ed. Leif Kramp, Nico Carpentier, Andreas Hepp, Ilija Tomanić Trivundža, Hannu Nieminen, Risto Kunelius, Tobias Olsson, Ebba Sundin, and Richard Kilborn, 33–39. Bremen: Edition Lumière.

Couldry, Nick, and Andreas Hepp. 2013. Conceptualizing mediatization: Contexts, traditions, arguments. *Communication Theory* 23: 191–202.

Couldry, Nick, Sonia Livingstone, and Tim Markham. 2007. *Media consumption and public engagement: Beyond the presumption of attention.* Basingstoke: Palgrave Macmillan.

Deacon, David, and James Stanyer. 2014. Mediatization: Key concept of conceptual bandwagon? *Media, Culture and Society* 36 (7): 1032–1044.

Ekström, Mats, Johan Fornäs, André Jansson, and Anne Jerslev. 2016. Three tasks for mediatization research: Contributions to an open agenda. *Media, Culture and Society* 38 (7): 1090–1108.

Encheva, Kameliy, Olivier Driessens, and Hans Verstraeten. 2013. The mediatization of deviant subcultures: An analysis of the media-related practices of graffiti writers and skaters. *Mediekultur* 54: 8–25.

Esser, Frank. 1999. "Tabloidization" of news. A comparative analysis of Anglo-American and German press journalism. *European Journal of Communication* 14 (3): 291–324.

Fiske, John, and John Hartley. 1978. *Reading television*. London: Methuen.

Gamson, William. 1992. *Talking politics*. Cambridge: Cambridge University Press.

Haddon, Leslie. 2016. The domestication of complex media repertoires. In *The media and the mundane: Communication across media in everyday life*, ed. Kjetil Sandvik, Anne Mette Thorhauge, and Bjarki Valtysson, 17–30. Göteborg: Nordicom.

Hall, Stuart. 1973. Encoding and decoding in the television discourse. Stencilled occasional paper, Media Series No. 7, Centre for Contemporary Cultural Studies, University of Birmingham. Abridged version. In *Culture, media, language*, eds. Stuart Hall, Dorothy Hobson, Andrew Lowe, and Paul Willis (1980), 128–138. London: Hutchinson.

Hartmann, Maren. 2009. Everyday: Domestication of mediatization or mediatized domestication? In *Mediatization: Concept, changes, consequences*, ed. Knut Lundby, 225–242. New York: Peter Lang.

Hasebrink, Uwe, and Andreas Hepp. 2016. How to research cross-media practices? Investigating media repertoires and media ensembles. Working Paper no. 15, Communicative Figurations series, University of Bremen. http://www.kommunikative-figurationen.de/fileadmin/redak_kofi/Arbeitspapiere/CoFi_EWP_No-15_Hasebrink_Hepp.pdf. Accessed 22 Apr 2017.

Hepp, Andreas. 2013. *Cultures of mediatization*. Cambridge: Polity.

Hepp, Andreas. 2014. Communicative figurations. In *Media practice and everyday agency in Europe*, eds. Leif Kramp, Nico Carpentier, Andreas Hepp, Ilija Tomanić Trivundža, Hannu Nieminen, Risto Kunelius, Tobias Olsson, Ebba Sundin, and Richard Kilborn, 83–99. Bremen: Edition Lumière.

Hepp, Andreas, Stig Hjarvard, and Knut Lundby. 2015. Mediatization: Theorizing the interplay between media, culture and society. *Media, Culture and Society* 37 (2): 314–324.

Hjarvard, Stig. 2013. *The mediatization of culture and society*. New York: Routledge.

Hjarvard, Stig. 2016a. Mediatization. In *The international encyclopedia of media effects*, eds. Patrick Rössler, Cynthia A. Hoffner, and Liesbet van Zoonen, 1–20. Malden MA: Wiley.

Hjarvard, Stig. 2016b. Medialisering: Teori og historie. In *Medialisering. Mediernes rolle i social og kulturel forandring*, ed. Stig Hjarvard, 17–38. København: Hans Reitzel.

Hutchby, Ian. 2001. *Conversation and technology: From the telephone to the internet.* Cambridge: Polity.

Kobbernagel, Christian, and Kim C. Schrøder. 2016. From everyday communicative figurations to rigorous audience news repertoires: A mixed method approach to cross-media news consumption. *Mediekultur* 32(60): 6–31.

Krotz, Friedrich. 2014. From a social worlds perspective to the analysis of mediatized worlds. In *Media practice and everyday agency in Europe*, ed. Leif Kramp, Nico Carpentier, Andreas Hepp, Ilija Tomanić Trivundža, Hannu Nieminen, Risto Kunelius, Tobias Olsson, Ebba Sundin, and Richard Kilborn, 69–82. Bremen: Edition Lumière.

Langer, John. 2003. Tabloid television and news culture. In *Ness public relations and power*, ed. Simon Cottle, 135–152. London: Sage.

Livingstone, Sonia. 2005. On the relation between audiences and publics. In *Audiences and publics: When cultural engagement matters for the public sphere*, ed. Sonia Livingstone, 17–41. Bristol UK: Intellect.

Livingstone, Sonia. 2013. The participation paradigm in audience research. *The Communication Review* 16: 21–30.

Livingstone, Sonia, and Peter Lunt. 2014. Mediatization: An emerging paradigm for media and communication research? In *Mediatization of communication*, ed. Knut Lundby, 703–723. Berlin, Boston: De Gruyter/Mouton.

Lundby, Knut. 2014a. Engaging with conflicts in mediatized religious environments. Paper for the Norwegian Association for Media Research, Trondheim 23–24 October 2014.

Lundby, Knut. 2014b. Mediatization of communication. In *Mediatization of communication*, ed. Knut Lundby, 3–35. Berlin, Boston: De Gruyter/Mouton.

Lundby, Knut. 2016. Where are audiences in mediatization research? Paper for the Mediatization section of the 6th ECREA conference, Prague 9–12 November 2016.

Madianou, Mirca. 2014. Polymedia: Communication and mediatized migration: An ethnographic approach. In *Mediatization of communication*, ed. Knut Lundby, 323–346. Berlin, Boston: De Gruyter/Mouton.

Moe, Hallvard, and Hilde Van Den Bulck. 2016. *Teletext in Europe.* From the analog to the digital era. Gothenburg: Nordicom.

Pfeffer, Jürgen, Thomas Zorbach, and Kathleen M. Carley. 2014. Understanding online firestorms: Negative word-of-mouth dynamics in social media networks. *Journal of Marketing Communications* 20 (1–2): 117–128.

Picard, R. 2014. Twilight or new dawn of journalism? Evidence from the changing news ecosystem. *Journalism Studies* 15 (5): 500–510. doi:10.1080/1461670X.2014.895530.

Potter, Jonathan, and Margaret Wetherell. 1996. Discourse analysis. In *Rethinking methods in psychology*, ed. Jonothan A. Smith, Rom Harré, and Luk Van Langenhove, 80–92. London: Sage.

Reuters Digital News Report. Published annually. *The Reuters Institute for the Study of Journalism*, University of Oxford. http://reutersinstitute.politics.ox.ac.uk/. Accessed 22 Apr 2017.

Rosen, Jay. 2006. The people formerly known as the audience, *PressThink*. http://archive.pressthink.org/2006/06/27/ppl_frmr.html.

Schrøder. Kim C., and Ib T. Gulbrandsen. In press. Audience. In *The international encyclopedia of strategic communication*, ed. Robert L. Heath, and Winni Johansen. Hoboken, NJ: Wiley.

Schrøder, Kim C. 2016. Q method and news audience research. In *The SAGE handbook of digital journalism*, ed. Tamara Witschge, Chris W. Anderson, David Domingo, and Alfred Hermida, 528–545. Los Angeles: Sage.

Schrøder, Kim C., and Bent Steeg Larsen. 2010. The shifting cross-media news landscape. *Journalism Studies* 11 (4): 524–534.

Schrøder, Kim C., and Louise Phillips. 2007. Complexifying media power: A study of the interplay between media and audience discourses on politics. *Media, Culture and Society* 29 (6): 890–915.

Shaw, Adrienne. 2017. Encoding and decoding affordances: Stuart Hall and interactive media technologies. *Media, Culture and Society* 39 (4): 592–602. doi:10.1177/0163443717692741.

Thorlacius, Lisbeth. 2016. Visuel remediering af de danske netaviser. In *Den fælles dagsorden—Og alle de andre*, ed. Mark Blach-Ørsten, and Ida Willig, 105–130. Frederiksberg: Samfundslitteratur.

Warner, Michael. 2002. *Publics and counterpublics*. New York: Zone Books.

Webster, F. 2014. *The marketplace of attention: How audiences take shape in a digital age*. Cambridge, MA: MIT Press.

Witschge, Tamara. 2014. Passive accomplice or active disruptor: The role of audiences in the mediatization of politics. *Journalism Practice* 8 (3): 342–356.

PART II

Dynamics in Politics and Organizations

CHAPTER 6

The Localities of Mediatization: How Organizations Translate Mediatization into Everyday Practices

Magnus Fredriksson and Josef Pallas

6.1 Introduction

The underlying argument behind this volume rests on an assumption that media, their values, preferences and working routines influence almost all aspects of our everyday lives. In a sociological sense, mediatization can be thought of as a normative and cognitive system that—not least through its technological affordance—provides stability and meaning to the social lives of those who operate within its jurisdiction. At an aggregated level, mediatization as a semi-autonomous institution transforms other institutions such as politics, business, culture and religion. That is, actors within these institutional orders internalize ideas and beliefs about media (what media do, how, why and with what consequences) to such an extent that it challenges and possibly also redefines

M. Fredriksson (✉)
University of Gothenburg, Gothenburg, Sweden
e-mail: magnus.fredriksson@jmg.gu.se

J. Pallas
Uppsala University, Uppsala, Sweden

O. Driessens et al. (eds.), *Dynamics Of Mediatization*,
Transforming Communications – Studies in Cross-Media Research,
DOI 10.1007/978-3-319-62983-4_6

how these actors understand, relate to and act upon the world around them. Research on mediatization has provided valuable insights and offers detailed descriptions, explanations and understandings of how such ideas and beliefs play out in and become intertwined with rationalities or logics governing contexts such as politics (Esser and Strömbäck 2014; Laursen and Valentini 2015), the public sector (Schillemans 2012, 2016; Thorbjornsrud et al. 2014), religion (Hjarvard and Lövheim 2012) or science (Marcinkowski et al. 2014).

However, in their recent book, Couldry and Hepp (2016) argue that it is necessary to pay closer attention not only to how mediatization intervenes with other day-to-day activities in specific contexts but also to how mediatization itself is re-created and reshaped in these activities. For us—being interested in organizational processes—such a call means to transcend the distinction between the institutional and social-constructivist approaches (see Lundby 2014 for details) and address the contexts of formal organizing as a site where mediatization comes into being through interpretations, negotiations and contestations efforts of those occupying these contexts (Pallas et al. 2014; Fredriksson and Pallas 2014; Pallas et al. 2016). Putting this into a more formal ambition for this chapter, we seek to understand how mediatization comes in and is formed in specific local contexts where it meets actors who hold different motives, values and beliefs about media, their role, functioning and effects. We do so by bringing insights from organizational institutionalism (Greenwood et al. 2008) and particularly the translation theory (Czarniawska and Sevón 1996, 2005; Spyridonidis et al. 2014). The translation literature has been traditionally (but not exclusively) concerned with how global models for governing and managing organizations travel across various organizational fields and how these models acquire meaning as they enter local settings of specific organizations. A central argument in our reasoning is to address mediatization in terms of such global ideas which allows us to highlight and recognize the relatively vague, ambiguous and imprecise properties of mediatization.

The rest of the chapter is structured as follows. First, we address the literature on mediatization by focusing on how mediatization is viewed and understood as it enters local (organizational) contexts through adoption of and adaptation to media logics. Second, we visit organizational research on translation of ideas to discuss how institutionalized models and practices travel and enter organizations. In particular, we suggest that mediatization, similarly to other institutionalized ideas, enters organizations—and can be understood—in terms of different elements that are interpreted, negotiated, translated and given meaning in relation to coexisting value systems characterizing the operations and activities of the context into which the ideas are introduced. We summarize the theoretical arguments by arguing that the notion of local translating of institutionalized ideas offers valuable insights if we want to understand the localities of mediatization. That is, we argue that the way in which mediatization is brought into being in specific organizational settings is essential also for how mediatization itself is reconstructed in and proliferated across these settings.

However, before we move on, a short comment on the notion of organization is in order. When we discuss the way mediatization works and influences organizations, we do so by recognizing differences between organizations with respect to: underlying organizational characteristics (i.e. entrepreneurial, professional bureaucracy, or divisional) (Mintzberg 1983), the different societal sectors organizations occupy (i.e. private, public and civic) (Esping-Andersen 1990), the distinct political systems of which the organizations are a part of (Djelic 1998); and the different media systems in which they operate (Hallin and Mancini 2004). However, in the context of this chapter, we use the notion inclusively to discuss general processes in which mediatization permeates and is given meaning in social entities that are characterized by properties of "complete organizations"—that is, entities that can be defined and described in terms of clear and definable structures, autonomous decision-making capacities, and distinct identities (Brunsson and Sahlin-Andersson 2000; Ahrne and Brunsson 2011).

6.2 Media Logics

The point of departure for much of the literature on mediatization follows the reasoning that media have become the most important form of communication between social actors in different sectors such as politics, business, religion, sport or education. Consequently, actors in these sectors transform as they adapt to the norms, rules, values and working procedures of media. Such a transformation—it is argued—has decisive effects on knowledge, attitudes and behaviours within these sectors, especially as the actors occupying these sectors need to handle their interactions not only with media but also with other—equally media-dependent—entities. Mediatization is a process where original rationales of non-media actors are complemented, suppressed or even supplemented by the working rationales of media organizations (Mazzoleni and Schulz 1999; Hjarvard 2008). These processes of internalization of media values, practices, routines and preferences have been addressed mainly in terms of a media logic as entering, complementing, competing with and eventually taking over the existing rationales for how organizations (such as political parties) structure, perform and communicate their activities (Strömbäck 2008; Schulz 2004).

More recent efforts have come to see and study mediatization of organizations beyond the totalizing implementation of and adjustment to the underlying working routines and preferences of the media by paying attention to how media logic is embedded in and intertwined with governing logics of a particular field (Esser and Strömbäck 2014; Laursen and Valentini 2015). Empirically, the analyses have focused on how media logic competes with pre-existing or parallel logics when it comes to influences on, for instance, decision-makers (Scheu et al. 2014), resources (Thorbjornsrud et al. 2014), structures (Esser 2013), activities or organizational processes (Schillemans 2012; Strömbäck 2008), and perceptions (Esser and Matthes 2013). Other examples of such a contestation include several studies on political logic versus media logic (Brants and Van Praag 2006; Haßler et al. 2014; Mazzoleni 1987; Strömbäck 2008; van Aelst et al. 2008; Zeh and Hopmann 2013) as well as judicial logic versus media logic (Peleg and Bogoch 2014), bureaucratic versus news logic (Thorbjornsrud et al. 2014), media logic versus the logic of network governance (Korthagen 2015) or audience-oriented market logic versus normative (media) logic (Landerer 2013).

Even though these studies offer useful insights into how mediatization is embodied in and channelled through media logic and how such a logic influences and guides organizational actions and at times also provides impetus for change at an aggregated level (i.e. institutional change), the media logic literature has not escaped some (occasionally) fundamental criticism. While understanding media logic as an articulation of a higher social order that points at stability, historical patterns and extensive reach of belief systems and practices, the notion has been criticized as being context-independent, linear and rather fixed/insensitive to macro-level dynamics (e.g. Couldry 2012; Lundby 2009; Pallas and Fredriksson 2013). Lundby (2009: 117) put it this way: "it is not viable to speak of an overall media logic, it is necessary to specify how various capabilities are applied in various patterns of social interactions". (See also Kriesi et al. 2013; Lunt and Livingstone 2016; Ekström et al. 2016 for more elaborative discussions.)

To avoid this critique, mediatization scholars have argued for the existence of multiple media logics (social media logics, networked media logics, journalistic logics, etc.), suggesting thereby that different media logics might coexist and "have different weight/importance due to situations, actors and other circumstances, something that also may change over time and thus is not fixed" (Klinger and Svensson 2015: 1244). Brants and Van Praag (2015) and Hjarvard (forthcoming) in a similar vein suggest that there are a number of media logics that are infused with values connected to different forms of media, different types of media contents, different types of media productions as well as institutional and national contexts. To address the rather deterministic underpinning of the early conceptualizations of media logic, mediatization scholars are now more sensitive to the reflexive, skilful and creative work of—among others—media and communication professionals (e.g. social media technicians, administrators and journalists) who negotiate with representatives of other logics (e.g. politicians, regulators, market actors, and citizens). See, for instance, Donges and Jarren (2014: 187) for an illustrative example where they argue that media logics "do not exist naturally but are socially constructed" which makes them – especially when they are introduced into specific organizational contexts – open for political enactment. Similarly, Laursen and Valentini (2015) have shown that mediated politics is about interactions and negotiations between journalists and civil servants where the latter can have considerable influence on how media are understood and acted upon (see also Kunelius and Reunanen 2011).

Despite the efforts to fend off some of the limitations of the notion of *media logic*—independently if we talk about a logic, the logics or logics—the literature tends to run into difficulties not to define and treat logic(s) as an expression of relatively stable, homogenous, and definable higher social order (Asp 2014). Therefore, we would argue that media logic, as an analytical and theoretical concept, continues to struggle with being insufficiently equipped to capture complexity in and between processes that follow local use (contextualization) of mediatization in its institutionalized form. So we believe that we can benefit from a theoretical framework that would offer a complementary view on specifics in which the mediatization enters and influences organizations. In the following, we outline such a framework by approaching mediatization in terms of ideas.

6.3 Ideas and Carries of Mediatization

As we stated at the beginning of the chapter, we argue for at least partial replacing of the notion of media logics with the notion of ideas. This would allow us to reconnect with Altheide and Snow's initial argument that "media logic has been accepted as the *perspective* through which various institutional problems are interpreted and solved" (1979: 15) (italics added by the authors). This means that we understand mediatization as a process where it is embedded in variety of loosely coupled and sometimes even unrelated and inconsistent best practices, recipes, routines, products and professional norms about how to understand and relate to media and media-related issues. These elements—as we have argued elsewhere—are eventually noticed, interpreted and made sense of (i.e. translated) in organizations by way of embedding these into local value systems permeating the context into which they are introduced and proliferated (Pallas et al. 2016; Schillemans 2012; Thorbjornrud et al. 2014). Owing to such translation processes, it is likely that mediatization will be understood and acted upon differently in and between different organizations. But before we continue to develop our reasoning about mediatization as a translation process, let us say a few words about the very notion of ideas and the carriers – i.e. symbols, routines, relations and artefacts – through which they are introduced to organizations.

First, ideas can be seen as transcriptions of widely spread and taken-for-granted practices, rules, norms and values that are constructed in specific institutional contexts—i.e. contexts that are populated by actors sharing common interests and organized around joint activities (Wedlin and Sahlin 2017). Ideas are created, proliferated and picked up in terms of models, recipes, concepts or templates and equipped with clear labels, formulations and rationales that would make sense also outside the context in which they were originally created or used. Ideas offer general rather than specific instructions for how organizations can or should make decisions, structure their operations, account for their activities or formulate their identities. Such universalism enables the ideas to reach a broad acceptance and to be adapted across organizations sharing the same organizational fields, industries, markets and sectors. This was the case with lean production and total quality management (TQM), which were originally models developed and used by Toyota. By the time the models (that can be seen as explicit articulations of rationalization and scientification of Western societies—Morris and Lancaster 2006; Benders and Bijsterveld 2000) have become institutionalized, de-contextualized and transformed into a recipe, they have started to get introduced and re-contextualized into remote and unrelated organizational contexts such as organizing of health care in hospitals and administration in public administrations. But similar examples can also be found in other areas and contexts; for instance, the emergence of public relations consultancies has been characterized by extensive import of models initially developed and used by management consultants (Tyllström 2013).

Second, the examples above illustrate not only that ideas can become widespread and gain popularity outside the contexts in which they have been created. Ideas are at the same time characterized by ambiguity as they don't offer specific instructions for a given situation. You must make obvious alliterations of an idea to make it fit into a new context. Ideas are sources of inconsistency and contestations in organizations as their meanings are translated differently depending on who is introducing them, how and into what organizational context. Different ideas often interact and oppose each other as they are interwoven within the same normative and regulative context in which organizations operate (Wedlin and Sahlin 2017). For instance, rationalized models and ideas about communication, such as transparency and integrated communication, both reinforce but oftentimes directly contradict each other (Fredriksson and Pallas 2017).

But ideas get also altered and transformed as they move from one (organizational) context to another. Therefore, different organizations might encounter and get seduced by ideas travelling under the same label although they differ substantially when compared. "Strategic communication" is not necessarily the same thing in a museum as it is in a business organization (Kjeldsen 2013). At the same time, there are ideas that are packaged differently but their content remains the same. What one organization might label as "strategic communication" can be labelled as "reputation management" by another. Another example is when political lobbying of organizations is incorporated in activities addressed as public relations, public affairs or governmental relations (l'Etang 2008).

In sum, in contrast to institutional logics, ideas by definition are dynamic, flexible and transformable when they are about to be introduced in organizations. As they are less characterized by stability and historical underpinning compared with institutional logics (cf. Friedland and Alford 1991; Thornton and Ocasio 1999; Thornton et al. 2012), ideas can be transformed into a variety of concrete objects that make sense in and are supported by resources and (fashionable) preferences available in an individual organization (Czarniawska and Sevón 1996; Lindberg 2014). Ideas, in other words, are codified, transcribed and symbolically and dramaturgically shaped and could be perceived (in contrast to more abstract institutional expressions) as designed with a specific organization in mind and thereby motivate the organization to change its behaviour.

6.3.1 *Carriers of Mediatization*

To be able to understand how ideas associated with how to understand and related to media are materialized and made transferable from one context to another, we (Pallas et al. 2016) have used Scott's (1995, 2003) distinction between four different carriers of institutions, namely symbolical systems, relational systems, routines and artefacts. In this study, we examined how different professional groups (communications practitioners, scientists, professional bureaucrats and members of management team) in one of the Swedish regulatory governmental agencies translated rationales of media into their everyday activities and how these translations were perceived in relation to members of others professions populating the agency.

Symbolic systems include rules, values and discourses regarding a social phenomenon. These rules and values are to a certain extent "external" to actors and are inscribed and codified in laws, regulations and standards. However, they are also to a certain degree subjective, internalized cognitive frames formulated as expectations, concepts and principles. Regarding media, it is evident that many concepts infusing modern organizations are interlinked with an idea rooted in communication in general and media in particular. How organizations are categorized, described and valued and whether they are perceived as successful or not are often evaluated from a media-related standpoint.

Relational systems are made of social networks where individuals, groups and organizations act as nodes, opinion leaders, bridges and liaisons. These networks include formal as well as informal connections and function as an infrastructure for information exchange between actors. But the relational systems also include individuals who have multiple organizational memberships as well as individuals who move from one position in one organization to a similar or another type of position in another organization. Regarding the latter, the increasing number of journalists working as press agents or public relations practitioners is an obvious example of how individuals can carry ideas from one context to another. But one could also point towards the increasing numbers of non-governmental organizations and public sector organizations hiring managers from private corporations. These often take a relatively strategic stance on marketing, branding and other expressive forms of communication which means that media are seen here as a tool to strengthen and increase organizations' competitiveness, reputation and autonomy.

Routines are patterned actions and procedures encoded in repetitive activities on the basis of actors' tacit knowledge. They include schematic as well as performative aspects and thereby hold a general idea of what to do, how to do it and when to do it. To align an organization's communication activities with the routines connected to specific news broadcasting or the print of a newspaper are two evident examples of media-oriented routines in organizations. Another example captures how organizing of communication departments at many organizations exhibits more similarities with traditional newsrooms rather than with other departments at these organizations.

Artefacts are tangible objects such as tools, equipment and technologies but also different types of products and materials. These objects are by no means determined in how they are about to be interpreted and used—rather the opposite. People tend to maintain a level of flexibility in the understanding of how to interact with artefacts. In a context of media and their artefacts, we know that the production of communication materials such as texts, images, and press materials does reassemble the production of news.

6.4 Translation of Ideas

Arguing for institutionalized ideas in the way we presented above enables a more systematic analysis of how mediatization is locally decoded and translated by organizational members who are embedded in different organizational contexts and possess different values and professional preferences. We can particularly note three aspects of such decoding and translating. The first one leads our attention to the character of the ideas that are translated. The ways in which different elements of ideas are understood and acted upon are not guided by institutionalized characteristics of the idea per se. It is the local interpretation of the elements that carry the idea and what meaning they have been given as they are brought into being in specific contexts that influences the translation. Second, ideas do not enter an organization in relation to other (competing) ideas in a way that they replace, transform or merge into new ideas as some of the mediatization literature would argue when analysing media logics in relation to, for instance, political or market logics. Instead, we see translation of mediatization as a process that takes place along the four elements and where we can find significant variation between how the different elements are made sense of (Pallas et al. 2016). This also means that the elements (or rather their meanings) change as they are translated. To make the above arguments more accessible, in the following we pay closer attention to the translation process itself as it has been addressed and developed by the (mostly Scandinavian) organizational institutionalists.

The organizational literature on translation puts meaning, values and motives at the centre of its empirical, methodological as well as theoretical interest. These theories, which have roots in the sociology of science (Callon 1986) and actor network approaches (Czarniawska and Hernes 2005; Latour 1996), refer to translation as an ongoing process through which institutional ideas and practices are created, legitimized, selected and given meaning as they travel across organizations and organizational fields. Within organizational institutionalism (see Greenwood et al. 2008 for an overview), the translation literature focuses primarily on describing and explaining how generalized and widely spread management models and organizational practices such as new public management, lean production and TQM not only transform the adapting organizations. The literature provides an explanation of how these models and practices change over time and space (Czarniawska and Sevón 1996, 2005). Thereby, translation scholars offer an understanding of the processes through which organizations and their members are involved in the creation and formation of institutional orders and are not merely passive adopters of these.

One of the most important contributions from organizational institutionalism is that most organizational activities do not only serve to solve specific operational or technical problems. The way they are introduced and performed in organizations is in large part also conditioned by the organization's search for legitimacy to secure necessary environmental support. Thus, most aspects of organizing—including structures, routines and standards concerning communication, staffing and accounting—are motivated by a necessity to comply with what significant others define as suitable. Here, the notion of *appropriateness* is central as it captures the processes of how and why organizations select models, ideas and practices. To some degree, this might be perceived as a process of solving specific problems, but a closer look often reveals the importance of general qualities that are recognizable and desirable from a perspective of resemblance with how other relevant organizations have approached the same or similar problems (Sevón 1996).

A crucial point in the translation literature (see above) is that ideas arrive from different places and seldom are directly applicable to or compatible with conditions of the receiving organization. Therefore, characteristics bounded to certain times or spaces (or both) in which the idea was embedded need to be omitted or downplayed (Czarniawska and Joerges 1996). This de-contextualization often involves detachment from rules or professional norms (or both) commanding certain professional conduct that is valid in the context from which the idea was brought. Therefore, ideas often are presented as equipped with characteristics that would make them attractive outside their home context. Such a presentation is more connected to the symbolical materialization of an idea than to its factual employment. Organizations translate an idea by formulating its form and content so it appears clear and explicit with respect to the local prerequisites and interests. This means that a successful reformulation of an idea manages to downplay those aspects of the idea that can be seen as contradicting or discrediting the new settings in which it is about to be introduced. Reformulation of an idea may thereby change not only its form but also its focus, content and meaning.

From this we can learn that the adaptation of an idea is not bound by the conditions whereby the idea was created and proliferated—rather the opposite. The translation of an idea follows the reasoning that governs the new context; that is, it is presented, understood and used in accordance with logical and rational arguments valid in the settings where the idea finds its new relevance (Sahlin-Andersson 1996). Therefore, translation can be described as a performative practice that is guided by identification of an appropriate reasoning that enhances the interpretation and employment of an idea in relation to values and preferences that are relevant and legitimate in the context into which the idea is introduced. This in turn means that translation is a dialectical process between the idea and the value systems of those being exposed to the ideas (Diedrich et al. 2013; Mueller and Whittle 2011). This means that translation refers to a transformation of both the idea at hand and the organizations in which the idea finds its relevance (cf. Czarniawska and Sevón 2005; Waldorff 2013; Werr and Stjernberg 2003; Pipan and Czarniawska 2010).

Central to the arguments here is the active role of actors who are engaged in the creation, diffusion and implementation of ideas and models into organizational contexts. These actors—commonly referred to as carriers—include external as well as internal experts such as management consultants, academics and representatives of professions occupying contemporary organizations. These carriers motivate organizations to pay attention to certain external ideas and models often in relation to preferences that are based in professional jurisdictions and value systems (Røvik 2016; Levay and Waks 2009). They are also involved when organizations modify and equip these models with new attributes that are tailored to the local settings (Sahlin and Engwall 2002). Professions thereby provide us with patterns in the local responses and translations and link these to larger structures of meaning in which they are embedded (Bévort and Suddaby 2015).

6.5 What Does Translation Mean for Understanding the Localities of Mediatization?

The overall aim of this chapter has been to offer a framework for how mediatization is given meaning and gets acted upon in individual organizations and thereby increase our knowledge of the localities of mediatization. With support from organizational institutionalism and theory of translation of management ideas, we have offered a contribution to the mediatization literature by unpacking the notions of *translation* and *ideas* as analytical concepts. We would argue that by illustrating and conceptualizing how ideas are created, distributed and re-contextualized and eventually become translated, we can find the ways in which mediatization gets enacted and embedded in local contexts and thus become connected to day-to-day activities of organizations. Hereby, we can also more properly theorize how translations of mediatization are related to and constructed in relation to local systems of norms, beliefs and assumption. By focusing on how the elements of ideas associated with and related to mediatization are given meaning as they meet with different professional groups, work practices and cognitive frames, we can theorize the role of profession and value systems in understanding not only how mediatization comes in and influences specific organizations but also how mediatization gets enacted and reconstructed in organizational contexts. Thus, while we recognize that local reconstruction of social orders is central to translation theory, our perspective provides tools to further theorize this situational and processual perspective, which is highly relevant for the literature on mediatization (Couldry and Hepp 2016).

The translation framework with its focus on *travel*—that is, how locally translated ideas get de-contextualized and serve as a source of inspiration in other local contexts—can also help us to understand how mediatization transforms as it is given prominence across and between organizations occupying different societal sectors. Even though mediatization at times appears as stabilized and included in routines and established practices of organizations, the translation of the different elements continues through articulation of the role and meaning of these elements in specific situations (cf. Pipan and Czarniawska 2010).

In more general terms, our argument is that a more complete understanding of mediatization of organizations requires a political perspective as well as a focus on the nature of an idea at hand. The way in which mediatization plays out in organizations should be studied in relation to other ideas and existing value systems as these have an important role in where, how, by whom and to what extent mediatization is internalized and subsequently altered and reconstructed. Thus, rather than describing the results of translation of ideas (such as those about mediatization) in terms of a relatively consistent and stabilized state (or states), we see mediatization as being a highly elastic and sensitive process that is open to organizations' and their members' capacities to actively and continuously interpret, enact and reconstruct it.

Acknowledgements This chapter was written as a part of our project "Management structures and mediatization of governmental agencies—translations and consequences", funded by the Swedish Research Council.

References

Ahrne, Göran, and Nils Brunsson. 2011. Organization outside organizations: The significance of partial organization. *Organization* 18 (1): 83–104.

Altheide, David L., and Robert P. Snow. 1979. *Media logic*. Beverly Hills: Sage.

Asp, Kent. 2014. News media logic in a new institutional perspective. *Journalism Studies* 15 (3): 256–270.

Benders, Jos, and Mark Van Bijsterveld. 2000. Leaning on lean: The reception of a management fashion in Germany. *New Technology, Work and Employment* 15 (1): 50–64.

Bévort, Frans, and Roy Suddaby. 2015. Scripting professional identities: How individuals make sense of contradictory institutional logics. *Journal of Professions and Organization* 3 (1): 17–38.

Brants, Kees, and Philip van Praag. 2006. Signs of media logic: Half a century of political communication in the Netherlands. *Javnost—The Public* 13 (1): 25–40.

Brants, Kees, and Philip van Praag. 2015. Beyond the media logic. *Journalism Studies* 18 (4): 1–14.

Brunsson, Nils, and Kerstin Sahlin-Andersson. 2000. Constructing organizations: The example of public sector reform. *Organization Studies* 21 (4): 721–746.

Callon, Michel. 1986. Some elements of a sociology of translation: Domestication of the scallops and the fishermen of St Brieuc Bay. In *Power, action and belief. A new sociology of knowledge?*, ed. John Law, 196–233. London: Routledge and Kegan Paul.

Couldry, Nick. 2012. *Media, society, world: Social theory and digital media practice*. Cambridge: Polity.

Couldry, Nick, and Andreas Hepp. 2016. *The mediated construction of reality*. Cambridge: Polity Press/Wiley.

Czarniawska, Barbara, and Bernward Joerges. 1996. Travels of ideas. In *Translating organizational change*, ed. Barbara Czarniawska, and Guje Sevón, 13–48. Berlin: Walter de Gruyter.

Czarniawska, Barbara, and Tor Hernes. 2005. *Actor-network theory and organizing*. Malmö: Liber.

Czarniawska, Barbara, and Guje Sevón. 1996. *Translating organizational change*. Berlin: Walter de Gruyter.

Czarniawska, Barbara, and Guje Sevón. 2005. *Global ideas: How ideas, objects and practices travel in the global economy*. Malmö: Libris.

Diedrich, Andreas, Ulla Eriksson-Zetterquist, Lena Ewertsson, Johan Hagberg, Anette Hallin, Fredrik Lavén, Kajsa Lindberg, Elena Raviola, Egle Rindzeviciute, and Lars Walter. 2013. *Exploring the performativity turn in management studies*. Gothenburg: Gothenburg Research Institute.

Djelic, Marie-Laure. 1998. *Exporting the American model: The post-war transformation of European business*. Oxford: Oxford University Press.

Donges, Patrick, and Otfried Jarren. 2014. Mediatization of political organizations: Changing parties and interest groups. In *Mediatization of politics: Understanding the transformation of Western democracies*, ed. Frank Esser, and Jesper Strömbäck, 181–199. New York: Palgrave Macmillan.

Ekström, Mats, Johan Fornäs, André Jansson, and Anne Jerslev. 2016. Three tasks for mediatization research: Contributions to an open agenda. *Media, Culture and Society* 38 (7): 1090–1108.

Esping-Andersen, Gøsta. 1990. *The three worlds of welfare capitalism*. Cambridge: Polity Press.

Esser, Frank. 2013. Mediatization as a challenge: Media logic versus political logic. In *Democracy in the age of globalization and mediatization*, ed. Hanspeter Kriesi, Daniel Bochsler, Jörg Matthes, Sandra Lavenex, Marc Bühlmann, and Frank Esser, 155–176. New York: Palgrave Macmillan.

Esser, Frank, and Jörg Matthes. 2013. Mediatization effects on political news, political actors, political decisions, and political audiences. In *Democracy in the age of globalization and mediatization*, ed. Hanspeter Kriesi, Daniel Bochsler, Jörg Matthes, Sandra Lavenex, Marc Bühlmann, and Frank Esser, 177–201. Hampshire: Palgrave Macmillan.

Esser, Frank, and Jesper Strömbäck. 2014. *Mediatization of politics: Understanding the transformation of Western democracies*. New York: Palgrave Macmillan.

Fredriksson, Magnus, and Josef Pallas. 2017. Translated inconsistency: Management communication under the reign of institutional ambiguity. *Management Communication Quarterly*. 37 (11): 1661–1684.

Fredriksson, Magnus, and Josef Pallas. 2014. Media enactments: Where to look for inspiration in mediatization studies. In *Organizations and the media. Organizing in a mediatized world*, ed. Josef Pallas, Stefan Jonsson, and Lars Strannegård, 234–248. London: Routledge.

Friedland, Roger, and Robert R. Alford. 1991. Bringing society back in: Symbols, practices, and institutional contradictions. In *The new institutionalism in organizational analysis*, ed. Walter W. Powell, and Paul J. DiMaggio, 232–266. Chicago: The University of Chicago Press.

Greenwood, Royston, Christine Oliver, Kerstin Sahlin-Andersson, and Roy Suddaby. 2008. *The SAGE handbook of organizational institutionalism*. London: Sage.

Hallin, Daniel C., and Paolo Mancini. 2004. *Comparing media systems: Three models of media and politics*. New York: Cambridge University Press.

Haßler, Jörg, Marcus Maurer, and Corinna Oschatz. 2014. Media logic and political logic online and offline. *Journalism Practice* 8 (3): 326–341.

Hjarvard, Stig. 2008. The mediatization of society: A theory of the media as agents of social and cultural change. *Nordicom Review* 29 (2): 105–134.

Hjarvard, Stig, and Mia Lövheim. 2012. Mediatization and religion: Nordic perspectives. *European Journal of Communication* 28 (2): 214–215.

Hjarvard, Stig. Forthcoming. Mediatization: Reframing the analysis of 'media effects'. In *The international encyclopedia of media effects*, eds. Patrick Rössler, Cynthia A. Hoffner, and Liesbet van Zoonen. Chichester: Wiley.

l'Etang, Jacquie. 2008. *Public relations.* Wiley Online Library.

Kjeldsen, Anna K. 2013. Strategic communication institutionalized: A Scandinavian perspective. *Public Relations Inquiry* 2 (2): 223–242.

Klinger, Ulrike, and Jakob Svensson. 2015. The emergence of network media logic in political communication: A theoretical approach. *New Media and Society* 17 (8): 1241–1257.

Korthagen, Iris. 2015. *Media logic versus the logic of network governance.* Doctoral dissertation, Erasmus University, Rotterdam.

Kriesi, Hanspeter, Daniel Bochsler, Jörg Matthes, Sandra Lavenex, Marc Bühlmann, and Frank Esser. 2013. *Democracy in the age of globalization and mediatization.* New York: Palgrave Macmillan.

Kunelius, Risto, and Esa Reunanen. 2011. Media in political power: A Parsonian view on the differentiated mediatization of Finnish decision makers. *The International Journal of Press/Politics* 17 (1): 56–75.

Landerer, Nino. 2013. Rethinking the logics: A conceptual framework for the mediatization of politics. *Communication Theory* 23 (3): 239–258.

Latour, Bruno. 1996. *Aramis or the love of technology.* Cambridge, MA: Harvard University Press.

Laursen, Bo, and Chiara Valentini. 2015. Mediatization and government communication: Press work in the European parliament. *The International Journal of Press/Politics* 20 (1): 26–44.

Levay, Charlotta, and Caroline Waks. 2009. Professions and the pursuit of transparency in healthcare: Two cases of soft autonomy. *Organization Studies* 30 (5): 509–527.

Lindberg, Kajsa. 2014. Performing multiple logics in practice. *Scandinavian Journal of Management* 30 (4): 485–497.

Lundby, Knut. 2009. *Mediatization: Concept, changes, consequences.* New York: Peter Lang Publishing.

Lundby, Knut. 2014. *Handbooks of communication science: Mediatization of communication.* Berlin: De Gruyter.

Lunt, Peter, and Sonia Livingstone. 2016. Is 'mediatization' the new paradigm for our field? A commentary on Deacon and Stanyer (2014, 2015) and Hepp, Hjarvard and Lundby (2015). *Media, Culture and Society* 38 (3): 462–470.

Marcinkowski, Frank, Matthias Kohring, Silke Fürst, and Andres Friedrichsmeier. 2014. Organizational influence on scientists' efforts to go public: An empirical investigation. *Science Communication* 36 (1): 56–80.

Mazzoleni, Gianpietro. 1987. Media logic and party logic in campaign coverage: The Italian general election of 1983. *European Journal of Communication* 2 (1): 81–103.

Mazzoleni, Gianpietro, and Winfried Schulz. 1999. Mediatization of politics: A challenge for democracy? *Political Communication* 16 (3): 247–261.

Mintzberg, Henry. 1983. *Structures in fives: Designing effective organizations*. Englewood Cliffs: Prentice Hall International Editions.

Morris, Tim, and Zoë Lancaster. 2006. Translating management ideas. *Organization Studies* 27 (2): 207–233.

Mueller, Frank, and Andrea Whittle. 2011. Translating management ideas: A discursive devices analysis. *Organization Studies* 32 (2): 187–210.

Pallas, Josef, and Magnus Fredriksson. 2013. Corporate media work and micro-dynamics of mediatization. *European Journal of Communication* 28 (4): 420–435.

Pallas, Josef, Magnus Fredriksson, and Linda Wedlin. 2016. Translating institutional logics: When the media logic meets professions. *Organisation Studies* 37 (11): 1661–1684.

Pallas, Josef, Stefan Jonsson, and Lars Strannegård. 2014. *Organizations and the media: Organizing in a mediatized world*. London: Routledge.

Peleg, Anat, and Bryna Bogoch. 2014. Mediatization, legal logic and the coverage of Israeli politicians on trial. *Journalism Practice* 8 (3): 311–325.

Pipan, Tatiana, and Barbara Czarniawska. 2010. How to construct an actor-network: Management accounting from idea to practice. *Critical Perspectives on Accounting* 21 (3): 243–251.

Røvik, Kjell A. 2016. Knowledge transfer as translation: Review and elements of an instrumental theory. *International Journal of Management Reviews* 18 (3): 290–310.

Sahlin-Andersson, Kerstin. 1996. Imitating by editing success: The construction of organizational fields. In *Translating organizational change*, ed. Barbara Czarniawska, and Guje Sevón, 69–92. Berlin: Walter de Gruyter and Co.

Sahlin-Andersson, Kerstin, and Lars Engwall. 2002. *The expansion of management knowledge: Carriers, flows, and sources*. Stanford: Stanford University Press.

Schillemans, Thomas. 2012. *Mediatization of public services. How organizations adapt to news media*. Frankfurt: Peter Lang.

Schillemans, Thomas. 2016. Fighting or fumbling with the beast? The mediatisation of public sector agencies in Australia and the Netherlands. *Policy and Politics* 44 (1): 79–96.

Scheu, Andreas M., Anna-Maria Volpers, Annika Summ, and Bernd Blöbaum. 2014. Medialization of research policy: Anticipation of and adaptation to journalistic logic. *Science Communication* 36 (6): 706–734.

Schulz, Winfried. 2004. Reconstructing mediatization as an analytical concept. *European Journal of Communication* 19 (1): 87–101.

Scott, W.Richard. 1995. *Institutions and organizations*. Thousand Oaks, CA: Sage.

Scott, W.Richard. 2003. Institutional carriers: Reviewing modes of transporting ideas over time and space and considering their consequences. *Industrial and Corporate Change* 12 (4): 879–894.

Sevón, Guje. 1996. Organizational imitation in identity transformation. In *Translating organizational change*, ed. Barbara Czarniawska, and Guje Sevón, 49–68. Berlin: Walter de Gruyter.

Spyridonidis, Dimitrios, Graeme Currie, Stefan Heusinkveld, Karoline Strauss, and Andrew Sturdy. 2014. New developments in translation research. *International Journal of Management Reviews* 16 (2): 245–248.

Strömbäck, Jesper. 2008. Four phases of mediatization: An analysis of the mediatization of politics. *The International Journal of Press/Politics* 13 (3): 228–246.

Thorbjornsrud, Kjersti, Tine U. Figenschou, and Øyvind Ihlen. 2014. Mediatization in public bureaucracies: A typology. *Communications—The European Journal of Communication Research* 39 (1): 3–22.

Thornton, Patricia, and William Ocasio. 1999. Institutional logics and the historical contingency of power in organizations: Executive succession in the higher education publishing industry, 1958–1990. *American Journal of Sociology* 105 (3): 801–843.

Thornton, Patricia, William Ocasio, and Michael Lounsbury. 2012. *The institutional logics perspective: A new approach to culture, structure and process*. Oxford: Oxford University Press.

Tyllström, Anna. 2013. *Legitimacy for sale: Constructing a market for PR consultancy*. Doctoral dissertation. Uppsala University, Uppsala.

van Aelst, Peter, Bart Maddens, Jo Noppe, and Stefaan Fiers. 2008. Politicians in the news: Media or party logic? Media attention and electoral success in the Belgian election campaign of 2003. *European Journal of Communication* 23 (2): 193–210.

Waldorff, Susanne B. 2013. Accounting for organizational innovations: Mobilizing institutional logics in translation. *Scandinavian Journal of Management* 29 (3): 219–234.

Wedlin, Linda, and Kerstin Sahlin. 2017. Circulating ideas: Imitation, translation and editing. In *The Sage handbook of organizational institutionalism*, ed. Royston Greenwood, Christine Oliver, Roy Suddaby, and Kerstin Sahlin, 218–242. London: Sage.

Werr, Andreas, and Torbjörn Stjernberg. 2003. Exploring management consulting firms as knowledge systems. *Organization Studies* 24 (6): 881–908.

Zeh, Reimar, and David N. Hopmann. 2013. Indicating mediatization? Two decades of election campaign television coverage. *European Journal of Communication* 28 (3): 225–240.

CHAPTER 7

Is There Any Future for Research on the Mediatization of Politics?

Barbara Brodzińska-Mirowska and Łukasz Wojtkowski

7.1 Introduction

Although the mediatization of politics is one of the most developed approaches in mediatization research, it seems that currently it faces substantial difficulties. Indeed, the current perspective on the process of mediatization of politics is no longer sufficient and this is for several reasons. Firstly, in the area of the mediatization of politics, empirical analyses are primary to the theoretical arrangement. This undoubtedly makes it more difficult to organize studies of mediatization, which as a result are fragmented and focused on relations between the politics and media but without any connection to broader conceptual frameworks. Secondly, the political communication perspective narrows the field to singular case studies but without any linkage to the mid-range research programs. This has been especially the case since political communication has been dominated by campaign studies, political marketing, and online communication research. Thirdly, the separation between the processes

B. Brodzińska-Mirowska (✉) · Ł. Wojtkowski
Department of Journalism and Social Communication, Nicolaus Copernicus University, Toruń, Poland
e-mail: brodzinska@umk.pl

O. Driessens et al. (eds.), *Dynamics Of Mediatization*,
Transforming Communications – Studies in Cross-Media Research,
DOI 10.1007/978-3-319-62983-4_7

of mediatization from other significant meta-processes has become increasingly apparent. Given that mediatization is part of the long-term process of broader social transformation (Hjarvard 2008, 2013, 2014a, b; Lundby 2009a), a media-centric perspective must give way to holistic analysis and take a number of concomitant transformation processes into account.

The attempt of going beyond the linear approach to the mediatization of politics means the necessity of placing this phenomenon in a broader social context, which takes into account the current social, cultural and technological developments. It requires a critical look at the recent analytical approaches and the answer to the main question: what are the limitations of a linear approach?

The main purpose of this inquiry is to initiate a discussion about adapting the concept of the mediatization of politics to the transformational character of the mediatization in general. Hence, in this chapter, we would like to present our proposition of multi-dimensional framework for research into the mediatization of politics. As a case study, we take the new social movement of the Committee for the Defence of Democracy (KOD) in Poland.

7.2 Common Weaknesses in the Conceptualization of the Mediatization of Politics

The discussion related to the process of the mediatization as a major, multi-dimensional and multi-stage social change takes place on three levels—*macro*, *meso* and *micro* (Krotz 2009; Strömbäck and Esser 2014a; Hepp 2013; Marcinkowski 2014; Meyen et al. 2014)—and raises the necessity of asking questions about the future of the study of mediatization. If we understand mediatization as "a concept used to analyse the (long-term) interrelation between the change of media and communication on the one hand, and the change of culture and society on the other hand in a critical manner" (Hepp 2013: 619), then a question arises as to whether the existing theoretical notions in terms of politics are sufficient.

The four-dimensional approach proposed by Jesper Strömbäck is the basis of many studies in the field of the mediatization of politics. It is founded on the assessment of the relationship between media and politics and especially on an analysis of how media logics are implemented to the politics (Strömbäck 2008: 228–246), where the fourth dimension of mediatization assumes subordination to the media logic (Strömbäck 2008; Strömbäck and Esser 2014a). Moreover, a lot of research conducted in recent years follows Strömbäck's approach of mediatization and confirms the dominant role of media logic in relation to politics (cf. Strömbäck and Esser 2014b: 386–395).

Frank Esser and Jörg Matthes's (2013) analysis—grounded in Strömbäck's conceptualization—describes four areas where the most visible changes caused by the mediatization process can be identified: (1) content, (2) actors, (3) organization and processes, and (4) the audience of political communication. The dominance of media logic at the level of media content "is often theorized to result in a simplification, dramatization, or negative representation of politics favouring conflict, scandals, and episodic over thematic frames" (Esser and Matthes 2013: 181). Owing to their increasingly large role, the ability to work with the media is one of the most important resources for political actors (Mazzoleni and Schulz 1999; Blumler and Gurevitch 1995; Marcinkowski 2014). In addition to this, an awareness of the media effects determines the nature of the activities undertaken by the political actors (Esser and Matthes 2013: 188–192; see also Strömbäck 2011). Finally, in the context of the consequences of mediatization for the citizens, Esser and Matthes notice that:

> The impact of mediated communication on citizens' civic attitudes is of special interest for the fourth dimension of mediatization [...] the conditions of a mediated public sphere, in particular the degree to which people use various kinds of media for information about politics, develop political perceptions and preferences, make their preferences heard, participate in the policy-making process, and evaluate the production and self-presentation of politics (Esser and Matthes 2013: 193).

Among the observed consequences of the mediatization, the authors mention (1) more or less explicit relationships with the media and a lower level of participation and satisfaction with the work of politicians and (2) the correlation between the nature of the content during the campaign and trends in voting or not voting (Esser and Matthes 2013: 192–196). Therefore, the analyses of the mediatization of politics are linear. In addition to this point, we can ask whether such an approach provides sufficient analytical capabilities in terms of the exploration of political organizations' activities in its management-related news professionalization, the phenomenon of self-mediatization (cf. Strömbäck and Esser 2014a: 21), the media image of politics, and finally the media effect on decision-making. The political sphere is complex and not isolated from other social spheres, and as Strömbäck and Esser (2014c: 249) rightly suggest, the "mediatization of politics should not be considered as a linear, unidirectional process". As such, in our opinion, the media-centric approach may be insufficient.

The linear attitude has a major weakness. Previous analyses of the mediatization of politics have not taken into account the third actor of Richard Perloff's[1] golden triangle (2008) of political communication, namely the audience. Until now, the media and politicians have taken an active part in the creation of media communication, and researchers observe the audience's reaction to such creations. Tamara Witschge takes into consideration the problem of the role of the audience in the process of mediatization:

> We see that in this approach the focus is on media and political actors and that the role of the audience remains rather implicit and passive [...] At the base of the institutional perspective of mediatization, there are effect studies, agenda-setting theory and framing analysis. In these theoretical perspectives and empirical analyses, the public takes on a central role as voters and as consumers of (political) information and feature prominently. However, in empirical research into the mediatization of politics, there seems less attention for the audience and the focus is rather on the interplay between media and political actors [...]. (Witschge 2014: 343, 345)

It should be highlighted that Strömbäck's four-dimensional concept does not include analysis of the audience as an active actor of the process of mediatization (see also Marcinkowski 2014). Therefore, in-depth analyses of the mediatization of politics require a change in this area. This is the reason why some of Witschge's arguments are appealing: "[...] with the changing role of the audience, we need to consider new ways in which we can understand their position in this process" (Witschge 2014: 346). Little attention in previous research has been paid to how the audience has changed during the mediatization of politics. The analyses of the audience are, in some sense, commercial in nature (Witschge 2014: 344–346). But this is not enough, especially for research into the mediatization of politics. We should remember that, owing to dynamic technological development, the role of the audience in the process of communication has been significantly transformed and that this has led to a substantial empowerment of society, understood here as a process of strengthening social actors' political agency in terms of challenging the media and political powers (cf. Witschge 2014; Kaun et al. 2016). Hence, Witschge leads the discussion about the role of the audience in the mediatization of politics research on the basis of technological changes. She suggests rightly that "If we consider or accept that audiences are both consumers and producers of media content as well as citizens in both categories, we need to provide them with a more prominent role in our empirical and theoretical considerations of the role of media in society" (Witschge 2014: 349).

In our opinion, we have to go one step further and draw attention to the audience from another angle. Instead, we go beyond linear system analyses of mediatization because politics is not only a social field where media and political logics collide (cf. Strömbäck and Esser 2014a, b, c; Schrott 2009). Unlike Witschge, we don't ask only whether the audiences internalize media logic and how they participate in the process of the creation of online content. We don't seek for the domination of the media logic, and we don't ask how the media "influence" attitudes or opinions. Rather, we ask about the manifestations of mediatization in actors' social practices not only in the online sphere and not only during election campaigns, which are usually (depending on the country) relatively short communication episodes (cf. Brodzińska-Mirowska 2013). We ask about the role of the active audience in the process of the mediatization of politics. We ask about how media power and logics are manifested in social practices and interrelate with other logics.

7.3 Towards the Multi-dimensional Framework of the Mediatization of Politics: Logics and Powers, Practices

Our proposal on the mediatization of politics has two main objectives: (1) to embrace the role of the active audience that shapes the mediatization process and (2) to take into account economic and cultural factors, which occur simultaneously with the process of mediatization of politics and which also determine it. The mediatization of politics will be understood as a process of deep, multi-dimensional changes that appear in the area of politics as a result of the development of the media and new communication technologies. The changes are the consequence of the coexistence of media, political and institutional logics and thus the interaction between political actors, the media and the audience. This process is highly contextual and determined by socio-cultural and economic developments.

Studies into the mediatization of politics should be carried out in relation to processes of transformation that can be observed in the media, politics, culture and society. Hence, it is an analysis of mediatization as a process of transformation of politics on three levels. Firstly, the mediatization of politics has to be understood as a transformative process of media and politics characteristic for late modernity, which is waved into broader temporal alterations. It requires, however, perceiving this phenomenon not as a change in political course itself (e.g. the professionalization of politics) but rather as a transformation in cultural and economic terms that in turn have an effect on politics and media. That is why tools of political economy analysis (i.e. power analysis, macro-level analysis together with sector-level analysis, politics of developments, or database of political institutions), instead of political communication apparatus, can be used to grasp meaning and dynamics at a meta level. Subsequently, this implies that the mediatization of politics is an institutional process at the meso level where *games of powers* and flows of logics take place between social institutions. Finally, all of these should be reflected in every single case study (micro-level) that describes the affairs of political-related individual media practices but with a greater emphasis on symbolic processes, which are not visible at the level of media coverage and political communication (see also Marcinkowski 2014; Meyen et al. 2014). Hence, our proposal requires that attention be paid to several key issues, namely (1) media logic, (2) power, and (3) practices.

The ongoing discussion on the mediatization of politics is strongly associated with the concept of media logic (cf. Altheide and Snow 1979; Lundby 2009b). Some researchers stress the coexistence of multiple logics (Landerer 2013) with a strong emphasis on institutional media logics (Hjarvard 2014a, b). Others suggest that concepts of "media logic" focus mainly on the technological and institutional dimension of the media but that the role of the media in shaping reality is complex and varied and beyond these areas (Couldry and Hepp 2013: 196; Couldry 2013; Hepp 2009). All things considered, we agree with Stig Hjarvard, who has developed the concept of an institutional perspective on mediatization and emphasizes that logics should be understood "as the *particular rules and resources that govern a particular domain*" (2014b: 204).

Institutional logics are some sort of a transmitter, which causes institutional changes through symbolic power. In these terms, we can assume that every social institution has (or at least may have) its internal logic, influenced by logics of other institutions. Hjarvard claims that media are crucial in the visibility of other social institutions; they are strongly present inside institutions (e.g. family and work); hence, they become a "semi-independent institution" that could bring their own logics into relations (Hjarvard 2014b: 216–219). That is why institutional logics are prone to being dependent upon media logics. Owing to such an omnipotent role that the media's communicative power plays in spreading of logics, the role of the media is vital in forming modern society.

The second important concept is media power, which "is not a binary relation of domination between 'large' and 'small' 'actors', with 'large actors' (the media) having the automatic ability to dominate 'small actors' (audience members) simply because of their 'size'" (Couldry 2001: 17). It corresponds with what Couldry and Curran described as an illusion that the media portrays only what is going on in society. On the contrary, media power is one of the strongest driving forces of society in processes of constructing reality (Couldry and Curran 2003: 3f.). Hence, media power is perceived as a "concentration in media institutions of the symbolic power of 'constructing reality' (both factual representations and credible fictions)—[as] a social process, which we need to understand in all its local complexity" (Couldry 2001: 4). The formation of institutions and powers has to be constantly renegotiated, which enforces the creation of specific repetitive communicative patterns that stabilize flux associations between every element in the relation. Regardless of whether we name them "rules", "resources", "ideological structures" or "media practices", we analyse the same social phenomenon: how individuals affected/empowered by (the) media form social institutions and enter into power relations with other institutions. It is possible because the institution's formation and powers are symbolic at their core. Following Couldry's argument, it creates a symbolic power inseparably entwined with every social process.

However, we argue that media power rallies around two complementary factors when it comes to relations with other institutions: the economic and technological dimensions of the power. Social institutions are able to emulate symbolic media power or media institutional logics. These processes are intense in the social sphere: they empower people's activities, boost civic engagement and protest movements, and enable them to use media accordingly to the actual social agendas.

Thus arises a third important component of our proposal: the practices. Practices are sets of similar social and individual actions. They are never the same since one practice differs from the other on the level of social actors, temporal and spatial alterations, media environments, and so on. In this sense, practices are forming forces of communication and social processes. Following Couldry's notion of media as a practice, we use the practice approach to capture what types of things people do in relation to media and what types of things "people say (think, believe) in relation to media" (2012: 40). Such media-related practice has to be regular, social and related to human needs and provide normative thinking about media (Couldry 2012: 33–58). However, in the mediatization of political process, analyses of media practices require the tracking of not only practices of politicians, journalists, or media workers but first of all the practices of activists (cf. Mattoni 2012; Mattoni and Treré 2014).

The impact of institutional and socio-cultural perspectives is clearly visible in our proposition. Nick Couldry and Andreas Hepp emphasized that "[…] these two different traditions of mediatization research co-exist, they have come closer to each other in recent years" (Couldry and Hepp 2013: 196). Drawing from multiple perspectives is inevitable if the foundation of our proposition is to extend and go beyond the linear analysis of the phenomenon of the mediatization of politics. Analysing different perspectives of mediatization studies, Göran Bolin rightly points out that one perspective rarely allows for a comprehensive and multi-dimensional analysis (Bolin 2014). However, the integration of both perspectives in order to create a coherent concept of mediatization of politics needs further scientific reflection since such a merge would be a serious challenge because of the ontological differences involved (Lundby 2014).

7.4 A Multi-dimensional Framework of Mediatization of Politics

In order to stress our approach, we consider the mediatization of politics as a process of transformational relations between media, society, politics and economy (Fig. 7.1). On the one hand, the complexity of these relations increases from a micro to a macro level and transforms in time.

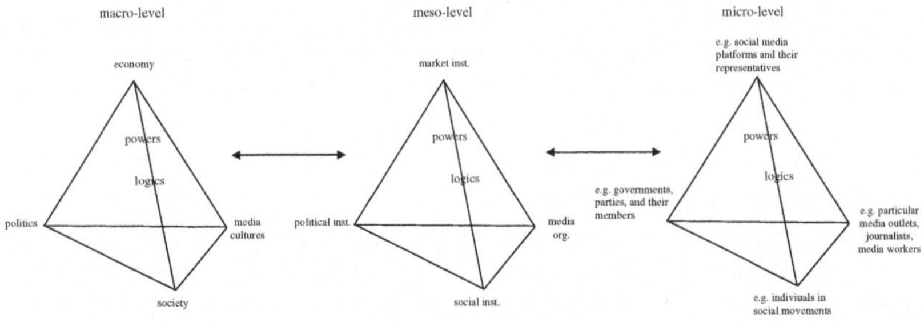

Fig. 7.1 Multi-dimensional concept of the mediatization of politics

On the other hand, interactions between those levels result in constant *flows of powers and logics* between (1) meta-processes (e.g. mediatization, acculturation and marketization), (2) social institutions (e.g. social movements, media organizations, market institutions, and governments), and (3) people's media practices (how the agency of social institutions is shaped in interaction with others "through", "with" and "in" media).

Starting with the first pyramid (macro level), we observe how the mediatization runs on the macro level, and how it is associated with other long-lasting meta-processes: (1) it relies on constant media-related power drifts between all four apexes, which are possible because of flows of logics between them; and (2) these broader alternations correspond with two other transformation processes that are associated with mediatization, and are equally important in forming the cultures of mediatization, politics and media cultures. Firstly, since the economic dimension of the power relies directly on the market, marketization serves as a meta-process that shapes the society, media culture, and politics. However, the appropriation of technology depends on cultural mechanisms; hence, secondly, acculturation will exemplify the process that grasps changes within the culture. Acculturation is a form of cultural diffusion based on contact between separate cultures that are distanced in terms of economy and social development. In the final stages, such a process might result in rejection and protest. Those counter-acculturative tendencies are especially present when acculturation follows the strategies of separation and marginalization of non-dominant cultures rather than assimilation and integration (cf. Berry 1997). Processes of marketization and acculturation emphasize stronger socio-economic and techno-cultural aspects of relations between media, politics and society on the macro level. They allow for grasping the role of market operations and capital structures which shape particular media cultures.

In terms of complexity, acculturation and marketization depend on compound power developments: market or ownership structure, historical marketization processes, the shape of media and political culture, the development of society, and technological appropriation, to name just the crucial ones. In every culture of mediatization, these developments shape a specific phenomenon, which is characteristic of regional or national patterns. In terms of mediatization theory at a meta level, it is decisive how media market and technological dimensions of powers are used by social and political institutions to mould the ownership and governance over the public and private media. Moreover, the way in which these powers are emulated to supplement and amplify media practices with the technical structures of social media platforms is compelling to accelerate the mediatization as well as the acculturation and the marketization.

Secondly, the meso-level pyramid simplifies (1) how the mediatization of politics is shaped within social institutions, (2) how long-lasting metaprocesses carve all apexes of institutional actors, and (3) how media-related social practice and agency affect institutional structures. In our case, the way in which the mediatization of politics, acculturation and marketization worked on the macro level caused very stable counter-tendencies in apexes of political and social institutions (i.e. the rise of populist parties), media institutions (i.e. cooperation with a conservative press company that supports local initiatives focusing on Catholic and patriotic values and Polish sovereignty), and economic institutions (i.e. credit unions established to bypass foreign finance capital). All of these tendencies relied on the use of media powers and logics, not only at the level of media broadcasts, but also on media usage to form activist groups, grassroots movements, and media outlets. Moreover, they were the basis of effective internet campaigns that gave the Law and Justice (PiS) ultimate victory in the latest presidential and parliamentary elections in 2015.

Finally, these meta-processes and meso-level interactions were in harmony with a more nuanced analysis of institutional logics and power relations at the micro level. Hence, the third pyramid depicts the politics-related media practices of society. On this level, we are able to observe (1) how logics and powers are framed into dialectics between agencies and institutions' structures, (2) how media powers are being interrupted during people's interactions with media processes and "media frame" (Couldry 2001), (3) how individual media practices affect political institutions on an everyday basis, and (4) how online media (e.g. social media platforms) and mobile media empower social movements in the process of the mediatization of politics.

In the Polish culture of mediatization, the issues mentioned above follow the case of the protest movement, which was a reaction to right-wing counter-acculturation and marketization leanings. The rise of the Committee for the Defence of Democracy (KOD) protest movement fits the mediatization of politics pattern. KOD was formed in November 2015 after PiS's victory in the presidential and parliamentary elections in Poland. It is a grassroots initiative established via the internet, initially based only on online communication and activities, and as a result it uses social media and personal media as tools which interrupt the "traditional" media power. On the meta level, KOD's formation was an indirect consequence of mediatization, marketization and acculturation processes. Yet the counter-acculturation tendencies in Poland resulted in a clash between two visions of politics, media culture, and economy. In short, the introduction of the first private media companies (e.g. Polsat, TVN and RMF) has started the competition with an undeveloped public media sector (TVP television channels and Polish radio stations). As a result, in the 2000s, public media adjusted to acculturation process and adopted market-oriented strategies of media production, technology, broadcast and advertisement. However, such dynamic integration and assimilation led to counter-tendencies since some of the traditional, conservative and Catholic media (*Gazeta Polska* or *Gość Niedzielny*) rejected the Western ideological model of liberal democracy. Similarly, the politics elaborated two main strategies regarding the development. First, politics created direct links with the market (i.e. strong relations between politics and foreign capital) and media (i.e. political influences and management over public media sector, private media influences on legislative processes, or mutual orientation on political communication mechanisms). Second, the slow rise of the protest tendencies formed as counter-acculturation social movements (i.e. Solidarity from 2000s) or political parties (Liga Polskich Rodzin, Samoobrona, and PiS) with conservative media as their voice.

Hence, mediatization, marketization and acculturation resulted in two dominant adaptation patterns in Poland. On the one hand, politics, media and society assimilated and integrated with Western economical and cultural models. On the other hand, we faced phase shift in the modernization process, where patterns of enculturation and socialization developed slower than other domains. It resulted in an indifference to the free market, a misunderstanding of contemporary politics, low media literacy, and low civic engagement. Eventually, these inclinations were articulated in PiS's electoral victory, after which the ruling party changed the course of modernization processes in terms of mediatization (unprecedented political influence on the public media and conservative-oriented private media), marketization (political agenda over economic one, slow economic growth, rapid increase of national debt, and clientelism) and acculturation (reintroduction of a traditional attitude to state policy, the role of the Catholic Church in the society, the environment, and education). As a protest against such politics, acculturation drift regained a voice as the KOD new protest movement.

Since KOD is a grassroots movement, it is worth emphasizing at this point the micro level of mediatization. Thus, we will analyse how the KOD's media practices evolved and how it composed the movement as a structured organization. Although initially KOD protested against PiS's decision on blocking Poland's highest court (the Constitutional Tribunal), multiple demonstrations in defence of other freedoms swept Poland.

Owing to social media practices, KOD gained a massive interest and marked its offline presence through marches, protests and politically oriented campaigns. The KOD case fits Couldry's idea of media as practice (2012: 33–58). All actions undertaken by KOD's members are regular and closely related to the time schedule of a protest. They are socially oriented because they discursively bridge agency with institutional structure and enable the institution to be "visible" to the other institutions. The composition of these two features, which are regularity and sociality, leads to social needs that are substantial to protest movements: coordination of actions, ongoing interaction between members and institutions, community-building, trust and freedom (Couldry 2012: 34). Finally, in normative terms, KOD's example answers the question of "how we should live with media" (Couldry 2012: 35). We observe two basic kinds of KOD members' media practices. Firstly, mobile devices and social media platforms (mainly Facebook, Twitter, mailing services, and text messages) are management tools both on an everyday basis and during protest activities. For instance, Facebook groups serve as message boards and gather followers who share documents or information on events. SMSs, phone calls and e-mails are elementary forms of communication between KOD's associates. At the same time, events on Facebook and hashtags are used as ignition and management tools during protests. They help to gather protesters and make it easier to follow KOD's information agenda. Secondly, media practices oscillate around the protests, where people on the streets use social media and mobile devices to show their presence at the events. They take photos, write posts, and use hashtags to make their attendance more visible for others and share the content online.

These media practices are forms of media power interruptions, which take place simultaneously during the protests, when social media are inherent spaces of protest management and online activism. They are dynamic and spontaneous in many cases but constitute larger sets and inherently have led to institutionalization of the movement. Over the last year, we have observed how KOD has transformed from a fragile social movement to a full-fledged social institution with a rigid structure. That, however, has caused dialectic tension between structure and agency: the more KOD has become regulated, the less dynamic and unified its actions have been. When it gained the status of an association and regional leadership elections took place, multiple personal and local conflicts arose. Moreover, many followers perpetually question KOD's national leadership. However, in terms of mediatization, the institutionalization process has unified the way KOD communicates its agenda on four levels. Firstly, KOD created a number of media outlets (online information website https://koduj24.pl/; online newspapers: *Obywatel*, *Dekoder* and *Przegląd Demokratyczny*). In addition, each of the 16 regional chapters publishes its own media outlets (i.e. *Prasówka* and *Droga do wolności*). Such a plethora of media channels (not to mention official Facebook, Twitter, Google+, YouTube and Instagram profiles) serves two functions: the opportunity to reach people from outside the movement and communicative reinforcement of KOD's base of their own narrative frames. Secondly, the institutionalized structure of the movement enables its educational operations. The movement aims not at a radical and rapid political change but at long-term educational activity. Thirdly, it stabilizes and unifies the way that KOD communicates with other media and political institutions in terms of media appearances, interviews, political talks, or negotiations. Fourthly, it gives better control over protests because of onsite management, application of the basic communication scheme, and the strong presence of narrative frames delivered by KOD.

Altogether, we can see how an institutionalized social movement and its protests tend to counter traditional media power and define it on its own terms. With regard to the media institutions, KOD has established media outlets to set its own narrative rules. For political institutions, it legalized its status and formalized the leadership. In reference to economic institutions, it based its founding on members' contributions.

In summary, the proposed framework above accentuates the role of the audience, users or even individuals who don't interact with media in the politically oriented activities. It is a response to the need to integrate the analysis of the mediatization of politics with an increasingly active audience and their relations with media and the political world. Hence, this case study put thogether three levels illustrated in the framework. Firstly, we illustrated how mediatization together with acculturation and marketization are manifested in the case of a new social movement in Poland. Secondly, we analysed how this new protest movement was formed and based on media practices and how media powers were interrupted during protests. Finally, we captured how the mediatization shaped the structuring of the movement and what the role of the movement's media was in shifts of power.

7.5 Conclusion

Given the case study and framework, the title question of this chapter should perhaps be reframed. We should not ask "is there" a future for research in the mediatization of politics framework but rather "what" is it? During our discussion, we attempted to show how complex the issues related to the mediatization of politics are and we argued why linear and media-centric approaches are insufficient in this field. Why, then, is a theoretical reflection about the mediatization of politics so crucial and needed? Firstly, and most importantly, we need to adopt this framework to mediatization as a transformation perspective. Secondly, politics isn't separate from other spheres of society or other social processes. Thirdly, it is not only mutual relations between media and politics but also the audience and other concomitant phenomena that shape the process of mediatization of politics. Such a conceptual rebuilding is difficult and brings about many further questions, but from our point of view this framework provides a new opportunity to start a fresh stage in analysing the effect of mediatization on politics; it captures the process of mediatization of politics on three essential levels: *macro*, *meso*, and *micro*. It creates an opportunity to take into consideration an active audience, which enters into close interaction with the course of this process and builds its specificity (e.g. the cultures of mediatization, political cultures). Last but not least, the multi-dimensional approach supports a broader view of this process, where other meta-processes, such as marketization and acculturation, determine these interrelations.

Note

1. Richard Perloff is the author of the golden triangle of political communication concept, in which he pointed out the three main actors in the process: media, political leaders, and the audience (Perloff 2008).

References

Altheide, David L., and Robert P. Snow. 1979. *Media logic*. Beverly Hills, CA: Sage.

Berry, John W. 1997. Immigration, acculturation, and adaptation. *Applied Psychology. An International Review* 46 (1): 5–68.

Blumler, Jay G., and Michael Gurevitch. 1995. *The crisis of public communication*. New York: Routledge.

Bolin, Göran. 2014. Institution, technology, world: Relationships between the media, culture, and society. In *Mediatization of communication. Handbooks of communication science*, ed. Knut Lundby, 175–197. Berlin: De Gruyter Mounton.

Brodzińska-Mirowska, Barbara. 2013. *Marketing międzywyborczy w teorii i praktyce. Przypadek Platformy Obywatelskiej*. Wydawnictwo UMK: Toruń.

Couldry, Nick. 2001. *The place of media power: Pilgrims and witnesses of the media age*. London: Routledge.

Couldry, Nick. 2012. *Media, society, world. Social theory and digital media practice*. Cambridge: Polity Press.

Couldry, Nick. 2013. Mediatization and the future of field theory. *Communicative Figurations*, 1–18. Bremen: University of Bremen. http://www.kommunikative-figurationen.de/fileadmin/redak_kofi/Arbeitspapiere/CoFi_EWP_No-3_Couldry.pdf. Accessed 22 Apr 2017.

Couldry, Nick, and James Curran. 2003. *Contesting media power*. Lanham, MD: Rowman & Littlefield.

Couldry, Nick, and Andreas Hepp. 2013. Conceptualizing mediatization: Contexts, traditions, arguments. *Communication Theory* 23 (3): 191–202.

Esser, Frank, and Jörg Matthes. 2013. Mediatization effect of political news, political actors, political decision and political audience. In *Democracy in the age of globalization and mediatization*, ed. Hanspeter Kriesi, Sandra Lavenex, Frank Esser, Jörg Matthes, Marc Bühlmann, and Daniel Bochsler, 177–201. London: Palgrave Macmillan.

Hepp, Andreas. 2009. Differentation: Mediatization and cultural change. In *Mediatization: Concept, changes, consequences*, ed. Knut Lundby, 139–155. New York: Peter Lang.

Hepp, Andreas. 2013. The communicative figurations of mediatized world. *European Journal of Communication* 28 (6): 615–629.

Hjarvard, Stig. 2008. The mediatization of society. A theory of the media as agents of social and cultural change. *Nordicom Review* 29 (2): 105–134.

Hjarvard, Stig. 2013. *The mediatization of culture and society*. Abingdon: Routledge.

Hjarvard, Stig. 2014a. From mediation to mediatization: The institutionalization of new media. In *Mediatized worlds: Culture and society in a media age*, ed. Andreas Hepp, and Friedrich Krotz, 123–142. London: Palgrave Macmillan.

Hjarvard, Stig. 2014b. Mediatization and cultural and social change: An institutional perspective. In *Mediatization of communication. Handbooks of communication science*, ed. Knut Lundby, 199–226. Berlin: De Gruyter Mounton.

Kaun, Anne, Maria Kyriakidou, and Julie Uldam. 2016. Political agency at the digital crossroads? *Media and Communication* 4 (4): 1–7.

Krotz, Friedrich. 2009. Mediatization: A concept with which to grasp media and societal change. In *Mediatization: Concept, changes, consequences*, ed. Knut Lundby, 21–40. New York: Peter Lang.

Landerer, Nino. 2013. Rethinking the logics: A conceptual framework for the mediatization of politics. *Communication Theory* 23 (3): 239–258.

Lundby, Knut. 2009a. *Mediatization: Concept, changes, consequences*. New York: Peter Lang.

Lundby, Knut. 2009b. Media logic: Looking for social interaction. In *Mediatization: Concept, changes, consequences*, ed. Knut Lundby, 101–119. New York: Peter Lang.

Lundby, Knut. 2014. *Mediatization of communication. Handbooks of communication science*. Berlin: De Gruyter Mounton.

Marcinkowski, Frank. 2014. Mediatization of politics: Reflections on the state of the concept. *Javnost—The Public* 21 (2): 5–22.

Mattoni, Alice. 2012. *Media practices and protest politics: How precarious workers mobilise*. Farnham: Ashgate.

Mattoni, Alice, and Emiliano Treré. 2014. Media practices, mediation processes, and mediatization in the study of social movements. *Communication Theory* 24 (3): 252–271.

Mazzoleni, Gianpietro, and Winfried Schulz. 1999. Mediatization of politics: A challenge for democracy? *Political Communication* 16 (3): 247–261.

Meyen, Michael, Markus Thieroff, and Steffi Strenger. 2014. Mass media logic and the mediatisation of politics. A theoretical framework. *Journalism Studies* 15 (3): 271–288.

Perloff, Richard M. 2008. *Political communication: Politics, press and public in America*. New York: Routledge.

Schrott, Andrea. 2009. Dimensions: Catch-all label or technical term. In *Mediatization. Concept, changes, consequences*, ed. Knut Lundby, 41–61. Oxford: Peter Lang.

Strömbäck, Jesper. 2008. Four phases of mediatization: An analysis of the mediatization of politics. *The International Journal of Press/Politics* 13 (3): 228–246.

Strömbäck, Jesper. 2011. Mediatization and perceptions of the media's political influence. *Journalism Studies* 12 (4): 423–439.

Strömbäck, Jesper, and Frank Esser. 2014a. Mediatization of politics: Towards a theoretical framework. In *Mediatization of politics: Understanding the transformation of Western democracies*, ed. Jesper Strömbäck, and Frank Esser, 3–28. Basingstoke: Palgrave Macmillan.

Strömbäck, Jesper, and Frank Esser. 2014b. Mediatization of politics. Transforming democracies and reshaping politics. In *Mediatization of communication. Handbooks of communication science*, ed. Knut Lundby, 375–397. Berlin: De Gruyter Mounton.

Strömbäck, Jesper, and Frank Esser. 2014c. Making sense of the mediatization of politics. *Journalism Studies* 15 (3): 243–255.

Witschge, Tamara. 2014. Passive accomplice or active disruptor. The role of audiences in the mediatization of politics. *Journalism Practice* 8 (3): 342–356.

CHAPTER 8

The Dynamics of Resistance and Response to Mediatization in Government: Whitehall Press Officers Caught in the "Cross-Field" Since 1997

Ruth Garland

8.1 Introduction

This examination of mediatization in government addresses questions about how social and cultural change linked to media change may impact on central bureaucracies over time and specifically on power balances or asymmetries between the political and administrative dimensions of government. As a non-normative "sensitizing concept", the idea of mediatization has the potential to enrich understandings of the interplay between long-term media change and more normative concepts such as politicization (Hjarvard 2008; Lundby 2014; Lunt and Livingstone 2016). This chapter looks at the dynamics of media-related change over time in the organization and operation of government media engagement, drawing on witness accounts from former Whitehall media intermediaries. This involves two types of actor: press officers,

R. Garland (✉)
London School of Economics/University of Hertfordshire, London, UK
e-mail: ruth.garland1@btinternet.com

O. Driessens et al. (eds.), *Dynamics Of Mediatization*,
Transforming Communications – Studies in Cross-Media Research,
DOI 10.1007/978-3-319-62983-4_8

the impartial civil servants delegated to speak to journalists on behalf of the government, and special advisers, the politically aligned but publicly funded officials appointed by ministers. I will argue that since the rise of 24/7 news in the late 1980s, there has been a shift from impartial to partisan styles of media management that challenges impartiality as a long-held bureaucratic value in both the UK and other liberal democracies.

Mediatization scholars have called for more longitudinal empirical studies carried out at the institutional or meso level (Hepp 2012; Hepp et al. 2015; Hjarvard 2013). In this chapter, I argue that the incoming Labour government of 1997 instituted changes to the formal and informal rules of media engagement that challenged the *resilience* of the communications structure which had been in place since 1945, enabling the service to become more *responsive* to ministers and the media while reducing its autonomy and hence its capacity to *resist* both politicization and mediatization. Here, the resilient institution is considered to be one that "maintains its effectiveness over time despite changing external conditions, where 'effectiveness' is the extent to which the institution fulfils the core mission" (Steinberg 2009: 65). Within the context of the resilient institution, resistance and responsiveness are seen as subsidiary concepts to mediatization, providing a conceptual link with politicization that is doubly determined. Any process of change meets resistance as well as response (Hepp et al. 2015), and the dual role of the civil servant combines responsiveness to political masters with resistance through the doctrine of speaking "truth to power" (Hennessy 2001; Wildavsky 1979).

Using in-depth interviews with former civil servants, journalists and partisan special advisers, I examine changes over time in the interactions which take place in the so-called "cross-field" (Rawolle 2005), theorized as the intersection between three fields—politics, media and bureaucracy—where intermediaries craft the narratives that become news (Cook 1998). The questions for this chapter, then, are what form did resistance and responsiveness in relation to mediatization and politicization take after 1997, and what impact did such change have on the roles of both types of government media intermediary?

8.2 Background

In 1997, Labour came into power on a landslide, determined to develop and exploit the resources of the civil service information machine to help them neutralize what they saw as the partisan bias of the national media, especially the press, which they believed had kept them out of power for 18 years (Blair 2012; Campbell and Stott 2007; Gould 1998; Macintyre 1999). The changes in news management wrought by the post-1997 UK governments, as in other jurisdictions such as Australia, New Zealand and Northern Europe, are thought to have increased partisan control over government communications (Eichbaum and Shaw 2010; Foster 2005) through the process known as politicization.

Government communications are little researched (Moore 2006; Sanders 2011; Strömbäck 2011), but recent studies have used multiple methods to identify ways in which central bureaucracies and executive agencies adapt to mediatization, indicating that politicization and mediatization may interact in a number of ways. A Norwegian observational study from within a government department found that competition between the "impartial expertise, the rule-based backstage of politics" and media specialists led to a speeding up of responsiveness to media, anticipatory media management and the simplification of policy, which was felt throughout the organization, driving a wedge between media and policy specialists (Thorbjørnsrud et al. 2014: 163). A study of the views of officials from public and third sector bodies in Australia and The Netherlands found that the more likely they were to encounter politicians as part of their work, the stronger the expectation of knowing the news (Schillemans 2012). Similarly, a Swedish observational and documentary study of executive agencies claimed that the drive to understand and exploit the promotional possibilities of news media was linked to organizational autonomy: officials opted to increase the media profile of their organizations as a way of pleasing politicians, thereby hoping to resist further interference (Fredriksson et al. 2015).

Thus, politicization, the exertion of greater power and control over bureaucracies by ruling politicians, is said to facilitate "politicization through indirect mediatization"—a process whereby officials delegated to manage the media respond to growing ministerial control over media management by increasingly identifying with and serving ministers' personal and political media needs (Fredriksson et al. 2015: 27). Hjarvard sees "indirect mediatization" as "the development of intertextual discourse between media and other institutions", considering it to be more subtle than but at least as important as direct mediatization (Hjarvard 2008: 115).

8.3 Theoretical Approach: Why Mediatization?

When one analyses governing bureaucracies, it is tempting to consider concepts such as impartial-partisan or bureaucratic-political as dichotomies when in practice they may be blurred or mutually reinforcing (Wæraas and Byrkjeflot 2012). Foucault, for example, proposed that conceptualizations based on dichotomies be substituted by the analysis of "the field of simultaneous and successive differences" (Miller et al. 1991: 62). Within a given field, the process of change does not act in a linear, causal fashion but interacts with internal and external forces to produce certain communicative configurations (Couldry 2014; Hepp 2013). Mediatization scholars suggest that rather than being the "zero sum game" identified in much media/political agenda-setting research (Thesen 2014), the fields of media and politics reinforce each other "enabling a simultaneous mediatization of politics and a politicization of media" (Hepp et al. 2015: 5). Thesen agrees that political and media agendas converge and reinforce each other by valorizing personalization and conflict (Thesen 2014). A field approach facilitates the analysis of qualitative data from complex institutional settings over time by using a non-normative perspective that does not assume mediatization to be inherently negative and by not relying unduly on dichotomies that may misrepresent or simplify a complex reality (Hjarvard 2008).

Mediatization, then, may impact on government media engagement in several ways. Firstly, a higher premium is placed on persuasive forms of communication among both journalists and politicians as they battle for attention in a declining market (Kunelius and Reunanen 2012). Secondly, political actors have, over time, increasingly deployed media-led strategic communications as a defence against potentially career-ending media coverage that privileges and personalizes blame and personal integrity over policy or political considerations (Hood 2011; Lindquist and Rasmussen 2012). Thirdly, as an institutionalized response to the dynamics of mediatization, the growth in the scale, scope and status of "promotional intermediaries" within a range of sectors, including government, contributes towards a pervasive "promotional culture" (Wernick 1991; Davis 2013; Dinan and Miller 2007).

Mediatization is a relatively new area of theoretical development, but two dominant traditions are emerging that are referred to here as the *media logic* tradition and the *embedded media* tradition. Couldry and Hepp also identify two traditions, referring to them as "institutionalist" and "social-constructivist" (Couldry and Hepp 2013: 196), and Driessens considers the recent work of Hjarvard and Hepp as representative of each tradition (Driessens 2013). The first considers the process by which media logic intrudes into other fields and institutions, influencing both implicit and explicit understandings of what is seen as appropriate and ultimately replacing existing rules (Esser 2013). Schulz identified four successive levels of media-related social change, in which media first *extend* the possibilities for human communication, *substitute* social activities and institutions, *amalgamate* with non-media social activities, eventually *accommodating* the behaviours of actors and institutions to media logic (Schulz 2004). Looking specifically at the communication activities of political parties, Strömbäck and Van Aelst outlined four dimensions of mediatization, culminating in a fourth stage where political actors incorporate news media logic into their ideas, perceptions and behaviour (Strömbäck and Van Aelst 2013).

The approach taken here is derived from the embedded media tradition, which argues that society has already exceeded the fourth dimension of mediatization and that the process is intensifying, for example, through the further acceleration of the news cycle and the incorporation of social media into everyday life. Rather than an accommodation or surrender to media logic, mediatization is a wider and more far-reaching historical meta-process in which media proliferate and are institutionalized and normalized to the extent that they increasingly contribute towards "the social construction of everyday life, society and culture as a whole" (Krotz 2009: 24). The empirical task is not to focus on media institutions or actors but to examine shifting power relations between various actors within a mediatized environment (Hoskins and O'Loughlin 2015). Within any given institution, or field, that is subjected to a process of change, such as mediatization, some actors will respond whereas others resist (Hepp et al. 2015). Change over time, then, becomes a crucial dimension in the empirical study of mediatization. Proponents of historical institutionalism, the study of shifts in informal routines and formal institutional structures that involve disparate institutional actors, have argued that, within communications studies, mediatization scholars are among the few who have successfully adopted this approach (Bannerman and Haggart 2015).

A field-based approach to mediatization seeks to examine the process of change as it applies to *all* actors, and across all relevant institutional boundaries within a particular domain, where boundaries between formal and informal institutions and the roles and practices of actors within them become blurred or distorted in response to mediatization. Within the embedded media tradition, some scholars draw on Bourdieu's idea of social fields and the forms of capital deployed within them as a way of theorizing change in dynamic and unstable media-focused settings. Couldry argues that the symbolic power of media constitutes a field of influence which overwhelms the social landscape (Couldry 2003). He considers such a field to be dynamic, fluid and unstable: "a bounded space of competition over specific forms of capital by defined sets of actors" (Couldry 2014: 9). Others have depicted the field as "a site of contestation over power" where "institutions, individuals or objects derive their distinctive properties from an internal relationship to all other positions in the field" (Akram et al. 2015: 351). For the Australian scholars Lingard and Rawolle, this approach to mediatization contains the possibility of interference between fields to create "cross-fields"—interfaces where two or more distinct fields collide and interact to produce a unique set of patterns.

Rawolle and Lingard deployed the notion of the "cross-field" empirically to examine negotiations between government media intermediaries and journalists to create and convey policy narratives relating to a particular news event—Australia's official review into its knowledge economy policy in 1999 (Lingard et al. 2005). In the struggle to define problems and propose solutions, the authors found that "journalists and policy agents adopted a range of strategies that produced cross-field effects" (Lingard et al. 2005: 734). Such effects were distinctive to the cross-field, such as texts or other representations which emerge during the lifetime of a "hot topic", snap decisions taken during a "media frenzy", or the internal negotiations between politicians and officials in response to "noise" within the mediatized cross-field. This is the context within which this chapter conceptualizes politicization and mediatization. Within the cross-field, mediatization may interact with politicization in a range of ways, for example, leading to policy failures by speeding up political decision-making in response to demands for quick solutions (King and Crewe 2013; Koch-Baumgarten and Voltmer 2010) and justifying such decisions through forms of mediated public communication which foreclose deliberation and reduce public trust (Moss and O'Loughlin 2008).

The drive by politicians to protect themselves from potentially career-ending media scrutiny may help to explain why state bureaucracies in liberal democracies have tended to become more responsive to political will over time (Eichbaum and Shaw 2010; Page 2007; Page et al. 2012; Van

Der Meer and Dijkstra 2011). In the UK, this has been most manifest in the steady rise of special advisers in the civil service who can manage both politics and the media (Greer 2008). Their numbers have more than doubled since 1997, and it has been argued that, far from being mere bag carriers or the demonized "spin doctors" of popular legend, they are significant media and political operators in their own right who together form a "political civil service" (Hood 2015). This has led some to claim that the UK now has a "dual government communication system" (Sanders et al. 2011: 534). Demands from ministers for more politically responsive bureaucratic arrangements have been observed in other ministerial democracies such as Denmark and Spain but with different local effects (Hustedt and Salmonsen 2014).

8.4 Mediatization: The Case of the UK Government After 1997

This section uses the three subsidiary concepts referred to in the introduction—resilience, resistance and responsiveness—to examine mediatization and politicization in Whitehall after 1997 and to draw conclusions about continuity and change in government communications, taking the UK as a case study. This approach accepts the historical possibility of de-mediatization or differential mediatization within political or bureaucratic settings (Fornäs 2016). These subsidiary concepts arose inductively during the research process, as we discuss below, but they also developed theoretically, firstly, from the mediatization paradigm itself and, secondly, from the dual, even contradictory, role of the impartial civil servant. Within Whitehall, "restraints", or resistance, combine with the doctrine of loyalty, or responsiveness, to uphold political leadership while providing "checks and balances" to majoritarian political power (Eichbaum and Shaw 2010; Lodge 2013). Factors, such as mediatization, which bypass or interfere with such "checks and balances" may be said to have constitutional impacts.

8.5 Methodology

To facilitate a longitudinal approach and overcome the traditional reticence of *serving* civil servants, I conducted 16 in-depth semi-structured interviews with long-serving *former* civil servants who collectively had worked in government for a total of 230 years between 1961 and 2014[1]. For a more rounded and critical understanding of the press officer's role, these were supplemented by interviews with six long-serving policy journalists and three politically appointed ministerial special advisers. Sampling was purposive, ensuring a mix of respondents who had worked at different times and at various levels of seniority, both in departments and at Number 10. The interview topic guide focused on changes over time in the everyday practice of government-media relations, asking how interviewees saw their role; how politicians, special advisers, and press officers worked together; and how all parties managed the interface between government bureaucracy, party politics, and the media. The interview material was augmented by a thorough analysis of contemporary government and parliamentary reports into media management, archive material dating back to the 1980s, and internal documents such as capability reviews and propriety guidance in order to track changes in custom and practice over time. All material was subjected to thematic analysis via Nvivo. Codes were not pre-assigned but emerged inductively, resulting in a coding frame with 76 separate codes under 16 main headings. The most frequently cited themes in order of prominence were the impact on government communications of changes in the governing party in 1997 and 2010; impartiality and maintaining "the line" between impartial and partisan communication; the changing role of politically appointed special advisers; perceptions of government communicators by other civil servants; the role of the Prime Minister's office; the priority accorded to media by ministers; and the principles and purposes of government communications.

8.6 Resilience: Enduring Structure but Changing Culture

Government communications has shown remarkable resilience. The structure put in place after World War II remains largely intact, consisting of central news management support for the Prime Minister and Cabinet at Number 10; departmental press offices to disseminate information about government policy; and, until 2011 at least, a central planning agency to deliver and coordinate propaganda (Grant 1999; Moore 2006). However, less visible incremental and, in some cases, dramatic changes took place after 1997 and continue today, particularly in relation to the role of ministers. In 1945, a Cabinet Committee stated that governments had the obligation to provide "material on which the public could reach an informed judgement on current affairs" (Cabinet Committee: 18 September 1945)[2] but must preserve the boundaries between public information and propaganda. The minister who later took charge of government communications, Herbert Morrison, stated in a memo that there could be "no questions of Government publicity being used to boost individual ministers" (Memo: 14 September 1945). Then as now, the service was staffed by a cadre of in-house communications specialists who answered to dual political and administrative leaderships and who, through a process of self-regulation, policed the invisible "line" dividing impartial public information from political communication. It is this line that has been increasingly challenged both directly by the process of mediatization and indirectly through the increasing involvement of ministers and political parties in the coordination of government publicity from the 1980s onwards but especially after 1997.

Recently released archived documents dating from the Thatcher governments of the 1980s show how ministers began to demand a more proactive and politically focused government news service, for example, one questioned whether "Whitehall's information forces are ideally deployed for the proper presentation of the overall economic message"[3]. This was rebutted by the Prime Minister's spokesman Bernard Ingham, although Ingham admitted to colleagues that the finance ministry was "desperately in need of some dynamic professionalism. Too much emphasis is apparently put on economic expertise, and far too little on a robust ability—and enthusiasm—to communicate simply"[4]. The archives show how, during the Thatcher years, senior government ministers met regularly, in secret, with party officials, to discuss the coordination of government presentation[5]. The fact that this meeting was held in secret and was seen as so controversial illustrates the cultural constraints on what then was considered to be improper ministerial "interference" in government communications. Contrast this with the most recent government propriety guidance for communicators, which states that "the press officer must always reflect the ministerial line clearly" and should "present, describe and justify the thinking behind the policies of the minister" (Government Communication Service 2014).

Despite Ingham's efforts to "introduce some of the disciplines of a newspaper office into Government Information work" and to raise its reputation and status[6], the mainstream civil service failed to rise to the challenge of the new 24/7 news media before 1997. John Major, who became Prime Minister in 1990, admitted that he was suspicious of "political spin" and did not prioritize media relations, even at Number 10 (Bale and Sanders 2001; Hogg 1995). A Number 10 press secretary at the time remembers how "the media was growing like topsy in front of us. We were running like fury to try and keep up. It was a tiny office. It was absolutely ridiculous when you think about it" (CS1). He refers to Number 10's "hair shirtism", a form of parsimony that failed to acknowledge the growing needs of journalists to the extent that no toilet facilities were available for female correspondents and broadcasters had to run cables through the windows to achieve a feed. The dramatic changes that took place after 1997, as we demonstrate below, reflect the release of pent-up pressures that unleashed a range of "cross-field" effects.

8.7 Vulnerability: A "Clear Run" for Labour

The failure to take media change seriously before 1997 effectively gave Labour a "clear run" at reform, allowing them to bring into government their own nimble and aggressive 24-hour strategic communications operation and use it as a basis for reconfiguring the service to suit their needs. This required a draconian attitude towards the existing government information service, especially those on the news frontline, about whom Labour had already formed a "poor opinion", having "run rings round it while Major was still Prime Minister" (Negrine 2008; Seldon 2005: 301). The outward form of the service remained the same, but internally there were major changes: within two years, almost the entire leadership of the government information service was replaced, and as the number of special advisers doubled, substantive and permanent changes in the terms of engagement with news journalists came into effect (Franklin 2004; Oborne 1999; Public Administration Select Committee 1998).

A senior civil servant at Number 10 until 1998 described the changes as a form of politicization "in the sense that special advisers… were very much more active in dealing with press relations than their predecessors had been" and of mediatization because "they had a very sophisticated media operation. Very rapid response geared to being 24/7" (CS2). A Number 10 press officer who later became a departmental Director of Communication flourished in the post-1997 atmosphere but recalled the poisonous atmosphere in many departments where "you had the special advisers whispering into the minister's ears saying 'this lot are not really supporting you'" (CS3). One departing Director of Information was described by a special adviser as "dead meat", a comment which found its way into the tabloid press (Public Administration Select Committee 1998). A departmental press officer, who joined in 1999, after the initial "cull", witnessed its aftermath:

> Slowly they were shuffled out (...) there was a head of news that had been there for quite a while, a lovely woman, but somehow, she was shuffled out against her will and they brought in a journalist who'd worked for a left-wing newspaper to replace her (CS4).

Journalists spoke most forcefully about the vulnerability of government press officers after 1997. One broadcast journalist described "a complete clear-out" (J1), and a broadsheet specialist identified "a takeover by special advisors (that) happened in most departments" (J2). Another took the view that "if you weren't quite New Labour enough then you probably didn't last very long" (J3), and a veteran parliamentary correspondent said that "they dismissed lots of very senior experienced, seasoned press officers who'd worked loyally for years for Labour or Conservative, and put in their own Labour party stooges" (J4). The last time there had been a major change of government was in 1979, and the media ecology of the time was very different, but it should be noted that in 1979 Margaret Thatcher took the advice of her most senior civil servant to appoint a career civil servant, Bernard Ingham, formerly a known Labour sympathiser, as her Chief Press Secretary.

Five of the 16 civil servants interviewed experienced the change of government after 2010 and described a similar hostility from incoming ministers. One Director who had experienced both changes of government recalled how:

> People were completely taken aback by the level of hostility to (...) communications people because they had beaten us; because we had been bad at our jobs. The clear-out has been at least as big and I think a bit bigger than it was in 1997. In 1997 the attitude was 'you're all a bit rubbish and you're going to have to improve and modernise quickly because we know how to do things'—not entirely welcome but not completely unrealistic. In 2010 it's 'civil servants are useless otherwise you'd have a proper job' (CS5).

Another described the experience as "a bloodbath", where "the general impression given by ministers (was) 'we don't think you're very good at your job and there's too many of you'" (CS6). In 2010, in contrast to 1997, there was little media interest in job losses in government communications, suggesting that the issue had become less controversial. My own analysis of turnover among departmental communications directors found that this was significant: by March 2014, only two remained of the 20 departmental directors of communication in post in 2010 (Garland 2016). This apparent weakening of the principle of permanence within the civil service communications leadership may also be seen as a "cross-field" effect.

8.8 Resistance: Speaking Truth to Power

We have seen how job losses after the 1997 election increased the perceived vulnerability of those who remained, potentially reducing their capacity to resist ministerial demands that crossed "the line": that is, the line which protects civil servants from engaging in party political communication. An interview study conducted in 1989–1990 with 49 senior Whitehall officials suggests that this capacity was limited, even then, and mitigated by loyalty (Barker and Wilson 1997). More recently, a study examining the lead-up to the publication of the UK Government's 2002 dossier *Iraq's Weapons of Mass Destruction* found that decisions about what information to place in the public domain were taken by a small, politically aligned group, with little resistance from officials, a conclusion borne out by the recent Chilcot report into the Blair government's decision to invade Iraq in 2003 (Chilcot 2016; Herring and Robinson 2014). A recent report by the government's official auditor concluded that the incentives for senior civil servants to challenge ministers were "weak compared with those associated with the day-to-day job of satisfying ministers" (National Audit Office 2016).

This timidity was noticed by Blair's former policy head at Number 10 (2003–2006), Matthew Taylor:

> It was clear that well-informed and well-paid civil servants were self-censoring in the face of political determination. As the minister (or prime minister) described the policy they wanted to unveil, or the commitment they wanted to make, you could see the officials wrestling with the need to provide a reality check—but all too often deciding it was better to nod sagely than look career-threateningly unhelpful. (Taylor 2015)

The press officers interviewed for this study all felt that they knew where "the line" lay and were confident that, however tricky to do so, they could manage it, commenting that "it's in the DNA" and "in the genes" and you "use your own radar". They were reluctant to argue that their own ability to challenge ministers had been compromised, but several expressed concern at practices they had observed since leaving the service. One press officer who left soon after 2010 felt that "over the course of the time that I was in government there was an erosion of those standards" (CS7). A civil servant specializing in strategy and communications across five departments during the Labour years felt that media coverage that had clearly originated from government sources showed an increasingly casual approach to the facts, which "would never have been tolerated when I was a civil servant (...) I just feel that the line has shifted a bit in the last couple of years" (CS8).

A senior civil servant who worked at Number 10 from the 1980s to the early Blair years believes that maintaining "the line" is harder today:

> Because the political battle is conducted through the media on a 24/7 basis, then ministers and politicians obviously give more attention to that battle and they put pressure on civil servants to support them in that, and it's more difficult therefore for all civil servants but perhaps particularly media frontline civil servants not to cross the line (CS2).

On matters of media presentation, which are known to be of deep concern to ministers (Leveson 2012), and in the absence of official sanctions or externally validated criteria, government press officers deploy "pragmatic flexibility", using gut instinct on a case-by-case basis to resist the demands of ministers which they consider to be inadvisable or improper (Sanders et al. 2011: 534). Since these instincts are contextual, responding to changes in what seems appropriate at the time, this line is movable. The democratic theorist Peter Aucoin argues that there has been a transformation in the meaning of impartiality within Westminster systems, from an article of faith policed by civil servants to the exercise of "promiscuous partisanship" in relation to governing politicians (Aucoin 2012). The wider research project on which this chapter is based has identified a gradual change in conceptualizations of impartiality that favours governing political actors—an argument that is, however, beyond the scope of this chapter (instead see Garland 2016).

8.9 Responsiveness: Pleasing Ministers

The significance of the 1997 "cull" was not just that it replaced almost the entire leadership of the information service but that it brought about a permanent change in the way government news was managed. The journalists interviewed for this study expressed this most clearly. One remembers the change taking place "almost immediately. Suddenly you had this new tier of semi-political operators working with chosen journalists" (J2). Another argued that the propensity for special advisers to select whom they spoke to—a practice prohibited by government press officers who have a duty to serve all media—"changed fundamentally the rules of engagement and continues to do so". Special advisers rather than civil servants took responsibility for the story of the day:

> in some cases, working with the civil service press people, but typically around them, over them, dealing with handpicked journalists who were being fed the story (…) the press officers who were left out of the loop would be trailing in the wake of this (J3).

A BBC correspondent, who was under increasing pressure to break stories for the morning news programs, found that "if you wanted the sort of thrust of (a story), especially to get it the day before so you could put it out in the morning and help set the agenda, then the special adviser became the main conduit" (J1).

The Leveson inquiry into the ethics and practices of the press following the post-2007 newspaper phone-hacking scandal revealed a consensus among leading politicians that life in the media spotlight had become almost unbearable and that, in consequence, they needed trusted and loyal aides who could handle the pressure (Blair 2012; Leveson 2012; Major 2012; Osborne 2010). David Cameron told the inquiry that he appointed the disgraced former tabloid newspaper editor Andy Coulson as his chief press secretary in 2007 because he needed "someone who could cope with the huge media pressure" (Cameron 2012). This illustrates Hjarvard's observation that, when "a single media scandal may put an end to a lifelong career in just a few days", politicians try to "create a deep backstage (…) in which they can trust their closest allies and friends in private" (Hjarvard 2013: 68). This too may be considered to be a "cross-field" effect arising from indirect mediatization.

8.10 Conclusion

The recollections of officials who had worked in close proximity to journalists and ministers during a time of significant media change suggest that, indeed, the process of mediatization took place in tandem with politicization as politicians felt increasingly compelled to take control of the news agenda as a matter of survival. As the archived documents show, ministers were already trying to develop synergies between the official government voice and the voice of the governing political party during the 1980s but this took place tentatively and secretly and did not translate into reform or modernization of government information services. Partly in response to civil service sensitivities and suspicions in relation to promotional culture, by the time Labour came into power in 1997, reform was well overdue, resulting in what appeared to be a sudden and politically driven transformation in the rules of engagement with journalists and the arrival of a small but well-connected political civil service to manage the news agenda.

The leadership structures within government communications appear to be especially vulnerable to political pressure, and ultimately to dismissal or resignation, following a change in the party of government, even in ostensibly impartial systems such as Whitehall. As the pressure of media scrutiny on ministers increases, press officers become more concerned with meeting their needs yet still see upholding impartiality as a key part of their role and indeed as its defining feature. Within a self-regulating syst'fem, government press officers use their own highly context-dependent gut instincts to maintain an ill-defined line between "impartial" and "political" government communications. The meaning of impartiality itself is called into question as it is redefined in line with political expediency. If mediatization is considered as a meta-process impacting over time on the "cross-field" where political, media and bureaucratic fields intersect, we can discern certain cross-field effects emerging over time, such as a climate of fear and blame that underlies much ministerial decision-making and the imperative to establish a "deep backstage". A growing network of politically appointed officials who are exempt from impartiality increasingly coordinates government media relations, above and below the radar, trading nuggets of information to selected journalists. This insulates and marginalises the role of government press officers while opening up a volatile and largely unseen and unregulated space where policy is framed and the news is made.

The advantage of a mediatization field approach to examining complex governing bureaucracies is that it can facilitate a more open, pluralistic and empirically grounded understanding of changing relationships and discreet power struggles within the administrative and political ecology of government. The extent to which officials and politicians resist or respond to the pressures of mediatization or indirect mediatization through politicization is a question that can be applied to any liberal democratic jurisdictions either comparatively or as case studies. Specifically, it can facilitate an understanding of how certain communicative configurations are institutionalized, normalized and intensified over time.

Notes

1.

Interviewee	Description (including final post)
CS1	Chief press secretary and director of communications (1978–1998)
CS2	Senior civil servant, Number 10 (1961–1998)
CS3	Number 10 press officer and director of communications (1994–2005)
CS4	Press officer (1999–2004)
CS5	Director of communications (1991–2011)
CS6	Director of communications (2001–2014)
CS7	Press officer (1999–2011)
CS8	Strategy director (1998–2010)
J1	Broadcast correspondent (1972–2002)
J2	Broadsheet specialist correspondent (1981–2012)
J3	Broadsheet specialist editor (1978 to date)
J4	Political editor and columnist (1962 to date)
J5	Broadcast reporter (1968–2002)

2. National Archives: CAB 78/37.
3. National Archives: PREM 19/720.
4. National Archives: MIO 1982; CAB 134/4382.
5. The Liaison Committee on the presentation of government policy was a long-standing but intermittent post-war body which was revived in 1981 but whose existence was not shared even with the Cabinet until March 1982. According to one commentator, Bernard Ingham's presence at these meetings was "a testimony to the intimate linkage even beyond the bounds of Whitehall propriety, between party and government machines" (Young 1989).

6. Ingham Archive, Margaret Thatcher foundation: May 1979–April 1985. Memo to Angus Maude, 15/10/1979.

References

Akram, Sadiya, Guy Emerson, and David Marsh. 2015. (Re)conceptualising the third face of power: Insights from Bourdieu and Foucault. *Journal of Political Power* 8 (3): 345–362.

Aucoin, Peter. 2012. New political governance in Westminster systems. *Governance* 25 (2): 177–199.

Bale, Tim, and Karen Sanders. 2001. Playing by the book: Success and failure in John Major's approach to Prime Ministerial media management. *Contemporary British History* 15 (4): 93–110.

Bannerman, Sara, and Blayne Haggart. 2015. Historical institutionalism in communication studies. *Communication Theory* 25 (1): 1–22.

Barker, Anthony, and Graham K. Wilson. 1997. Whitehall's disobedient servants? *British Journal of Political Science* 27 (2): 223–246.

Blair, Tony. 2012. Evidence session: 28 May. *Leveson Inquiry into the culture, practices and ethics of the press*. London: The Stationary Office (TSO).

Cameron, David. 2012. Evidence Session: 14 June. *Leveson Inquiry into the culture, practices and ethics of the press*. London: The Stationary Office (TSO).

Campbell, Alastair, and Richard Stott. 2007. *The Blair years: Extracts from the Alastair Campbell diaries*. London: Hutchinson.

Chilcot, John. 2016. *The report of the Iraq Inquiry*. London: House of Commons.

Cook, Timothy E. 1998. *Governing with the news: The news media as a political institution*. Chicago: The University of Chicago Press.

Couldry, Nick. 2003. Media meta-capital: Extending the range of Bourdieu's field theory. *Theory and Society* 32 (5): 653–677.

Couldry, Nick. 2014. Mediatization and the future of field theory. In *Mediatization of communication*, ed. Knut Lundby, 227–245. Berlin: Walter de Gruyter.

Couldry, Nick, and Andreas Hepp. 2013. Conceptualizing mediatization: Contexts, traditions, arguments. *Communication Theory* 23 (3): 191–202.

Davis, Aeron. 2013. *Promotional cultures: The rise and spread of advertising, public relations, marketing and branding*. Cambridge: Polity.

Dinan, William, and David Miller. 2007. *Thinker, faker, spinner, spy: Corporate PR and the assault on democracy*. London: Pluto Press.

Driessens, Olivier. 2013. Book review 'Cultures of Mediatization' (Andreas Hepp) and 'The Mediatization of Culture and Society' (Stig Hjarvard). *Communications* 38 (4): 451–455.

Eichbaum, Chris, and Richard Shaw. 2010. *Partisan appointees and public servants: An international analysis of the role of the political adviser*. Northampton: Edward Elgar.

Esser, Frank. 2013. Mediatization as a challenge: Media logic versus political logic. In *Democracy in the age of globalization and mediatization*, ed. Hanspeter Kriesi, Sandra Lavenex, Frank Esser, Jörg Matthes, Marc Bühlmann, and Daniel Bochsler, 155–176. Basingstoke: Palgrave.

Fornäs, Johan. 2016. The mediatization of third time tools: Culturalizing and historicizing temporality. *International Journal of Communication* 10: 5213–5232.

Foster, Christopher D. 2005. *British government in crisis*. Oxford: Hart.

Franklin, Bob. 2004. *Packaging politics: Political communications in Britain's media democracy*. London: Arnold.

Fredriksson, Magnus, Thomas Schillemans, and Josef Pallas. 2015. Determinants of organizational mediatization: An analysis of the adaptation of Swedish government agencies to news media. *Public Administration* 93 (4): 1049–1067.

Garland, Ruth. 2016. *Between media and politics: Can government press officers hold the line in the age of 'political spin'?* Ph.D. thesis, London School of Economics, London. http://etheses.lse.ac.uk/3463/.

Gould, Philip. 1998. *The unfinished revolution: How the modernisers saved the Labour Party*. London: Little, Brown.

Government Communications Service. 2014. *Propriety Guidance*. London: Cabinet Office.

Grant, Mariel. 1999. Towards a Central Office of Information: Continuity and change in British government information policy, 1939–1951. *Journal of Contemporary History* 34 (1): 49–67.

Greer, Scott. 2008. Whitehall. In *Constitutional futures revisited: Britain's constitution to 2020*, ed. Robert Hazell, 123–138. London: Palgrave Macmillan.

Hennessy, Peter. 2001. *Whitehall*. London: Pimlico.

Hepp, Andreas. 2012. Mediatization and the 'molding force' of the media. *Communications: The European Journal of Communication Research* 37 (1): 1–28.

Hepp, Andreas. 2013. *Cultures of Mediatization*. Cambridge: Polity.

Hepp, Andreas, Stig Hjarvard, and Knut Lundby. 2015. Mediatization: Theorizing the interplay between media, culture and society. *Media, Culture and Society* 37 (2): 314–324.

Herring, Eric, and Piers Robinson. 2014. Report X marks the spot: The British government's deceptive dossier on Iraq and WMD. *Political Science Quarterly* 129 (4): 551–584.

Hjarvard, Stig. 2008. The mediatization of society. *Nordicom Review* 29 (2): 105–134.

Hjarvard, Stig. 2013. *Mediatization of culture and society*. London: Routledge.

Hogg, Sarah. 1995. *Too close to call: Power and politics—John Major in No. 10*. London: Little, Brown.

Hood, Christopher. 2011. *The blame game. Spin, bureaucracy, and self-preservation in government*. Princeton: Princeton University Press.

Hood, Christopher. 2015. *A government that worked better and cost less?*. Oxford: Oxford University Press.

Hoskins, Andrew, and Ben O'Loughlin. 2015. Arrested war: The third phase of mediatization. *Information, Communication and Society* 18 (11): 1320–1338.

Hustedt, Thurid, and Heidi H. Salmonsen. 2014. Ensuring political responsiveness: Politicization mechanisms in ministerial bureaucracies. *International Review of Administrative Sciences* 80 (4): 746–765.

King, Anthony, and Ivor Crewe. 2013. *The blunders of our governments*. London: Oneworld.

Koch-Baumgarten, Sigrid, and Katrin Voltmer. 2010. *The interplay of mass communication and political decision-making—Policy matters!* Oxford: Routledge.

Krotz, Friedrich. 2009. Mediatization: A concept with which to grasp media and societal change. In *Mediatization: Concepts, changes, consequences*, ed. Knut Lundby, 21–40. New York: Peter Lang.

Kunelius, Risto, and Esa Reunanen. 2012. The medium of the media: Journalism, politics and the theory of 'mediatisation'. *Javnost—The Public* 19 (4): 5–24.

Leveson, B. 2012. *An inquiry into the culture, practices and ethics of the press (Leveson report)*. London: The Stationary Office (TSO). ISBN 9780102981063.

Lindquist, Evert, and Ken Rasmussen. 2012. Deputy ministers and new public governance: From neutral competence to promiscuous partisans to a new balance? In *From new public management to new political governance*, ed. Herman Bakvis, and Mark D. Jarvis, 179–203. Canada: McGill-Queen's University Press.

Lingard, Bob, Shaun Rawolle, and Sandra Taylor. 2005. Globalizing policy sociology in education: Working with Bourdieu. *Journal of Education Policy* 20 (6): 759–777.

Lodge, Guy, Susanna Kalitowski, Nick Pearce, and Rick Muir. 2013. *Accountability and responsiveness in the senior civil service: Lessons from overseas*. London: Institute for Public Policy Research.

Lundby, Knut. 2014. Introduction: Mediatization of communication. In *Mediatization of communication*, ed. Knut Lundby, 3–38. Berlin: Walter de Gruyter.

Lunt, Peter, and Sonia Livingstone. 2016. Is 'mediatization' the new paradigm for our field? *Media, Culture and Society* 38 (3): 462–470.

Macintyre, Donald. 1999. *Mandelson and the making of new labour*. London: HarperCollins.

Major, John. 2012. Witness statement. 14 May. *Leveson inquiry into the culture, practices and ethics of the press*. London: The Stationary Office (TSO).
Miller, Peter, Colin Gordon, and Graham Burchell. 1991. *The foucault effect: Studies in governmentality*. Chicago: University of Chicago Press.
Moore, Martin. 2006. *The origins of modern spin: Democratic government and the media in Britain, 1945–51*. Basingstoke: Palgrave Macmillan.
Moss, Giles, and Ben O'Loughlin. 2008. Convincing claims? Democracy and representation in post-9/11Britain. *Political Studies* 56 (3): 705–724.
National Audit Office. 2016. *Accountability to parliament for taxpayers' money*. London: NAO.
Negrine, Ralph. 2008. The transformation of a political communication: The global context. In *The transformation of political communication: Continuities and changes in media and politics*, ed. Ralph Negrine, 143–169. Basingstoke: Palgrave Macmillan.
Oborne, Peter. 1999. *Alastair Campbell: New labour and the rise of the media class*. London: Aurum.
Osborne, George. 2010. Witness statement: 12 June *to Leveson inquiry into the culture, practices and ethics of the press*. London: The Stationary Office (TSO).
Page, Edward. 2007. Where have all the powers gone? The UK top civil service in comparative perspective. Paper presented at the American Political Science Association Annual Meeting, September 1, in Chicago, USA.
Page, James, Jonathan Pearson, Brian Jurgeit, and Marc Kidson. 2012. *Transforming Whitehall: Leading major change in Whitehall departments*. London: Institute for Government.
Public Administration Select Committee. 1998. *Sixth report, session 1997–98*. London: House of Commons.
Rawolle, Shaun. 2005. Cross-field effects and temporary social fields: A case study of the mediatization of recent Australian knowledge economy policies. *Journal of Education Policy* 20 (6): 705–724.
Sanders, Karen. 2011. Political public relations and government communication. In *Political public relations: Principles and applications*, ed. Jesper Strömbäck, and Spiro Kiousis, 177–192. New York: Routledge.
Sanders, Karen, María J.C. Crespo, and Christina Holtz-Bacha. 2011. Communicating governments. *The International Journal of Press/Politics* 16 (4): 523–547.
Schillemans, Thomas. 2012. *Mediatization of public services: How organizations adapt to news media*. Frankfurt am Main: Peter Lang.
Schulz, Winfried. 2004. Reconstructing mediatization as an analytical concept. *European Journal of Communication* 19 (1): 87–191.
Seldon, Anthony. 2005. *Blair*. London: Simon and Schuster.
Steinberg, Paul F. 2009. Institutional resilience amid political change. *Global Environment Politics* 9 (3): 61–81.

Strömbäck, Jesper. 2011. Mediatization and perceptions of the media's political influence. *Journalism Studies* 12 (4): 423–439.

Strömbäck, Jesper, and Peter Van Aelst. 2013. Why political parties adapt to the media. *International Communication Gazette* 75 (4): 341–358.

Taylor, Matthew. 2015. The critical fault line damaging departmental effectiveness? *Civil Service World*. November 4. https://www.civilserviceworld.com/articles/opinion/matthew-taylor-critical-fault-line-damaging-departmental-effectiveness-relationship.

Thesen, Gunnar. 2014. Political agenda-setting as mediatized politics? *International Journal of Press/Politics* 19 (2): 181–201.

Thorbjørnsrud, Kjersti, Øyvind Ihlen, and Tine U. Figenschou. 2014. Mediatization in new areas: The changed role of public bureaucracies. In *Organizing in mediatized worlds*, ed. Josef Pallas, and Lars Strannegård, 162–175. New York: Routledge.

Van Der Meer, Frits, and Gerrit S.A. Dijkstra. 2011. Civil service systems in Western Europe: Variations and similarities. In *Civil service systems in Western Europe*, ed. Frits Van Der Meer, 271–286. Cheltenham: Edward Elgar.

Wæraas, Arild, and Haldor Byrkjeflot. 2012. Public sector organizations and reputation management: Five problems. *International Public Management Journal* 15 (2): 186–206.

Wernick, Andrew. 1991. *Promotional culture: Advertising, ideology and symbolic expression*. London: Sage Publications.

Wildavsky, Aaron B. 1979. *Speaking truth to power: The art and craft of policy analysis*. Boston: Little, Brown.

Young, Hugo. 1989. *One of us: A biography of Margaret Thatcher*. London: Pan Macmillan.

CHAPTER 9

Autonomy Losses or Heightened Control? On the Limits of the Idea of Media Autonomy in the Mediatization of Politics Narrative

Ximena Orchard

9.1 Introduction

This chapter discusses the narrative of media autonomy that underpins the mediatization of politics theory, interrogating the concept by adopting an institutional perspective (Hjarvard 2008, 2013; Lundby 2009). Using examples from fieldwork conducted in Chile, a post-authoritarian country, and exploring practices in the relationships established between politicians, journalists and communications officers working in Chile, this chapter questions assumptions regarding the autonomy losses attached to political actors as an outcome of mediatization processes.

The data discussed in this chapter belong to a larger project concerned with exploring how Chilean political elites have adapted to the mediatization of politics.[1] This study looked at complementary subject areas connected to the mediatization of political actors. This chapter

X. Orchard (✉)
Universidad Alberto Hurtado, Santiago, Chile
e-mail: morchard@uahurtado.cl

O. Driessens et al. (eds.), *Dynamics Of Mediatization*,
Transforming Communications – Studies in Cross-Media Research,
DOI 10.1007/978-3-319-62983-4_9

focuses on one of those subject areas: dynamics of autonomy and control between political and media actors. In particular, the aim of the chapter is to identify and characterize key dimensions in the relationships between political and media actors in Chile and interrogate the concept of media autonomy from these findings, highlighting how an interactional approach may offer valuable insight into institutionalized practices among milieus of politicians and journalists. In doing so, this chapter expands the research on mediatization of politics by focusing on media autonomy, a dimension of mediatization theory that has been mostly neglected in comparison with other dimensions. Furthermore, the object of study is approached through interviews with politicians, journalists and communications officers, a design that has been scarce in research on mediatization of politics. Likewise, it shifts the focus of empirical enquiry away from the much-explored democracies of the Global North.

The mediatization of politics theory focuses on how political institutions and actors have become increasingly dependent on mass communication resources as a reaction to the increasing autonomy of news media institutions (Strömbäck 2008; Schulz 2004; Esser and Strömbäck 2014; Hjarvard 2008). The media "[become] a social institution in their own right" (Hjarvard 2008: 113) in a process driven by complementary sources of institutional homogeneity: professionalization and commercialization (Thompson 1995; Hallin and Mancini 2004). In this context, professionalization is usually equated with the acquisition of distinct professional norms, some of them of a normative nature (Dimaggio and Powell 1983; Hallin and Mancini 2004), and commercialization is understood as the incorporation of operational rules oriented to profit and audience maximization (McManus 2009).

For political actors, dependence on mass communication resources has been explained and empirically observed as the incorporation of logics of action pertaining to news media institutions. Such adoption of media logic has been theoretically discussed in opposition to political logic (Strömbäck 2008) and associated with autonomy losses on the part of political actors (Mazzoleni and Schulz 1999), while empirical studies show how political actors are often in a position to take advantage of media logic (Elmelund-Præstekær et al. 2011; Landerer 2014).

Chile makes an interesting case to explore the dimension of media autonomy. Previous research shows that political elites perceive the media as an institution that has acquired increasing power (PNUD 2004, 2015), which confirms that Chilean media have become increasingly autonomous from politics at an institutional level. Nonetheless, studies of journalistic culture show that although Chilean journalists recognize autonomy as a core professional value, they confront important challenges for an autonomous journalistic practice (Hanitzsch and Mellado 2011; Mellado and Humanes 2012). Thus, macro-level media autonomy does not necessarily equate to micro-level journalistic autonomy.

The chapter starts by introducing basic concepts about the Chilean political and media systems and then develops a discussion about institutional logics of action, establishing a dialogue between institutional approaches to mediatization (among others Hjarvard 2008, 2013; Strömbäck 2008; Lundby 2009) with the institutional logics perspective (Friedland and Alford 1991; Thornton et al. 2012). Following this discussion, a revision of theoretical and empirical approaches that highlight how politicians' and journalists' interactions can inform a discussion about the concept of autonomy in the framework of mediatization of politics is presented. Analysis of interviews emphasises an understanding of the mediatization of political actors as a field-level reaction that seeks to heighten and retain control over information flows. In relation to their exchanges with journalists in particular, this control-seeking understanding of mediatization is reinforced by the strong insider culture identified in the political beat, built on the construction of instrumental platforms of collaboration between actors, mutually recognized transactional relationships between journalists and politicians, and a shared recognition of the important power inequalities of this relationship.

Finally, findings will be discussed and it will be argued that patterns of practice within political communication cultures offer important indications about how institutional logics of action have been shaped as well as how media and political actors relate to them. These observations lend support to the idea that identifying the foundation for media autonomy on a situated basis becomes an important distinction regarding different modes of mediatization.

9.2 Media and Politics in Chile: The Basics

Chile has been traditionally well positioned in regional rankings and praised for its political and economic stability. The World Bank regards Chile as a high-income country[2] and since 2009 has had full membership in the Organisation for Economic Co-operation and Development (OECD), where it features as the country with the highest inequality in income distribution.[3] The country has a strong presidential system, where the executive power is granted a set of exclusive legislative initiatives that allows the president great control over legislative agendas. Additionally, Chile has a bicameral congress integrated by 120 deputies and 38 senators,[4] where every legislative decision has to be corroborated by both assemblies (Aninat et al. 2006). Chile recovered democracy in 1990 after 17 years of military dictatorship led by Augusto Pinochet and supported by the political right, during which congress was suspended and party politics was mostly absent from public life. From 1990 onwards, two relatively stable political coalitions have conducted the country.[5] They show competitive voting patterns and capture around 90% of votes in parliamentary elections. In spite of this, four out of five post-Pinochet governments have been led by the centre-left and only one by the centre-right.

The Chilean media system is notoriously market-driven. Also, television is the most important media industry, in terms of both revenue and audience share (Godoy 2016). Chilean media show high levels of ownership concentration, and each media industry is dominated by a handful of major actors, most of them economic conglomerates with ties to different productive sectors of the economy (Mastrini and Becerra 2006). This situation has triggered concerns about the subordination of the media to corporate powers and the ideological homogeneity among the more relevant mass media outlets, which generally are regarded as economically liberal and politically conservative (Sunkel and Geoffroy 2002; Couso 2012). Nonetheless, it is important to note that different media industries perform differently in terms of ownership concentration: telecommunications and print are among the most concentrated, whereas radio and TV—industries open to international actors—are among the more diverse (for a detailed overview, see Godoy 2016).

9.3 Core Assumptions About Institutional Logics of Action

The mediatization of politics is a process of inter-institutional change, which requires thinking about how two different institutions—politics and the media—interact and mutually influence one another. The literature about mediatization of politics prominently features discussions about media and political logic. The process of mediatization of politics itself has largely been conceptualized as a confrontation between media and political logics, where political actors incorporate media logic at the expense of political logic (Mazzoleni and Schulz 1999; Strömbäck 2008). Yet the concept of media logic has also been controversial and open to criticism because of its all-encompassing nature (see Hepp 2012; Lundby 2009).

In discussions of mediatization within an institutionalist framework, there is greater consensus in the recognition that both media and political logic are each informed by a plurality of competing rationales. The very same process of institutionalization of the media is defined as one propelled by commercialization on the one hand and professionalization on the other (Blumler and Gurevitch 1995; Thompson 1995). Esser (2013) recognizes this plurality and, following Meyer (2002), asserts that media logic is informed by commercial, professional and technological considerations and political logic is informed by the complementary dimensions of policy, electoral politics and the polity. Landerer (2013), in turn, puts forward a compelling argument for overcoming the problematic premise of considering both media and political logics as opposites by highlighting how normative and market rationales break through both institutions. In the same vein, the present study takes the position that media and political logics of action do not necessarily negate each other and therefore cannot constitute oppositional forces that vary along a continuum between poles (more media logic versus less political logic). Institutional logics are "representations or constraints that influence action in a given domain" (DiMaggio and Powell 1983: 277), "organizing principles ... available to organizations and individuals to elaborate" (Friedland and Alford 1991: 248f.), and media logic has become increasingly central and integrated in different social fields, prompting a wide range of transformations (Hjarvard 2008). What follows is that rather than surrendering political logic and being subsumed by media logic, political actors accommodate the logic of the media to their routines: they understand, react to, resist or use the logic of the media.

In the Chilean case, the commercialization of the media has been the main basis for claims about the modernization in the communications field. This process developed steadily from the 1980s onwards and was characterized by a substantial decrease in the intervention of the state in the media operations, paired with a significant growth in infrastructure necessary to receive broadcast media, an increase in advertising spending and consolidation of private ownership of news media outlets (Tironi and Sunkel 1993). The market-driven nature of the Chilean news media becomes visible in previous research inspecting the autonomy of journalists, where economic pressures are identified as the matter most pressing for Chilean journalists (Hanitzsch and Mellado 2011; Lagos and Cabalin 2013; Mellado and Humanes 2012).

9.4 An Interactional Approach: From Institutional Logics to Practices

Developed as a theoretical framework to understand and explain institutional change (March and Olsen 1989), an institutionalist approach allows for locating empirical enquiry on mediatization within the boundaries of specific institutional domains, paying attention to practice. Hjarvard (2013) highlights this linkage by emphasizing how media logic becomes a link between the news media as an institution and actual social practices and interactions; an example is the extent that actors outside the media have to engage in media praxis (e.g. increasing use of public relations and media consultants) in order to tap into the resources of visibility granted by means of access to media platforms. Lundby (2009) also discusses media logic as practice when advocating for an interactional approach for the study of mediatization, one that takes into account how the media intervene and transform context-dependent social interactions.

Paying attention to practices may also contribute to a better understanding of contradictions or tensions between macro-level analyses of the relationship between media and politics and micro-level analyses based on the observation of concrete practices and shared understandings of such practices. These contradictions may be brought to light when inconsistencies are observed across different levels of social interaction (micro and macro level), and the concept of micro-foundations of institutional logics (Thornton et al. 2012) can be especially valuable to this end. Observing the micro level of institutional logics mostly refer to rendering visible how actors' goals, identities, roles and decision-making processes are constrained and enabled by the institutions they inhabit (Friedland and Alford 1991; March and Olsen 2006). Research on political communication cultures has placed exchanges between political elites and journalists at the centre of empirical enquiry, attributing important explanatory value to the orientations, attitudes and norms regulating such exchanges (Pfetsch 2004; Schwab Cammarano and Díez Medrano 2014). The value of an interactional approach has also been recognized in comparative analysis of mediatization processes (Strömbäck and Dimitrova 2011; Maurer and

Pfetsch 2014), confirming that looking into micro-level dynamics may inform how mediatization processes have developed within institutional environments that are context-specific. For an empirical application of practice theory to mediatization research, see Driessens et al. (2010.)

For contemporary Chile, news media are regarded as a crucial institution for national elites in general and political actors in particular. Chilean political elites perceive news media as accumulating unprecedented power by introducing new rules for the representation of political discourses that respond to their own operational criteria, instead of political criteria (PNUD 2004, 2015). For political elites, this move justifies the need for greater resources and professional support in the management of press relations, and it has become common for politicians to recruit press managers or similar advisors in order to facilitate relations with the media (ICSO/UDP 2004; Santander 2013). These elements lend support to the idea that politics in Chile have become increasingly mediatized.

Nonetheless, previous research regarding the relationship between media and politics in Chile shows that the professional ethos of Chilean journalists has been shaped by a tradition of political authoritarianism, resulting in journalistic practices that lean towards non-adversarial political reporting and a respectful stance towards political and economic authority figures. For Chile, the literature highlights the "officialist" character of news-making and the high dependency on official sources and limited interpretive capabilities (Faure et al. 2011; Leon-Dermota 2003; Mellado and Rafter 2014). In recent years, some research developed within the framework of the mediatization of politics has highlighted how journalistic practice has moved into a more autonomous pole, while noticing that some of the previously described features are resilient to change (Mellado and Humanes 2014; Porath et al. 2015).

This brief description sheds light on the tension of a news media institution perceived as increasingly powerful and a journalistic field described as struggling to assert its autonomy from political and economic powers. I argue that this tension derives from the way media autonomy is understood, and generally taken for granted as a premise of the mediatization of politics process, and from the lack of connection between a macro-level narrative about the mediatization of politics and a micro-level inspection of political and media actors' interactions. In the following section, core features of day-to-day interactions between journalists, communications officers and politicians in Chile will be identified and discussed in order to shed light on the above.

9.5 Data and Methods

This study uses a qualitative research strategy to explore understandings of politicians' relationships with the media, which are confronted with the accounts of communications officers working with politicians—most of them journalists by training—as well as journalists who frequently interact with politicians as practitioners across different media platforms. This methodological strategy has been oriented to provide a general explanation of a process, action or interaction shaped by the views of participants (Creswell 2007; Strauss and Corbin 2008). Thus, the research process followed a path from participant-generated data to researcher-generated data.

Sixty interviews were conducted in Santiago and Valparaíso, Chile between May and July 2013 with politicians (30), press or communications officers (12) and journalists (18). Valparaíso is a coastal city where Congress is located, and Santiago is the capital and main power centre of the country, home to the presidential palace (La Moneda) as well as ministries, political parties' headquarters and national news media outlets, all of which were places where interviews were conducted.

Sampling for this study was purposive and was oriented to establish a strategic correspondence between research questions and interview respondents. That is, the research was "designed to encapsulate a relevant range in relation to the wider universe, but not to represent it directly" (Mason 2002: 124). The population of reference for this study is made of Chilean political and media elites. Politicians interviewed occupied positions as senators, deputies, current and former minsters, high-level assessors and political party leaders belonging to political parties represented in congress. Journalists interviewed occupied positions as editors and reporters in print newspapers, online newspapers, and radio and TV stations. Communications and press officers occupied positions as senior and junior employees in parliament, political parties and central government.

Interviews were semi-structured and ranged between 15 and 70 min, and the average duration was 33 min. All were audio-recorded and fully transcribed for analysis. Interviews were inductively coded by using qualitative data analysis computer software (NVivo). Analysis followed general principles of constructive grounded theory (Charmaz 2006; Strauss and Corbin 2008), which were complemented with some data reduction techniques (Guest et al. 2012), in order to identify central categories for analysis. Interviews were conducted, transcribed and analysed in Spanish. Quotations used throughout the text were translated by the author.

In the following sections, findings relating to day-to-day relationships between media and political actors are presented, which together provide important insight about the micro-foundations of relationships of politicians and journalists in the Chilean context. These findings highlight how politicians and journalists build platforms of collaboration based on rationales of expected utility on both ends but also marked by clear power inequalities that allow politicians to retain control in the relationship.

9.6 Findings: The Micro-Foundations of Politicians' and Journalists' Relationships in Chile

Through the analysis of interviews with Chilean politicians, communications officers and journalists, vocabularies of practice used by these groups of actors were identified. Vocabularies of practice give indications about ways in which institutional logics are wholesale or partially adopted by individual actors (Thornton et al. 2012). As such, they are to be understood not only as rhetorical devices but as shared concepts guiding attention, individual decision-making and collective sense-making.

For participants, understanding the relationship as one of mutual utility was prevalent. Accounts of routine interactions are permeated by a strong transactional rationale, characterized by the construction of instrumental platforms of collaboration. These descriptions emerge in the interviews as normalized narratives to describe action—first, through references to trust-testing exercises in the construction of long-term relationships and, second, through the use of business-like language for the description of most interactions. However, the relationship is also infused with strong power differentials between these groups, expressed in the variances regarding rhetorical strategies used by the groups of reference to distance themselves from each other. While journalists resort to professional values as a protective shield, politicians express a rather dismissive stance towards the professional capabilities of the average journalist.

9.6.1 Trust-Testing Exercises and the Construction of Platforms of Collaboration

When asked to describe their daily interactions, members of all groups interviewed highlighted the high frequency and routine nature of their exchanges. Most notably, mentions of "trust" are frequent in the accounts of journalists, communications officers and politicians alike, indicating that this is a crucial asset for constructing working relationships around political reporting, where exchanges of information are routine. For example, politicians and communications officers describe being more inclined to share information (especially, off the record) with journalists they know; journalists are more inclined to make use of unattributed information coming from sources they have known for some time and to assume that this information will be of better quality: up-to-date, truthful, more nuanced and outside of official lines. The quotations below from a senator and a communications officer illustrate and reflect the prevalence of this narrative.

> I have a Head of Communications and a Press Officer who are in direct contact [with journalists], who are doing the job every day, and the job of having corridor conversations in Congress. However, it is also important to do it myself sometimes, because you obviously generate trust relationships and you must generate those yourself (Politician 26, Senator).

> Sure, and trust-based because often we ask for some topic to be covered, but with no source, and then you have to trust your colleague, who will publish the story without a source but off the record, you know what I mean? (...) That is why the issue of trust with the colleague is there (Communications Officer 3, Deputies Chamber).

What emerges from these and many similar quotations is that relationships between politicians, journalists and press officers are based on frequent, often daily contact and are built mostly on informal conversations, mutual monitoring and backstage negotiations carried out both face-to-face and through other platforms. For politicians who engage in intensive relationships with the media, being perceived as a reliable source who regularly delivers truthful background information and newsworthy tips is considered an important asset, as this gives them a greater ability to occasionally position topics of interest in news coverage or to offer interpretative frameworks for understanding political developments.

Trust-building and trust-testing exercises are best seen as practices that enable the construction of platforms for collaboration between actors while also acknowledging conflicting interests. To this is added a practice of permanent courtship, especially in the press officer–journalist axis and the cultivation of personal relationships that may result in grey areas that can challenge autonomous decision-making.

Social proximity between political and media elites is indeed identified in the literature as a source of blurring boundaries between the two (Sigal 1973; Gans 1979; Manning 2001; Davis 2009; Wahl-Jorgensen 2014). In their comparative study of political communication cultures in European countries, Pfetsch, Maurer, Mayerhöffer and Moring (2014) examine degrees of concurrence and conflict between politicians and journalists, positing that the prevalence of social norms—such as trust—lessens distance between actors and therefore decreases journalists' professional autonomy. In a European context, Maurer and Pfetsch (2014) observe that the prevalence of personal relations between politicians and journalists is more prominent in countries such as Spain and France, which they associate with strongly networked political communication cultures, where client-patron relationships may surface more easily.

In the Chilean context, social proximity is built on the shared experiences of an insider culture of political reporting. For example, all actors occasionally play the "friendly card", whether highlighting the "colleague to colleague" nature of journalist-press officers' relationships or providing unattributed information on the basis of mutual trust in the case of politician-journalist relationships. Failure to follow these trust-testing practices usually comes with practical costs for journalists and may translate to some form of sanction against specific journalists or media organizations.

9.6.2 *News Trading as Business*

When participants describe their interactions, information trading as a business-like activity is mentioned as prominently as trust. Many actors expect reciprocity in their relationships and often invest in their counterparts by collaborating with each other with the aim to increase bargaining power for future transactions. The perception of an ongoing trade-off is articulated in the frequent use of business language to describe reporting and information exchange routines. Words such as "business", "currency", "selling", "buying", "exchange" and "deals" were mentioned across research participants' accounts: politicians and press officers described selling stories (and journalists and news organizations buying them). Some stories were used as "tokens" in exchange for others, and ongoing deals were always being suspected. Typical responses include the following:

> Sometimes you can be upset with someone, and you say, OK, this person never again, but you know that this is going to be short-lived and within

> two months, you will have to give him something and he, in turn, is going to need something from you. It is a business after all (Communications, Senate).

> I mean, look, some people do not like this expression, but I really think that journalism, especially in politics, is a sort of—in the best sense of the word—business. I mean, I give you something and you give me something (Journalist 3, Editor, elite newspaper).

The acknowledgement of deals between politicians and journalists is mentioned in most of the interviews conducted. These deals, which are not always explicit, are based on the exchange of potentially newsworthy information and media visibility. Though pervasive, the practice nonetheless reveals itself as a conflict for the parties involved. Many openly refer to these exchanges as an implicit rule dominating many relationships within the political communications community. Equally, participant groups were critical of and resistant to this practice, expressed through normative condemnation of its use or abuse, particularly when it is perceived as driven by self-interest of politicians and commercial interest of news media outlets. These critiques feature more prominently among politicians, many of whom acknowledge the existence of deals in others but not in themselves:

> People who really know this business realise what you are saying. Everyone could make a list with the cast of leaders who are repeatedly in the media. And—not all of them, because I do not want to be unfair—but many have this sort of deal with the media; about providing information and, in exchange, having a certain level of prominence (Politician 29, Former Minister).

Alternatively, some condemn the "deals" selectively, judging the motives of the actors involved. On those occasions, they make a distinction: instead of condemning the trade-off in itself, they judge some specific actions as negative if those actions are perceived as motivated solely by personal interests. In this sense, the trade-off or information exchange would not be inherently negative, but its normative value would be assessed on a situated, case-by-case basis.

The prominence of references both to trust-testing exercises that operate according to implicit rules and to the adoption of business-like language points towards the construction of platforms of collaboration between political and media actors, built on the instrumental identification of converging interests. These features shed light on the extent to which backstage routines of political news production are informed by a rationale of expected utility, in which an instrumental stance prevails on both sides. This should be understood as evidence of the role played by vocabularies of practice in the institutionalization of logics of action. (Thornton et al. 2012)

9.6.3 *Steerable Journalists, Unequal Actors*

When describing their interactions, politicians, journalists and communications officers reflect on the limits of their relationships. They do so by defining their own role or their expectations about other actors' roles. For journalists, references to news values are the most prevalent rhetorical device that allows for the construction of professional boundaries in connection to their sources, resorting to their professional status as a framework for information exchanges and trust-testing exercises with political actors.

Politicians do not generally address the need for distancing themselves from journalists in the same way journalists do, which could be explained by the power differentials between these groups. Instead, they describe distancing themselves from the news media institution as a whole. This is achieved by downplaying the relevance of media visibility in the performance of their roles and particularly by criticizing the conflict-driven nature of news and showing attitudes of distrust and discomfort towards media demands. In doing so, they make normative claims about the legitimacy of political work, situating politics as a domain truly interested in the common good and oriented to the public. Chilean politicians describe the logic of the media as conflict-oriented, attached to the present, and permeated by commercial considerations. These attributes allow political actors to use the cleavage between market and normative considerations to position themselves as guardians of the public interest, in opposition to news organizations concerned with strategies for audience maximization. This line of argument is frequently found among politicians who articulate their views on the media in normative terms, accusing news media outlets of contributing to lowering the level of public debate and damaging the public perception of politics. As mentioned before, journalists also show criticism towards self-motivated politicians concerned with electoral rationales, yet both parties are ready to compromise when spaces for convergence become evident.

An additional point frequently mentioned by politicians and press officers alike was a general view of journalists as accepting with little scrutiny the input of politicians when constructing news stories and interpreting events. This issue deserves attention, as it reveals a perception of passivity in journalists which would be counter-intuitive to the idea of an increasingly autonomous media institution.

The following quotations from political actors who engage with journalists and editors on a regular basis reflect a strikingly similar line of thinking:

> [The quality of the political press is] poor, deeply poor, with few exceptions. I think they accept what they are told, there is little research, they accept little things, they are interested in minor things; the assistance of deputies (…) It has improved a little but I think there are only a handful of serious political journalists today (Politician 20, Deputy).

> I found them little creative. It strikes me how they buy stories. I mean, I say, hey but do a little bit more research, ask a little bit more to really know what had happened (Politicians 26, Senator).

This reliance on official sources, both recognized and criticized by political actors, can be explained by a variety of factors, including entrenched journalistic routines. On the one hand, this observation is consistent with literature on source relationships that support the idea of political elites as primary definers of news stories (Gans 1979; Sparrow 1999; Wolfsfeld 2003; Davis 2007). On the other hand, it is a statement consistent with local literature that stresses the "officialism" of Chilean journalism (Faure et al. 2011; Mellado and Humanes 2012). In either case, it reveals that the power inequalities observed at the micro level within the relationships between political and media actors conflict with the idea of an increasingly autonomous news media institution.

9.7 Discussion

In the previous section, some core features emerging from the analysis of interviews with politicians, journalists and communications officers working in politics in Chile were identified. Vocabularies of practice highlight how rationales of expected utility permeate the exchanges between these groups. The cultivation of trust speaks of a relatively small and networked community, where social norms overlap with professional norms of interaction, while the prevalent use of business-like language expresses the naturalization and widespread incorporation of market-driven parameters in the interactions between these actors. Additionally, problematic perceptions about journalists as a professional group were voiced by political actors, highlighting power asymmetries between these groups. On the whole, these findings reveal ways in which institutional logics of action are negotiated on the ground within the community of practice integrated by politicians, journalists and communications officers. Now the question to be answered is: in which ways could these findings inform a reflection on the concept of media autonomy in (and possibly beyond) the Chilean context?

From the premise that the practices mentioned in this chapter are one type of input for a necessary discussion about the idea of media autonomy in the mediatization narrative, this section highlights some areas requiring further development to advance our understanding of the mediatization of politics in different national contexts: on the one hand, whether it is possible and necessary to identify the basis upon which claims of institutional autonomy are made in specific contexts and, on the other hand, how the concepts of media autonomy and journalistic autonomy can be reconciled, a distinction particularly relevant in the context of Latin American new democracies whose media systems' submissiveness to political and economic power has been identified as a challenge to overcome on the road to full democratization (Voltmer 2013; Waisbord 2012; Márquez-Ramírez and Guerrero 2014).

From the perspective of media actors, vocabularies of practice inspected above highlight important obstacles for an autonomous journalistic practice. Indications are that professional autonomy has to be defended against a set of social norms and also against market-oriented rationales that provide common ground for journalists' and politicians' interactions. If we accept Landerer's (2013) redefinition of mediatization of politics as the predominance of audience-oriented market logic over normative concerns, we could state that interactions between politicians and journalists in Chile are highly mediatized. However, at the same time, these findings lend support to the idea that the Chilean journalistic field shows high degrees of heteronomy or, in other words, that it is a highly commercial and weakly autonomous field (Bourdieu 2005). This idea seems reinforced by the finding that the professional status of journalists appears often undermined in political actors' accounts.

From an analysis of the relationship between media and political actors at the micro level, it can be argued that the autonomy gained at an institutional level—mostly by means of commercialization processes that prompted the media to act within market parameters—cannot necessarily be equated to professional (journalistic) autonomy. Moreover, when the perspective of politicians is incorporated, assumptions of autonomy losses attached to political actors seem less clear, especially considering that journalists (as a group) are openly perceived by both politicians and communications officers as steerable actors with limited ability to go beyond political actors' inputs. These insights hold true when explaining relationships between media and political actors within circuits of elite communication in which exchanges become routine. Criticism of the passivity of journalists and their dependence on official versions of events was a somewhat unanticipated finding given that available data show that 62.1% of politicians believe that the news media control the public agenda and help to create a negative image of politics (ICSO/UDP 2004).

If media autonomy is understood as a result of institutional differentiation, the concept will rest primarily on whether the media are able to operate according to their own rules and standards, however defined (Hjarvard 2008). Nonetheless, when the concept of media autonomy is problematized by paying attention to power relations and particularly to democratization processes, we would expect the media to resist clientelistic practice and perform functions of accountability to power, providing citizens with meaningful information and acting as a forum for discussion among a diversity of voices (Voltmer 2013; Jebril et al. 2013; Örnebring 2012, 2013). From this perspective, connecting the concept of media autonomy with the capacity of journalists and media outlets to resist political influence, Chilean media are shown not to be in particularly good standing. The latter is consistent with features identified in the Latin American context; Márquez-Ramírez and Guerrero (2014) have used the term "captured-liberal" to describe the dependence of Latin American media systems on economic and political powers: they are described as sharing characteristics of liberal media systems, yet market liberalization has not proven a powerful enough force to prompt consistent levels of journalistic autonomy across the region.

I argue that important cues to understand these tensions can be gained from inspecting day-to-day communication practices. Far from being just anecdotal, these practices can and should be interrogated as micro-foundations of situated institutional logics. In the Chilean case, the inspection of micro-level practices shows the extent to which market rationales permeate the ways in which politicians, journalists and communications officers relate to one another, and these market rationales seem more pronounced and better articulated than normative or professional rationales in research participants' accounts. These findings offer an important indication of what media autonomy looks like in practice and raise questions regarding the ways in which institutional logics develop in close connection to historical and contextual issues.

A second consideration to be addressed is the extent to which media autonomy parallels journalistic autonomy. Often this distinction is lost in the narrative of the mediatization of politics despite the many ways in which external pressures regularly manifest around journalistic work, and as a result the pursuit of journalistic autonomy is understood as a constant struggle against both commercial and political considerations (Bourdieu 2005; Schudson 2005). Findings discussed here allow for a situated observation of the ways in which journalistic autonomy struggles for validation in the context of routine relationships with political counterparts. In other words, Chilean elites' perceptions about "the power of the media" as an institution have not completely changed prevailing relationship patterns that are rooted in professional cultures, and therefore appear resistant to change. Relationships based not only on mutual dependency but also on loyalty strategies developed between reporters and sources become especially problematic when journalists are not seen as equals by their sources. These asymmetries feed into a long tradition of officialism (Gronemeyer 2002; Faure et al. 2011) expressed in a strong attachment to official sources and their versions of events (Santander 2013; Mellado and Humanes 2014).

9.8 Conclusion

This chapter discussed practices in the relationship between journalists, press officers and politicians in the Chilean context, paying particular attention to the ways in which the analysis of these practices relates to narratives of media autonomy in the mediatization of politics. Findings point towards highly routinized relationships infused by rationales of audience maximization, in which media actors confront obstacles for an autonomous practice while political actors are still able to influence the reporting of politics.

This study certainly has important limitations; most importantly, it develops an interpretative framework based on the views of a group of participants in a single moment in time. As such, this study has not been designed to provide evidence of longitudinal change in the mediatization process, let alone measure levels of mediatization. Instead, research participants' accounts about their practices have been interrogated as micro-foundations of those institutional logics that shape their day-to-day interactions. When viewed from this perspective, strong rationales of expected utility are observed in their information exchanges, while media visibility is discussed as a key resource disputed in media outlets that operate, first and foremost, according to market parameters. Power differences between journalists and politicians also facilitate dynamics of dependence from politicians and press officers' inputs in the reporting of politics, to the point that levels of professional autonomy of journalists are often called into question by those actors who provide information subsidies to this group on a regular basis.

Throughout this chapter, I have propounded some initial routes to be explored in order to reconcile, on the one hand, findings that point towards limited journalistic autonomy in journalists' relationships with political actors and, on the other, perceptions of the media as the most powerful institution in the country among national elites. In this sense, it seems relevant to scrutinize situated institutional logics as well as practices in the relationship between political and media actors. Findings discussed here in connection to Chile lend support to the idea that highly routinized information exchanges, where important power asymmetries between actors can be observed, demand caution at the time of making inferences about decreasing autonomy levels for political actors connected to the mediatization of politics.

Notes

1. Some of the findings discussed in this chapter come from a PhD project conducted in The University of Sheffield, UK.
2. See http://data.worldbank.org/country/chile. Accessed December 2016.
3. According to the OECD Income Distribution Database. See http://www.oecd.org/social/income-distribution-database.htm. Accessed: 26 April 2017.
4. As of 2018, the Chilean Congress will be integrated for 155 deputies and 50 senators, due to an electoral reform approved in 2015.
5. During most of the post-authoritarian era, these coalitions were *Concertación* and *Alianza por Chile*. The former, located at the centre-left of the political spectrum, has been integrated by a core of four parties: *Partido Socialista*, *Democracia Cristiana*, *Partido Radical* and *Partido por la Democracia*. It was re-named as *Nueva Mayoría* and incorporated

new members during the run-up to the 2014 presidential election. The latter, located on the centre-right of the political spectrum, is led by *Renovación Nacional* and *Unión Demócrata Independiente*. This coalition was re-branded as *Chile Vamos* in October 2015 and also incorporated new members.

References

Aninat, Cristóbal, John Landregan, and Patricio Navia. 2006. *Political institutions, policymaking processes and policy outcomes in Chile*. Washington, DC: Inter-American Development Bank.

Blumler, Jay, and Michael Gurevitch. 1995. *The crisis of public communication*. London: Routledge.

Bourdieu, Pierre. 2005. The political field, the social science field, and the journalistic field. In *Bourdieu and the journalistic field*, ed. Rodney Benson, and Erik Neveu, 29–47. Cambridge: Polity.

Charmaz, Kathy. 2006. *Constructing grounded theory A practical guide through qualitative analysis*. London: Sage.

Couso, Javier. 2012. El mercado como obstáculo a la libertad de expresión: La concentración de la prensa escrita en Chile en la era democrática. In *Democracia y medios de comunicación. Más allá del estado y el mercado*, ed. Bernardo Sorj, 109–142. Buenos Aires: Catálogos SRL.

Creswell, John. 2007. *Qualitative inquiry & research design choosing among five approaches*. London: Sage.

Davis, Aeron. 2007. *The mediation of power: A critical introduction*. London: Routledge.

Davis, Aeron. 2009. Journalist-source relations, mediated reflexivity and the politics of politics. *Journalism Studies* 10 (2): 204–219.

DiMaggio, Paul J., and Walter W. Powell. 1983. The iron cage revisited: Institutional isomorphism and collective rationality in organizational fields. *American Sociological Review* 48 (2): 147–160.

Driessens, Olivier, Karin Raeymaeckers, Hans Verstraeten, and Sarah Vandenbussche. 2010. Personalization according to politicians: A practice theoretical analysis of mediatization. *Communications: The European Journal of Communication Research* 35 (3): 309–326.

Elmelund-Præstekær, Christian, David N. Hopmann, and Asbjørn S. Norgaard. 2011. Does mediatization change MP-Media interaction and MP attitudes toward the media? Evidence from a longitudinal study of Danish MPs. *The International Journal of Press/Politics* 16 (3): 382–403.

Esser, Frank. 2013. Mediatization as a challenge: Media logic versus political logic. In *Democracy in the age of globalization and mediatization*,

ed. Hanspeter Kriesi, Sandra Lavenex, Frank Esser, Jörg Matthes, Marc Bühlmann, and Daniel Bochsler, 155–176. Basingstoke: Palgrave Macmillan.
Esser, Frank, and Jesper Strömbäck. 2014. A paradigm in the making: Lessons for the future of mediatization research. In *Mediatization of politics. Understanding the transformations of Western democracies*, ed. Frank Esser, and Jesper Strömbäck, 223–242. London: Palgrave Macmillan.
Faure, Antoine, Claudio Salinas, and Hans Stange. 2011. El imperio del sentido común: Influencia del sistema mediático sobre las prácticas profesionales de los periodistas 1970–2000. Paper presented at *I Congreso Mundial de Comunicación Iberoamericana, Sao Paulo*, August 3–6.
Friedland, Roger, and Robert Alford. 1991. Bringing society back in: Symbols, practices, and institutional contradictions. In *The new institutionalism in organizational analysis*, ed. Walter W. Powell, and Paul J. DiMaggio, 232–263. Chicago: University of Chicago.
Gans, Herbert J. 1979. *Deciding what's news*. London: Constable.
Godoy, Sergio. 2016. Chile. In *Who owns the world's media? Media concentration and ownership around the world*, ed. Eli M. Noam, 641–673. Oxford: Oxford University Press.
Gronemeyer, María E. 2002. Periodistas chilenos: El reto de formar profesionales autónomos e independientes. *Cuadernos de Información* 15: 52–70.
Guest, Greg, Kathleen M. MacQueen, and Emily E. Namey. 2012. *Applied thematic analysis*. London: Sage.
Hallin, Daniel C., and Paolo Mancini. 2004. *Comparing media systems: Three models of media and politics*. Cambridge: Cambridge University Press.
Hanitzsch, Thomas, and Claudia Mellado. 2011. What shapes the news around the world? How journalists in eighteen countries perceive influences on their work. *The International Journal of Press/Politics* 16 (3): 404–426.
Hepp, Andreas. 2012. Mediatization and the "molding force" of the media. *Communications: The European Journal of Communication Research* 37 (1): 1–28.
Hjarvard, Stig. 2008. The mediatization of society: A theory of the media as agents of social and cultural change. *Nordicom Review* 29 (2): 105–134.
Hjarvard, Stig. 2013. *The mediatization of culture and society*. London: Routledge.
ICSO/Universidad Diego-Portales—UDP. 2004. *Medios masivos y élites políticas. Un estudio de opinión a 100 líderes políticos*. Santiago de Chile: ICSO/UDP.
Jebril, Nael, Václav Stetka, and Matthew Loveless. 2013. *Media and democratisation: What is known about the role of the mass media in transitions to democracy*. Oxford: Reuters Institute for the Study of Journalism, University of Oxford.
Lagos, Claudia, and Cristian Cabalin. 2013. Precarious and realistics: Chilean journalists' perceptions of their professional practice and freedom of expression. *Perspectivas de la Comunicación* 6 (1): 7–21.

Landerer, Nino. 2013. Rethinking the logics: A conceptual framework for the mediatization of politics. *Communication Theory* 23 (3): 239–258.

Landerer, Nino. 2014. Opposing the government but governing the audience? *Journalism Studies* 15 (3): 304–320.

Leon-Dermota, Ken. 2003. *And well tied-downChile's press under democracy.* London: Praeger.

Lundby, Knut. 2009. Media logic: Looking for social interaction. In *Mediatization: Concept, changes, consequences*, ed. Knut Lundby, 101–119. New York: Peter Lang.

Manning, Paul. 2001. *News and news sources: A critical introduction.* London: Sage.

March, James G., and Johan P. Olsen. 1989. *Rediscovering institutions. The organizational basis of politics.* New York: The Free Press.

March, James G., and Johan P. Olsen. 2006. Elaborating the "New Institutionalism. In *The Oxford handbook of political institutions*, ed. R.A.W. Rhodes, Sarah A. Binder, and Bert A. Rockman, 3–22. Oxford: Oxford University Press.

Márquez-Ramírez, Mireya, and Manuel A. Guerrero. 2014. The "captured-liberal" model: Media systems, journalism and communication policies in Latin America. *The International Journal of Hispanic Media* 7: 1–12.

Mason, Jennifer. 2002. *Qualitative researching.* London: Sage.

Mastrini, Guillermo, and Martín Becerra. 2006. *Periodistas y magnates: Estructura y concentración de las industrias culturales en América Latina.* Buenos Aires: Prometeo Libros.

Maurer, Peter, and Barbara Pfetsch. 2014. News coverage of politics and conflict levels: A cross-national study of journalists' and politicians' perceptions of two elements of mediatization. *Journalism Studies* 15 (3): 339–355.

Mazzoleni, Gianpietro, and Winfried Schulz. 1999. "Mediatization" of politics: A challenge for democracy? *Political Communication* 16 (3): 247–261.

McManus, John H. 2009. The commercialization of news. In *The handbook of journalism studies*, ed. Karin Wahl-Jorgensen, and Thomas Hanitzsch, 218–223. London: Routledge.

Mellado, Claudia, and María L. Humanes. 2012. Modeling perceived professional autonomy in Chilean journalism. *Journalism* 13 (8): 985–1003.

Mellado, Claudia, and María L. Humanes. 2014. The use of objective and analytical reporting as a method of professional work: A cross-longitudinal study of Chilean political coverage. *The International Journal of Press/Politics* 20 (1): 67–84.

Mellado, Claudia, and Kevin Rafter. 2014. Understanding the influence of journalists and politicians on content: A cross-longitudinal analysis of Chilean political news coverage. *International Communication Gazette* 76 (7): 531–551.

Meyer, Thomas. 2002. *Media democracy: How the media colonize politics*. Cambridge: Polity.

Örnebring, Henrik. 2012. *Elites, democracy and the media in Central and Eastern Europe*. Oxford: Media and Democracy in Central and Eastern Europe, University of Oxford—The London School of Economics and Political Science.

Örnebring, Henrik. 2013. *Journalistic autonomy and professionalisation*. Oxford: Media and Democracy in Central and Eastern Europe, University of Oxford—The London School of Economics and Political Science.

Pfetsch, Barbara. 2004. From political culture to political communication culture. A theoretical approach to comparative analysis. In *Comparing political communication: Theories, cases and challenges*, ed. Frank Esser, and Barbara Pfetsch, 344–366. Cambridge: Cambridge University Press.

Pfetsch, Barbara, Peter Maurer, Eva Mayerhöffer, and Tom Moring. 2014. A hedge between keeps friendship green—Concurrence and conflict between politicians and journalists in nine European democracies. In *Comparing political communication across time and space: New studies in an emerging field*, ed. María J. Canel, and Katrin Voltmer, 172–191. Basingstoke: Palgrave Macmillan.

PNUD. 2004. *Desarrollo humano en Chile. El poder: ¿para qué y para quién?* Santiago de Chile: Programa de las Naciones Unidas para el Desarrollo.

PNUD. 2015. *Desarrollo humano en Chile: Los tiempos de la politización*. Santiago de Chile: Programa de las Naciones Unidas para el Desarrollo.

Porath, William, José-Joaquín Suzuki, and Tania-Marie Ramdohr. 2015. Newspaper coverage of three presidential campaigns in Chile: Personalisation and political strategies. *Bulletin of Latin American research* 34 (4): 451–466.

Santander, Pedro. 2013. Influir sobre los medios: La tensa relación entre asesores comunicacionales de la élite y periodistas políticos. *Comunicación y Sociedad* 20: 95–112.

Schulz, Winfried. 2004. Reconstructing mediatization as an analytical concept. *European Journal of Communication* 19 (1): 87–101.

Schudson, Michael. 2005. Autonomy from what? In *Bourdieu and the journalistic field*, ed. Rodney Benson, and Erik Neveu, 214–223. Cambridge: Polity Press.

Schwab Cammarano, Stephanie, and Juan Díez Medrano. 2014. Distant north-conflictive south: Patterns of interaction and conflict. In *Political communication cultures in Europe: Attitudes of political actors and journalists in nine countries*, ed. Barbara Pfetsch, 271–286. London: Palgrave Macmillan.

Sigal, Leon V. 1973. *Reporters and officials: The organization and politics of newsmaking*. Lexington: Heath and Company.

Sparrow, Bartholomew H. 1999. *Uncertain guardians*. Baltimore: The Johns Hopkins University Press.

Strauss, Anselm, and Juliet Corbin. 2008. *Basics of qualitative research: Techniques and procedures for developing grounded theory.* London: Sage.
Strömbäck, Jesper. 2008. Four phases of mediatization: An analysis of the mediatization of politics. *The International Journal of Press/Politics* 13 (3): 228–246.
Strömbäck, Jesper, and Daniela Dimitrova. 2011. Mediatization and media interventionism: A comparative analysis of Sweden and the United States. *The International Journal of Press/Politics* 16 (1): 30–49.
Sunkel, Guillermo, and Esteban Geoffroy. 2002. Concentración económica de los medios de comunicación. Peculiaridades del caso chileno. *Comunicación y Medios* 13: 135–150.
Thompson, John B. 1995. *The media and modernity: A social theory of the media.* Cambridge: Polity.
Thornton, Patricia H., William Ocasio, and Michael Lounsbury. 2012. *The institutional logics perspective. A new approach to culture, structure and process.* Oxford: Oxford University Press.
Tironi, Eugenio, and Guillermo Sunkel. 1993. Modernización de las comunicaciones y democratización de la política: Los medios en la transición a la democracia en Chile. *Estudios Públicos* 52: 215–246.
Voltmer, Katrin. 2013. *The media in transitional democracies.* Cambridge: Polity.
Wahl-Jorgensen, Karin. 2014. The production of political coverage: The push and pull of power, routines and constraints. In *The handbook of communication sciences—political communication*, ed. Carsten Reinemann, 305–324. New York: DeGruyter Mouton.
Waisbord, Silvio. 2012. Political communication in Latin America. In *The SAGE handbook of political communication*, ed. Holli A. Semetko, and Margaret Scammel, 437–449. New York: Sage.
Wolfsfeld, Gadi. 2003. The political contest model. In *News, public relations and power*, ed. Simon Cottle, 81–96. London: Sage.

PART III

Dynamics in Everyday Life and Culture

CHAPTER 10

Mediatization of the Automobile

James Miller

10.1 Introduction

There are few signs that carry the weight of signification as heavily as the automobile. To take one example, Reyner Banham (1971: 195–196) found a means to utopia—to "autopia"—on the LA freeways of the 1960s. They constituted "a single comprehensible place, a coherent state of mind, a complete way of life [...] [that brought on] a state of heightened awareness that some locals find mystical". Banham's observation invokes James Carey's (1989: 208) description of a similar sensibility in the preceding century, one that began with the introduction of the telegraph. "Each improvement in communication, by ending isolation, by linking people everywhere, was heralded as realizing the Universal Brotherhood of Universal Man".

Mobility and media, here both claimed to be capable of inducing transcendent states of being, share numerous other associations.

References in the text are made to published material. Otherwise, the study draws on primary sources found in the archives mentioned below. Additional information about them is available from the author.

J. Miller (✉)
Hampshire College, Amherst, USA
e-mail: jmiller@hampshire.edu

O. Driessens et al. (eds.), *Dynamics Of Mediatization*,
Transforming Communications – Studies in Cross-Media Research,
DOI 10.1007/978-3-319-62983-4_10

There are cars-in-media: Today, the US cable channel Velocity offers about a dozen auto-centric programs plus live coverage of events like collector-car auctions. It claims to be the number one non-sports channel for 18- to 49-year-old men. The channel reaches about 66 million subscribers in the US and an additional 71 million globally (Discovery Communications 2016; Discovery Press Web 2016).

And media-in-cars: In 1935, about 900,000 American cars were sold with radios. Five years before, the figure was just 34,000. In 1947, after the interruption of the war, there were seven million car radios in use (Ford 1987: 4). Today, an Audi TT features a "virtual cockpit" that includes a one-foot-wide digital display directly in front of the driver. It offers a 3D-like image of traditional gauges as well as the view provided by a back-up camera plus infotainment, including navigation, telephone and wireless connection to the driver's mobile devices. Touch controls are on the steering wheel and between the seats, while microphones and speakers in the harness allow voice control of telephone and internet services.

The automobile and media are inextricably linked. They have a common, lengthy, over-lapping history as instruments and indicators of modernity.[1] And while the experience of automobility is fundamentally a material one, it is equally one of media-influenced meanings: of driver subjectivity, the romance of travel, the thrill of speed and design aesthetics.

The literature, popular and scholarly, on cars-in-media and the related car culture is vast and unceasing. In contrast, there is relatively little research on media-in-cars.[2] And as the Audi example suggests, cars have now become well-established mobile media venues.

This chapter is a step towards the US history of media-in-cars.[3, 4] Its primary argument is that the introduction and steady integration of media into the automobile interior transformed drivers' and passengers' experience of automobility. This change, which involved design, marketing and popular culture, constitutes the mediatization of the automobile. Periodizing this history into pre- and post-Second World War and the turn of the last century leads to a second argument. Media in cars proliferated and became more sophisticated and were increasingly presented as an essential component of the desirable contemporary automobile. This process accelerated as the operation of cars grew more dependent on computer technology. Together, these developments pushed the car's mediatization into the more radical stage of digitalization—GPS, mobile hot spots, touch screens and voice recognition, along with various driver-assistance technologies—whose next, even more revolutionary change in automobility is the autonomous automobile. This will be a multiply networked vehicle piloted by powerful artificial intelligence, perhaps allowing more efficient traffic flows and promoting greater travel safety. Crucially, the self-driving car, as currently conceived, will be a site of intense media consumption, a place where digital media are both operational infrastructure and means of infotainment (IDEO 2014).

10.2 The Mediatization Orientation

Knut Lundby (2014b: 3) says that "'Mediatization' has become a much-used concept to characterize changes in practices, cultures and institutions in media-saturated societies, thus denoting transformations of these societies themselves". This chapter takes its understanding of the process of mediatization from Andreas Hepp's (2010) attempt to integrate aspects of sometimes competing theoretical approaches. Mediatization entails, first and obviously, the development of more media and more uses of them. This fact, Hepp says, has temporal, spatial and social implications. By this, he means that media are now continually available nearly everywhere and so have become a naturalized part of very many social contexts. This general dynamic brings about change, in which new media technologies increasingly structure practices of human social communication. The changing mediality, or the material and aesthetic aspects of individual media, is a significant consideration here, especially when digital media affordances are becoming embedded in places and things and so perhaps experienced as an immaterial presence (Miller 2015a). Under conditions of mediatization, media play a fundamentally constitutive role in shaping everyday life (Deuze 2012). Hepp (2010: 43) terms this "everyday mediacentrism", implying both people's casual perception of this new reality and the conceptual recognition that life is now lived amid the unavoidable interplay of media ensembles in a variety of social situations, some of which were previously unaffected directly by media.[5] Nick Couldry and Hepp (2016: 34) observe that comprehensive digitalization and what they call datafication (a world of big data and pervasive algorithms) have produced the present era of deep mediatization: "A much more intense embedding of media in social processes than ever before".

An assessment of the mediatization of automobility that focuses on media-in-cars must take into account the growing number of media in automobile interiors and their popularity, an emphasis on manufacturers' design and marketing that stress the desirability of these media to car drivers and passengers and the greater technological sophistication of media affordances available in cars. The development of these conditions over time implies that the social experience of automobility is becoming mediatized. That is, what it means to inhabit an automobile is not only inseparable from media-in-cars but the car has taken on the nature of a possibly unique site of intense media consumption—which experientially may be nearly as significant as the car's function as a vehicle.

10.3 The Automobile: How to Think About It

Few people around the globe would fail to recognize an automobile. There were after all 900 million passenger cars in 2014 (OICA 2016). And more than three decades ago, it was discovered that 95% of a group of Dutch children included "auto" among their first 50 nouns (presented somewhat inaccurately by Mom 2015: 1; see Schlichting 1996: 25). However numerous or familiar, a car is much more than a single vehicle: it implies what John Urry (2004: 25–26) calls the system of automobility. There are the designed and manufactured object itself; the meaning-laden product that is bought, used and maintained; a mostly taken-for-granted complex of many socio-technical phenomena that includes multiple industries, road construction, petroleum refining, suburbia, etc.; its place at the top of the list of preferred mobility options, with implications for the organization of social life; a car culture that often remains synonymous with the good life; and of course the sweeping environmental consequences captured by the term climate change. This system, Urry (2004: 27, 26) argues, reproduced itself around the world with such success that it created a "century of the car" and gave rise to what might be automobility's central feature, the hybrid assemblage, the car driver.

The modern car originated around the turn of the twentieth century. In the US, Charles and Frank Duryea built the first automobile powered by an internal combustion engine in 1893, and were soon manufacturing them. Henry Ford began the mass production of the Model T in 1908. Cars' purpose was uncertain, and their reliability questionable. They were called "devil wagons" (Chiu 2008: 32) for the danger they posed and the disruption they inflicted on fellow travelers.[6]

After the First World War, production of automobiles expanded rapidly. Rudi Volti (2004: 63) observes that by "the mid-1920s, the manufacture of automobiles had become America's largest industry". Many urban planners were eager to reorganize cities to accommodate the automobile, especially the City Beautiful movement. Daniel Burnham's 1909 *Plan of Chicago* is a prime example, and Frank Lloyd Wright was an eager ally (McShane 1994: 203–228; Fraser and Kerr 2002). The design of houses increasingly took the car into account (Kihlstedt 1983). It was the automobile that made possible the "centerless residential suburb" and its successor, the "edge node", a dispersed array of malls, corporate offices and homes located around freeways (Hayden 2003: 154–180) that are emblematic of post-war socio-geographic reorganization. The heyday of the American automobile spanned 1945 until about the mid-sixties, when Volti (2004: 88) says, "an automobile-based culture had taken hold in the industrialized world". American car models were styled to look and to be lower, longer and wider. They were a triumph of "fantastic styling" (Gartman 1994: 136–181), often taking their design cues from aircraft and promoted by futuristic, one-off concept cars (Dixon, in press; Chrysler Corporation 1961).[7] Harley Earl, a General Motors (GM) vice president and first head of its Styling Section, explained: "You can design a car so that every time you get in it, it's a relief—you have a little vacation for a while" (Sloan 1964: 278).

Much else about the automobile during this period was inflected by media culture. Sixties youth culture is unimaginable without the freedom of personal mobility—as the Beach Boys celebrated in 1964: "She'll have fun, fun, fun till her daddy takes the T-bird away". Car culture embraced hot rods and custom cars, racing and rallying, the enthusiast press, automobile-themed movies and car-identified stars, pop music, drive-in movie theatres (nearly 5000 at the end of the 1950s) and even board games (Park and Shop, introduced in 1953). Cars were a pop art theme, and between 1975 and 2010 BMW famously employed artists, including Frank Stella, Andy Warhol and David Hockney, to paint 18 of its race cars. (See Lewis and Goldstein (1983) for a collection of articles on how cars are "the mirror of art".)

Rising oil prices, successful foreign imports, safety and environmental concerns, over-crowded streets and today an unexpected return to life in revitalized city centres all dampened American car culture during the last years of the century.[8] At the same moment, somewhat paradoxically, the deepening mediatization of cars because of digital technology shaped the experience of automobility as a comfortable, personal sphere where the media-enhanced passage of time may be as significant as the automobile's function as a means of transportation.

10.4 A Chronology of Media in Cars

10.4.1 Pre-war

During 1920s and 1930s America, the automobile and the popular culture of everyday life became intimately intertwined. A resident of Middletown wondered why Robert and Helen Lynd (1929: 251) needed to ask how life was changing in 1925: "I can tell you what's happening in just four letters: A-U-T-O". The Lynds showed how the radio, the phonograph, Hollywood movies and the automobile together were rapidly altering long-established patterns of leisure activity, domestic finances, church-going and adolescent behaviour.

Los Angeles, the capital of filmmaking, had in 1925 the highest per-capita car ownership in the world. As Leo Braudy (2011: 73, 75) puts it, Hollywood "would not have existed without the car". Film director Cecil B. DeMille supposedly remarked that the American "love of motion and speed" was embodied in both automobiles and movies. Stars and their cars were a regular feature in the sorts of popular magazine biographies—"idols of consumption"—that Leo Lowenthal (1944: 517) documented: "the headliners of the movies, the ball parks and the night clubs".

The Lynds (1929: 259, 253) quote one such magazine, the *Saturday Evening Post*, as describing the car as "an enricher of life" and conclude that already in 1925 Middletown, it had "reached the point of being an accepted essential of normal living". By 1932, more than half of American homes owned a radio, where manufacturers of automobiles and related products advertised heavily. David Lewis (1976: 311, 313–314) says they spent nearly $2 million in 1933, up from only $134,000 in 1927. When Ford sponsored a twice-weekly musical variety show between 1933 and 1937, it was carried on a record 86 CBS stations and quickly gained one of the largest national audiences. In 1934, Ford became the initial commercial sponsor of the baseball World Series, which was broadcast nationally for the first time by 180 stations representing all of the networks.

The luxurious marques Peerless or the US-made Rolls Royce or both offered factory-installed radios in late 1923 or early 1924. Ford and Chevrolet first offered AM radios at additional cost, installed by the dealer, in 1932 and 1933. Chevrolet's price was equivalent to about $1000 (in 2016 terms), when its two-door, five-passenger automobile cost about $11,000 (in 2016 terms). It was not until the 1980s that Chevrolet made radios a standard feature, although more expensive cars did so sooner.

Radios of the 1930s were built into a car's instrument panel. By 1937, Ford's radio sported an "invisible 'ear-line' speaker" (mounted above the windshield) with "variable tone control". Push-button radios ("auto-tuning") became available during the late thirties. The radio in 1939 Pontiacs featured a "volume levelizer", which automatically increased the radio's volume as the car's speed increased. The radio's controls were located in "an artistically designed decorative plate" at the centre of the dashboard, where cars' heater and fresh-air intake controls were typically grouped. Foot controls for the driver were available from the thirties into the seventies. Automobile radio sales leapt from 34,000 in 1930 to 900,000 in 1935 (Ford 1987: 3).[9]

In the 1930s, Chevrolet radio advertising invited the driver to "Change the boredom of long drives to periods of pleasure and interest [...] you are never out of touch with the world". Chevrolet suggested that "Today everybody wants a radio equipped car. People today are spending more time in their automobiles than ever before. This, in many cases, deprives them of the pleasure of their home Radios". In 1939, Pontiac claimed that its Master Radio had "better tone quality that many good household radios".

10.4.2 Post-war

Buick described its 1947 Sonomatic radio in considerable detail, lauding its "exceptionally fine fidelity in the low tones, such as organ music or brass instruments. It is also very clear and lifelike in higher frequencies, particularly voice". By 1950, a radio manufacturer's repair manual began by noting that "radios have become a major accessory item". Their growing popularity required user instruction in such skills as resetting the push buttons and understanding the signal-seeking tuner. The manual advised to "explain the effect of street car lines, neon signs, buildings, power lines, mountains and the power of various stations".

Delco, purchased by GM in 1918, reported building more than 2.25 million auto radios in 1955 (Delco Radio Division 1955: 2). Chevrolet, in 1958, offered three different radio models. Touching the "wonder bar" of one would automatically seek strong station signals. Antennas could be mounted in a "streamline" fashion on either rear fender.

In the 1960s, transistor radios were commonplace, rear speakers were regularly available and stereo (eventually quadraphonic) and AM/FM radios and 8-track tape players could be had. A 1968 Ford press release about these new "elaborate in-car entertainment systems" began by pointing out that "Swingers in the 'now' generation go for groovy cars and groovy music". Integrated circuitry soon allowed the several entertainment functions to be packaged in single units. Antennas began to effectively disappear, becoming wires embedded in the windshield. Using the increasingly popular CB (citizens band two-way) radio, HELP (Highway Emergency Locating Plan) was proposed as a means to aid automobile travellers in summoning roadside help, although it never came to fruition.

By the late 1980s, what were called mobile cellular telephones could be installed as aftermarket devices. Attached by a phone cord to a box-like apparatus, they could be used in the car or the entire unit removed for portability. The preferred term for audio was now "music system", and GM was touting cassettes as "the wave of the eighties", an example of "the art of music through the science of sound", sometimes in collaboration with Bose. "The acoustics of the car were measured, the speakers precisely placed and the locations of the listeners were considered". Cassette players featured graphic equalizers and a subwoofer system, and CB radio could be integrated as well. An operating manual ran to 14 pages. One firm that in 1991 converted Cadillacs into limousines featured a back-seat fax machine.

Ford characterized these changes at the end of the eighties by saying, "the automotive radio has moved from under the floor boards to a central position in the electronic, computerized, digitalized instrumentation of today's cars and trucks" (Ford 1987: 10).

Cadillac's market research at this time revealed that for the youngest and wealthiest potential buyers, "technology is of prime importance". This led to a stress on the totality of its advanced technology, such as the "new, standard computer command ride" (a "road sensing suspension system") and "uplevel, Bosch II anti-braking system", along with a remote keyless entry system that would "activate [the] illuminated entry system and arm and disarm [the] theft-deterrent system". One model, with a quieter interior due to better door seals and thicker glass, offered a "driver information center" that included a garage door opener. A front armrest provided storage for cassettes and CDs. In 1994, an "active audio system" included 11 speakers and a 6-disc CD player (two years later, it played 12 discs). The next year, an installed cell phone that allowed hands-free conversation and was compatible with faxes and pagers was a Cadillac option (various phone choices filled four pages of a brochure). Digital instrument displays were standard.

In 1995, Cadillac's advertising and marketing were explicitly emphasizing that the "relationship of man and machine has gained new importance with each step in the automobile's evolution [...] one simple, yet elusive goal: a rewarding and accommodating interaction among driver, passengers and the car itself. Movement toward perfection of these 'human factors'" was the Cadillac theme.

10.4.3 At the Millennium

During the years immediately before and after 2000, emphasis on comprehensive interior design increased. In 2009, market research revealed very strong interest among new car buyers for rear-view cameras, rear-seat entertainment, and navigation and infotainment systems (Frank 2009; Velotta 2009). One study showed nearly two thirds wishing to connect personal music players with their vehicle. Ford reported that cars equipped with its SYNC infotainment systems sold twice as fast as those without. SYNC upgrades could be accomplished by downloading the upgrade onto a USB flash drive and then plugging it into the car. Delivering a keynote address to the annual 2009 Consumer Electronics Show (CES), the Ford CEO announced, "We are a car company, but we are working to think and act like a technology company".[10]

10.4.4 Autonomous Automobiles

Autonomous cars are being developed to address two basic problems: safety and traffic jams. According to the World Health Organization, road traffic injuries kill more than a million people each year and are the leading cause of death among 15- to 29-year-olds (WHO 2015: vii). Emerging-world megacities are regularly paralyzed by the massive number of vehicles on their streets ("Jam today" 2016). It is also a truism that more than 90% of cars are parked at any one time. Self-driving cars lend themselves to car-sharing arrangements, which would allow their continual use—dramatically reducing the overall number of cars and freeing up space currently allocated to parking.

The autonomous car is still early in its realization.[11] Perhaps the best known project is Google's, which claims to have driven its fleet of 60 automobiles 1.7 million miles in four US cities (Google Self-Driving Car Project 2016). One analysis foresees a situation where "sensor and connected-vehicle technologies will continue to develop and converge, leading to an eventual inflection point beyond which it is likely that the driver will increasingly be taken out of the loop" (KPMG and CAR 2012: 18) at around 2025.

Three concept cars demonstrate multiple advanced design features, including semi-autonomous operation. The Mercedes-Benz F 015 features four rotating lounge chairs and an "interior as a digital living space" with six displays wrapping three sides of the car and laser and LED exterior lighting.[12] Mercedes-Benz describes the more recent IAA (Intelligent and Aerodynamic Automobile) as the result of "a continuous digital process chain from research and development through production to marketing and sales, logistics and the service area […]". The prototype features car-to-car communication and OFM (optical finger navigation) for its driver.[13] BMW's Vision Next 100 emphasizes a "companion" that "organizes your appointments or takes over your travel planning for you. It also forwards your incoming calls and e-mails—but only when the time is right" and filters social media and other news in real time. Traveling, the car "preconsciously prepares you for the next situation […] you're able to see things that you couldn't otherwise see".[14]

10.5 Mediatization of the Automobile

This chapter argues that the introduction and accelerating growth of the number and sophistication of media in cars' interiors, from the 1930s to the new century, significantly shaped the vehicle occupants' experience, constituting the mediatization of automobility. Secondly, more recent developments in digitalization have intensified the process of mediatization by both bringing new media into automobiles and turning cars into "rolling computers" (i.e. vehicles with digital operating infrastructures).

And the line between infotainment and infrastructure is becoming less distinct, as is illustrated by predictions of self-driving vehicles.

10.5.1 Has the Automobile Undergone Mediatization?

The evidence for the mediatization of automobility can be summarized as follows. During the 1930s, the number of new cars made and sold in the US with AM radios grew steadily. They were optional accessories and they were expensive. Immediately after the war, the number of AM radio-equipped automobiles skyrocketed, even though for all but the most costly automotive brands, radios remained an option until the seventies or eighties. From the fifties into the eighties and nineties, the variety of media available for installation in cars increased in parallel with new media found in the home, plus a few media unique to automobiles. At the same time, there was greater design and marketing attention to the experience of traveling in a comfortable, safe and technologically advanced automobile. New media were central to this formulation. By the end of the 20th century, buyers expected a modern car to be suffused with modern media.

The general terms of this selective evidence, most of which is based on primary documents, are easy to accept. On their face, they make for a convincing argument. To conclude that the automobile has been mediatized, however, immediately raises questions that reduce the certainty of the conclusion. There are two sources for this hesitation. One arises from the nature of historical mediatization research, the other from the nature of the subject.

The valuable quest of historical research is to show the unfolding of the mediatization process over time. Stefanie Averbeck-Lietz (2014) makes a compelling case for taking a very long view in order to understand present-day mediatization developments. Stig Hjarvard (2013: 103–136) takes a more limited historical perspective with his study of LEGO—"from bits to bytes" or "the transformation of play"—which focuses on the distinctive toy maker and its strategic move at the turn of the century away from its globally famous plastic bricks, first produced in 1955, to lifestyle, entertainment and other less "solid" products. Hjarvard (2013: 134) concludes with this necessary caveat: "[W]e cannot infer a change in children's play directly from the changes in their toys". Clearly, this is the fundamental challenge faced by all historical mediatization research.

This study has documented the mediatization of the automobile by establishing the increasing presence of media in cars over several decades and the marketing language that accompanied it. Allusions to related phenomena like car culture, the automobile as a theme in literature and film, and the related popularity of media in the home offer an interpretive context for the documentation. But there is, as with Hjarvard's LEGO study, no direct empirical evidence about a change in automobility that made media experience a central feature for drivers and their passengers.[15]

Furthermore, it is nearly impossible to imagine media-less automobiles in order to produce a counter-factual account that would somehow demonstrate automobility both mediatized and not. Why the automobile should have become a premier example of media embedded in a constructed space is neither obvious nor answered by this study. For other transportation modes like trains or airplanes, media came late and in a more limited way. How then can the ostensible mediatization of the automobile best be explained? Does the answer reside mainly in the realm of particular media? Of automobility itself? Something about their intersection in very specific contexts like the baby boom youth culture or the reshaping of American cities as suburbs and ex-urbs and the necessity of long-distance commuting over complex highway systems—contexts that have collectively but episodically a cumulative mediatizing effect over historical time?

Undeniably, the automobile underwent a decades-long transformation into a significant and perhaps unique site of embedded media technology and its use. The record of the never-waning popularity of media in cars is indisputable. These observations may have to suffice in making this preliminary mediatization argument.

The second source of reticence for the claim of mediatized automobility is the lack of research on the mediatization of place—of material, physically constructed environments, like the car. There is not one such study in the three major collections of mediatization literature (Lundby 2009, 2014a; Hepp and Krotz 2014).[16] That makes analysis of this sort a pioneering enterprise that will have to find its inspiration in other literatures, like architecture and design, pervasive computing, mobility studies and science and technology studies[17] (Miller 2016).

Even if there were studies of the mediatization of place, the automobile is a peculiar example of a built environment. Unlike most others, it is mobile and so must conform to a variety of special design parameters, some of them legally mandated with regard to safety, noise, fuel efficiency, emission standards, and so on (Yang et al. 2007; Hossoy et al. 2011; Akamatsu et al. 2013). In addition, people experience automobility while seated in a car's interior, whose proper history has yet to be written (Möser 2003: 61). More than 60 years ago, it was noted that "interiors of American cars are often designed to duplicate in domestic comfort the living room of the driver's home". This "glorification of comfort" seeks to achieve a "sensationless limbo [...] as the highest form of motoring pleasure" (Drexler 1953: 3). Kurt Möser (2003: 74, 75) adds that the "trend is towards a total 'uncoupling' of drivers and passengers from the elements, the surrounding landscape, the driving environment and from other drivers in their cars". In these ways, the travellers' compartment is both similar to other material places where media might be found (home-like, demarcated by its own artificial environment) and very different (mobile and designed around the primary need to drive the car safely). Investigation of the mediatization of the automobile needs to include micro-spatial analysis that takes these interior features systematically into account, analogously to contemporary micro-apartments whose design may influence space habitats (Simon and Toups 2014).

10.5.2 Is It Useful to Speak of the Digitalization of the Automobile?

Niels Ole Finnemann's (2014: 299, 310) observation that "digital media introduce a radical change in the materialization of media" and perhaps consequently that "there is no exclusive limit between media and non media" bears directly on the nature of media in cars at the millennium. In an advanced car today, or very soon (Tesla and Audi), a single screen or a heads-up display on the windshield will present images that afford information about the journey (maps), control of the car and its interior environment (speed, ride mode, temperature), mechanical operations and problems (fuel, tire pressure) and infotainment, including text messages, e-mail, internet content, music and video. For the car's occupants, the interface remains the same, regardless of the service. And beyond their awareness, the automobile will be monitoring its own operation and streaming a report to its manufacturer, insurer and others. All of this happens digitally.

Media in cars are no longer more numerous than in the past, or better integrated or even more sophisticated. Rather, the digitalization and resultant merging—at least from the perspective of the driver and passengers, but not only—of infotainment and infrastructure constitute a basic change in the mediatization of the automobile. In retrospect, this may be seen as the intermediate stage on the way to autonomous vehicles. Looking forward from history, it may be understood as the culmination of the mediatization process that began in the 1920s. Either way, something significant and discrete has happened. What is lacking is satisfactory conceptual language to label it.

10.6 Future Research

Continued exploration of the mediatization of automobility would do well to focus on two questions. One relates to the necessity of determining the changing experience of media-in-cars, the ways in which mediatized automobiles altered drivers' and passengers' affective, haptic and other behaviour, which in turn influenced the design of auto interiors. As Mimi Sheller (2003: 2) puts it, how do "feelings for, of and within cars come to be socially and culturally embedded sensibilities, in familial and sociable practices of car use and in entire regional and national car cultures that form around particular systems of automobility and generate different aesthetic and kinaesthetic dispositions toward driving"?

The second question concerns the extent to which the long history of automotive mediatization, especially its culmination in autonomous vehicles, can be understood as presaging the internet of things (IoT). Experts predict significant progress toward the IoT by 2025. Typical is the chief data officer of Deutsche Bank, JP Rangaswami, who foresees that "'[e]verything' will become nodes on a network [...]. People will engage with information using all of their senses [...] today's connected devices [will] become smaller and smaller and slowly merge into the part of the body from where the particular sense related to the device operates" (Pew Research Center 2014: 6–7).[18]

A pervasive IoT must confront many of the same constraints affecting the self-driving car: the development of advanced machine learning/artificial intelligence, technology standard-setting and compatibility, reliability, safety and security, existing material environments, law and regulations, and so on. Nonetheless, the car is one of the most complete present-day instances of a bounded space with systematically integrated, interactive media that are both taken for granted and essential to the functioning of a built environment. There are several aspects of the mediatization of the automobile relevant to conceptualizing the IoT (see Miller (2015b) for a further discussion), and they would be profitably studied.

Notes

1. Robert Gordon (2016: 193) comments, "It could be argued that the radio defined the first half of the twentieth century as much as the automobile did". Gijs Mom (2015) discusses the car as a "herald of modernity".
2. John Heitmann (2009: 99) states explicitly that "there is not one scholarly essay that explores how the two dynamic technologies of radio and automobiles were brought together beginning in the 1920s".
3. *Sound and safe: A history of listening behind the wheel* (Bijsterveld et al. 2014) is the most extended treatment of the subject. This excellent study considers mechanical and car body issues, marketing, "boom cars" and a brief history of auto radios as well as the general place of audio in automobile travel. See also Michael Bull (2001, 2007) and Alexander Russo (2010).
4. The study benefitted greatly from the generous cooperation of the following archivists and librarians and their staffs: Christo Dantini, GM Heritage Center/Media Archive, Sterling Heights, MI; Natalie Morath, GM Design Archive and Special Collections, GM Technical Center, Warren, MI; Linda Skolarus, Benson Ford Research Center at the Henry Ford Museum, Dearborn, MI; Courtney McAlpine, Ford Motor Company Archives; Mark Bowden, National Automotive Historical Collection, Detroit Public Library, Detroit, MI; the Automobile Reference Collection, Free Library of Philadelphia, Philadelphia, PA; and Heather McCann at Hampshire College's Harold F. Johnson Library. Research for this study was partly supported by Hampshire College and the Five College Blended Learning Initiative, for which I developed the seminar, Media in Cars, taught during spring term 2016. I am grateful to its students for spirited discussions about this neglected and fascinating subject.
5. Nick Couldry and Andreas Hepp (2013) provide a thorough introduction to the concept of mediatization (see also Hepp 2013).
6. Clay McShane (1994: 125–148) documents the role of popular culture until 1917 in making the car the "epitome of possessions", in Henri Lefebvre's words.
7. How an automobile should look is open to debate and relates directly to issues of cars in media and media in cars. A famous statement from the catalogue of Eight Automobiles, "the first exhibit anywhere of automobiles selected for design" (Museum of Modern Art 1951), is that "Automobiles are hollow, rolling sculpture. They have interior spaces

corresponding to an outer form, like buildings, but the designer's aesthetic purpose is to enclose the functioning parts of an automobile, as well as its passengers, in a package suggesting directed movement along the ground" (Drexler 1951: n. p.).

8. Both the degree of "motorization"—the absolute and relative number of vehicles—and the percentage of people with a driver's license may have peaked in the US (Sivak 2013; Sivak and Schoettle 2016).
9. In December 1987, Ford's public relations department produced a detailed, 11-page, 50-year history of "Ford audio systems" (Ford 1987).
10. For a lengthy description of Ford digital initiatives, see the 2010 CES keynote by the Ford CEO (Mulally 2010) and four others with senior supervisory responsibilities.
11. Autonomous cars are being developed largely as hybrid and alternative fuel, especially electric, vehicles. These combined features will lead to fundamental design changes, with interiors no longer designed around the driver, the elimination of engines and traditional drive trains and reduction in weight due to the enhanced safety promised by deep-learning platforms.
12. https://www.mercedes-benz.com/en/mercedes-benz/innovation/research-vehicle-f-015-luxury-in-motion/. Accessed: 26 April 2017.
13. https://www.mercedes-benz.com/en/mercedes-benz/design/mercedes-benz-design/concept-cars/concept-iaa-intelligent-aerodynamic-automobile/. Accessed: 26 April 2017.
14. http://www.next100.bmw/en/topics/bmw-vision-next-100.html. Accessed: 26 April 2017.
15. The next best thing might be internal auto industry documents like market research, design memos, and so on. This material, for reasons of liability and competition, seems to be inaccessible to researchers. My historian colleague Michael Lesy points out that police reports began to include "driving while drunk" in the 1920s. Did "distracted by radio" appear in the 1930s?
16. With the possible exception of Peil and Röser (2014), which is more an ethnography of gender roles with respect to new media in the home.
17. For a succinct discussion of the current state of the "new sociology of technology", i.e. social construction of technology (SCOT), Large-Scale Technological Systems (LTS) and actor-network theory (ANT), see Bijker and Pinch (2012).
18. A comprehensive design forecast that takes into account six "metatrends" by one of the largest US-based architectural firms begins with "iHumanity", or continuous digital engagement, and "'smarter' lives" in which "buildings, settings and products will integrate connectivity and 'know' that we're present" (Gensler 2016).

References

Akamatsu, Motoyuki, Paul Green, and Klaus Bengler. 2013. Automotive technology and human factors research: Past, present and future. *International Journal of Vehicular Technology*. http://www.hindawi.com/journals/ijvt/2013/526180/. Accessed 26 Apr 2017.

Averbeck-Lietz, Stefanie. 2014. Understanding mediatization in the 'first modernity': Sociological classics and their perspectives on mediated and mediatized societies. In *Mediatization of communication*, ed. Knut Lundby, 109–130. Berlin: De Gruyter Mouton.

Banham, Reyner. 1971. *Los Angeles: The architecture of four ecologies*. Berkeley: University of California Press.

Bijker, Wiebe E., and Trevor Pinch. 2012. Preface to the anniversary edition. In *The social construction of technological systems: New directions in the sociology and history of technology*, anniversary edition, eds. Wiebe E. Bijker, Thomas P. Hughes, and Trevor Pinch, xi-xxxiv. Cambridge: MIT Press.

Bijsterveld, Karin, Eefje Cleophas, Stefan Krebs, and Gijs Mom. 2014. *Sound and safe: A history of listening behind the wheel*. New York: Oxford.

Braudy, Leo. 2011. *The Hollywood sign: Fantasy and reality of an American icon*. New Haven: Yale University Press.

Bull, Michael. 2001. Soundscapes of the car: A critical study of automobile habitation. In *Car cultures*, ed. Daniel Miller, 185–202. Oxford: Berg.

Bull, Michael. 2007. *Sound moves: iPod culture and urban experience*. London: Routledge.

Carey, James W. 1989. Technology and ideology: The case of the telegraph. In *Communication as culture*, 155–177. Boston: Unwin Hyman.

Chiu, Imes. 2008. *The evolution from horse to automobile: A comparative international study*. Amherst, NY: Cambria.

Chrysler Corporation. 1961. Idea cars and parade cars, 1940–1961. Engineering Division, Technical Information Services, November 1.

Couldry, Nick, and Andreas Hepp. 2013. Conceptualizing mediatization: Contexts, traditions, arguments. *Communication Theory* 23 (3): 191–202.

Couldry, Nick, and Andreas Hepp. 2016. *The mediated construction of reality*. Cambridge: Polity.

Delco Radio Division. 1955. *Delco radio training manual* no. 551. Kokomo, IN.

Deuze, Mark. 2012. *Media life*. Cambridge: Polity.

Discovery Communications. 2016. *Annual report 2015*. Silver Spring, MD.

Discovery Press Web United States. 2016. *2015–2016 Velocity upfront slate*. https://press.discovery.com/us/vel/programs/velocity-2015-2016-upfront-slate/. Accessed 26 Apr 2017.

Dixon, Leon. in press. *Creative industries of Detroit: The untold story of Detroit's secret concept car builder*. Forest Lake, MN: CarTech.

Drexler, Arthur. 1951. *Eight automobiles.* New York: Museum of Modern Art.

Drexler, Arthur. 1953. *Ten automobiles.* New York: Museum of Modern Art.

Finnemann, Niels O. 2014. Digititization: New trajectories of mediatization? In *Mediatization of communication*, ed. Knut Lundby, 297–321. Berlin: De Gruyter Mouton.

Ford. 1987. Milestones in the evolution of Ford audio systems. *Public Affairs, Diversified Products Operations*, Dec 4. Dearborn, MI.

Frank, Randy. 2009. Technology-based features drive automobile sales. *Design News* 64 (3), March 1.

Fraser, Murray and Joe Kerr. 2002. Motopia: Cities, cars and architecture. In *Autopia: Cars and culture*, ed. Peter Wollen, and Joe Kerr, 315–326. London: Reaktion Press.

Gartman, David. 1994. *Auto Opium: A social history of American automobile design.* London: Routledge.

Gensler. 2016. *Live, work, play in 2025: Gensler Design Forecast 2016.* http://www.gensler.com/uploads/document/427/file/gensler-designforecast-2016.pdf. Accessed 26 Apr 2017.

Google Self-Driving Car Project. 2016. *Google self-driving car project monthly report*, June 2016. https://static.googleusercontent.com/media/www.google.com/en//selfdrivingcar/files/reports/report-0616.pdf. Accessed 26 Apr 2017.

Gordon, Robert J. 2016. *The rise and fall of American growth: The US standard of living since the Civil War.* Princeton: Princeton University Press.

Hayden, Delores. 2003. *Building suburbia: Green fields and urban growth, 1820–2000.* New York: Pantheon.

Heitmann, John. 2009. *The automobile and American life.* Jefferson NC: McFarland.

Hepp, Andreas. 2010. Researching 'mediatized worlds'. In *Media and communication studies: Interventions and intersections*, ed. Nico Carpentier, Ilija Tomanić Trivundža, and Pille Pruulmann-Vengerfeldt, 37–48. Tartu: Tartu University Press.

Hepp, Andreas. 2013. *Cultures of mediatization.* Cambridge: Polity.

Hepp, Andreas, and Friedrich Krotz. 2014. *Mediatized worlds: Culture and society in a media age.* London: Palgrave Macmillan.

Hjarvard, Stig. 2013. The mediatization of play. In *The mediatization of culture and society*, 103–136. London: Routledge.

Hossoy, Ilkin, Panos Papalambros, Richard Gonzalez, and Thomas J. Aitken. 2011. Modeling customer perceptions of craftsmanship in vehicle interior design. *Journal of Engineering Design* 22 (2): 129–144.

IDEO. 2014. *The future of automobility by IDEO*. http://automobility.ideo.com/. Accessed 26 Apr 2017.

"Jam today". 2016. *Economist*, 9–10, Feb 27.

Kihlstedt, Folke T. 1983. The automobile and the transformation of the American house, 1910–1935. In *The automobile and American culture*, ed. David L. Lewis, and Laurence Goldstein, 160–175. Ann Arbor: University of Michigan.

KPMG and Center for Automotive Research (CAR). 2012. *Self-driving cars: The next revolution*. https://www.kpmg.com/US/en/IssuesAndInsights/ArticlesPublications/Documents/self-driving-cars-next-revolution.pdf. Accessed 26 Apr 2017.

Lewis, David L. 1976. *The public image of Henry Ford: An American folk hero and his company*. Detroit: Wayne State University Press.

Lewis, David L., and Laurence Goldstein. 1983. *The automobile and American culture*. Ann Arbor: University of Michigan.

Lowenthal, Leo. 1944. Biographies in popular magazines. In *Radio research 1942–1943*, ed. Paul F. Lazarsfeld, and Frank N. Stanton, 507–548. New York: Duell, Sloan and Pearce.

Lundby, Knut. 2009. *Mediatization: Concepts, changes, consequences*. New York: Peter Lang.

Lundby, Knut. 2014a. *Mediatization of communication*. Berlin: De Gruyter Mouton.

Lundby, Knut. 2014b. Mediatization of communication. In *Mediatization of communication*, ed. Knut Lundby, 3–35. Berlin: De Gruyter Mouton.

Lynd, Robert S., and Helen Merrell Lynd. 1929. *Middletown: A study in American culture*. New York: Harcourt, Brace and Company.

McShane, Clay. 1994. *Down the asphalt path: The automobile and the American city*. New York: Columbia University Press.

Miller, James. 2015a. The dematerializing interface. *Westminster Papers in Communication and Culture* 10 (1): 66–80.

Miller, James. 2015b. Prefiguring the internet of things and beyond: The case of the automobile. Paper presented at the Society for Social Studies of Science, November, Denver.

Miller, James. 2016. Media and automobility: The space of the car. Paper presented at T2M—International Association for the History of Transport, Traffic and Mobility, October, Mexico City.

Mom, Gijs. 2015. *Atlantic automobilism: Emergence and persistence of the car, 1895–1940*. New York: Berghahn.

Möser, Kurt. 2003. The driver in the machine: Changing interiors of the car. In *Tackling transportation*, ed. Helmuth Trischler and Stefan Zeilinger, 61–80. East Lansing: Michigan State University Press.

Mulally, Alan. 2010. *Keynote address at the Consumer Electronics Show*. Dearborn, MI: Ford Motor Company Media Center, Jan 7.

Museum of Modern Art. 1951. *Museum to open first exhibition anywhere of automobiles selected for design*. Press release 510823-46. New York.

OICA (International Organization of Vehicle Manufacturers). 2016. *Motorization rate 2014—Worldwide*. http://www.oica.net/category/vehicles-in-use/. Accessed 26 Apr 2017.

Peil, Corinna, and Jutta Röser. 2014. The meaning of home in the context of digitalization, mobilization and mediatization. In *Mediatized worlds: Culture and society in a media age*, ed. Andreas Hepp, and Friedrich Krotz, 233–252. London: Palgrave Macmillan.

Pew Research Center. 2014. *The internet of things will thrive by 2025*, Mar 14. www.pewinternet.org/2014/05/14/internet-of-things/. Accessed 26 Apr 2017.

Russo, Alexander. 2010. *Points on a dial: Golden age radio beyond the networks*. Durham: Duke University Press.

Schlichting, J.E.P.T. (Liesbeth). 1996. *Discovering syntax: An empirical study in Dutch language acquisition*. Doctoral dissertation. Catholic University of Nijmegen, NL. http://www.liesbethschlichting.nl/discovering-syntax/. Accessed 26 Apr 2017.

Sheller, Mimi. 2003. Automotive emotions: Feeling the car. Department of Sociology, University of Lancaster, 19 May.

Simon, Matthew A., and Larry Toups. 2014. Innovation in deep space habitat interior design: Lessons learned from small space design in terrestrial architecture. *AIAA SPACE 2014 Conference and Exposition, SPACE Conferences and Exposition*.

Sivak, Michael. 2013. *Has motorization in the US peaked?* Ann Arbor, MI: University of Michigan Transportation Research Institute.

Sivak, Michael, and Brandon Schoettle. 2016. *Recent decreases in the proportion of persons with a driver's license across all age groups*. Ann Arbor, MI: University of Michigan Transportation Research Institute.

Sloan Jr., Alfred P. 1964. *My life with GM*. New York: Doubleday.

Urry, John. 2004. The 'system' of automobility. *Theory, Culture and Society* 21 (4/5): 25–39.

Velotta, Richard N. 2009. Ford: Think of us as a technology company. *Las Vegas Sun*, January 16. http://lasvegassun.com/news/2009/jan/16/ford-think-us-technology-company/. Accessed 26 Apr 2017.

Volti, Rudi. 2004. *Cars and culture: The life story of a technology*. Baltimore: Johns Hopkins University Press.

WHO (World Health Organization). 2015. *Global status report on road safety 2015*. Geneva.

Yang, Jingzhou, Joo H. Kim, Karim Abdel-Malek, Timothy Marler, Steven Beck, and Gregory R. Kopp. 2007. A new digital human environment and assessment of a vehicle interior design. *Computer-Aided Design* 39 (7): 548–558.

CHAPTER 11

The Mediatization of Fashion: The Case of Fashion Blogs

Nete Nørgaard Kristensen and Christa Lykke Christensen

11.1 Introduction

During the past 200 years, fashion and the media have formed an increasingly interdependent alliance since the dissemination of fashion has been tied to various types of media: fashion sketches and fashion photography in magazines; actresses' presentations of fashion brands in movies; fashion journalists commenting on collections in newspapers; television programs on fashion history; and, since the late twentieth century, the internet, which has played a crucial role in fashion communication because of all-encompassing media technologies. Unmistakably, *mediated* communication is today the precondition for the distribution of fashion knowledge, fashion as consumer goods and fashion as markers of identity; thus, the media legitimize fashion as a field of cultural and societal value. Owing to the media, contemporary fashion is ubiquitous and intertwined with conceptions of individual distinctiveness and modern lifestyle—a process supported by the mass distribution

N.N. Kristensen · C.L. Christensen (✉)
University of Copenhagen, Copenhagen, Denmark
e-mail: christal@hum.ku.dk

N.N. Kristensen
e-mail: netenk@hum.ku.dk

O. Driessens et al. (eds.), *Dynamics Of Mediatization*,
Transforming Communications – Studies in Cross-Media Research,
DOI 10.1007/978-3-319-62983-4_11

and commercialization of fashion. This ubiquity has contested the aura of exclusiveness of the fashion world in terms of taste and trends, the uniqueness of new fashion items, and changing hierarchies of designers, fashion houses, tailors, models and photographers. It has put pressure on fashion as an institution "with its own rules and resources" (Hjarvard 2013: 44).

To develop the argument of fashion as an institution under pressure from media logics, this chapter analyses the interplay of fashion and the media in the digital age, exemplified by fashion blogs. It aims to answer the broad research question: How do digital media influence fashion communication? More specifically, we ask: how are fashion blogs as a specific type of fashion communication influenced by the formal and informal logics of the blog as a media technological and genre hybrid, and how do they communicate fashion?

Taking our point of departure in mediatization theory, we analyse the fashion blog as a *media* phenomenon in light of the alliance of fashion, market and the media—that is, as an example of the mediatization of culture and society (e.g. Hjarvard 2013; Lundby 2014). The point of departure is not fashion as a cultural phenomenon but rather how the professional strategies, practices and technological affordances of the media impact fashion communication, exemplified by fashion blogs as a distinctive communication genre. The chapter is based on existing research on the generic features of blogs (Herring et al. 2005; boyd 2006; Lomborg 2009; Rettberg 2014) and *fashion* blogs in particular (Pham 2011; Rocamora 2012), including their potential in a market context (Colliander and Dahlén 2011; Halvorsen et al. 2013). We have chosen, as analytical cases, two Danish fashion blogs which received the Danish Fashion Blog Award in 2015 for "best female fashion blog" (nemesisbabe.dk) and "best personal blog" (twinpeaks.dk). The two blogs epitomize the amalgamation (Schulz 2004) of a distinct fashion look and individual lifestyle and thus how fashion blogging is as much about the performance of identity by means of mediated fashion communication as it is about specific fashion trends and items. The main argument is that fashion blogging, as an example of intensified digital communication, may influence the authority of the institution of fashion. This may challenge previously important ways of fashion communication.

11.2 Mediatization: From the Logic of Fashion to the Logic of Digital Media

Mediatization theory concerns the ways the media are influencing and changing late modern culture and society. Applying Hjarvard's institutional approach, we define mediatization as:

> the process whereby culture and society to an increasing degree become dependent on the media and their logic. This process is characterized by a *duality*, in that the media have become *integrated* into the operations of other social institutions and cultural spheres, while also acquiring the status of social institutions *in their own right*. (Hjarvard 2013: 17)

The mediatization of fashion thus refers to the long-term processes through which the media influence the social forms of interaction and communication related to the cultural sphere of fashion and change how fashion and media institutions interact.

The mediatization of fashion is more than the *mediation* of fashion, i.e. the fact *that* fashion is communicated by means of various types of media and *that* these media precondition fashion communication, for example, on fashion blogs. Rather, *mediatization* involves *how media logics*—in this case, the logics of blogs—affect fashion communication and fashion as an institution. Media logic(s) refers to specific media's "particular *modus operandi* and characteristics [...] that come to influence other institutions and culture and society in general" (Hjarvard 2013: 17).[1] Of particular importance are the affordances of the blog that challenge traditional and institutionalized types of fashion communication: the printed and professionally edited fashion magazine.

11.2.1 The Logic of Fashion Encapsulated by the Fashion Magazine

The fashion magazine may be considered an institutionalized communication channel to the fashion world because of its primary function as a cultural and promotional intermediary between fashion producers and users. Moeran (2006: 737) argues that:

> As intermediaries between producer and consuming public, fashion magazines exist to teach the lay public why fashion should be important in their lives, what the latest trends may be, who are the names that drive them

> and where the clothes themselves may be purchased. In other words, they legitimate fashion and the fashion world in cultural terms.

Since fashion magazines are part of media corporations, they may be characterized as institutions; they are, ideally, professionally *edited* publications based on the insights of fashion experts who, first and foremost, adhere to the logics of the fashion world. As a consequence, fashion magazine reporters and photographers have long been primary authoritative sources of knowledge about fashion: They put fashion into perspective by addressing the history of fashion and designers; appraise the aesthetic potentials of fashion materials, forms and colours; and pay attention to innovative and qualitatively new fashion ideas and items. Fashion magazines typically strive to communicate a factual profile, exuding a professional and anonymous aura (Bradford 2015: 204). Thus, fashion magazines represent a hierarchical approach to fashion communication. They guide consumers by presenting fashion trend guidelines and by emphasizing themselves as *the* authoritative point of reference with respect to aesthetic adjustments of personal style and bodily appearance (Davis 1995; Gough-Yates 2003).

It may be argued that fashion magazines have contributed to the so-called democratization of fashion, a process parallel to industrialization, modernization and commercialization of fashion products (Wilson 2005; Turner 1991). Both fashion industries and media have profited from this transformation of fashion—from a dictate available only to the few and wealthy to being accessible to a wider population. Fashion magazines have had the authority to:

> legitimate fashion and the fashion world in cultural terms [...] They provide historical and aesthetic order in a world whose products, by their very seasonality and potentially chaotic quantity, are likely to go unnoticed. (Moeran 2006: 738)

However, this striving for "order" and homogeneity has come under pressure, especially from the market and from digital media.

11.2.2 The Logic of Digital Media Circumventing Fashion Hierarchies

The fashion magazine's role as a provider of order and authority of "what is fashionable" has been contested as it has become increasingly difficult to make absolute and final statements about fashion. Since the 1970s, market logics have influenced fashion as an institution and turned fashion into simple fashion goods and fashion magazines into advertising catalogues. However, notwithstanding the blurring boundaries between magazines' fashion reports and advertisements, the aura or logic of fashion has been preserved. Equally important, since the late 1990s, digital technologies, especially the internet, have provided consumers with *immediate* worldwide access to the increasingly immense and diverse assortment of fashion products in a mediated form. Immediacy, as Tomlinson (2007: 98) defines it, involves the closure of the interval between now and a future that may entail waiting and require patience. Within this logic of immediacy, the media's role as *mediators* has been supplemented by a role as everyday acquaintances and interlocutors (Tomlinson 2007: 100), implying that consumers themselves increasingly have to evaluate what fashion is and choose between competing styles. From a media perspective, these new circumstances have occasioned a paradoxical situation for the fashion industry.

On the one hand, the spread of digital media has enabled wide-ranging dissemination of fashion and better strategic planning of targeted communication (and subsequent sale) to individualized consumers. The fashion blog, for example, provides designers and industry with unique access to consumers' communication on taste and style, including their reflections on fashion consumption. This information, previously difficult to access, may prove crucial to future fashion innovation and production. Furthermore, many bloggers blog for or are associated with print and digital fashion magazines, thereby serving and supporting the interests of both magazines and the fashion industry. As such, digital media have developed into tools that stimulate the demand for, at least, more knowledge of fashion, thus consolidating fashion as a natural and integral part of modern consumer society. In that sense, digital technologies have presented the fashion industry with more power compared with when fashion was spread mainly through mass media (e.g. magazines), targeting all audiences at once.

On the other hand, as Bradford points out (2015: 199), the industry has also lost some of its previous control of the media (re)presentation of fashion: Today, anyone can design a website, open a blog or create a profile on Facebook or Instagram to present and share knowledge and experiences of fashion. Thus, contemporary fashion blogging involves both fashion industry insiders and outsiders (Bradford 2013), implying that mediatization has made the cultural intermediaries of the fashion world more heterogeneous by providing virtual spaces for fashion experts *and* non-professionals to articulate and negotiate fashion preferences.

In the words of Jenkins, the fashion blog has facilitated a social participatory culture (2006: 3) in the form of virtual communities of taste with an advisory role in the everyday lives of bloggers and blog readers (Bradford 2015; Halvorsen et al. 2013). This meddling of non-professional intermediaries in the public dialogue on fashion is often criticized by designers and journalists because, as Bradford (2015: 200) points out,

> bloggers are, like journalists, telling a story about fashion, but it's a different kind of story—not one based on technical knowledge or informed criticism, perhaps, but rather one where fashion meets real life.

Bloggers provide experience-based perspectives on fashion and thus challenge the expert paradigm already circulating among the fashion world's professionals and fashion magazine editors and journalists. Accordingly, Rocamora (2011) and Pham (2011) speak of fashion blogs democratizing fashion communication. Blogs are easy to use since they have a low entry-point (Lomborg 2009), and they have global reach, superseding the prior monopoly of elite fashion media, houses and metropolises (Rocamora 2011).

This indicates that fashion blogging is, obviously, not only about fashion. Closely related to modern consumption, lifestyle and identity performance, fashion blogging shares many features with lifestyle television and the celebritization of lifestyle gurus and can, in the words of Lewis, "be seen as a marker of a growing convergence between a public sphere of commodity production and spectacle, and an intimate, private sphere of consumption and ordinary, everyday life" (Lewis 2010: 581). This convergence is characterized by the increasing interconnectedness of information, entertainment, privatized lifestyle consumption and ethical modes of citizenship (Lewis 2010).

The mediatization of fashion implies that the position as primary, and authoritative conveyers of fashion, previously associated with designers, the fashion industry *and* the accompanying media portfolio of magazines and newspapers, has been challenged by digital media in general and by fashion blogs in particular. Mediatization, to some extent, entails a democratization of fashion since everybody now has the opportunity to present and discuss fashion or even confess peculiar fashion interests to fellow bloggers and blog readers. Thus, anyone can contextualize fashion in a personal everyday setting or in a context of subjectively motivated knowledge of, for instance, fashion history or industrial aspects. Adding a communication aspect to fashion itself, blogging accentuates fashion not primarily as a field of concrete consumption but as a field of communication, thereby expanding the radius of the fashion logic. Thus, fashion logic expands by means of the media logic, and vice versa: the media logic expands by means of the fashion logic.

11.3 Fashion Blogs as Communicative Genre

Since the mid-2000s, scholars have presented various definitions and types of blogs. While blogs, in their most basic form, are defined as "[…] frequently modified web pages in which dated entries are listed in reverse chronological sequence" (Herring et al. 2005: 142), Lomborg (2009) argues for a more dynamic definition to encompass the diversity of blog sub-genres. She contends that "the weblog can be defined as an author-driven, asynchronous and informal genre of CMC that uses various modalities and entails some interactivity" (Lomborg 2009: 3) and points to three generic features that may be useful to consider when analysing blogs: (1) the content/purpose of the blog, (2) the directionality of the communication—between blogger and blog reader, and (3) the style of communication.

11.3.1 Content and Purposes of (Fashion) Blogs

Rettberg (2014: 17) distinguishes between three types of blogging: *The personal blog* mostly serves as a personal diary in view of the blogger's storytelling of self and intimate musings on everyday life. Thus, the personal blog is closely associated with the individual blogger as a mediated *persona* in the words of Horton and Wohl (1956: 216). More specifically, Horton or Wohl argue that this persona is a creation by the media of "a special category of "personalities" whose existence is a function of the media themselves", aiming to create the illusion of intimacy (Horton and Wohl 1956: 216). Whereas *the filter blogs* "filter the web from the blogger's own point of view" (Rettberg 2014: 17), *the topic-driven blog* focuses on specific subjects, such as hobbies or professions and often prioritizes information and debate. It is produced by individuals or smaller groups of people with specific interests (Rettberg 2014: 24) and places the topic rather than the blogger at the centre of attention.

The analysis presented in this chapter includes fashion blogs carrying features from the personal and the topic-driven blog. However, it may be difficult to decipher the specific purpose of a blog or the blogger's motivation for blogging and thus the rules that apply to the communication. Some fashion bloggers are private individuals, whereas others are journalists, public relations professionals or brand promoters. Often, these non-professional/professional distinctions are further blurred by bloggers starting out as individuals performing their digital selves (McGaughey 2010) but increasingly becoming part of institutionalized structures by engaging in blog communities, blogging for media corporations and developing professional features as (or, if) the blog becomes successful. Even though fashion bloggers may be less dependent on advertisers and less obliged to blog about specific brands compared with printed magazines (Rocamora 2012), branding and advertisement increasingly have become part of the blogosphere: Advertising revenues have increased considerably, and lifestyle blogs have proven to be more valuable public relations channels than print media journalism (Halvorsen et al. 2013). Similarly, bloggers increasingly are motivated by the potential for influencing blog readers and making money on their blogs (Lowrey et al. 2011; Technorati 2014). Although advertising on blogs may contribute to formalizing blogs to make them more attractive to advertisers, this "professionalization" may threaten the originality and authenticity that made the fashion blog successful in the first place (Lowrey et al. 2011). Especially, "amateur" bloggers typically gain credibility because of their authenticity, experience-based personal tastes and independence from commercial interests; blog readers expect transparency and honesty when it comes to bloggers' commercial liaisons (Colliander and Dahlén 2011; Halvorsen et al. 2013). However, bloggers are not formally subject to regulations or professional ethics, and blog posts and product promotion are easily mixed, blurring the boundaries between blogging, journalism and marketing and challenging the influence of the institutionalized fashion world of magazines, designers and fashion houses.

11.3.2 Tone and Directionality

Rettberg's definition of the various types of blogs emphasizes the role of the blogger since blogs are "generally written in first person" (Rettberg 2014: 34). The blogger's style of writing may display an autobiographical, intimate and confessional (informal) tone, typical of the personal blog, or a neutral, distanced or formal tone, typical of the topic-driven blog (Lomborg 2009); the more it simulates spoken language and private conversation, the more informal or intimate.

Colliander and Dahlén (2011) argue that an important communication feature of fashion blogs is the bloggers' ability to perform as "fashionable friends" to blog readers by mimicking face-to-face interaction or para-social interaction (Horton and Wohl 1956). Such friendship-like relations are accomplished precisely by means of a conversational style, engaging blog readers in *live*-like dialogues. This potential dialogue is facilitated by the technological affordances of blogs, i.e. the communication speed and lack of editing, (potentially) making blog readers active participants (Wright 2006 in Halvorsen et al. 2013). By sharing details of their private lives and commenting on posts, bloggers simulate more private relations with their readers and thus imitate word-of-mouth or peer-to-peer communication. As a consequence, bloggers perform a double role (Halvorsen et al. 2013: 215): they represent (extra-ordinary) fashion icons or idols to blog readers and at the same time perform as (ordinary) friends. This points to the significance of the individual blogger's credibility since he or she is an integral part of the content. Thus, engaging in conversational forms of communication with blog readers is an important task for fashion bloggers. This suggests the potential for interaction as a defining feature of blogs—in contrast to the more anonymous relations of magazine journalists and their readers.

Rocamora (2012) emphasizes hypertext on fashion blogs as another generic feature that has altered fashion communication. Blog linking is essential to the survival of bloggers (Halvorsen et al. 2013: 219) because large blog networks provide access to new and larger segments of blog readers or communities. Whereas fashion magazines organize content to provide order and a linear reading, fashion blogs are characterized by inviting a non-linear reading or open text, which may constantly be altered and is fragmented or even chaotic and characterized by snapshot aesthetics. In many ways, it reflects the changed time cycle of the fashion world itself (Rocamora 2012). This points back to the question of immediacy: The fast pace of blogging facilitates not only "inter-personal" communication with blog readers but also "fast reaction to global and local trends" (Halvorsen et al. 2013: 214). The changed time structure of both industry and communication has brought fashion blog reading and the actual consumption of fashion (shopping) even closer (Rocamora 2012) since the acquisition of fashion displayed on blogs is only one click or link away. Thus, immediacy as media logic characterizes the consumption of fashion blogs and of fashion, indicating how mediatization has contributed to changing the logic of fashion.

To sum up, the following generic features and affordances of the fashion blog are of particular importance, pointing to the mediatization of fashion: the (seeming) *authenticity* of the fashion blogger's communication since fashion blogging is more about the blogger than about fashion—the blogger *is* the blog; equally important is the *informality* of the genre since fashion blogging mimics conversation, often in an informal and intimate tone, rather than applies an expert or commercial discourse; blogs provide the potential *for interaction*, including liking, commenting and small-talking about fashion facilitated by the technological affordances of the blog; blogs hold the potential for *democratizing* fashion communication, including decentering institutionalized communication hierarchies and the network potentials of hyperlinking; they include the potential for *sharing* fashion tastes, advice and inner thoughts, which may provide an experience-based evaluation of fashion; finally, blogs allow the potential for *consumption*, which provides opportunities for integrating fashion consumption with blog activities. Thus, the fashion blog may be defined as a hybrid genre between the fashion magazine, the personal diary, lifestyle promotion, and fashion branding and marketing.

11.4 Methodology

The following analysis focuses on two Danish fashion blogs that received the Danish Fashion Blog Award in 2015 for "best personal blog" (twinpeaks.dk) and "best female fashion blog" (nemesisbabe.dk). The Danish Fashion Blog Award was introduced in 2011 by miinto.dk, a major Scandinavian fashion webshop, and is awarded to fashion bloggers who "during the past year have drawn attention to themselves either creatively, innovatively or commercially".[2] Thus, the "awardable fashion blog" is one of aesthetic and communicative distinction but also of commercial value, signifying the market logic of fashion. The founders of the award perceive bloggers as part of the international elite and find it "more relevant than ever to focus on the bloggers as media, as trendsetters and as idol-phenomena and not least award the particularly skilled".[3] This reasoning connotes that the blogger is an important cultural and promotional intermediary between the producers and consumers of contemporary fashion culture, but it also confirms the blogger as a "media-made arbiter of taste" (Kristensen and From 2015) negotiating the ordinary/extra-ordinary duality of fashion and celebrity culture. The award designates a dawning *institutionalization* of the fashion blog as part of contemporary fashion communication, at least if awards are taken as signs of excellence or cultural capital (Benson 2006; Bourdieu 1984). Notwithstanding, the rationale for introducing the award also designates the mediatization of fashion by means of the blog. Danish fashion bloggers make a particular interesting case in light of the recent international achievements and recognition of the Danish fashion industry, which has become renowned for its stylish, minimalistic and wearable design and for prioritizing sustainability and quality.[4]

Twinpeaks.dk (winner of "best personal blog") opened in January 2014 and exists only in Danish, making it available mainly to a Scandinavian audience. It is written by Mette Marie Lei Lange, who is in her mid-thirties, lives in the Danish capital, Copenhagen, and used to work as a digital editor at the fashion magazine *ELLE*. Today, her primary occupation is the blog, which mixes topics such as fashion, everyday activities and family life (as she is a mother of small twins). According to her blog posts, she makes a living from her blog.

Nemesisbabe.dk (winner of "best female fashion blog", second year in a row) opened in 2010 and exists in identical Danish and English versions, making it available to an international audience. It is written by Marie My (Jensen), who is in her mid-twenties and originally lived in a larger Danish city (Aalborg) but today resides in Copenhagen. She explicitly frames her blogger identity as a fashionista with a colourful and striking style, combining vintage and street wear. Fashion blogging, including photographing and modelling for her blog, seems to be the focus of her professional and private self-performance on the blog while she, contrary to twinpeaks.dk, rarely touches upon her everyday life or social networks.

11.5 Findings

Based on the theoretical framework, including mediatization and the generic features of fashion blogs, the following presents a qualitative analysis of the two blogs (posts from spring/summer 2015 and spring 2016), focusing on the blogs' (1) content and purpose; (2) form, aesthetics and tone; (3) directionality and networks; and (4) commercial ties.

11.5.1 Content and Purpose: Fashion as Everyday Life and Personal Style

Twinpeaks.dk started out as a "mommy-blog" but gradually developed into a blog promoting a range of lifestyle- and consumer-related topics and products during the period from 2015–2016: fashion, beauty, parenting, relationships and cooking. Thus, fashion is intermeshed with a line of everyday activities forming the identity and life of the blogger. The blog also reports on events that the blogger has attended as a key figure or guest, and it displays the media coverage she has received on other blogs, in fashion magazines, and in tabloids. All of these features are a testament to her performance as a "micro-celebrity" (Marwick 2015). The main narrative is the blogger's personal life, thoughts and blogger life, and this narrative is linked to her patterns of consumption and how these patterns are part of her identity project and increasingly mediated persona with fashion being one constituent of many.

At nemesisbabe.dk, fashion plays a more central role since this blog includes photo reportages from the blogger's visits to designers or fashion capitals. These reportages stress vintage and street wear as her distinct feature. The blog also displays the blogger's favourite looks from the catwalks as well as her own "looks" and "wardrobe", including numerous photos of her wearing various outfits and photo collages of her private clothing. Thus, fashion is perceived primarily as an aesthetic form related to style, emphasizing that the blogger's particular (colourful, extraordinary) style provides her with a unique identity and makes her stand out as both blogger and fashionista.

In the words of Rettberg (2014), both blogs may be characterized as personal since they exemplify fashion as a mediated integral part of everyday life and thus signal that fashion communication and a personalized lifestyle are part of the bloggers' identity project. However, the two blogs target very different blog readers. Nemesisbabe.dk also includes feature elements from the topic-driven blog because of its intentionally informative and passionate preoccupation with fashion as an expression of art, design and distinct taste. However, as we will demonstrate later, the two blogs display different types of market logic, blurring the boundaries between the subjectively "authentic" personal blogger, the fashion-passionate topical blogger, and the blogger as brand endorser. This also entails a blurring between the role of blog readers as fashion-interested individuals and potential fashion consumers.

11.5.2 Aesthetics and Tone: Unpolished Glimpses of Everyday Life and Magazine Aesthetics

In view of the two bloggers' quite different approaches to fashion, the aesthetics and tone of the blogs differ considerably, including how text and visuals interplay.

Twinpeaks.dk is mainly a "verbal" blog since posts are often quite long, offering the blogger's point of view on the topic(s) of the day. Unsophisticated pictures of low photo quality typically illustrate the posts. Even though these visuals may appear staged (e.g. by illustrating the blogger posing at events or flashing consumer products or fashion items), they are primarily amateurish snapshots or selfies of her everyday life. The background is often the blogger's apartment, her office or a shop hosting a sponsored event rather than a staged and aesthetically refined setting. Thus, the visual aspect primarily serves to confirm the blogger's aim of communicating her private life and doings as authentically as possible. That is, she is depicting herself as a younger woman, a mother, a wife and a blogger, motivated by her personal interests and everyday life rather than by a professional passion for or knowledge of fashion, aesthetics or a distinct style. Accordingly, the verbal tone is immediate and "talkative"/chatty and includes swearing as well as spoken language rather than linguistic sophistication. This is a deliberate communicative approach because the blogger, in one of her posts, proclaims (our translation):

> I've been complimented at lot (and thank you so much for that!) on writing in a manner that makes you feel that I'm enjoying it. In fact, I've also been complimented for always writing in a personal style—also in my sponsored posts. And that really makes me proud and happy!! (Lange 2015a)

The aesthetics and tone of twinpeaks.dk are clearly unfiltered and authentic, reflecting the everyday excitements, passions and flaws of the blogger and her personal lifestyle. This tone confirms Colliander and Dahlén's (2011) argument that the mimicking of face-to-face interaction and performing as "fashionable friends" are important communication features of fashion blogs. The success of twinpeaks.dk in her para-social interaction is exemplified by a comment posted by one of her readers: "Am quite crazy about your blog and even though I do not know you, for 'real' (as my daughters would phrase it)—then I'm also quite crazy about you 😀". Another blog reader confirms, "My girls would say the same—for real!", to which twinpeaks.dk, unfiltered, replies: "Thank you so much, damn what a compliment—for real! 😀" (Lange 2015b).

This conversational tone also characterises the verbal approach of nemesisbabe.dk to some extent. However, although twinpeaks.dk's readers often respond, this kind of dialogue is more unusual at nemesisbabe.dk. The blogger rhetorically tries to initiate conversations by concluding blog posts with questions addressed to the blog readers, such as "Which photo is your favourite?" or "What spring trend is your favourite?". Her readers post few comments, however, and if they do respond, it is mostly very briefly. This lack of dialogue may be the result of nemesisbabe.dk's mode of communication, which imitates fashion magazines' one-way communication, and it places the blogger and her visual identity at the centre rather than inviting blog readers into her private sphere. As indicated, nemesisbabe.dk is mainly visually driven since most posts consist of colourful photographs accompanied by few comments. This visual style mimics fashion photography as presented in fashion magazines with models posing cool and distantly in front of the camera, expressing highly staged attitudes. The visual and aesthetic primacy of nemesisbabe.dk confirms the blogger's inclination to colour and aesthetic extraordinariness. By being the visual centre point in most blog posts, the blogger exploits fashion magazine logics, to promote not fashion but her own media persona as lead in her own fashion show.

11.5.3 Directionality and Networks

Twinpeaks.dk was originally part of the blog network and advertising community bloggers.delight but is, at the time of this analysis (spring 2016), hosted by stylista.dk, an online magazine on beauty, gossip, parenting, fashion, food and lifestyle targeted at younger women. Stylista.dk is owned by Benjamin Media, which is part of Bonnier Publications, one of the largest magazine publishers in the Nordic countries. Twinpeaks.dk is one of five blogs connected to this site. Nemesisbabe.dk was also part of the network bloggers.delight for a few years (2011–2014) but then became part of a small link community consisting of six fellow Danish bloggers. At the time of this analysis, it appears as an independent fashion and style blog. Both blogs signal that forming networks with other bloggers and profiting from each other's legitimacy, credibility and networks are an important part of the (professional) blogosphere. But the two blogs are involved in quite different types of network. Whereas twinpeaks.dk takes part in a commercialized but less distinctive online magazine universe, nemesisbabe.dk appears stylistically personalized and less streamlined commercially.

Furthermore, both blogs signal the bloggers' social media presence. Twinpeaks.dk has profiles on Facebook, Instagram and Bloglovin' that are all listed under "Contact", whereas nemesisbabe.dk has profiles on Instagram, Bloglovin', Pinterest, Twitter and Facebook, all of which are easily accessible almost anywhere on the blog. This confirms social network presence and availability to be an important constituent of the fashion blogosphere (Halvorsen et al. 2013). The importance of such peer-to-peer circuits distances fashion blogging from the more hierarchical one-way communication of the fashion magazine. Whereas the blog appears to be the centre of the social network manifestations at twinpeaks.dk, the Instagram profile seems to be of particular importance at nemesisbabe.dk since blog posts often make reference to visuals posted on Instagram. This again confirms the primacy of nemesisbabe.dk's visual identity as fashion blogger. Nemesisbabe.dk's social media omnipresence, however, somewhat contradicts the exclusiveness that the blog tries to convey through her very distinct style. At the same time, the blogger's consistent visual performance on the various platforms composes her "unique" social media persona.

11.5.4 Commercial Ties

Both blogs are engaged in various commercial ties or collaborations. Since the spring of 2015, twinpeaks.dk's commercial affiliations have developed considerably. The blog has evolved from a few blog posts a week, composed from the blogger's living room and without financial gain, to a more professional and commercial venture with office hours and sponsored content. After having become part of the digital universe at stylista.dk, twinpeaks.dk posts one or two posts almost every day, usually intertwined with sponsored posts (e.g. for rye bread, sweets or various fashion brands). Posts are surrounded by ads for consumer products (glasses, shoes) or online magazines owned by Benjamin Media. These commercial collaborations confirm that the blog addresses various (consumer) aspects of everyday life, including fashion. However, these conventional ads also confirm that aesthetic perfection is not centre priority since they visually disrupt the often more intimate snapshots and selfies of the blogger's everyday life. This commercialization of the blog exemplifies the paradox pointed to by Lowrey et al. (2011), namely that the commercial ties formalize and thereby challenge the authenticity and originality that, in the first place, made the blog successful.

Nemesisbabe.dk also has various commercial ties, implied by a "disclaimer" stating that "Ads and affiliate links are used on Nemesis, babe blog" on the front page. In this case, the commercial collaborations appear more in accordance with the aesthetic style of the blog. The blogger promotes various designers and brands by wearing their clothes in several photo series, and at the same time these brands help promote the blog by engaging in such collaborations. This co-promotion of blogger and fashion brands signals mutual recognition of style and an alignment between the blogger's aesthetic identity and that of the blog. Under the heading "Let's shop", the blog also has affiliate links to webshops, retailing products endorsed or wanted by the blogger in various blog posts (e.g. ASOS, an online retailer which the blogger also does photo shoots for). However, contrary to twinpeaks.dk, nemesisbabe.dk does not include advertising in the traditional sense. This may be because ads cannot be controlled and shaped by the blogger and therefore may disturb the aesthetic identity and visual project of the blog, which would prevent the mutual added value between brand and blogger. Instead, the blogger incorporates brands into her own aesthetic blog universe in aesthetically sophisticated photo series showing her as both model and photographer. This allows blogger and brand to merge rather than appear as preproduced advertisements.[5] Although commercial ties have long been an integral part of fashion magazine communication, these collaborations, on the fashion blog, are as much about promoting the bloggers as they are about promoting fashion.

The analysis thus suggests that nemesisbabe.dk is, to a larger extent, based on the logics of the fashion world and traditional fashion communication (modelling and display of clothing, colour, aesthetics and beauty in a stylized manner) but that twinpeaks.dk is, to a larger extent, based on the logics of consumer culture (i.e. communicating how various lifestyle-related products and the blogger's patterns of consumption are part of her everyday identity project). *At the same time*, the blogger is the main centre of attention in both cases because nemesisbabe.dk primarily displays fashion items on her blog to support the performance of her personal style and identity as fashionista. A main feature of both fashion blogs is the mediation of the bloggers' personae despite nemesisbabe.dk prioritizing the logics of fashion and twinpeaks.dk prioritizing the logics of everyday consumption. Thus, both sites communicate the bloggers as mediated personas rather than fashion as primary object, but they do this in very different ways.

11.6 Conclusion

This chapter has investigated the *fashion blog* as a distinct media genre in light of the changing interplay of fashion, media and market. Using mediatization theory, theories on blogs as a communicative genre and a case study of two Danish fashions blogs, the chapter has argued that, paradoxically, mediatization has rendered fashion omnipresent and less authoritative at one and the same time.

Although the logic of fashion is ubiquitous—everything may become fashion(able)—it is increasingly presented on the terms of the media: Fashion logics, such as fashion cycles and conceptions of exclusivity, no longer *dictate* media coverage of fashion; the traditional, hierarchical way of fashion communication has been challenged by digital communication, such as blogging, which influences and defines what fashion is from the consumers' viewpoint. Spurred by digital media logics, such as immediacy, interactivity, democratized access and distribution, digital media genres have challenged traditional mass media such as the fashion magazine as authoritative intermediaries of fashion; blogs are booming, making fashion communication available and feasible for everyone anytime. Thus, fashion blog communication is based on the logics of the blog with its call for communicative performance, placing the blogger at the centre while relocating fashion to a secondary position. As exemplified by the analysis of the two Danish fashion blogs, fashion and the blog intertwine in the identity project of the blogger, fashion blogs being as much about communicating and performing self and consumer lifestyle as about communicating fashion. Digital media intensify the amalgamation of fashion, identity, everyday life and consumer culture, thus reducing the institutional power of fashion in favour of media users' communicative activities concerning identity and lifestyle performance.

This is not to say that fashion is powerless; it is after all a global commercial driving force. But the case of fashion blogs exemplifies how the mediation of fashion has intensified with the emergence of digital media and how mediatization has forced fashion institutions and industrial markets to adjust to the logics of digital media. The reservation of front-row seats for individual bloggers at fashion shows emphasises that the fashion industry has realized that the future lies in personal communication. As Bradford points out, this involves recognizing that "people's personality, opinions and taste can draw a reader into their world, creating a committed and engaged audience who will trust what they say" (2015: 204). Thus, mediatization has made fashion omnipresent and marginalized at one and the same time: Although fashion is ubiquitous in the media, it is increasingly discussed and presented on the terms of the media rather than on the terms of fashion. Put differently, mediatization has facilitated the omnipresence of fashion so that fashion strategies and norms are taken into account in almost every possible aspect of everyday life. However, despite this ubiquity of the fashion logic, fashion is increasingly presented and discussed on the terms of the media rather than on the terms of institutionalized fashion. Digital media have made it clear that the media logic supports the fashion logic and vice versa but also that modern fashion would not exist without the media.

Notes

1. In view of the current media environment, there is obviously not one single media logic. Similar to the market logic, economic logic, or fashion logic, the logic of the media involves several underlying rules, norms, strategies and practices. Van Dijck and Poell, for example, speak of a "social media logic" that encompasses "the norms, strategies, mechanisms, and economies—underpinning its dynamics" (2013: 2), i.e. alluding to the particular affordances of social media.
2. Our translation (http://www.miinto.dk/modeblogprisen/vindere). Accessed: 26 April 2017.
3. Our translation (http://www.modeblogprisen2015.dk/om-mpb2015). Accessed: 26 April 2017.

4. See, for example, Russel (2015) and the Ministry of Foreign Affairs of Denmark (2015).
5. Examples are her collaborations with the hair product label Aussi and the candy brand Malaco (Jensen 2015a, b).

References

Benson, Rodney. 2006. News media as a "journalistic field": What Bourdieu adds to news institutionalism and vice versa. *Political Communication* 23: 187–202.

Bourdieu, Pierre. 1984. *Distinction. A social critique of the judgment of taste.* Cambridge: Harvard University Press.

Boyd, Danah. 2006. A blogger's blog: Exploring the definition of a medium. *Reconstruction* 6 (4).

Bradford, Julie. 2013. Fashion journalism. In *Specialist journalism*, ed. Barry Turner, and Richard Orange, 79–95. Oxon: Routledge.

Bradford, Julie. 2015. *Fashion journalism.* London: Routledge.

Colliander, Jonas, and Micael Dahlén. 2011. Following the fashionable friend: The power of social media. *Journal of Advertising Research* 51 (1): 313–321.

Davis, Fred. 1995. *Fashion, culture, and identity.* Chicago: University of Chicago Press.

Gough-Yates, Anna. 2003. *Understanding women's magazines: Publishing, markets and readerships.* London: Routledge.

Halvorsen, Katarina, Jonas Hoffmann, Ivan Coste-Manière, and Rasa Stankeviciute. 2013. Can fashion blogs function as a marketing tool to influence consumer behaviour? Evidence from Norway. *Journal of Global Fashion Marketing* 4 (3): 211–224.

Herring, Susan C., Lois A. Scheidt, Elijah Wright, and Sabrina Bonus. 2005. Weblogs as a bridging genre. *Information Technology & People* 18 (2): 142–171.

Hjarvard, Stig. 2013. *The mediatization of culture and society.* London: Routledge.

Horton, Donald, and R. Richard Wohl. 1956. Mass communication and para-social interaction: Observations on intimacy at a distance. *Psychiatry* 19: 215–229.

Jenkins, Henry. 2006. *Convergence culture, where old and new media collide.* New York: New York University Press.

Jensen, Marie M. 2015a. Aussify my body. *Nemesisbabe*, blog post, 12 February. http://nemesisbabe.dk/?s=Aussie&submit=Søg&lang=da. Accessed 26 Apr 2017.

Jensen, Marie M. 2015b. Nemesis, Babe X Malaco: Kreativitet, idéer og lakrids. *Nemesisbabe*, blog post, March 4. http://nemesisbabe.dk/?s=Malaco&submit=Søg&lang=da. Accessed 26 Apr 2017.

Kristensen, Nete N., and Unni From. 2015. From ivory tower to cross-media personas: The heterogeneous cultural critic in the media. *Journalism Practice* 9 (6): 853–871.

Lange, Mette M.L. 2015a. Mette Maries manifest: Lidt om blog, spons, forventninger og forandringer. *Twinpeaks*, blog post, 15 May. http://twinpeaks.dk/2015/05/mette-maries-manifest-lidt-om-blog-spons-forventninger-og-forandringer/. Accessed 26 Apr 2017.

Lange, Mette M.L. 2015b. Endelig er den her twinpeaks ordbogen. *Twinpeaks*, blog post, 10 August. http://twinpeaks.dk/2015/08/endelig-er-den-her-twinpeaks-ordbogen/. Accessed 26 Apr 2017.

Lewis, Tania. 2010. Branding, celebritization and the lifestyle expert. *Cultural Studies* 24 (4): 580–598.

Lomborg, Stine. 2009. Navigating the blogosphere: Towards a genre-based typology of weblogs. *First Monday* 14 (5).

Lowrey, Wilson, Scott Parrott, and Tom Meade. 2011. When blogs become organizations. *Journalism* 12 (3): 243–259.

Lundby, Knut. 2014. *Mediatization of communication: Handbooks of communication science*. Berlin: De Gruyter Mouton.

Marwick, Alice E. 2015. You may know me from Youtube: (Micro-) celebrity in social media. In *A companion to celebrity*, ed. P. David Marshall, and Sean Redmond, 333–350. Hoboken, NJ: Wiley.

McGaughey, Kerstin. 2010. Food in binary: Identity and interaction in two German food blogs. *Cultural Analysis* 9: 69–98.

Ministry of Foreign Affairs of Denmark. 2015. *Sector analysis: UK—An overview of the fashion industry*. Royal Danish Embassy, The Trade Council. http://storbritannien.um.dk/da/~/media/storbritannien/Documents/Trade%20Council/Sektorrapporter%202015/Fashion%20UK.pdf. Accessed 26 Apr 2017.

Moeran, Brian. 2006. More than just a fashion magazine. *Current Sociology* 54 (5): 725–744.

Pham, Minh-Ha T. 2011. Blog ambition: Fashion, feelings, and the political economy of the digital raced body. *Camera Obscura, Feminism, Culture, and Media Studies* 76 (26: 1): 1–37.

Rettberg, Jill W. 2014 [2008]. *Blogging*. Cambridge: Polity Press.

Rocamora, Agnès. 2011. Personal fashion blogs: Screens and mirrors in digital self-portraits. *Fashion Theory* 15 (1): 407–427.

Rocamora, Agnès. 2012. Hypertextuality and remediation in the fashion media. *Journalism Practice* 6 (1): 92–106.

Russel, Helen. 2015. Danish fashion takes centre stage—and with hardly a woolly jumper in sight. *The Guardian*, February 1 2015. www.theguardian.com. May 17 2016.

Schulz, Winfried. 2004. Reconstructing mediatization as an analytical concept. *European Journal of Communication* 19 (1): 87–101.

Technorati. 2014. *Digital influence report 2013.* http://technorati.com/report/2013-dir/. Accessed 26 Apr 2017.

Tomlinson, John. 2007. *The culture of speed.* London: Sage.

Turner, Bryan S. 1991. Recent developments in the theory of the body. In *The body: Social process and cultural theory*, ed. Mike Featherstone, Mike Hepworth, and Bryan S. Turner, 1–35. London: Sage.

van Dijck, José, and Thomas Poell. 2013. Understanding social media logic. *Media and Communication* 1 (1): 2–14.

Wilson, Elizabeth. 2005. *Adorned in dreams: Fashion and modernity.* London: I.B. Tauris.

Wright, Jeremy. 2006. *Blog marketing: The revolutionary new way to increase sales, build your brand, and get exceptional results.* New York, NY: McGraw-Hill.

CHAPTER 12

Musicalization and Mediatization

Tobias Pontara and Ulrik Volgsten

12.1 Introduction

According to media scholar Benjamin Krämer, "music is ubiquitous in today's media societies" (Krämer 2011: 471). Such statements have become something of a truism among contemporary music and media scholars. But implicit in Krämer's statement also lies a more substantive claim, namely that there is an undeniable connection between this abundance of music in modern society and the continuous emergence of new media and media technologies. Furthermore, Krämer notes that as a result of its mediatization the entire field of music has changed drastically during the twentieth century, giving priority to a diversity of genres as institutional determinants of music reception and consumption (Ibid.). Although this line of reasoning is cogent and convincing, it is somewhat limited in scope, dealing with the surface effects of a more far-reaching phenomenon that we propose to call ***musicalization***.

Musicalization must be distinguished from mediatization, although the two should be regarded as partly overlapping processes. Mediatization,

T. Pontara (✉)
University of Gothenburg, Gothenburg, Sweden
e-mail: tobias.pontara@gu.se

U. Volgsten
Örebro University, Örebro, Sweden

O. Driessens et al. (eds.), *Dynamics Of Mediatization*,
Transforming Communications – Studies in Cross-Media Research,
DOI 10.1007/978-3-319-62983-4_12

as we understand the concept, concerns primarily the transformation of communication and communicative action in its relation to media change. More broadly, mediatization can be described as "the process whereby communication refers to media and uses media so that the media *in the long run* increasingly become relevant for the social construction of everyday life, society and culture as a whole" (Krotz 2009: p. 24; emphasis added). Musicalization too should be understood as a long-term historical process, but one most palpably characterized by an ever-increasing presence of music in culture and everyday life. As such, musicalization is intimately connected with changing technological conditions and with transformations in how music is mediated and communicated as well as with broader socio-cultural processes at work in a given historical period. At its broadest, the concept of musicalization captures the gradually altered position of music in social life from unmediated forms of music making (i.e. singing and dancing) in pre-modern societies to the ubiquity of music of all kinds in today's digitalized and globalized world.[1]

More profound and wide-ranging effects of musicalization in the twentieth century concern emerging new ways in which people listened to and behaved towards music and, even more importantly, fundamental changes in how music was comprehended and conceptualized. However, those changes should not merely be understood as transformations in the reception and consumption of established and newly emerging musical genres (as per Krämer). Rather, they should be seen in a more radical way as influencing the practices of media producers as well as the habits and rituals of everyday life, in this way giving music an important role for how culture and everyday lifeis represented, communicated and made sense of in an increasingly mediatized society.

In this chapter, we will look more closely at some central aspects of musicalization and consider how processes of musicalization interact with processes of mediatization. The nature of the relation between the two—musicalization and mediatization—is a complex matter, and a basic question is indeed to what extent musicalization should be understood as a relatively autonomous phenomenon that exerts its own cultural agency within and with regard to processes of mediatization or whether it is better conceived of as conditional on and produced by such processes. The issue is further complicated by the fact that other factors of social and cultural change (institutional, economic, ideological, etc.) should be taken into consideration when searching for an explanation of the often very gradual alterations in the dissemination, conceptualization and possible influences of music on other cultural and social practices indicated by the concept of musicalization. Having said this, in the following, we will focus mainly on the relation between musicalization and mediatization. Furthermore, our discussion will predominantly concentrate on the twentieth century, which means that questions arising specifically in relation to recent developments in digital music media will be discussed more in passing. Our argument proceeds in two steps. We begin with a more thorough and systematic examination of what the concept of musicalization implies. We then proceed to discuss the relation between musicalization and what we see as the most salient aspects of mediatization.

12.2 The Concept of Musicalization

Music is everywhere, changing our lives with its sounds, one is tempted to say. But is this situation new, hasn't music always been around? Yes and no. In the Western world, a process of musicalization begins already in the renaissance (during a second period of mediatization that Johan Fornäs (2014: p. 492) calls "Print mediatization"), as a result of the burgeoning music print. Around the year 1500, the Venetian printer Ottaviano Petrucci published the first of three commercial volumes of chamber music that was not intended for playing or performance but rather for study by a wider circle of readers than that of the professional musician (Bernstein 2001; Volgsten 2012). Of course, Petrucci is not alone in this regard, and the technology of music print develops and goes through several phases during the following centuries. Another important step in this process of musicalization occurs as a result of the daily press and its regular music criticism, which diffuses music in terms of a public discourse for the educated man to take account of (Habermas 1962; Volgsten 2015a; Widestedt 2001). Through the phonogram, the dissolution of music's traditional social functions, initiated by the process of its commercialization two centuries earlier (public concerts, etc.), is taken to an extreme as music becomes a commodity to be consumed by the individual listener at will in the kitchens and living rooms of the twentieth century (Volgsten 2015b; Volgsten, forthcoming) and, as the century draws to its close, on the move through mobile devices such as the Walkman.[2]

From this historical snapshot, it is clear that musicalization is about a lot more than a mere increase in the amount of music available and listened to in modern society. In this section, we would like to attract attention to what we see as two central aspects of musicalization in the twentieth century. The first concerns what one may call the discursive aspect of musicalization. By this we mean the ubiquity of media representations and mediated cultural discourses on music and music-related matters in modern society. As will become clear below, thinking of such representations and discourses as an aspect of musicalization requires that we entertain a broader understanding of what music is than has traditionally been the case in the academy. The second concerns an increasing influence of what could best be described as a kind of "musical dramaturgy" on other areas of culture and on everyday life. Musicalization in this sense can be understood as a continuous *soundtracking of culture and everyday life*, a process that is inextricably linked to music's increasing presence in different kinds of mediatized narratives (fictional as well as non-fictional) during the course of the twentieth century. This is a process in which the everyday social world becomes ever more structured and organized in accordance with a musically mediated awareness, a mode of perception that may at least partly be traced back to the way background music structures the awareness and assessment of the fictional worlds encountered in film. We will now discuss the two aspects of musicalization in turn.

12.3 Musicalization and Discourse

The discursive aspect of musicalization pertains to the ways in which conceptions of and practices related to music are affected by an intensification of music's visibility, discursivity and mediatic presence in society over time. Since the advent of broadcast technology and the emergence of mass media at the beginning of the twentieth century, music has become increasingly intersected by a steadily multiplying number of discursive practices. With every playing of a piece of music, whether in "old" or in "new" media and regardless of musical genre, comes a deluge of commentaries, personal reflections, reviews, opinions, descriptions, analyses, interpretations, explanations, contextualizations and more or less metaphorical characterizations. We have already mentioned the music criticism of the early daily press as a means by which music loses its ties from preestablished social functions. Criticism is also a good example of the *discursivation* described here.[3] Foreshadowed by music theory since antiquity, music criticism marks the change from scholarly to public discourse in a process that continues through the twentieth century, with a proliferation of music magazines directed towards different audience groups and subcultures, including radio and television hosts introducing and commenting on the music played, reaching its most recent manifestation when digital streaming services tend to link up with the personal commentaries of Facebook and its likes (cf. Kaun and Fast 2014: pp. 26–28).

Likewise—and also part of what we mean by discursivation—in visually based media such as film, TV and the Internet, music is always accompanied by photographic images, paintings or other visual imaginings and, of course, by moving images. Although music has always been a visual spectacle (even so-called "absolute music" always reached its listener in a combination of aural and visual modes, as exemplified by the visual appearances of star conductors and soloists on stage and pictured on album covers), this aspect was accentuated in music drama, opera and the musical, continuing with music video and YouTube. Examples of both discursivation and what might be called visualization could be endlessly multiplied. Thus, it is not only "the music itself" (however one is supposed to understand this phrase) that becomes ever more present in people's lives through the continuous development of new technologies and media, but also the verbal and visual determinations of it.

It is close at hand to regard this latter aspect as an example of the mediatization of music (cf. Krämer op cit. p. 473). However, such a conclusion would follow only if a clear-cut distinction could be drawn between discourses about music and "the music itself". We believe that such a distinction cannot be so easily drawn. Instead, we view the connection between "the music itself"—which for present purposes may be roughly defined as any sequence of organized sound that is culturally acknowledged as music (such as when one identifies a piece of music as "this" tune or "that" song[4])—and the discourses about it as a mutually constitutive relationship through which music understood as a wider and more encompassing phenomenon emerges. Strictly speaking, there is no such thing as "the music itself"; representing music (verbally, visually, etc.) and thinking about music are to be already involved in the cultural construction of what music means and what it is (cf. Pontara 2007, 2008). As musicologist Nicholas Cook has put it, "music is never alone" (Cook 1998: p. 23), which is to say that a construct like "the music itself" is always surrounded and permeated by talk, images, visualizations, reveries and ideas about its significance, ontology and structure.

It is through these discursive and signifying practices that listeners are able to conceptualize music, any music, and become aware of its existence and, consequently, it is through these practices that music is constituted as what it is (cf. Pontara 2015; Volgsten 2006, 2012). When listening to, experiencing, studying, talking about, moving to and performing music—all of these activities that Christopher Small would term "musicking" (Small 1998)—one is always at the same time entertaining the culturally constituted discursive and representational resources and practices surrounding, permeating and constituting it.

The historical process through which discourses and representations of music become progressively more present in and dependent on different kinds of media could certainly be described as an increasing mediatization of music. But since on our view discursive and representational practices must be part of any convincing account of what music is, such a mediatization of music could with equal plausibility be theorized as a musicalization of culture and society. As we will argue below it is through the continuous development of new technologies and media—gramophone, tape recorder, radio, LPs and CDs (and the liner notes and front covers accompanying these), television, film, and the Internet, etc.—that this kind of musicalization is made possible. Processes of mediatization can therefore be regarded as important preconditions for the wide dissemination of music (understood in the broadest sense as comprising both sonic and discursive dimensions) throughout modern society. Musicalization is here equivalent, then, to an ever-increasing presence of music in society in terms of both its sounding aspects and the formative discourses through which it is made intelligible.

12.4 Musicalization and Dramaturgy

The concept of musicalization should however not be restricted to cover only the increasing ubiquity of music in the modern world, not even when music is understood in the "wide" discursive sense described above. Beyond this, the concept also points to the ways in which music becomes an important resource for how media texts and cultural messages are constituted. Musicalization is a process that affects other social practices and institutions as well as it influences the perception and experience of the everyday world and how one partakes in the construction of that world.

The extensive use of (sounding) music in different kinds of media and media texts is one of the clearest examples of this aspect of musicalization. By permeating and underscoring everything from fiction films to computer games, documentaries, news broadcasts, children's programs, televised sport events, on-screen political speeches, Internet home pages, advertisements, and nature-and wildlife films, music becomes progressively more important for the ways representations of the social and natural environment are constructed. Correspondingly, when following the news, watching a film, playing a computer game, seeing a clip on YouTube, dining at a restaurant, being put on hold in a telephone queue, travelling to school, working with the music from mobile devices flowing through the headphones, or buying food at the local supermarket, one is constantly drawn into a musicalized reality, a reality in which music not only is included as a natural component but also participates in structuring and organizing perceptions, experiences and expectations.

Without forgetting its renaissance and enlightenment precursors, the historical preconditions for this increasingly musicalized society should be sought primarily in the twentieth century. Music's increasing presence and importance in sound film and other media during the last century involved a gradual accustomization to musicalized realities and to different musical dramaturgies whose job it was to administer and organize emotions and attitudes towards the represented worlds (fictional or not) that they dramatized. In many media and mediatized contexts, such dramaturgies have become so naturalized that they are simply taken for granted; often, music is just "sawing away in the backfield of consciousness" (Gorbman 1987: p. 1; cf. Kassabian 2013) and precisely for this reason becomes all the more effective in steering perceptions and emotions in ways that affect beliefs of what is going on as well as for how one relates to and judges the people, things and events that are encountered in such contexts.

Many of the examples given above concern audio-visually mediated narratives and fictional worlds. However, some of these examples suggest that elements of musical dramatization and dramaturgy have increasingly come to penetrate everyday life on a broader supra-fictional level (cf. Bossius and Lilliestam 2011). For example, a common phenomenon today is what may be called "emotional painting": one "paints" the world and regulates one's affective relation towards it in accordance with the emotional and expressive logic of the music that one has, for each particular occasion, decided should fill one's auditory and perceptual space (cf. Sloboda et al. 2009). Such use of music, to aesthetically elevate the mundane everyday world, is arguably closely connected to the possibility of self-determined access to personal audio media during formative years of youth and early adulthood, which suggests that to some extent it must be regarded as generation-specific. In any case, this kind of "real-world" dramatization (cf. DeNora 2000; Weber 2009; Bull 2009) is not essentially different from the way music dramatizes and underscores a news report, a sequence from a gameplay or a scene in a feature film. On the contrary, it should be seen as partly *derived* from and basically dependent on the established function and significance of music in such multi-media contexts.

So far, we have discussed the phenomenon of musical dramatization on a general level. But an adequate understanding of how musical dramatization works requires reference to the notion of a *specific* musical dramaturgy. This is so because different musical dramaturgies may have different consequences for how culture and everyday life is represented. A good example of a more specific musical dramaturgy is Western tonal music. As many musicologists have noted, Western tonal music has a teleological syntax that makes it a highly effective means to unify and dramatize almost every possible situation and course of action.[5] In Susan McClary's words, "tonality itself—with its process of instilling expectations and subsequently withholding promised fulfilment until climax—is the principal musical means during the period from 1600 to 1900 for arousing and channelling desire…" (McClary 1991: p. 13; see also Tagg 1979, 2013: p. 305). And in the twentieth century, tonal music has been the dominating musical form in visually based media such as the feature film and the television. The syntax of tonal music has a strong tendency to endow the narratives and representations it underscores with a sense of finality and inevitability, making it an unsurpassed means through which such narratives can be elevated to the transparent realms of legend and myth, uncontaminated by the complexities of society and everyday life (cf. Brown 1994).

Furthermore, with an intensified mediatization of music the forms and elements of tonal music have accrued a high degree of cultural coding that greatly aids the transmission of non-verbal but nevertheless very determinate meanings in almost all media contexts. Thus, with regard to most visual media, and to visually based spectacle more generally, tonal music helps to "ward off the displeasure of the image's potential ambiguity" in that it "anchors the image in meaning, throws a net around the floating visual signifier, assures the viewer a safely channelled signified" (Gorbman 1987: p. 58). Of course, this semiotic dimension—this sedimentation of musical meaning—is not an exclusive feature of tonal music but should, in addition to syntax, be seen as a constitutive part of any musical dramaturgy. (We will return to the constitution of specific musical dramaturgies below.)

Music's dramaturgical potential has become one of the main resources by which emotional realities are regulated and relationships to other people are structured and for how these realities and relationships are narrated and staged. In this regard, music can be seen as a constitutive element of many persons' individual identities, thereby affecting social interaction on a micro level (cf. DeNora 2000; Frith 1996; Larson 1995; McRobbie and Garber 1976; Bull 2000; DeBoise 2015). Not only is music available to almost everyone, everywhere, anytime, but owing to the abundance of its defining discourses, music's significance and value become very much a personal matter, affecting even the individual identity formation of many listeners (cf. Volgsten 2014; Volgsten and Pripp 2016). This change in how music is both discursively communicated and used as positional marker in communicative interaction thus indicates how the dramaturgical and the discursive aspects of musicalization are intertwined.

We have now discerned three aspects or dimensions of musicalization in modern society: (1) the dissemination and ubiquity of music as a sounding phenomenon (what we initially referred to as an ever-increasing presence of music in culture and everyday life), (2) the dissemination and ubiquity of discourses about music, and (3) the influence of music and "musical dramaturgy" on other parts of culture and society and on everyday life. The question before us now is how such processes of musicalization relate to processes of mediatization.

12.5 The Relation Between Musicalization and Mediatization

According to Krämer, the mediatization of music "can … be described as a transformation or innovation of institutions" resulting from and in response to changes in "modern technical media", which ultimately affect individual "reception" and "consumption" (Krämer 2011: pp. 473–483). Taking an institutional perspective on mediatization, as does Krämer, may have several advantages. Stig Hjarvard notably proposes an institutional perspective since, as he says, it makes it possible to "steer free of … overgeneralization as well as under-theorization" (Hjarvard 2013: p. 4). Whereas universal claims are too encompassing to say anything of relevance in particular cases, Hjarvard says, "the endless minor variations of situated interaction" easily become the trees that detract our view of the forest. The middle-range theory that Hjarvard accordingly proposes has consequences not only for the actorial-structural range (the institutional meso level) but also for the temporal range of the research: "mediatization only became prominent … when the media have both become more differentiated from other institutions … and re-embedded into culture and society" (Hjarvard 2013: p. 7). Thus, Hjarvard limits his focus to the historical period of high modernity, more specifically from the 1980s onwards (Hjarvard 2013: p. 26).

A different approach is taken by Friedrich Krotz and Andreas Hepp, according to whom "we can identify an ongoing long-term process of media development as a part of the whole social and cultural history of human existence." Mediatization is thus seen as "a long-term metaprocess of changing forms of communicative action, as communication in the course of mediatization relies more and more on media" (Krotz and Hepp 2011; p. 138, italics omitted). Although spanning over far longer time-spans than do Hjarvard or Krämer in their respective focus on the meso level of institutions, Krotz and Hepp do not advocate any traditional historical or evolutionary stance. Instead, "metaprocess" should be seen as a conceptual construct, grasped by corresponding "metatheories," "by which science as well as persons in their everyday life sum up certain developments, their causes, forms of expression and consequences and therewith make the world manageable" (Krotz 2007, quoted in Hepp 2012: p. 9). In contrast to scientific theories of temporally more limited domains, metatheories are generalizing, narrative-like and not empirically testable or provable in their entirety. Rather, a metatheory may serve as "a general theoretical pattern of reference for concrete empirical research," encompassing several more demarcated scientific theories (Hepp 2012: p. 10). The metaprocess described by a metatheory is thus not a simple macro phenomenon, but in its nesting of processes on different scientific as well as cultural levels it also involves processes at the micro level. Thus, as Hepp concludes, "it makes no sense to describe the specifics that a certain medium might have 'on its own' […]. We have to analyze the molding forces of the media always in their netting with human action, especially (but not exclusively) with communicative action" (Hepp 2012: p. 18).

This brief overview goes to indicate that mediatization theory and research embrace the whole gamut of micro, meso, and macro levels of social interaction (e.g. communicative action, groups, organizations, institutions, cultures and societies). Equally interesting is that the corresponding array of cultural norms (e.g. language, genres, media logics, dispositives, laws and regulations) do not apply on a one to one scale vis-à-vis the different levels of interaction. Rather, what Hepp (2009, 2010) describes as the "quantitative" aspects of mediatized change of any level of interaction may affect those on any level of norms, effecting a "qualitative" change of "how media structure the way we communicate" (Hepp 2009) and *vice versa*. Indeed, it is a process of mutual impact, and a similar network of simultaneous top-down and bottom-up connectivity could be seen in the case of musicalization. Depending on the particular aspects of focus, and without making any deterministic suppositions, we therefore suggest that musicalization can be regarded as (a) quantitatively *conditioned by*, (b) a qualitative *part of*, and (c) a *relatively autonomous phenomenon* in relation to, mediatization. Although these are aspects of a complex whole, they need to be analytically separated in order to be understood more fully.

12.6 Musicalization as Conditioned by Mediatization

Important quantitative conditions for musicalization, both in its sounding and its discursive dimensions, are the temporal, spatial and social aspects of mediatization (cf. Hepp 2009, 2012). For instance, with the advent of the phonogram, the radio, and early home recording devices in the twentieth century and, as we proceed beyond the millennium shift, streaming services over the Internet, music becomes *temporally* available to an extent previously unheard of, literally at all times of the day. In addition, allowing for a *spatial* diffusion of music, portable travel gramophones became available already from the mid-1920s, followed by transistor radios in the 1950s, the Walkman in the 1980s and mp3-players in the 2000s (Björnberg 2012; Weber 2009; Bull 2000, 2007). Finally, from a *social* point of view, it is obvious that these temporal and spatial aspects correspond to an increasing number of situations amenable for music consumption as well as music becoming available to all strata of the population in some way or another.

How the temporal, spatial and the social may intersect is shown in an on-going research project focusing on the latter part of the period that Fornäs characterizes by its 'audiovisual mediatization' and that precedes the present digital era (approximately 1900–1970).[6] This period witnesses the advent of the gramophone, the radio, and early home recording devices. However, the instant availability of music presupposes both public and private spatial locations for listening to recorded music, provided by public spaces such as bars and diners, as well as the transformation of the nineteenth-century bourgeois salon into the twentieth-century living room (Volgsten, forthcoming). In contrast, we can think of the domestic hobby room lodging home recording on magnetic tape recorders after World War II (Burlin, forthcoming). From a social point of view, these processes become naturalized and disciplined through media such as sound film, visually portraying the presence and use of music reproduction devices (Pontara, forthcoming), and the many journals and magazines discussing and ordaining correct modes and procedures of media use (Björnberg 2009; Björnberg, forthcoming).

Although these examples betray more complex relations between musicalization and mediatization, the point to be made here is that the increase in music's spatial, temporal and social presence to some extent can be regarded as conditioned by processes of mediatization.

12.7 Musicalization as a Part of Mediatization

As described above, many changes and transformations in the media landscape can be regarded as quantitative preconditions for musicalization. But there are also significant qualitative aspects that warrant the description of musicalization as being a substantial *part of* mediatization.

On a straightforward level, musicalization can be understood as being part of mediatization in the rather obvious and unqualified sense that a certain aspect of musicalization corresponds to certain aspects of mediatization, namely those discourses (and discursive changes) that are concerned with music. Although we have argued that such processes can plausibly be regarded as instances of musicalization, musicalization and the mediatization of music can here admittedly be explained as two sides of the same coin. In addition to this, music as a discursive phenomenon can be regarded as a more qualitative force within mediatization by the way it actively impacts and changes practices and institutions related to music *through* processes of mediatization. As a discursive phenomenon, music intersects and "cooperates" with processes of mediatization in ways that work to transform such practices and institutions over time, as indicated by music's role in individual and collective identity production and its consequences for communicative interaction (Volgsten 2014; Volgsten and Pripp 2016).

The partaking in processes of mediatization by musicalization is perhaps more obvious when it comes to the dramaturgical aspect. Music is an important element of many media forms and messages and a particular musical syntax often influences the way communication is moulded (to speak with Hepp) via different media. A case in point is the way the importance and newsworthiness of almost all televised news broadcasts in Western society are signalled by introducing them with the help of more or less dramatic nonverbal (and mostly tonal) musical cues and logotypes. On a broader and more long-term level music has been an integral part of mediatization since the advent of the radio and it has played a major role for how audio-visual media such as the fiction film, the television and, later, streaming sites like YouTube have developed. In its dramaturgical aspect, musicalization has thus arguably been an important component in the mediatization of certain areas of culture and society and also in the formation of different kinds of more specific "media logics." In light of this, the role played by musicalization in processes of mediatization is conspicuously undertheorized in contemporary mediatization theory, calling for further discussion of certain basic elements and preconditions of musicalization that can be regarded as enjoying some measure of independence with regard to processes of mediatization. This will clarify further how musicalization can function as an active participant within media related social and cultural transformations over time.

12.8 Musicalization as a Relatively Autonomous Agent in Media-Related Processes of Social and Cultural Change

Given that mediatization mainly concerns the transformation of communication and communicative action in its relation to media change, and more broadly the role played by the media in social and cultural change over time, it is important to consider how musicalization can influence or have an effect on processes of mediatization, i.e. how musicalization can function as a relatively autonomous agent in relation to such processes. In other words, if musicalization is to be theorized as an active participant in media related transformations of culture and everyday life, it must be accredited some measure of independence from other determinants of social and cultural change. Consequently, we will in this last section consider some basic elements of musicalization related to the aspect of musical dramaturgy—elements, we argue, that either cannot be regarded as obviously conditional on processes of mediatization (or any other social and cultural developments) or else may be so entrenched in social and cultural practices so as to acquire a sufficiently independent cultural agency to participate as active determinants in processes of social and cultural change. Thus, the wider purpose of these considerations is to work towards a closer determination of the concept of musical dramaturgy in order to illustrate how this aspect of musicalization may interact with processes of mediatization.

At first, we would like to bring up recent research on so called "communicative musicality" (Malloch and Trevarthen 2009), showing how music is a pre-verbal communicative capacity available already at infancy, but also how communicative interaction in its most elementary phases builds on the affective impact of "protomusical" qualities such as variations in rhythm, timing, intensity, prosody, etc. (Volgsten 2012). These qualities are perceived as affective contours and serve as bodily foundations for the detection of personal styles of behaviour (Stern 1985: 159), enabling not only small-group genres of communicative interaction (cf. Bachtin 1997: p. 203; Bakhtin 1981) but also the emergence of the very "senses of self" (Stern op cit. passim; Guattari 1995: p. 6) that subsequently may invoke culture-specific styles and genres of music for its identity formation.

Thus, even if music theory and analysis has followed in the footsteps of grammar and linguistics, as cultural phenomena music and verbal interaction are likely to share common social roots, the one influencing the other in a mutual fashion. In its pre-verbal, non-discursive capacity music (or rather "proto music," which should not be confused with a "music in itself") is almost exclusively an affective, bodily phenomenon that affords various (culture specific) discursive and syntactic articulations (Volgsten 2014; Volgsten and Pripp 2016). As such it points out one dimension of musicalization that can be seen as relatively unaffected by media related social and cultural changes, namely the more or less immediate affective impact of musical and protomusical qualities. We may here justifiably speak of a dimension of musicalization since this affective impact must be regarded as a constitutive element of, and at the same time a precondition for, *any* form of musical dramaturgy. Thus, to the extent that processes of musical dramaturgy interact with and have the power to influence "the various ways in which media shape social and cultural transformations" (Ekström et al. 2016: p. 5) such processes will essentially rely on the impact of musical and protomusical affective qualities.

However, at this point, someone might still feel that the concept of musical dramaturgy is too vague to function in a convincing account of how processes of musicalization can influence and partake in media related social and cultural transformations. One way to further clarify what we mean by musical dramaturgy is to distinguish it from the musical syntax that serves as a nexus between the affective and connotative aspects of music. A specific musical dramaturgy should not be equated with the musical syntax on which it relies. Rather, a certain musical syntax, or kind of syntax, should be understood as a necessary, but not sufficient, condition for the musical dramaturgy it supports and enables. To clarify this point, we may pick up on the claim, already indicated above, that a musical dramaturgy not only comprises affective and syntactic qualities but also involves a semiotic dimension, a dimension grounded in long-standing signifying practices which affect a more or less explicit cultural coding of musical works, gestures and styles (cf. Taruskin 2013; see also Pontara 2015: pp. 13–14). This semiotic dimension is however underdetermined by the constituting syntax of any musical dramaturgy, which is to say that a particular musical syntax is compatible with a variety of semiotic possibilities. An obvious example of this is the very different meanings that the same musical passage or piece can take on in different cinematic contexts.

Given that a central part of what a specific musical dramaturgy consists in can be captured by identifying the musical syntax on which it relies, this element of musical dramaturgy too can be understood as enjoying a relative autonomy from mediatization and other cultural processes. To illustrate this let us again take tonal music as an example (or more specifically what musicologists call "common practice tonality"). The syntax of this music is basically constituted by how certain pitches and chords relate to one another within a specified and hierarchical musical system, most fundamentally by how a relation of tension and release is built up around the so-called dominant and tonic sonorities in a particular musical piece or sequence and how this tension is elaborated upon through techniques of modulation and prolongation. While the historical development of this syntax must at some level be explained with reference to broader social and cultural transformations (including media related transformations), this development can also to some extent be accounted for in terms of how musicians and composers have responded to and worked to transform specific characteristics of earlier musical systems and syntaxes, which means that the evolution of the syntax of common-practice tonality must be regarded as a relatively autonomous process.[7]

We are now in a position to give a more qualified description of the concept of musical dramaturgy and thereby to indicate some of the ways in which processes of musicalization may partake in media-related social and cultural change. A specific musical dramaturgy is constituted by three distinct yet closely interconnected elements: (1) the affective impact of the musical and protomusical qualities, (2) the specific musical syntax it embodies, and (3) the semiotic properties that accrue to it through long-standing signifying practices and conventions. We suggest that when such musical dramaturgies become sufficiently entrenched in our social and cultural practices they to some extent acquire the status of cultural agents in their own right in that they may exert their own influence on the complex long-term processes of media-related social and cultural change connoted by the concept of mediatization.

To illustrate this thought let us return one last time to the dramaturgy of tonal music. The basic teleological syntax, the affective qualities and the semiotic properties of tonal music have been co-constitutive in how certain practices and parts of modern everyday life have successively transformed in the presence of shifting media and media technologies in that this musical dramaturgy has increasingly and variously come to penetrate our everyday environments (our homes, our study- and workplaces, our urban surroundings, etc.), and by doing so has participated in reshaping our experiences of those environments. For instance, the teenage room as a site of mediatization involves a steadily growing number of media devices as well as a plurality of uses, activities and communicative practices afforded by such devices. In this increasingly mediatized environment, the dramaturgy of tonal music (in the form of Jazz, pop, Rock, hip-hop, etc.) has arguably played a central role by providing the emotional and semiotic resources through which young people have regulated and constructed their subjectivities, which in turn has led to changes in how they demarcate the limits of their personal and private spaces as well as how they negotiate their relations to parents and peers. Thus, the mediatization of the teenage-room, as it has developed in the West and in Westernized countries, is inconceivable without this particular musical dramaturgy.

Or to give a final, more generalized example: by helping to mould our perception of everything from political campaigns to major sport events, the dramaturgy of tonal music has played a significant role for how we interpret, decipher and make sense of certain parts of our social reality. More specifically, by entering as a constitutive element in the *mediatization* of such phenomena music, and tonal music in particular, has been an active participant in how certain areas of social reality have been represented, constructed and renegotiated by media-related communicative practices over time.

12.9 Conclusion

The relation between musicalization and mediatization is a complex one. Partly depending on which aspects of musicalization that are emphasized, musicalization can be seen as a *product* of mediatization, as an agent of social and cultural change working *within* processes of mediatization or as a phenomenon that enjoys a degree of relative autonomy with regard to such processes. Thus, the relation between the two is intricate because musicalization is itself a complex process involving several aspects. In this essay, we have highlighted three such aspects: the increasing ubiquity of music as a sounding phenomenon in modern society, the increasing ubiquity of music understood in a wider sense as also encompassing a discursive dimension, and the ways music impacts on other areas of culture and society (including processes of mediatization) through its musical dramaturgy.

This is not to say that the concept of musicalization cannot be extended to include other aspects as well. For example, we may regard the emergence of new subjectivities through the creation and dissemination of novel musical genres, instruments, technical innovations, sound worlds etc. as an integral part of processes of musicalization. Such subjectivities may be bodily enacted (i.e. through dancing or playing) in ways that engender changes in existing social and cultural practices and that may have an impact on the way we communicate as well. At the risk of over-generalizing, one important element of much popular music since the 1950s and onwards—whether at live concerts, in discotheques and clubs, or at get-togethers like rave-parties or silent dance gatherings (where each participant wears her own headphones and decides which music to listen to)—has been to create a kind of sonorous envelope for the bodily active listener through a combination of steady pulses, fixed rhythmic patterns, melodic loops and, not least, often extremely high sound volume, thereby making possible a musicalization of public spaces and an expansion of interior life that work to subjectivize such spaces and transform them into arenas of personal experience. That such developments have affected behavioural and communicative practices should be obvious, not least through the way they have often prompted a decrease in face-to-face verbal communication and instead encouraged the development other forms of bodily and gestural communication.

The relation between different aspects of musicalization and broader media-related social and cultural transformations is a challenging and important subject that should be further explored by media scholars, music sociologists and musicologists interested in music's role and function in society and everyday life. Perhaps the most pressing questions here lie in an area that this chapter has addressed only in passing, namely the relation between musicalization and processes of mediatization in our present digital era.

Notes

1. The term 'musicalization' has been used in a variety of scholarly contexts. For instance, there has been research on the musicalization of visual arts (Hennion 2008), the musicalization of theatre (Roesner 2008) and the musicalization of literary fiction (Wolf 1999). This research is not directly relevant for the understanding of musicalization that we develop in the following. However, the musicalization of particular artistic fields could perhaps be seen as instances of the broader processes of musicalization explored in our essay.
2. Thus understood, musicalization can be seen as inextricably bound up with what Kurt Blaukopf described as the mediamorphosis of music and musical culture, by which the emergence of print, electronic and digital media in turn have effected radical changes in the production, dissemination and consumption of music (Blaukopf 1989, 2012; see also Katz 2010).
3. Here we follow the terminological use of e.g. Wolf (1999, passim).
4. Needless to say, we do not propose this as a real definition of music; that is, as a set of necessary and sufficient conditions that would determine what music essentially is. It is rather the way that, we would claim, many people tend to think about and identify music.
5. The concept of tonal music, or tonality, has been widely discussed throughout the history of musical scholarship. Following Arnold Whittall, one may say that what all systems of tonality have in common is "the idea that music progresses away from and towards fundamental pitches, which control the relative importance of all the sounds used within a [musical] work" (Whittall 2006).
6. This project (*Everyday Devices. Mediatisation, Disciplining And Localisation Of Music In Sweden 1900–1970*, funded by the Swedish Research Council) aims to show how sound-reproduction technology interacted with and transformed practices and ideas related to music, sound and listening during a period of increasing mediatization, by asking

how the perception and apprehension of music and sound have affected and been affected by processes of mediatisation, including changes in the social and spatiotemporal organisation of listening.

7. Not everyone would agree: that the historical evolution of Western tonality should be explained primarily with reference to its own internal logics and to the specific influences that earlier composers working within the system of tonality have had on later ones is a notion that has been repeatedly rejected by contemporary musicologists and music historians (see, for example, Susan McClary 1987). In any case, the relative autonomy of common-practice tonality with regard to broader social and cultural processes argued for here can perhaps be seen as a more specific variant of the relative autonomy accredited to "superstrucural" phenomena such as law, politics and ideology in relation to an allegedly economic base that one finds in the thinking of Louis Althusser and other Marxist theorists following his lead (see Althusser 1969).

References

Althusser, L. 1969. Contradiction and overdetermination. In *For Marx*, 87–128. New York: Random House.

Bachtin, M. 1997. Frågan om talgenrer. In *Genreteori*, ed. E.H. Aurelius, and T. Götselius, 203–239. Lund: Studentlitteratur.

Bakhtin, M. 1981. *Discourse in the novel: The dialogic imagination*. Austin and London: University of Texas Press.

Bernstein, J. 2001. *Print culture and music in sixteenth-century Venice*. Oxford: Oxford University Press.

Björnberg, A. 2009. Learning to listen to perfect sound: Hi-fi culture and changes in modes of listening, 1950–1980. In *The Ashgate research companion to popular musicology*, ed. D.B. Scott, 105–129. Farnham: Ashgate.

Björnberg, A. 2012. Moderna människor med mobil musik: Om rörligt musiklyssnande före transistoreringen. In *Senmoderna reflexioner: Festskrift till Johan Fornäs*, ed. E. Bjurström, M. Fredriksson, U. Olsson, and A. Werner, 125–136. Linköping: Linköping University Electronic Press.

Björnberg, A. Forthcoming. What do I listen to when I listen to my gramophone? The development of the genre system of early phonography.

Blaukopf, K. 1989. Westernisation, modernisation, and the mediamorphosis of music. *International Review of the Aesthetics and Sociology of Music* 20 (2): 183–192.

Blaukopf, K. 2012. *Kurt Blaukopf on music sociology: An anthology*. Frankfurt am Main: Peter Lang.

Bossius, T., and Lilliestam L. 2011. *Musiken och jag: Rapport från forskningsprojektet Musik i människors liv*. Göteborg: Ejeby.

Brown, R. S. 1994. *Overtones and undertones: Reading film music*. Berkeley: University of California Press.
Bull, M. 2000. *Sounding out the city: Personal stereos and the management of everyday life*. Oxford: Berg.
Bull, M. 2007. *Sound moves: iPod culture and urban experience*. London: Routledge.
Bull, M. 2009. The auditory nostalgia of iPod culture. In *Sound souvenirs: Audio technologies, memory and cultural practices*, ed. K. Bijsterveld, and J. van Dijck, 83–93. Amsterdam: Amsterdam University Press.
Burlin, T. Forthcoming. Sound and Songs from the Amateur Super Sonic Scientist(s): The Tape Recorder and Home Tape Recording Culture in Sweden 1950–1970.
Cook, N. 1998. *Analysing musical multimedia*. Oxford: Clarendon Press.
de Boise, S. 2015. *Men, masculinity, music and emotions*. Houndmills: Palgrave Macmillan.
DeNora, T. 2000. *Music in everyday life*. Cambridge: Cambridge University Press.
Ekström, M., et al. 2016. Three tasks for mediatisation research: Contributions to an open agenda. *Media, Culture and Society* 38 (7): 1–19.
Fornäs, J. 2014. Mediatization of popular culture. In *Mediatization of communication*, ed. K. Lundby, 483–504. Berlin: De Gruyter.
Frith, S. 1996. *Performing rites: On the value of popular music*. Cambridge, MA: Harvard University Press.
Gorbman, Claudia. 1987. *Unheard melodies. Narrative film music*. Bloomington, IN: Indiana University Press.
Guattari, F. 1995. *Chaosmosis: An ethico-aesthetic paradigm*. Bloomington, IN: Indiana University Press.
Habermas, J. 1962. *Strukturwandel der Öffentlichkeit: Untersuchungen zu einer Kategorie der bürgerlichen Gesellschaft*. Darmstadt: Politica.
Hennion, A. 2008. The musicalization of visual arts. *Music, Sound, and the Moving Image* 2 (2): 175–182.
Hepp, A. 2009. Differentiation: Mediatization and cultural change. In *Mediatization: Concept, changes, consequences*, ed. K. Lundby, 135–153. New York: Peter Lang.
Hepp, A. 2010. Researching 'mediatized worlds': Non-media-centric media and communication research as a challenge. In *Media and communication studies: Interventions and intersections*, eds. N. Carpentier, I. Tomanić Trivundža, P. Pruulmann-Vengerfeldt, E. Sundin, T. Olsson, R. Kilborn, H. Nieminen, and B. Cammaerts, 37–48. Tartu: Tartu University Press.
Hepp, A. 2012. Mediatization and the 'molding force' of the media. *Communications* 37 (1): 1–28.

Hjarvard, S. 2013. *The mediatization of culture and society*. London, New York: Routledge.

Kassabian, A. 2013. *Ubiquitous listening: Affect, attention, and distributed subjectivity*. Los Angeles: University of California Press.

Katz, M. 2010. *Capturing sound: How technology has changed music*. Los Angeles: University of California Press.

Kaun, A. and K. Fast. 2014. *Mediatization of culture and everyday life*. Huddinge: sh.se/publications.

Krämer, B. 2011. The mediatization of music as the emergence and transformation of institutions: A synthesis. *International Journal of Communication* 5: 471–491.

Krotz, F. 2007. *Mediatisierung: Fallstudien zum Wandel von Kommunikation*. Wiesbaden: VS.

Krotz, F. 2009. Mediatization: A Concept with which to grasp media and societal change. In *Mediatization. Concept, changes, consequences*, ed. Knut Lundby, 21–40. New York: Peter Lang.

Krotz, F., and A. Hepp. 2011. A concretization of mediatization: How mediatization works and why 'mediatized worlds' are a helpful concept for empirical mediatization research. *Empedocles: European Journal for the Philosophy of Communication* 3 (2): 137–152.

Larson, R. 1995. Secrets in the bedroom: Adolescents' private use of media. *Journal of Youth and Adolescence* 24 (5): 535–550.

Malloch, S., and C. Trevarthen. 2009. Musicality: Communicating the vitality and interests of life. In *Communicative musicality: Exploring the basis of human companionship*, ed. S. Malloch, and C. Trevarthen, 1–12. Oxford: Oxford University Press.

McClary, S. 1987. The blasphemy of talking politics during the Bach year. In *Music and society: The politics of composition, performance and reception*, ed. R. Leppert, and S. McClary, 13–62. Cambridge: Cambridge University Press.

McClary, S. 1991. *Feminine endings: Music, gender, and sexuality*. Minneapolis: University of Minnesota Press.

McRobbie, A., and J. Garber. 1976. Girls and subcultures. In *Resistance through rituals: Youth subcultures in post-war Britain*, ed. Stuart Hall, and Tony Jefferson, 209–222. London: Harper Collins Academic.

Pontara, T. 2007. *Brev från den autonoma musikens värld: Den diskursiva konstruktionen av musikalisk autonomi i den samtida klassiska CD-skivan*. Diss. Stockholms universitet.

Pontara, T. Forthcoming. *Listening to Technologically Mediated Music in Film: Representations of Social and Solitary Listening in Swedish Cinema 1930–1970*.

Pontara, T. 2008. Constructing the relevant listener: Power, knowledge and the construction of identity in the discourse of musical autonomy. In *Music and identity: Transformation and negotiation*, ed. E. Akrofi, et al., 69–87. Stellenbosch: Stellenbosch University Press.

Pontara, T. 2015. Interpretation, imputation, plausibility: Toward a theoretical model for musical hermeneutics. *International Review of the Aesthetics and Sociology of Music* 46 (1): 3–41.

Roesner, D. 2008. The politics of the polyphony of performance: Musicalization of contemporary German theatre. *Contemporary Theatre Review* 18 (1): 44–55.

Sloboda, J., A. Lamont, and A. Greasley. 2009. Choosing to hear music: Motivation, process, and effect. In *The Oxford handbook of music psychology*, ed. S. Hallam, et al., 431–440. Oxford: Oxford University Press.

Small, C. 1998. *Musicking: The meanings of performing and listening*. Hanover, NH: University Press of New England.

Stern, D. 1985. *The interpersonal world of the infant: A view from psychoanalysis and developmental psychology*. New York: Basic Books.

Tagg, P. 1979. *Kojak—50 seconds of television music: Toward the analysis of affect in popular music*. Göteborg: Skrifter från Musikvetenskapliga institutionen.

Tagg, P. 2013. *Music's meanings: A modern musicology for non-musos*. New York: The Mass Media Music Scholar's Press.

Taruskin, R. 2013. Afterword. In *Representation in Western music*, ed. J. Walden, 287–309. Cambridge: Cambridge University Press.

Volgsten, U. 2006. Between ideology and identity. Media, discourse and affect in the musical experience. In *Music and manipulation: On the social uses and social control of music*, ed. S. Brown, and U. Volgsten, 74–100. New York, Oxford: Berghahn.

Volgsten, U. 2012. The roots of music: Emotional expression, dialogue and affect attunement in the psychogenesis of music. *Musicae Scientiae* 16 (2): 200–216.

Volgsten, U. 2014. Music, culture, politics: Communicating identity, authenticity and quality in the 21st Century. *Nordic Journal of Cultural Policy* 17 (1): 114–131.

Volgsten, U. 2015a. Work, form and phonogram. On the significance of the concept of *communication* for the modern Western concept of music. *IRASM: International Review of the Aesthetics and Sociology of Music.*

Volgsten, U. 2015b. Between critic and public: Listening to the musical work in Stockholm during the long 19th century. *Swedish Journal of Music Research* 97 (1): 1–25.

Volgsten, U., and Pripp, O., 2016. Music, Memory, and Affect Attunement: Connecting Kurdish Diaspora in Stockholm. *Culture Unbound: Journal of Cultural Research* 8 (2): 144-164.

Volgsten, U. Forthcoming. How phonography changed the wor(l)d of music: Locating gramophones, discs and listeners in Sweden 1900–1945.

Weber, H. 2009. Taking your favourite sound along: Portable audio technologies for mobile music listening. In *Sound souvenirs: Audio technologies, memory and cultural practices*, ed. K. Bijsterveld and J. van Dijck, 69–82. Amsterdam: Amsterdam University Press.

Whittall, A. 2006. Tonality. *The Oxford companion to music. Oxford Music Online*. Oxford University Press. http://www.oxfordmusiconline.com.ezproxy.ub.gu.se/subscriber/article/opr/t114/e6829. Accessed 26 Apr 2017.

Widestedt, K. (2001): *Ett tongivande förnuft. Musikkritik i dagspress under två sekel*, diss. Stockholm: JMK.

Wolf, W. 1999. *The musicalization of fiction: A study in the theory and history of intermediality*. Amsterdam: Rodopi.

CHAPTER 13

The Legacy of Mediatization: When the Media Became Cultural Heritage

Christian Hviid Mortensen PhD

13.1 Introduction

Mediatization, according to proponents of the theory, is a long-term meta-process whereby the media influence other fields of society (Couldry and Hepp 2013; Hepp et al. 2010; Lundby 2014). Thus, the study of mediatization is the examination of the dynamics of these media-related transformations within different social domains. Mediatization has been conceptualized as the degree to which the institutional logics of other societal institutions adapt to a media logic (Hjarvard 2014). Recently, Rudloff has argued that the increased digitization within the museum field of museum assets, communication and mediated exhibition experiences is evidence of the mediatization of museums (Rudloff 2013). In addition, one could argue that other salient aspects of contemporary museum practice such as the increased focus on museum marketing and blockbuster exhibitions as a survival strategy within the experience economy are modelled more on a media

C.H. Mortensen PhD (✉)
Department for Cultural Heritage, The Media Museum, Odense City Museums, Odense, Denmark
e-mail: chrhm@odense.dk

O. Driessens et al. (eds.), *Dynamics Of Mediatization*, Transforming Communications – Studies in Cross-Media Research, DOI 10.1007/978-3-319-62983-4_13

logic than a museum logic (Pine and Gilmore 2011; Skot-Hansen 2008; Kotler et al. 2008). Based on the increased popularity of museums—in Denmark, the yearly visitor attendance has doubled from 10 million in 1984 to 21 million in 2015[1]—cultural historian Huyssen claims that the museum institution has been transformed from a cultural institution catering to an exclusive elite into a "mass medium" aimed at the public at large (Huyssen 1995: 14). Furthermore, he argues that this popularity is part of a broader meta-process of musealization fuelled by the increased attention to memory, history and the past in contemporary society and evidenced by, among other phenomena, a boom in the number of museums (Huyssen 2000; Huyssen 1995). For example, with currently over 35,000 museums, there are now more museums in the US than locations of Starbucks and McDonald's combined (Institute of Museum and Library Services 2016; *The Washington Post* 2014).

Mediatization theory accords media a central role in everyday life within late modern industrialized societies (Hjarvard 2013). The permanent exhibition about everyday life in Denmark, *Histories from Denmark 1660–2000*, at the National Museum of Denmark reflects this development; the latest decades are each represented by a display of media technologies: the 1970s with LPs and a cassette tape recorder, the 1980s with a yellow Sony Walkman and a VCR, and the 1990s with a PC, PlayStation and a mobile phone (see Figs. 13.1, 13.2 and 13.3). This is not a case of the museum adapting to a media logic, however, but rather the museum is imposing a museal logic on the media. Thus, while the exhibit provides evidence for the mediatization of everyday life, it is not itself an instance of mediatization of the museum but rather a musealization of the media.

The three exhibits show how the double articulation of media, as both material technology and symbolic text (Silverstone 2003), manifests itself in the museological strategies of display. The contemporary Samsung flat-screen TVs in the bottom of the display cases are separated physically from the historic media technologies above. The separation is also a conceptual distinction of the different functions performed by the media technologies in the display case as a meaningful arrangement. Above the technology has the status of museum objects or artefacts, while below the flat screen is a didactic device for displaying media texts, in this case segments of TV shows from the period. As TV texts, they have no inherent connection with the LP turntable, VHS recorder or PC as museum objects besides being concurrent with them. But playback equipment

Fig. 13.1 Display case from the exhibition *Histories from Denmark 1660–2000 at the National Museum of Denmark*. 13.1: The 1970s

Fig. 13.2 Display case from the exhibition *Histories from Denmark 1660–2000 at the National Museum of Denmark.* 13.2: The 1980s

Fig. 13.3 Display case from the exhibition *Histories from Denmark 1660–2000 at the National Museum of Denmark*. 13.3: The 1990s

is not the neutral equivalent of Plexiglas display cases (Cohen-Stratyner 2013). Using media as interpretative or didactic devices often becomes a question of usability and is a determining factor in visitor meaning-making. The distinction between media in the museum as didactic devices and as museum objects is crucial. The former is the result of a mediatization process, whereby museums increasingly rely on different media technologies (Parry 2007; Kirschenblatt-Gimblett 2001; Falk and Dierking 2013). The other is the result of a musealization process, whereby media are incorporated into museum collections and thus given a new status as artefacts of cultural heritage.

Concurrently with the mediatization of everyday life, there has been a musealization of the media. This is most prominent in the establishment internationally of many museums dedicated to diverse aspects of mass media. Towards the end of the twentieth century, mass media has apparently matured enough as a cultural phenomenon to be considered a form of heritage. Thus, the media now constitute a legitimate field for museal collection.

In this chapter, I will account for this process of musealization of the media in terms of its geographical and temporal distribution. Having addressed the where and when of the musealization of the media, I will address the why, how and what in a discussion of media as cultural heritage. Here, I will argue that, from a museum studies perspective, the musealization of media can be seen as a consequence of mediatization.

13.2 The Musealization of Media

On the macro level, Huyssen sees the museum as a "paradigmatic institution that collects, salvages and preserves that which has fallen to the ravages of modernization" (Huyssen 1995: 15). According to Huyssen nothing escapes the logic of musealization (Huyssen 1995: 20), and the whole "world is being musealized, and we all play our parts in it" (Huyssen 2000: 25). Also, Huyssen sees media technologies as an important enabling factor in this meta-process:

> Untold recent and not so recent pasts impinge upon the present through modern media of reproduction like photography, film, recorded music and the Internet, as well as through the explosion of historical scholarship and an ever more voracious museal culture. The past has become part of the present in ways simply unimaginable in earlier centuries. As a result,

temporal boundaries have weakened just as the experiential dimension of space has shrunk as a result of modern means of transportation and communication (Huyssen 2003: 1).

In this view, the meta-processes of mediatization and musealization run parallel on the macro level, with the former to some extent enabling the later. It can seem misleading, however, to label a general societal turn towards memory, history and the past—where the museum institution is only one aspect alongside other aspects—for musealization. Museums are just one way of "consuming history" besides others, such as re-enactments and retro culture, some of them mediated, for example, historically themed TV drama or video games (De Groot 2009). These are all actualizations of cultural memory that otherwise exist only in the potentiality of the archive (Assmann 1995: 130). Rather, we should reserve the term "musealization" for the museal processes at the institutional meso level. According to the latest (2007) definition by the International Council of Museums:

A museum is a non-profit, permanent institution in the service of society and its development, open to the public, which acquires, conserves, researches, communicates and exhibits the tangible and intangible heritage of humanity and its environment for the purposes of education, study and enjoyment (Desvallées and Mairesse 2010: 57).

Following this definition, "musealisation is the operation of trying to extract, physically or conceptually, something from its natural or cultural environment and giving it a museal status, transforming it into a musealium or 'museum object', that is to say, bringing it into the musealfield" (Desvallées and Mairesse 2010: 50).

Media objects have been incorporated in the collections of national cultural history museums as just another kind of appliances used by citizens in their everyday life, as was the case in the *Histories from Denmark* exhibition mentioned above. Similarly, media technologies usually form part of the collections of many technological museums among other technological inventions. But already from the beginning of the twentieth century, and especially since 1970, we can observe the establishment of museums dedicated to mass media and communication. Figure 13.4 shows this development. I performed a series of systematic Google searches for each of the 193 UN member states. The searches had the following structure: "[country name] [museum category] museum". The museum category for each search was postal, communication and media. I knew that the former two were common kinds of media museum and wanted to establish just how common. The last category is uncommon and the objective was to discover any media museums not already known to me. The results were added to a list I have been compiling of all the media museums I have encountered since 2007 as a practitioner in the field. The systematic search corrected the Western bias of my list and proved the phenomenon of media museums to be more widespread than I had anticipated. The survey is not exhaustive, as it includes only museums with an internet presence in English. However, I am confident that the results are sufficient to empirically substantiate the claim of a musealization of media. The searches also identified other kinds of media museums for which I have not yet performed a systematic country-by-country search. A detailed comparison of the different categories of media museums falls outside the scope of this chapter. An advantage of the Google approach in comparison with consulting the directory *Museums of the World* (*Museums of the World, EBookPlus* 2016) is that the search also identified amateur initiatives and online-only museums—two approaches that contribute to the full picture of the musealization of media.

Figure 13.4 shows how the increase in media museums is doubled every decade from 1950 to 1990 and the trend continues at a high pace with over 20 new media museums every decade. Inevitably, the trend will slow down as the global "market" for media museums is saturated, but there is no sign of subsiding yet.

Table 13.1 shows how the media museums identified in the search are distributed globally categorized by continent. Over three quarters of the media museums are within the Northern Hemisphere (Europe plus North America, even more if we include the instances in Asia), and almost half of the museums are located in Europe. I expect that the overrepresentation of media museums in Europe reflects a general overrepresentation of museums.

The trend with museums dedicated to various aspects of the media began in 1872 with the Postal Museum in Berlin and the Telegraph Museum in Saint Petersburg. I use the umbrella term "media museums" to encompass all museums specializing in media, communication and ICT, but excluding museums of fine art collecting and exhibiting media art such as the ZKM Center for Art and Media in Karlsruhe. Within this

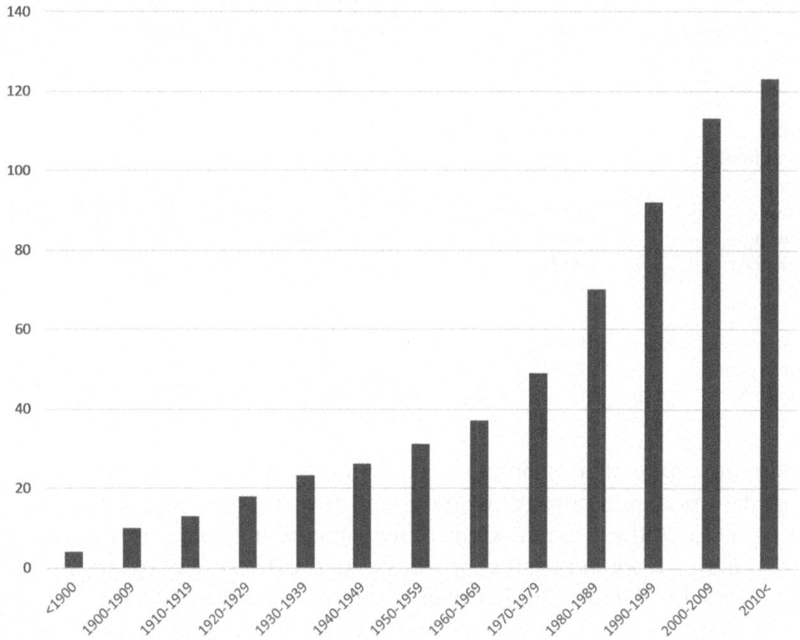

Fig. 13.4 The aggregate number of media museums divided by decade

Table 13.1 The number of media museums divided by continent and transposed to percentiles. The total of 126 museums differs from the aggregate number in Fig. 13.4 because I have included three future media museums that are currently in the planning stage

Continent	*Media museums*	%
Europe	57	45
Asia	29	23
North America	24	19
South America	6	5
Africa	6	5
Australia	4	3
Antarctica	0	0
Total	**126**	**100**

Table 13.2 The different kinds of media museums divided into categories and sub-categories

Media Museum category	*Media Museum sub-categories*		
Postal	Stamps/phliatelic		
Communication	Telegraphy	Telephone	ICT
Media			
News	Journalism		
Printing	Newspapers	Books	Magazines
Broadcast	Radio	TV	
Cinema	Film	Moving images	
Photography			
Comics	Cartoons	Manga	
Video games	Arcades		

group one can further distinguish different categories and sub-categories of media museum according to the focus of their collection. Table 13.2 is a typology of the different kinds of media museums I have identified so far. Though a work in progress, it still shows the diversity of media museums. Here, I will address only the first four main categories, however.

The most common kind, and also the first to develop, is the postal museum. The search identified 55 postal museums in the world. The one in Berlin, now the Museum für Kommunikation, established in 1872, is credited with being the oldest postal museum in the world. The humblest is probably the Mtengatenga Museum in Malawi—a restored postal rest hut forming a wayside museum commemorating the period before 1941 when the mail in Malawi was brought out on foot. This shows that in both industrialized and developing countries the postal service has formed a vital part of a country's infrastructure and therefore is considered worth remembering with a dedicated museum. In contrast to the humble hut in Malawi, many national postal museums are located in the former, or still functioning, central post office—an often opulent building such as the former Palacio de Communicaciones [Palace of Communication] (now the Cybele Palace) in Madrid that housed the Postal and Telegraphy Museum until 2007, when it became the Madrid City Hall.

The search revealed 34 communication museums. Like the Museum für Kommunikation in Berlin, several communication museums have a postal museum as their genesis. In time, they began to collect artefacts related to telegraphy and telephony, eventually changing from postal to communication museum. This history is still reflected in the name of the Serbian Postal-telegraphic-telephone Museum (1923) in Belgrade. Even the postal museum in Malawi, when it was renovated in 2013, was described by an official spokesperson as "the custodian of our history not just in the postal sector, but the whole communications sector" (Chilene 2013).

Almost every postal museum has close institutional ties to the national postal service. Although many communication museums also have institutional ties to national infrastructure providers, within this category we can also see the emergence of the independent communication museum founded by private amateurs (museum amateurs but often former professional practitioners), such as the Herbert H. Warrick Jr. Museum of Communications (1988) in Seattle, Washington. The museum is named after its founder, director of network engineering for the Pacific Northwest Bell Telephone Company, built and maintained by retired telephone company employees.

In addition to postal and communication museums, many media museums are dedicated to singular media or particular technologies such as printing, broadcast, cinematography, video games, newspapers or comics. Few museum collections span the divide between print media and audio-visual media, even if they brand themselves as a "media museum". A case in point: The National Museum of Photography, Film and Television established in 1983 in Bradford was renamed the National Media Museum in 2006, but the focus was still on audio-visual media, now also including video games and the internet. Thus, the interdependencies and competition between different media and technologies are seldom the object of museal attention. The genealogy of the Media Museum in Odense, Denmark, reflects both the ambition and the challenges of a comprehensive media museum. The museum began as a printing museum in 1984. Later, in 1989, the museum merged with the Danish Press Museum (established in 1954). Finally, in 2000, the museum's remit was extended to include the electronic and digital media. In 2003, the museum changed its name to the Media Museum of Denmark and again in 2010 to the Media Museum in recognition of the international influence and boundless nature of the media. The museum's existing collections, however, are still biased towards printing technology and do not yet adequately reflect the comprehensive remit of a holistic media museum.

Finally, news museums are another category of media museum that, instead of taking a technological approach to media heritage, focus on a particular form of media content, namely news and the journalistic practices of producing the news. A common denominator for news museums is that the founding organization is a newcomer to the museum sector and often has a political agenda with the museum. A news museum often promotes values, such as freedom of expression and the democratic role of the press as the fourth estate. The most prominent example is the Newseum (1997) in Washington, D.C., founded by the Freedom Forum, the raison d'être of which is to champion "the First Amendment as a cornerstone of democracy" (Newseum Institute 2016). The museum considers itself one of the most interactive in the world, offering a range of activities around news in which the visitor can engage. However, there are also more traditional museum galleries devoted to important media events, such as the 9/11 gallery featuring the original broadcast antennae from atop the World Trade Center and the Berlin Wall gallery featuring eight sections of concrete from the original wall. Despite the focus on media events and the news generated from them, it is apparently still considered an attraction to witness the physicality and authenticity of material objects connected to these events.

News museums, such as Istanbul's TGC Press Media Museum (1988) established by the Turkish Journalists' Association, often have an exhibition devoted to important journalists and publicists. Haus der Pressefreiheit (2001) [House for the Freedom of the Press], established by journalists and publishers in Germany, has even named this section Hall of Fame as is common practice within popular culture such as music, film and sports.

Haus der Pressefreiheit is also representative for another kind of media museums because it is an online-only museum. There were ambitions for making a physical museum in Hamburg, but the project proved to be economically unfeasible. Since 2012, the Haus has instead been an online resource. The internet affords the organization behind the museum to pursue their objectives without the economic encumbrance of maintaining a physical location. Therefore, the virtual museum is attractive to groups of amateur enthusiasts as a single cost-effective platform for collecting, storing and disseminating material.

The development of media technologies is enabling the musealization of many different aspects of culture and society, including the media, by lowering the entry costs and thus providing groups and individuals with an affordable solution to their museal sensibilities, thus democratizing the museum field (Huhtamo 2002). Amateur media museums are a significant way of performing heritage, and they speak volumes about the perceived cultural value of obsolete media. In the case of virtual museums, media technology has become the driver for musealization as claimed by Huyssen. In addition to performing the traditional museum functions, the virtual museum enables collaborative heritage practices through crowdsourcing. An example is www.radiomuseum.org, where radio enthusiasts are compiling a vast catalogue/database of antique radio technology.

13.3 Media Heritage and Cultural Heritage

Having addressed the when and where of media museums, I now turn to the issue of the what and how of media heritage. But first let us consider why we have museums dedicated to media heritage. According to Ernst, "we need a place which is different from the media in order to reflect on media" (2015: 17). Stating the raison d'être of media museums post-factum, Ernst claims that the museum introduces a distance by removing media objects from their usual circulation as commodities and that this distance is a precondition for reflection. We find a similar notion with McLuhan for whom the current media environment (including processes of mediatization) can become the object of study only "in so far as there is an anti-environment or counter-situation constructed to provide a means of direct attention" (McLuhan 1966: 1). Ideally, a media museum should constitute such an anti-environment. On the other hand, one might argue that owing to mediatization museums are too enmeshed in the current media environment as "media makers" (Kidd 2014: 3), themselves producing media content, to provide a McLuhanesque anti-environment. According to Sandell, museums still occupy a marginal but privileged position within the mediascape as trustworthy and valuable sources compared with the mass media (Sandell 2007). However, when the media are included within the museum, and museums frequently contribute content to the mass media, this blurs the border between the museums and the overall mediascape, stipulated by Ernst, and changes in meaning, authority and other aspects of media when they move between the two (Kidd 2014).

Furthermore,

> Museums, after all, are a medium—in their most common state a unique, three dimensional, multi-sensory, social medium in which knowledge is given spatial form. However, they are also themselves *full* of media [italics in original]. (To McLuhan the content of one medium is always another medium). We might even go so far as to say that media define the museum. Through their histories museums have taken their varied shapes and functions from the communications technologies that they have chosen to deploy (Parry 2007: 11).

Parry is obviously referring to media as didactic devices, or communication technologies, and not as artefacts of cultural heritage. However, the notion of the museum as a medium that contains other media can prove helpful if we consider this a form of remediation. According to Bolter and Grusin, every remediation contains an inherent element of hypermediacy, so when media are represented as museum artefacts (remediated), attention is drawn to them as media, which potentially illuminates aspects of the mediatization phenomenon for critical study (2000: 272).

One thing is a promising theoretical point; however, museum practice is often quite another. The notion of media heritage as the double articulation of media, simultaneously material and symbolic, challenges the traditional museological view of cultural heritage in some respects. This view breaks with the traditional division of labour between archives collecting the "software" of media content and museums collecting the hardware. Thus, the double notion of media heritage requires enlarging the scope in the definition of heritage compared with the UNESCO definition. Smith argues that UNESCO is propagating a specific version of what heritage is, namely an Authorised Heritage Discourse (AHD) that focuses exclusively on "aesthetically pleasing material objects, sites, places and/or landscapes" (Smith 2006: 29). The tangible and material bias in the AHD view of heritage is evident in the need for a second notion of "intangible heritage" in order to recognize the legacy of indigenous (primarily non-Western) cultures based on oral traditions without the monuments or documents characteristic of Western culture. Smith further argues for the futility of this dual concept as all heritage is inherently intangible as the values and meanings represented by heritage sites and objects as well as the cultural practices of our engagements with heritage (Smith 2006). In this view, heritage is a cultural process rather than a cultural object. Heritage needs to be experienced for it to become heritage. Heritage is something you do rather than something you have. Museums are one kind of site for public history-making (Kavanagh 2005) where heritage is performed through meaning-making experiences and remembering. Curating museum collections is a cultural practice that constructs the props for this performance (Smith 2006), thus creating the mise-en-scène for our encounters with cultural memory when it is staged in museums as the theatres of memory.

The material bias of UNESCO's definition of cultural heritage in regard to the symbolic form and ephemeral nature of many media texts has led UNESCO to introduce a third category of heritage: documentary heritage. A document is defined as an entity that deliberately records or documents something. The document has two components—the information content and the carrier on which it resides—and the two can be equally important as part of our cultural memory. Furthermore, documentary heritage should have the following characteristics (Edmondson 2002: 8): movable; made up of signs/codes, sounds, and/or images; preservable (the carriers are non-living); reproducible and migratable; and the product of a deliberate documenting process. Thus, the large (unmovable) runic stones at Jelling in Denmark are considered by UNESCO as monuments of heritage rather than documentary heritage, while they are definitely a kind of media text as the earliest written documents in Denmark (950–985 CE) and arguably also the earliest instance of political propaganda (UNESCO 1994).

Although the musealization of media reflects the mediatization of our life and society, recognizing the institutional and material importance of media, the museum approach has not yet found a way of capturing the qualitative aspects of (deep) mediatization, as the experienced media saturation of everyday life. Within media museums, there has been a focus on the first articulation of media as material objects (technology) and to some extent also the second articulation of media as text (symbolic content); however, what has been called the third articulation of media as the immediate context of use has hitherto often been lacking (Hartmann 2006: 96). We need to take all three articulations of media into consideration in order to understand and reflect upon mediatization as a phenomenon. Therefore, the museal practices concerning media heritage should reflect each articulation and not just the first concerning media as material objects.

Another challenge to the museum institution by the media, famously addressed by Walter Benjamin (Benjamin 1968), is the disappearance of the original and authentic object because of the reproducing capabilities of the media resulting in the object's loss of aura and presumably undermining the idea of museums as temples dedicated to the cult of authentic or auratic objects (Huhtamo 2002). Now 80 years after Benjamin wrote his essay in 1936, the media themselves, albeit inherently mass-produced and embedded in popular culture, both affronts to the view of the museum as a place for fine art and unique objects, are on display in many museums as shown in the previous section. Here, objects of vintage media technology are imbued by the museum with an aura of authenticity as they are displayed as cultural artefacts. However, the textual dimension of the media is seldom staged as artefacts of cultural heritage in the same way as the hardware of technology. Within museum exhibitions, audio-visual media texts are usually considered as secondary and supportive of the material artefacts on display. For example, in the exhibits shown above, the screens showing TV content are located at the bottom of the display case, where they are more difficult to see and where they indicate a secondary importance. In addition, no mention of the TV content is made in the text accompanying the exhibit, directing the visitor's attention towards it. Considering media content as artefacts of media heritage on par with material objects within the meaning economy of a museum exhibition requires a change in perspective and emphasis.

Finally, as noted by media archaeologist Wolfgang Ernst and as evident with the blank computer screen in the display depicted above, media technologies are seldom exhibited in their working state, which reduces them to just being pieces of furniture (Henning and Ernst 2015). This is of course in the interest of preserving the vintage technology by not subjecting it to undue wear and tear. But it can result in a disproportionate amount of attention given to the often utilitarian exterior design of the media devices rather than to their function as media. In an effort to overcome this blackboxing (Latour 2000) of functioning media, Ernst has established *The Media Archaeological Fundus* in Berlin. The fundus is a collection of vintage media technology but also a "tinkering space" where scholars and students can gain insight into old media by operating them (Parikka 2012: 131). Media archaeology is seen as "a way to investigate new media cultures through insights from past new media" (Parikka 2012: 2). Several similar *media labs* with open collections have been established around the World; however, they are usually affiliated with universities and thus not accessible to the general public as access is restricted to researchers and students. Media museums could adopt this approach and turn their material bias into an asset by opening up their collection for use by the general public, but this approach is anathema to the conservational efforts of the museum and probably would require a parallel collection of duplicate artefacts. At our museum, we are running workshops for elementary and high school groups centred on magnet tape technology for music listening, movie watching, and gaming (cassette recorder/Walkman, VCR and C64 computer) in order to observe how the younger generation engage with media technologies from the 1980s and what kind of reflections such engagements prompt.

The many technology-oriented media museums seem to have built similar collections, including the same major innovations as from a technology standpoint the development of communications has followed similar trajectories internationally with minor local variations. "The desire to preserve, to lend a historical aura to objects otherwise condemned to be thrown away, to become obsolete—all of this can indeed be read as reaction to the accelerated speed of modernization" (Huyssen 1995: 28). Therefore, technological progress has been a driver in this development, as technological innovation has made old technology obsolete. But this obsolete technology was still regarded as valuable in a historical sense by the professional community of practitioners and thus deviated from the designated pathway to the junkyard by donation to a museum instead (Appadurai 1986). This was the case with the Media Museum in Denmark (1984), where the closure of businesses in the printing industry became the foundation of the museum's collections.

Where the national differences become significant is on the level of domestication of media with the triple articulation of technology, content and context, including the interplay between content developed nationally and the influence from international content, resulting in, for example, discourses of moral panic about Americanization and the anglicization of local vernaculars.

13.4 The Legacy of Mediatization

The musealization of media can be seen as a consequence of mediatization. The establishing of museums dedicated to media and communication is a significant indicator of the impact of media in our late modern societies and the value attached to media and communication as something to be preserved for posterity as cultural heritage. Thus, media museums can be considered the legacy of mediatization as the final resting places of selected media objects.

The majority of media museums can be characterized as museums of science and technology with an emphasis on collecting and displaying media and communication technology. However, others have adopted a cultural history approach with a broader scope to include media content and context. A reason for this technology bias is that museums, as the institutional caretakers of our heritage, have traditionally collected material culture (Smith 2006). The primary material traces of media culture are the technology with much audio-visual content from broadcast TV and radio being experienced in the moment and newspapers and magazines being discarded after consumption.

However, with the material approach to media heritage in museums, we risk inadvertently proving McLuhan right as now the medium becomes the message (McLuhan 1964). It is a limited view of media culture, which excludes the ephemeral content of audio-visual media and the intangible practices around media technologies. Echoing the assertion of Silverstone that new media research should reflect the double articulation of media and integrate "the analysis of the media *qua* material objects located in particular spatio-temporal settings (thus including Hartmann's third articulation of context) with the analysis of the media *qua* texts or symbolic messages located within the flows of particular socio-cultural discourses" (Livingstone 2007: 18), I argue that our understanding of media heritage should build on a similar perspective. Also, there is an inherent producer bias in the material approach to media heritage as the practices of media use and reception leave few material traces. Thus, in order to correct this bias, there is a need to decentre the approach to media heritage and also consider the practices around media (Couldry 2004). There is no reason why modern practices of media production and use should not also be considered as intangible heritage. But it will require that media museums revise their collection policies and also adopt ethnographic methods of data collection for documenting these practices and contexts of use.

Crossing the border between the overall mediascape and the museum domain as collected artefacts of cultural heritage changes the meaning, authority and other aspects of these media objects. When the museum artefacts themselves become media, the barrier is blurred between artefacts and media as didactic devices. This establishes media heritage exhibitions as complex sites for meaning-making experiences: what is the added value of exhibiting media rather than experiencing media the conventional way? Can we understand the meaning-making of museum visitors to such exhibitions as a second-order media reception providing the reflective distance postulated by Ernst? To answer such questions, there is a need for empirical studies of meaning-making experiences of media heritage within museums and comparisons with non-museum encounters with past media, thereby illuminating how and whether media museums fulfil their promise as McLuhanesque anti-environments.

Note

1. According to Danmarks Statistik [The Office of Statistics in Denmark], 10,746,644 people visited a museum in 1984. The figure has risen to 21,083,515 in 2015.

References

2016. *Museums of the World, EBookPlus,* 23th ed. Berlin: De Gruyter Saur. https://www.degruyter.com/view/product/466149.

Appadurai, Arjun. 1986. *The social life of things: Commodities in cultural perspective.* Cambridge: Cambridge University Press.

Assmann, Jan. 1995. Collective memory and cultural identity. *New German Critique* 65: 125–133.

Benjamin, Walter. 1968. The work of art in the age of mechanical reproduction. In *Illuminations*, ed. Hannah Arendt, 217–251. New York: Schocken Books.

Bolter, Jay D., and Richard Grusin. 2000. *Remediation. Understanding new media.* Cambridge, MA: MIT Press.

Chilene, Josephine. 2013. Malawi: Macra renovates Mtengatenga postal hut. News site. *All Africa.* http://allafrica.com/stories/201310140594.html. Accessed 26 April 2017.

Cohen-Stratyner, Barbara. 2013. Authority and meaning-making in the digital era. *Exhibitionist* 31: 22–26.

Couldry, Nick. 2004. Theorising media as practice. *Social Semiotics* 14 (2): 115–132.

Couldry, Nick, and Andreas Hepp. 2013. Editorial. Conceptualizing mediatization: Contexts, traditions, arguments. *Communication Theory* 23: 191–202.

De Groot, Jerome. 2009. *Consuming history, historians and heritage in contemporary popular culture*, vol. 1. London: Routledge.

Desvallées, André, and Francois Mairesse. 2010. *Key concepts in museology.* Paris: Armand Colin.

Edmondson, Ray. 2002. *Memory of the world: General guidelines.* Paris: UNESCO.

Falk, John H., and Lynn D. Dierking. 2013. *The museum experience revisited.* Walnut Creek, CA: Left Coast Press.

Hartmann, Maren. 2006. The triple articulation of ICTs. Media as technological objects, symbolic environments and individual texts. In *Domestication of media and technology*, ed. Thomas Berker, 80–102. Maidenhead: Open University Press.

Henning, Michelle, and Wolfgang Ernst. 2015. Museums and media archaeology. An interview with Wolfgang Ernst. In *Museum media*, ed. Michelle Henning, 3–22. The International Handbooks of Museum Studies. Chichester: Wiley.

Hepp, Andreas, Stig Hjarvard, and Knut Lundby. 2010. Editorial. Mediatization—Empirical perspectives: An introduction to a special issue. *Communications* 35: 223–228.

Hjarvard, Stig. 2013. *The mediatization of culture and society.* New York: Routledge.

Hjarvard, Stig. 2014. Mediatization and cultural and social change: An institutional perspective. In *Mediatization of communication*, ed. Knut Lundby, 199–226. Berlin: Walter de Gruyter.

Huhtamo, Erkki. 2002. On the Origins of the Virtual Museum. *Nobel Symposium: Virtual museums and public understanding of science and culture*, May 26–29. Stockholm: Nobel Media AB. http://www.nobelprize.org/nobel_organizations/nobelfoundation/symposia/interdisciplinary/ns120/lectures/huhtamo.pdf.

Huyssen, Andreas. 1995. Escape from amnesia: The museum as mass medium. In *Twilight memories, marking time in a culture of amnesia*, ed. Andreas Huyssen, 13–35. New York: Routledge.

Huyssen, Andreas. 2000. Present pasts: Media, politics, amnesia. *Public Culture* 12: 21–38.

Huyssen, Andreas. 2003. Cultural Memory in the Present. *Urban palimpsests and the politics of memory.* Stanford, CA: Stanford University Press.

Institute of Museum and Library Services. 2016. Museum universe data file. *Institute of museum and library services.* https://www.imls.gov/research-evaluation/data-collection/museum-universe-data-file. Accessed 26 Apr 2017.

Kavanagh, Gaynor. 2005. *Making histories in museums.* London: Continuum International Publishing.

Kidd, Jenny. 2014. *Museums in the new mediascape. Transmedia, participation, ethics.* Farnham, Burlington: Ashgate.

Kirschenblatt-Gimblett, Barbara. 2001. The museum as catalyst. In *Museum 2000: Confirmation or challenge*, ed. Per-Uno Ålgren and Sophie Nyman, 1–19. Stockholm: Riksutställninger.

Kotler, Neil G., Philip Kotler, and Wendi I. Kotler. 2008. *Museum marketing and strategy, designing missions, building audiences, generating revenue and resources*, 2nd ed. San Francisco, CA: Jossey-Bass.

Latour, Bruno. 2000. *Pandora's hope. Essays on the reality of science studies.* Cambridge, MA: Harvard University Press.

Livingstone, Sonia. 2007. On the material and the symbolic: Silverstone's double articulation of research traditions in new media studies. *New Media and Society* 9 (1): 16–24.

Lundby, Knut. 2014. Mediatization of communication. In *Mediatization of communication*, ed. Knut Lundby, 3–35. Hawthorne: De Gruyter.

McLuhan, Marshall. 1964. *Understanding media: The extensions of man*, 2nd ed. New York: Signet Books, The American Library.

McLuhan, Marshall. 1966. The relation of environment to anti-environment. *University of Windsor Review* 2 (1): 1–10.

Newseum Institute. 2016. Freedom forum. Organisation. *Freedom Forum.* http://www.newseuminstitute.org/freedom-forum/. Accessed 26 Apr 2017.

Parikka, Jussi. 2012. *What is media archaeology?* Cambridge: Polity Press.

Parry, Ross. 2007. *Recoding the museum. Digital heritage and the technologies of change.* Abingdon: Routledge.

Pine, Joseph, and James Gilmore. 2011. *The experience economy.* Boston, MA: Harvard Business Review Press.

Rudloff, Maja. 2013. Det medialiserede museum: Digitale teknologiers transformation af museernes formidling [The mediatized museum: Digital technologies' transformation of museum communication]. *MedieKultur. Journal of Media and Communication Research* 29: 65–86.

Sandell, Richard. 2007. Museums in the mediascape. In *Museums, prejudice and the reframing of difference*, ed. Richard Sandell, 105–137. Oxon: Routledge.

Silverstone, Roger. 2003. *Television and everyday life.* Taylor & Francis e-Library. London: Routledge.

Skot-Hansen, Dorte. 2008. *Museerne i den Danske oplevelsesøkonomi. Når oplysning bliver til oplevelse [The Museums in the Danish Experience Economy. When enlightenment turns into experience].* Frederiksberg: Imagine, Samfundslitteratur.

Smith, Laurajane. 2006. *The uses of heritage.* New York: Routledge.

The Washington Post. 2014. There are more museums in the U.S. than there are Starbucks and McDonalds—combined. News site. *The Washington Post.* https://www.washingtonpost.com/news/wonk/wp/2014/06/13/there-are-more-museums-in-the-us-than-there-are-starbucks-and-mcdonalds-combined/. Accessed 26 Apr 2017.

UNESCO. 1994. Jelling mounds, runic stones and church. *World heritage list.* http://whc.unesco.org/en/list/697. Accessed 26 Apr 2017.

CHAPTER 14

The Mediatization of Urban Cultural Heritage: Participatory Approaches to Narrating the Urban Past

Arno van der Hoeven

14.1 Introduction

Cities are dynamic places that continuously change and develop. Furthermore, they are centres of creativity, culture and innovation (Glaeser 2011). Heritage plays a vital role in providing a sense of continuity in these dynamic urban environments. This chapter asks how the mediatization of urban cultural heritage enables people to participate in the conservation of the urban past. Various recent heritage policies, such as UNESCO's Recommendation on the Historic Urban Landscape, seek to foster community participation in heritage practices. The active involvement of people in the conservation of urban heritage is particularly relevant in cities, as urban places host a rich diversity of communities with different lifestyles, ethnic backgrounds and cultural interests. As I will argue in this chapter, digital media technologies facilitate the representation of their heritage.

A. van der Hoeven (✉)
Erasmus University Rotterdam, Rotterdam, The Netherlands
e-mail: vanderhoeven@eshcc.eur.nl

O. Driessens et al. (eds.), *Dynamics Of Mediatization*,
Transforming Communications – Studies in Cross-Media Research,
DOI 10.1007/978-3-319-62983-4_14

Heritage refers to those aspects from the past that are preserved because they form an essential part of the identities of communities (Graham and Howard 2008; Smith 2006). It provides a temporal grounding to the attachments people have to cities and their diverse communities. In that sense, heritage is about communication (Groote and Haartsen 2008) for the reason that it represents the histories of a place and the values we attribute to the past. Cultural heritage is a key asset that shapes the image of cities and contributes to the ways in which people identify with a place (Paganoni 2015). In fact, while national identities are being challenged by the forces of globalization, identification with cities seems to be growing (Ashworth et al. 2007; Prévélakis 2008). In the context of rapid urbanization, policy makers and researchers are increasingly concerned with finding new ways of preserving urban heritage (Bandarin and Van Oers 2015).

Various media forms have a vital role in disseminating narratives of cultural heritage (Malpas 2008; Wellington and Oliver 2015; De Groot 2009). Online media, for example, make it possible to share heritage in virtual environments. The advent of the internet in particular has spurred a renewed interest in cultural heritage (Flinn 2007; Van den Broek et al. 2009), providing the impetus for large-scale efforts to digitize all sorts of cultural heritage objects. Online media thus afford unprecedented access to historical material through platforms such as YouTube. Consequently, it is now easier for urban residents to engage with heritage narratives related to their physical surroundings.

In this chapter, I will argue that mediatization results in the growing diversity of the people who participate in the narration of the urban past. Along with the activities of museums and archives, grassroots heritage initiatives are emerging in virtual spaces such as Facebook groups (Gregory 2015). Meanwhile, existing heritage institutions also come to pay more attention to audience participation. I will explain that, although museums and archives thus change their practices through mediatization, this process is inseparable from other developments in this field. Mediatization feeds into wider developments towards the democratization of cultural heritage. Over the last few decades, there has already been growing attention paid in the heritage sector to questions of participation, cultural diversity and the representation of subaltern voices. These institutional transformations will be discussed in the next section. Subsequently, the ways in which mediatization fosters public involvement in urban heritage conservation will be explored by focusing on three developments: the digitization of heritage collections, the growing attention paid to audience participation by heritage institutions, and the grassroots practices of cultural heritage initiated by citizens. Finally, I discuss how the mediatization of cultural heritage changes the public role of heritage institutions and their professionals.

14.2 Institutional Transformations in the Heritage Field

In defining the mediatization of culture and society, Hjarvard (2013) argues that this involves a duality in which media increasingly affect the operations of various social institutions while also becoming separate social institutions in their own right. Increasingly, institutions such as politics have adapted to what has been defined as a media logic. In very general terms, this means that these institutions have integrated the way media operate in their own practices and pay more attention to questions of communication and publicity. However, the consequences of mediatization vary for different social institutions and fields. Therefore, we need to study the dynamics of mediatization in relation to other socio-cultural developments and cultural spheres. As Hepp (2013: 38) states, "mediatization seeks to capture the nature of the interrelationship between historical changes in media and communication and other transformational processes".

In order to understand how this interrelationship works in the heritage field, I first need to discuss the ongoing development towards the democratization of heritage. Heritage institutions seek to become more inclusive by representing the heritage of different communities. This leads to growing attention being paid to subaltern voices and the heritage of minority groups (Flinn 2007; Smith 2006). The focus on questions of inclusiveness follows on from a recognition that heritage narratives are selective constructions, shaped by present-day concerns (Graham and Howard 2008). Thus, heritage always involves a particular orientation to the past, which excludes other perspectives:

> Heritage is that part of the past that we select in the present for contemporary purposes, whether these be economic or cultural (including political and social factors), and choose to bequeath to a future, whatever posterity may choose to do with it. (Ashworth et al. 2007: 35)

As this definition shows, heritage narratives are now understood as representations that serve particular goals in the present, such as city marketing or identity building. In other words, heritage narratives are not fixed but are constructed in an active process of remembering through which particular aspects of the past are highlighted (Smith 2006). These critical approaches to heritage have spurred questions about whose voices are represented in heritage narratives and what kinds of perspective are being excluded (Hall 1999).

The democratization of heritage is also manifested in the broadening scope of what is considered to be heritage (Harrison 2013). As existing canons are being questioned, museums and archives are becoming more open to new types of cultural heritage. Mediated cultural forms such as popular music and film, for example, are increasingly archived and exhibited because they are now recognized as vital aspects of the socio-cultural landscape of contemporary society (Moore 2000). Interestingly, the "heritagization" of these popular cultural forms is, in itself, testament to their growing cultural legitimacy. This demonstrates that the mass-produced commercial products of the media and cultural industries are no longer considered to be at odds with the focus on authentic objects in conventional conceptions of heritage (Bennett 2009). As cultural institutions seek to target a broader audience instead of representing solely the interests of elites (Reijnders 2010), they also become more attentive to the heritage of everyday life and popular cultures.

This trend towards democratization has been strengthened by the adoption of media and communication technologies in heritage institutions (Flinn 2007; Pruulmann-Vengerfeldt and Runnel 2011). In the heritage field, there are many experiments that use digital media for more interactive exhibitions, crowdsource inputs and establish online heritage communities (Russo 2012; Snoek et al. 2010). These initiatives foster interactions with audiences and enable their participation in the construction of heritage narratives. Meanwhile, people use social media to start their own non-institutional heritage initiatives such as online popular music archives (Baker and Collins 2016) or social networking sites where historic photos are shared (Garduño Freeman 2010).

Arguably, these processes of democratization in the heritage field lead to a wider range of voices being represented. Through the mediums of oral history and digital storytelling (Couldry 2008), for example, people are invited to narrate their personal accounts of historical events.[1] This could result in a more multi-vocal understanding of the past (Farinosi and Micalizzi 2016; Paganoni 2015), which recognizes the contributions that different communities have made to the ways in which cities have evolved. This is vital, as it is not possible to reduce the history of a city to a single narrative (Massey 1995). Different communities have diverging identifications with cities. Urban places generally differ from rural contexts in their rich diversity of people and cultures. Media enable the representation of the multiple understandings of the past of cities and their relationship to the lives of urban residents.

Researchers studying the ways in which media developments affect the heritage sector have focused predominantly on museums and archives (e.g. Proctor 2010; Pruulmann-Vengerfeldt and Aljas 2011; Verboom and Arora 2013; Wellington and Oliver 2015). This is understandable, as these are important institutions for the presentation and preservation of cultural heritage. However, a consequence of mediatization is that more people can participate in the construction of cultural heritage narratives. Increasingly, all sorts of commercial and grassroots initiatives aim to contribute to the archiving and presentation of cultural heritage (Flinn 2007; Pessach 2008). Examples are popular representations of the past in games, magazines and historical television shows (De Groot 2009). Arguably, Google, with its Google Books and Google Arts projects, is one of the most well-known instances of a commercial organization making digitized cultural heritage available in the public domain. However, there are also many smaller-scale and local initiatives that emerge outside the realm of the classic heritage institutions. Examples are neighbourhood museums, city blogs and cultural entrepreneurs who use new media to present local heritage narratives.

These new heritage activities largely benefit from processes of digitization, in which non-digital original objects are converted to digital representations in the form of a binary code. Finnemann (2014) defines digitization as a set of particular modes of mediatization. It creates new possibilities such as making objects searchable, reproducible and editable. In the digital spatial humanities (Roberts 2015), these digital developments are used to enhance research on place. The present chapter contributes to this emerging research by examining how mediatization enables people to participate in the conservation of the urban past.

In so doing, this chapter will discuss professional and grassroots initiatives in various Dutch cities. The examples that will be introduced are drawn from my wider research on urban cultural heritage. For my earlier work on social media and urban heritage (Van der Hoeven 2016), I have conducted a qualitative content analysis on online heritage platforms from four Dutch cities. In the next section, I will start with a discussion of the general trend towards the digitization of urban heritage collections. This is necessary to understand how mediatization enables public involvement in urban heritage conservation.

14.3 Digitization of Cultural Heritage Collections

An important consequence of mediatization is the virtualization of social institutions, which means that institutions become less tied to a specific physical location (Hjarvard 2013). In the heritage field, the digitization of collections plays an important role in this process, making it easier to engage with heritage narratives without actually being present at heritage sites or archives. The advent of the internet, in particular, has contributed to the "virtualization" of urban heritage. In the last decade or so, heritage organizations have made huge efforts to make their collections available in virtual environments. Research conducted in 2013 showed that Dutch heritage institutions estimate that, so far, 28% of their collections have been digitized (DEN and Enumerate 2014).

Digital heritage collections have several advantages over their analogue equivalents. Of course, digitization is particularly important when original analogue media formats tend to deteriorate (Valtysson 2015). Furthermore, digital heritage objects can be edited, re-used and easily distributed through different media channels. A digital photo, for example, can be manipulated or combined with audio in a video or users can tag its content (Bratteteig 2008; Coyne 2012). Digitization thus gives heritage materials a new life. In virtual spaces, people can comment on these digitized heritage objects, adding personal meanings and memories. Digitization also enables multi-modal presentations, such as combinations of music, speech and moving images (Lundby 2008). Furthermore, digitized heritage collections become more accessible when they can be viewed outside an archive or museum. The availability of cultural heritage in virtual spaces thus provides several affordances to both heritage institutions and their audiences. As the Amsterdam Museum states in its business plan:

> Next to the duty to preserve and conserve, the museum also has a duty to show the collection, primarily in the museum, but also by showing it

> extramurally and digitally. An important step was to make the complete collection accessible through the internet. The Amsterdam Museum was the first Dutch museum to do so. As a follow up, a free app was developed in 2011 so that the complete collection can also be retrieved with a mobile phone.[2]

In this way, museums can reach audiences who would otherwise not visit their physical locations. Instead of needing people to come to the museum, heritage becomes accessible from home. Moreover, this enables people who have moved away to explore the heritage of the city where they grew up.

These developments diversify the ways in which the urban cultural heritage of cities is made visible and how people interact with it. As discussed in the introduction of this chapter, cities are dynamic places that continuously develop as history unfolds. The mediatization of urban cultural heritage makes it possible for people to engage with these changes. In Rotterdam, for example, World War II led to the almost complete destruction of the inner city. The author is involved in a multi-media heritage project about the 75 years of reconstruction of the city after the bombings.[3] In this project, people were invited to share their photos and videos of the reconstruction of Rotterdam, so that these analogue media formats could be digitized. The most interesting material was passed on to the city archive or made visible in the public space through exhibitions in shop windows. The project gave new life to audio-visual materials that otherwise would have remained hidden in the attics of their owners or even disappeared as old videotapes deteriorated over the years. Furthermore, the historical photos exhibited in shop windows were meant to provide inspiration for the future development of these areas.

The mediatization of urban cultural heritage thus makes the past more accessible, albeit within certain legal constraints, as this accessibility is often complicated by copyright regulations (Baker and Collins 2016; Truyen and Waelde 2016). Indeed, in 2015, the archive of the city of Rotterdam took many digitized photos offline after a legal battle with an organization representing the rights of photographers. This temporarily reversed the process of virtualization, as users again had to go the physical location of the archive to explore the photo collection.[4] This example shows that the mediatization of cultural heritage not only depends on the affordances of media but needs to be understood in relation to wider regulatory frameworks.

14.4 Audience Participation

The digitization of cultural heritage, which I discussed above, brings new opportunities for heritage institutions to let their publics participate in the preservation of the urban past. As media are increasingly integrated in the practices of these institutions, their users can take a more active role in constructing and sharing heritage narratives. Hjarvard (2013) argues that the focus on audience involvement and the production of social relations between people is a defining characteristic of how contemporary media operate. As Livingstone (2013: 26) observes about these questions of participation:

> The idea of participation has become a compelling topic for public attention, resulting in a clamor of reflexive questioning — is there enough participation in society, should institutions be more participatory, are young people too apathetic, who's listening to citizens' voices, whose voices are going unheard, and what should be done about it?

In the heritage sector, the attention paid to participation fits into longstanding developments towards democratization. Heritage institutions have indeed become more reflexive about the voices that go unheard in their work (Ashworth et al. 2007). The mediatization of cultural heritage could potentially further democratize this work, as there are now more tools with which to actively involve the public. Jenkins (2009) has described this as a participatory culture, which has lower barriers for people to produce and share cultural content by using new media such as social networking sites. Although this could potentially lead to more balanced power relations between heritage institutions and their audiences (Pruulmann-Vengerfeldt and Runnel 2011), in practice the level of participation varies widely.

Writing about participatory practices, Carpentier (2015) distinguishes between minimalist and maximalist forms of participation. In the case of the latter, people get control over the outcome of such practices while professionals retain strong control over the process in the former. I find that participatory practices in this field lean towards minimalist participation, as heritage professionals largely set the boundaries for these projects and bring them into line with an organization's aims. In so doing, they solicit inputs from their publics or facilitate initiatives such as digital storytelling and community exhibitions. Users can thus contribute more actively to heritage narratives, albeit within institutional boundaries. Of course, it is also in the interest of heritage institutions to provide opportunities for participation. These institutions are increasingly required by funders to actively involve their audiences (Watson 2007). By working with communities, they can enhance their public relevance and legitimacy.

An interesting example of such a participatory heritage initiative is the re:DDS project, curated by the Amsterdam Museum. This is a pilot project for web archaeology, in which the museum aims to reconstruct a digital city that had its base in Amsterdam. The original digital city, founded in 1993, was one of the first online communities to use the metaphor of a city for its design.[5] To reconstruct it, the museums asked former "inhabitants" to share memories and search for old servers and hard drives containing relevant information. Furthermore, computer science students have helped to make old digital archives accessible again. This example shows how participation makes it possible to involve the local public, solicit their contributions and thus provide a richer account of the urban past. In so doing, these initiatives give a voice to the diverse communities of cities. At the same time, the museum retains a central role in the execution of the project.

These participatory projects also make it possible to document the intangible heritage values that people attach to urban cultural heritage. Increasingly, heritage institutions invite people to share memories, personal stories or their experiences of particular historic events. On a dedicated website for participatory heritage activities, the Historical Museum of The Hague, for example, asks people from The Hague to share objects that relate to the history of the city.[6] The photos presented on this website are accompanied with stories about what these objects (e.g. historic newspapers, diaries and ticket stubs) mean to the participants. This fits into the democratization of heritage, as there is increasing attention paid to the ways in which people experience the heritage of cities in their everyday lives (Reijnders 2010). Consequently, heritage institutions no longer focus on merely objects and elites from the distant past but also the meanings that heritage has to urban communities in the present. These are the affective dimensions of heritage, representing how people identify with urban heritage narratives. According to Caswell and Mallick (2014), these emotional meanings are often neglected in official heritage practices, although they carry important information about how the past was experienced. These authors argue that digital participatory projects help to fill such historical gaps by involving community members.

However, of course, not all urban residents participate in such projects. Inequalities in the physical space can be echoed in the symbolic spaces of heritage initiatives (Morley 2001). In other words, people who live on the margins of cities might also be less likely to become involved in participatory heritage practices. De Kreek (2014) gives an example of this in the "Memory of East" project, which is a local memory website initiated by the Amsterdam Museum where people share stories and memories about the eastern borough of the city. In his study of the content and organizational context of the website, De Kreek (2014) observes that some neighbourhoods are underrepresented. Although the website aimed to involve minority groups, this proved to be difficult in practice:

> Although the present group invites anyone to contribute a memory about the far or recent past, not all the people who are reached with this invitation, feel they have something interesting to tell or are insecure about their writing. To deal with this, people are invited to participate in workshops, which is again a threshold for many locals. (De Kreek 2014: 17)

As a consequence, people who did not grow up in Amsterdam East are underrepresented on the website. In another project, which focused on South Asian immigrants' first day in the US, Caswell and Mallick (2014) made a similar finding that limited access to technology was a barrier for working-class immigrants to contribute to the digital archive. Thus, as heritage professionals develop participatory projects, they face the challenge of developing inclusive practices that reflect the diversity of contemporary cities.

14.5 Grassroots Heritage Initiatives

While the previous section focused on participatory projects initiated by established institutions, I will now turn to grassroots initiatives emerging outside the realm of professional organizations. These initiatives benefit from the growing availability of tools for media production. Not only are media more ubiquitous in our everyday lives because of mediatization processes, media users also have more digital technologies at their disposal to produce media content themselves (Rainie and Wellman 2012). As the software and hardware for recording, photo-editing, creating websites, scanning and storing data is now widely available, it is easier for people to archive and share material related to the history of particular cities. This is in contrast to previous eras, where the recording of the past was largely the preserve of elites (Garde-Hansen et al. 2009; Haskins 2015).

Indeed, we can observe a wide range of grassroots initiatives that aim to document the urban past. Examples are Facebook groups where old photos of cities are shared, blogs with local memories, and online popular music archives. The local Facebook pages in particular are very popular. Nowadays, almost every city has at least one Facebook group with historical photos, provoking reminiscences and nostalgia in the comment sections. Interestingly, these groups bring cultural heritage to the virtual spaces that people use on a daily basis. In so doing, they make the past of cities available on social media in an accessible manner. Writing about the "Beautiful buildings and cool places Perth has lost" Facebook group, Gregory (2015: 24) found that the discussions in the group go beyond mere talk:

> [I]n showcasing lost buildings and places from the past, social media such as Facebook enhances both awareness of and collective attachment to the past by facilitating the public expression of emotional responses to the past. Moreover, it helps to generate the social capital needed to mobilise against the destruction of heritage buildings and places.

Similarly, Silberman and Purser (2012) argue that digital technologies enable the construction of "memory communities". Thus, online heritage practices can foster social relations that extend to the physical city. The connections that are formed in online spaces then translate to actual urban encounters. In the case of the abovementioned local memory website in Amsterdam, for example, the online activities lead to walking tours past places discussed on the website.

These grassroots heritage initiatives diversify the narration of the urban past. As the barriers to content production become lower, people without formal training in the heritage field have more opportunities to find an audience by sharing historical material. This can complement the collections of established heritage institutions because grassroots initiatives might raise awareness of hidden or neglected histories. Writing about heritage initiatives in which communities themselves have a central role, Flinn (2007) discusses how these projects document the experiences of, for example, LGBTs, working-class communities and people involved in disappearing occupations. According to Flinn, Stevens and Shepherd, "[M]ost community archives offer an important and empowering assertion of community resistance to otherwise exclusionary and (often) marginalizing dominant narratives". These practices can thus lead to a wider representation of heritage themes and voices.

However, grassroots heritage initiatives also face notable sustainability and accessibility challenges. They have to work with less resources than established institutions. This means they generally use generic social media platforms (e.g. Facebook or WordPress) instead of dedicated heritage technologies (Lewi et al. 2015). Furthermore, as these bottom-up heritage projects often rely on a few enthusiasts, their continuation can be at risk when older volunteers are unable to find successors to run them (Baker and Huber 2012). Furthermore, the lack of formal archiving procedures affects the sustainability of projects. Although the informal nature of these initiatives is often their charm, it can lead to a situation where documents and files will no longer be available in the future. This is particularly the case on social media, where archival material and memories are being circulated on platforms that are not specifically designed for that purpose. Baker and Collins (2016) use the term "unintentional archives" for the initiatives that are run by individuals who do not necessarily conceive of their activities as archiving. The researchers discuss the fact that Facebook has limited archival functionality and that newer content usually replaces earlier posted material. Indeed, the design of the medium used for remembering affects how the heritage is presented and what kinds of conversation unfold (Simon 2012). Other challenges that Baker and Collins (2016) identify are a lack of resources to deal with copyright regulations and creators who gradually lose interest in the collection. Although grassroots initiatives diversify the narration of the urban past, these challenges show that they sometimes operate in a precarious position. Nevertheless, more institutional projects can also encounter issues of sustainability, as they often rely on temporary funding.

14.6 Urban Cultural Heritage Networks

In the previous sections, I have discussed the fact that the mediatization of urban cultural heritage is strongly related to several notable developments in this field: more voices can participate in the narration of the urban past, digitized content is being circulated through different media channels, and heritage institutions show increasing concern about questions of participation. In this final section, I will discuss how these developments affect the public role of heritage professionals and how grassroots initiatives relate to more institutional examples.

Museum curators and archivists are important gatekeepers when it comes to engagement with the past. Traditionally, people working in museums and archives are custodians of the heritage of cities. However, their authority is challenged in a participatory culture where lay people have more opportunities to share and comment on historical material. In such a culture, people can produce heritage narratives that are not defined and authorized by experts working in established heritage institutions (Silberman and Purser 2012). Moreover, information is no longer contained between the walls of institutions when collections are being digitized (Russo 2012; Verboom and Arora 2013). Hjarvard (2013) helpfully draws upon Bourdieu's field theory to explain how institutions become less autonomous when media affect the internal structure and norms of, for example, the heritage field. As this field is opening up to participation and a wider range of voices, heritage professionals have to redefine their public role and the ways in which they communicate with their audiences (Pruulmann-Vengerfeldt and Runnel 2011). Through new media, they are able to enter into a dialogue with their audiences and facilitate participation and co-creation. As Verboom and Arora (2013) find in a study on the museum blogosphere, "Today, museums still assert their authority, albeit in a different, more personal tone of voice, which may put pressure on their previously 'unassailable voice'".

I find that heritage professionals increasingly work in a networked structure as a consequence of the mediatization of cultural heritage. In a network, heritage organizations can collaborate with different partners to preserve and present the urban past. Furthermore, in the on- and offline networks of organizations, professionals and the public who participate in heritage practices, the activities of grassroots heritage initiatives and official heritage institutions can coexist. This enables different organizations to connect while maintaining their own organizational identity. This is useful because some grassroots heritage organizations prefer to remain relatively independent from established institutions in order to have more control over their collections (Flinn 2007). Grassroots projects that represent the heritage of specific communities can have aims that are different from those of "official" heritage institutions with a public orientation. Furthermore, some grassroots projects are more informal, as they are driven by the passion of volunteers and focus on the affective connections with the material that is preserved (Baker and Huber 2013). We thus see a range of practices within urban heritage networks that encompass different approaches to a city's past.

However, grassroots heritage initiatives can also benefit from the expertise of museums and archives. Even in a participatory culture, museums and archives are still widely recognized as institutions of authoritative knowledge (Wellington and Oliver 2015). The expertise of heritage professionals on, for example, heritage management and policy remains vital but is complemented with a more supportive role (Silberman and Purser 2012). Heritage institutions can function as central hubs of knowledge and expertise within networks. The Historical Museum of The Hague, for example, supports a heritage network that is focused on migration in this city, helping organizations representing migrants to set up their own archival practices, because these smaller bodies often lack the necessary expertise (Caswell and Mallick 2014).[7]

As central hubs in local heritage networks, heritage institutions could provide a platform for the different voices that want to raise awareness of their past. As this chapter has shown, there are an increasing number of heritage initiatives in contemporary cities. However, not all of these voices are being heard. Heritage institutions could connect the "small stories" shared on diverse media platforms to the wider narrative of urban history. Similarly, Silberman and Purser (2012: 14) define the task of heritage professionals as enabling "contemporary communities to digitally (re)produce historical environments, collective narratives and geographical visualizations that cluster individual perspectives into shared forms and processes of remembering". Particularly with the information overload in the contemporary media landscape, heritage professionals can function as gatekeepers who guide their publics to relevant information about the urban past. In so doing, they help to qualify and interpret the plethora of heritage narratives that circulate in the physical and virtual realms of contemporary cities.

14.7 Conclusion

This chapter has been concerned with the relationship between mediatization and urban cultural heritage. The concept of mediatization denotes long-term changes by which social institutions increasingly attune their practices to questions of publicity, media exposure and communication while media institutions themselves also gain a growing influence in society (Hjarvard 2013). As part of these developments, media are increasingly implicated in how cities are experienced and managed (De Lange and De Waal 2013; Koch and Latham 2014). Local governments and institutions use media to foster a sense of place and local belonging and to give cities a distinctive identity (Paganoni 2015). This image of cities is largely constituted by their cultural heritage.

In this chapter, I have discussed several consequences of mediatization for the ways in which people engage with the heritage of cities. First, the digitization of heritage collections renders them more accessible. Once digitized, heritage materials can be distributed through different media channels, re-used and edited by the public. Consequently, the engagement with heritage is no longer necessarily embedded in the physical locations of museums and archives. This gives people easy access to, for example, old photos of buildings and neighbourhoods that no longer exist. Particularly in rapidly changing cities, there is an urge to share these digital fragments of the past. Secondly, the focus on user involvement in the contemporary media landscape (Hjarvard 2013) also manifests itself in the field of cultural heritage. Heritage institutions use digital media to let their publics participate in the narration of the urban past. The practitioners working for these institutions are increasingly challenged to develop more inclusive heritage practices that represent the diversity of contemporary cities. Finally, urban communities, in turn, seize on the opportunities of a participatory culture to initiate their own grassroots heritage projects. This allows people who share a certain lifestyle, cultural interest or ethnic background to document their contributions to urban histories.

We can thus observe a growing diversity of initiatives that encompass grassroots, institutional and commercial projects. This leads to a broader representation of urban cultural heritage, as more people now participate in its preservation. In this context, heritage professionals have to redefine their pubic role because they operate in networks where many different people and organizations contribute to the preservation of urban cultural heritage. In their new role, more attention is paid to public engagement and facilitating participatory heritage practices. Heritage institutions thus draw upon various media technologies to give their audiences a more active role in the construction of heritage narratives.

To put it succinctly, these developments show how the mediatization of cultural heritage can enable richer accounts of the urban past. Mediatization proves to be a useful meta-concept for understanding developments in the urban cultural heritage field but has to be examined in relation to wider social forces. The mediatization of urban cultural heritage feeds into ongoing developments towards democratization in the heritage sector. In the last few decades, questions of inclusiveness, participation and representation have been high on the agenda in this field. As media are integrated in the practices of heritage institutions, the focus on audience participation and public engagement is further strengthened. However, even in a participatory culture, the involvement of people is constrained by the technological and socio-economic resources they have at their disposal. This challenges researchers, policy makers and heritage professionals to consider how media can be used in ways that are representative of the diverse heritage of contemporary cities.

Notes

1 Oral histories are recorded interviews with people that are conducted with the aim of capturing their subjective experiences of particular historical events (Haskins 2015). Digital storytelling is a way to enable ordinary people to develop short media products (e.g. video or audio or both) about particular personal memories or experiences (Couldry 2008; Lundby 2008).
2 All Dutch quotes have been translated by the author. The business plan was downloaded from https://www.amsterdammuseum.nl/sites/default/files/ondernemingsplanam_31_01_12_1.pdf. Accessed: 27 April 2017.
3 See www.digitup.nl. Accessed: 27 April 2017.
4 See http://www.stadsarchief.rotterdam.nl/nieuws/beeldbank-stadsarchief-rotterdam-op-zwart. Accessed: 27 April 2017.
5 http://hart.amsterdammuseum.nl/nl/page/33444. Accessed: 27 April 2017.
6 http://www.mijndenhaag.org/. Accessed: 27 April 2017.
7 https://www.haagshistorischmuseum.nl/stad-van-aankomst. Accessed: 27 April 2017.

Acknowledgements The author would like to thank Joost Groenendijk and Simone Driessen for their comments on earlier versions of this chapter.

References

Ashworth, G.J., Brian Graham, and J.E. Tunbridge. 2007. *Pluralising pasts: Identity and place in multicultural societies*. London: Pluto Press.
Baker, Sarah, and Alison Huber. 2012. Masters of our own destiny: Cultures of preservation at the Victorian Jazz Archive in Melbourne, Australia. *Popular Music History* 7 (3): 263–282.

Baker, Sarah, and Alison Huber. 2013. Notes towards a typology of the DIY institution: Identifying do-it-yourself places of popular music preservation. *European Journal of Cultural Studies* 16 (5): 513–530.

Baker, Sarah, and Jez Collins. 2016. Popular music heritage, community archives and the challenge of sustainability. *International Journal of Cultural Studies*. Advance online publication, March 9, 2016. doi: 10.1177/1367877916637150.

Bandarin, Francesco, and Ron van Oers. 2015. *Reconnecting the city: The historic urban landscape approach and the future of urban heritage*. Oxford: Wiley-Blackwell.

Bennett, Andy. 2009. "Heritage rock": Rock music, representation and heritage discourse. *Poetics* 37 (5–6): 474–489.

Bratteteig, Tone. 2008. Does it matter that it is digital? In *Digital storytelling, mediatized stories*, ed. Knut Lundby, 271–283. New York: Peter Lang.

Carpentier, Nico. 2015. Differentiating between access, interaction and participation. *Conjunctions. Transdisciplinary Journal of Cultural Participation* 2 (2): 7–28.

Caswell, Michelle, and Samip Mallick. 2014. Collecting the easily missed stories: Digital participatory microhistory and the South Asian American Digital Archive. *Archives and Manuscripts* 42 (1): 73–86.

Couldry, Nick. 2008. Mediatization or mediation? Alternative understandings of the emergent space of digital storytelling. *New Media & Society* 10 (3): 373–391.

Coyne, Richard. 2012. Mosaics and multiples: Online digital photography and the framing of heritage. In *Heritage and social media: Understanding heritage in a participatory culture*, ed. Elisa Giaccardi, 161–178. London: Routledge.

De Groot, Jerome. 2009. *Consuming history: Historians and heritage in contemporary popular culture*. London, New York: Routledge.

De Kreek, Mike. 2014. Evolving empowerment in an online community collecting memories of Amsterdam East. Challenges and Solutions. In *CIRN Prato Conference 2014*, ed. Larry Stillman, and Tom Denison, Centre for Community and Social Informatics, Faculty of IT, Monash University, Monash.

De Lange, Michiel, and Martijn De Waal. 2013. Owning the city: New media and citizen engagement in urban design. *First Monday* 18 (11). http://dx.doi.org/10.5210/fm.v18i11.4954.

DEN and Enumerate. 2014. *De digitale feiten 2013–2014. Resultaten van de Nederlandse inbreng in Enumerate*. The Hague: Stichting Digitaal Erfgoed Nederland.

Farinosi, Manuela, and Alessandra Micalizzi. 2016. Geolocating the past: Online memories after the L'Aquila earthquake. In *Memory in a Mediated World*, ed. Andrea Hajek, Christine Lohmeier, and Christian Pentzold, 90–110. New York: Palgrave Macmillan.

Finnemann, Niels O. 2014. Digitization: New trajectories of mediatization? In *Mediatization of communication*, ed. Knut Lundby, 297–321. Berlin, New York: Walter de Gruyter.

Flinn, Andrew. 2007. Community histories, community archives: Some opportunities and challenges. *Journal of the Society of Archivists* 28: 151–176.

Garde-Hansen, J, Andrew Hoskins, and A Reading. 2009. Introduction. In *Save as… digital memories*, ed. J Garde-Hansen, Andrew Hoskins, and A Reading, 1–21. New York: Palgrave Macmillan.

Garduño Freeman, Cristina. 2010. Photosharing on Flickr: Intangible heritage and emergent publics. *International Journal of Heritage Studies* 16 (4–5): 352–368.

Glaeser, Edward. 2011. *Triumph of the city: How our greatest invention makes us richer, smarter, greener, healthier, and happier*. New York: Penguin Press.

Graham, Brian J., and Peter Howard. 2008. Heritage and identity. In *The Ashgate research companion to heritage and identity*, ed. Brian J. Graham and Peter Howard, 1–15. Aldershot: Ashgate.

Gregory, Jenny. 2015. Connecting with the past through social media: The "Beautiful buildings and cool places Perth has lost" Facebook group. *International Journal of Heritage Studies* 21 (1): 22–45.

Groote, Peter, and Tialda Haartsen. 2008. The communication of heritage: Creating place identities. In *The Ashgate research companion to heritage and identity*, ed. Brian J. Graham, and Peter Howard, 181–194. Aldershot: Ashgate.

Hall, Stuart. 1999. Unsettling 'the heritage', reimagining the postnation. Whose heritage? *Third Text* 13 (49): 3–13.

Harrison, Rodney. 2013. Forgetting to remember, remembering to forget: Late modern heritage practices, sustainability and the "crisis" of accumulation of the past. *International Journal of Heritage Studies* 19: 579–595.

Haskins, Ekaterina V. 2015. *Popular memories: Commemoration, participatory culture, and democratic citizenship*. South Carolina: University of South Carolina Press.

Hepp, Andreas. 2013. *Cultures of mediatization*. Cambridge: Polity Press.

Hjarvard, Stig. 2013. *The mediatization of culture and society*. London: Routledge.

Jenkins, Henry. 2009. *Confronting the challenges of participatory culture: Media education for the 21st century*. Cambridge MA: The MIT Press.

Koch, Regan, and Alan Latham. 2014. Representing and imagining the city. In *Cities and social change: Encounters with contemporary urbanism*, ed. Ronan Paddison and Eugene McCann, 14–32. London: Sage.

Lewi, Hannah, Andrew Murray, Wally Smith, and Sarah Webber. 2015. Some implications of digital social media for heritage practice. Paper presented at the Australia ICOMOS Conference 2015, Nov 5–8, Adelaide. http://www.

aicomos.com/wp-content/uploads/Some-implications-of-digital-social-media-for-heritage-practice.pdf. Accessed 27 Apr 2017.

Livingstone, Sonia. 2013. The participation paradigm in audience research. *The Communication Review* 16 (1–2): 21–30.

Lundby, Knut. 2008. Introduction: Digital storytelling, mediatized stories. In *Digital storytelling, mediatized stories*, ed. Knut Lundby, 1–20. New York: Peter Lang.

Malpas, Jeff. 2008. New media, cultural heritage and the sense of place: Mapping the conceptual ground. *International Journal of Heritage Studies* 14 (3): 197–209.

Massey, Doreen. 1995. Places and their pasts. *History Workshop Journal* 39 (1): 182–192.

Moore, Kevin. 2000. *Museums and popular culture.* London: Cassell.

Morley, David. 2001. Belongings: Place, space and identity in a mediated world. *European Journal of Cultural Studies* 4 (4): 425–448.

Paganoni, Maria C. 2015. *City branding and new media: Linguistic perspectives, discursive strategies and multimodality.* Hampshire: Palgrave Macmillan UK.

Pessach, Guy. 2008. [Networked] memory institutions: Social remembering, privatization and its discontents. *Cardozo Arts and Entertainment Law Journal* 26 (1): 71–149.

Prévélakis, Georges. 2008. City museums and the geopolitics of globalisation. In *City museums and city development*, ed. Ian Jones, Robert R. MacDonald, and Darryl McIntyre, 16–26. Maryland: Alta Mira Press.

Proctor, Nancy. 2010. Digital: Museum as platform, curator as champion, in the age of social media. *Curator: The Museum Journal* 53 (1): 35–43.

Pruulmann-Vengerfeldt, Pille, and Agnes Aljas. 2011. Digital cultural heritage—Challenging museums, archives and users. *Journal of Ethnology and Folkloristics* 3 (1): 109–127.

Pruulmann-Vengerfeldt, Pille, and Pille Runnel. 2011. When the museum becomes the message for participating audiences. *Communication Management Quarterly* 6 (21): 159–179.

Rainie, Lee, and Barry Wellman. 2012. *Networked: The new social operating system.* Cambridge MA: MIT Press.

Reijnders, Stijn. 2010. Collecting the contemporary in the imagined city. *Quotidian* 2: 104–110.

Roberts, Les. 2015. Navigating the "archive city" Digital spatial humanities and archival film practice. *Convergence: The International Journal of Research into New Media Technologies* 21 (1): 100–115.

Russo, Angelina. 2012. The rise of the 'media museum': Creating interactive cultural experiences through social media. In *Heritage and social media: Understanding heritage in a participatory culture*, ed. Elisa Giaccardi, 145–157. New York: Routledge.

Silberman, Neil, and Margaret Purser. 2012. Collective memory as affirmation: People-centered cultural heritage in a digital age. In *Heritage and social media: Understanding heritage in a participatory culture*, ed. Elisa Giaccardi, 13–29. New York: Routledge.

Simon, Roger I. 2012. Remembering together: Social media and the formation of the historical present. In *Heritage and social media: Understanding heritage in a participatory culture*, ed. Elisa Giaccardi, 89–106. New York: Routledge.

Smith, Laurajane. 2006. *Uses of heritage*. London: Routledge.

Snoek, Cees G.M., Bauke Freiburg, Johan Oomen, and Roeland Ordelman. 2010. Crowdsourcing rock n' roll multimedia retrieval.In *Proceedings of the 18th ACM international conference on Multimedia*, 1535–1538, ACM, New York.

Truyen, Frederik, and Charlotte Waelde. 2016. Copyright, cultural heritage and photography: A gordian knot? In *Cultural heritage in a changing world*, ed. Karol J. Borowiecki, Neil Forbes, and Antonella Fresa, 77–96. Springer.

Valtysson, Bjarki. 2015. From policy to platform: The digitization of Danish cultural heritage. *International Journal of Cultural Policy*, advance online publication, 14 Sept 2015. doi: 10.1080/10286632.2015.1084300.

Van den Broek, Andries, Jos de Haan, and Frank Huysmans. 2009. *Cultuurbewonderaars en beoefenaars. Trends in cultuurparticipatie en mediagebruik* [Digging culture and doing culture. Trends in cultural participation and media use]. Den Haag: Sociaal en Cultureel Planbureau.

Van der Hoeven, Arno. 2016. Urban memories on social media: Remembering, sharing and mapping. Paper presented at the annual conference of the International Association for Media and Communication Research: Memory, Commemoration and Communication, July 27–31 2016, University of Leicester, United Kingdom.

Verboom, Jessica, and Payal Arora. 2013. Museum 2.0: A study into the culture of expertise within the museum blogosphere. *First Monday* 18 (8). http://dx.doi.org/10.5210/fm.v18i8.4538 .

Watson, Sheila. 2007. *Museums and their communities.* London, New York: Routledge.

Wellington, Shannon, and Gillian Oliver. 2015. Reviewing the digital heritage landscape: The intersection of digital media and museum practice. In *The international handbooks of museum studies: Museum practice*, ed. Conal McCarty, 577–598. Chichester: Wiley.

PART IV

Conclusion

CHAPTER 15

The Complexities of Mediatization: Charting the Road Ahead

Göran Bolin and Andreas Hepp

15.1 Introduction

How should we move ahead with mediatization research? One way to answer this question is to briefly reflect on the development of mediatization research over the last few years. Mediatization started as an ungainly word for native English speakers, but today we can see how gradually a more unified, albeit at the same time internally differentiated, common field of mediatization research has emerged and how that field that has also become institutionalized in research sections of international associations (e.g. ECREA) and in numerous panels at international conferences. On the one hand, this field, like all fields of relative coherence, also includes internal debates on how mediatization should be theorized (for an overview, see Lundby 2014) and, on the other hand, the degrees to which the concept has explanatory value (e.g. Deacon

G. Bolin (✉)
Södertörn University, Stockholm, Sweden
e-mail: goran.bolin@sh.se

A. Hepp
University of Bremen, Bremen, Germany
e-mail: ahepp@uni-bremen.de

O. Driessens et al. (eds.), *Dynamics Of Mediatization*,
Transforming Communications – Studies in Cross-Media Research,
DOI 10.1007/978-3-319-62983-4_15

and Stanyer 2014; cf. Hepp et al. 2015; Lunt and Livingstone 2016; Ekström et al. 2016). The chapters in this volume represent a selection of "new voices" that have emerged in this process and indicate some of the opportunities, but also complexities, that mediatization research encompasses.

In the preceding chapters, we have seen empirical and theoretical reflection on mediatization as a long-term process. The sum of these descriptions illustrates the very dynamics of this process, pointing to its multi-dimensional and multi-level nature. In this concluding chapter, we will reflect on the implications of these various contributions and suggest some trajectories that mediatization research might embark upon. We will do so, firstly, by accounting for the complexities that have been indicated by the preceding chapters in this volume, structured against various institutional, cultural and social *dimensions*, and different analytical *levels* of mediatization, as outlined with reference to a macro-micro scale. Secondly, and on this basis, we will systematize the main features that run through the complex nature of the mediatization process. There are at least three kinds of complexity we see related to the dynamics of mediatization: the complexity of the media environment or landscape, the complexity of an entanglement of practices with digital media technologies, and the complexity of the levels of analysis. Reflecting on these complexities, in a third section, we will try to delineate some future trajectories of mediatization research.

15.2 Dynamics of Mediatization—The Lines of Discourse in This Volume

When it comes to the various institutional, cultural and social dimensions discussed with reference to the dynamics of mediatization, it is obvious that the focus on institutional relations is a prominent feature of many chapters, most notably so concerning the political institutions in relation to the institutions of journalism (but also the media more broadly). Here, we can see analyses of the relations between media institutions and political institutions more generally, as in Ruth Garland's chapter in this volume, where civil servants and policy advisors in the UK have struggled with the working procedures of the news media. This specific tension is also discussed in Ximena Orchard's chapter, and although the Chilean setting reveals some differences to the UK case, the tensions between the "political logics" and the "media logics" are similar. The principles of such conflicting "institutional logics" are further discussed in Magnus Fredriksson and Josef Pallas's chapter—a chapter that also introduces distinctions between different types of organizations and the ways in which such variations, coupled with differences in political systems, media systems and societal sectors, should impact on our understanding of mediatization. We can notice here an increasing sensitivity for the complexities of institutions and their levels of analysis and how they relate to the mediatization process.

One dimension of the mediatization process not explored in its full potential in previous mediatization debate encompasses the various social and cultural processes that can be seen as being related to, but also as indicators of, mediatization. Thus, Kim Schrøder theorises "audiencization" as a parallel process related to mediatization, while Tobias Pontara and Ulrik Volgsten analyse the process of "musicalization". Similarly, Christian Hviid Mortensen gives an interesting account of "musealization" as a process indicating the increasing importance of mediatization in society through the fact that popular media are becoming the focus of museum interest, while Arno van der Hoeven in a similar argument mentions "heritagization" as yet another parallel process to mediatization. We can understand such contributions as an argument for contextualizing mediatization within the complexities of everyday practices in a better way. Focusing just on institutional dynamics is not enough to grasp the manifold character of mediatization. But moving to such further social and cultural aspects means a fundamental increase of complexity when analysing this meta-process.

To add to such complexities of dimensions, a number of complexities of various levels of mediatization are revealed in the preceding chapters. These levels range from the macro-analytical perspective of Zrinjka Peruško to the meso-analytical levels of specific institutions, illustrated by the chapters by Garland and Orchard. A further emphasis on the micro level is made in the chapter by Barbara Brodzińska-Mirowska and Lukasz Wojtkowski, who specifically address this in relation to the mediatization of politics. Also, Magnus Andersson reflects on questions of the micro in his discussion of the "mediatization from below".

While the institutional perspective of mediatization is dominant—in this volume as well as in most mediatization debates—several of the chapters adopt the historically more far-reaching socio-cultural perspective on mediatization as a meta-process (Krotz 2007), regarding the media as a "moulding force" (Hepp 2013) that is an integrated part of wider social and cultural processes. These perspectives also highlight some "specificities of media"—not only as institutions but also as technologies (including their sign systems, codes etc.) and the types of social interaction these codes and technological features privilege when they increasingly enter into more spheres of everyday life. We can notice here a sensitivity not only for media-related practices but also for their entanglement with objects and technologies. A focus on "media" as content structures and technological features from such structuralist perspectives is rare in previous discussions, although they have been pointed out occasionally (see, for example, Bolin 2014). However, similar approaches—though not as determining as the structuralist perspectives of, for example, Baudrillard (1971)—attract the attention of several chapters in this volume, both in a meta-theoretical respect, where Marian Adolf thoroughly discusses the implications of different conceptualizations of "media", and in empirical respects. The latter is most clearly illustrated in James Miller's account of how sound media have become integrated into cars. But the musical codes and technologies are also penetrating everyday life in intricate ways, as illustrated in Pontara and Volgsten's contribution to this volume.

Altogether, these chapters demonstrate that in the longer historical perspective, we have always been mediatized. But we have indeed been mediatized in different ways, depending on the specific combination of the media technologies, genres, and organizational forms that are characteristic for each specific society. All social and cultural processes presume some sort of mediation, and with the development of communications technologies, from cave paintings and clay tablets, and from the symbolic systems of cuneiform to the advanced and highly abstract symbol systems of contemporary societies, humankind has lived inside of the symbolic worlds as well as the organizational forms of communication. The increased complexity of the mediatization process goes in tandem with the complexities of modern societies.

15.3 Three Complexities of Mediatization

As we could notice in our discussion of the different chapters of this volume, the links between them show the complexities of mediatization: there is a variety of different, partly contradicting dynamics of mediatization which results in the challenge of analysing this meta-process properly. This explains the partly contradicting results of existing research.

But what are the complexities of mediatization more in detail? And what does complexity mean in this respect?

While being used more and more in media and communication research (cf. Qvortrup 2006), complexity is an opaque term (Manson 2001; Walby 2007). For our purpose, we have a twofold understanding of complexity (Loosen and Scholl 2017: 6). On the one hand, complexity refers to the variety and diversity of media, their interrelatedness and, because of that, also contingency of technologically mediated communication. On the other hand, complexity refers to the uncertainty, lack of clarity and openness which goes hand in hand with the variety and diversity of media. The challenge for mediatization research is to address this complexity. As we have seen in the chapters of this volume, there are at least three kinds of complexity we should have in mind: first, the complexity of the media environment or landscape; second, the complexity of the entanglement of practices with digital media technology; and, third, the complexity of levels of analysis. In the following, we want to elaborate these three kinds of complexity further.

The increasing *complexity of the media environment or landscape* is closely related to the process of mediatization as such. As discussed in various publications (for an overview, see Couldry and Hepp 2013: 197), there is a qualitative and a quantitative dimension of mediatization as a long-term process. In the quantitative respect, mediatization is about the increase and spread of technologically based communication media. While the first mass media were restricted to print media, over the last 150 years the number of media technologies and forms has increased fundamentally. Historically, the media have changed from mechanical media to electronic media and today's digital media which have become not only means of communication but also means of producing content and also data—resulting in the "datafication" of society (cf. van Dijck 2014; Schäfer and van Es 2017). Furthermore, not only has the number of media increased. As these technical communication media rely on organizations (Thompson 1995: 87–100), the number of organizations involved in these processes has grown. Furthermore, with digitization and datafication, the character of these organizations has transformed when it comes to their institutional forms and their ways of operating (Bolin 2011; Bolin and Schwarz 2015). While we as media and communication scholars were for a long time used to having "media organisations" (Curran 2000) in the traditional sense of content-producing corporations in mind, many of the most influential organizations of the present are "tech firms" like Apple, Facebook and Google. In light of this, we have to re-think what a "media organisation" really is and distinguish between, for example, content-producing organizations and those that build on media-user profiling and database marketing systems (Bolin 2014; Turow 2006, 2011).

The qualitative dimension of mediatization means that these changes are of importance not because of the massive quantitative increase in data generated and circulating within the media and communications industries. They are of importance because, parallel to the quantitative amassment of data, the ways in which we as humans communicatively construct our society transform. So in qualitative terms this means: What exactly transforms with a changing media environment or landscape? In this general sense, we can understand all mediatization research as being occupied with such qualitative and also ontological questions. The spread of technologically based communication media is not an interesting fact on its own. It becomes relevant in so far as it is related to the wider qualitative transformations of society.

Such questions provoke conceptual frameworks, and these frameworks also have an epistemological dimension in that they will impact on our understanding of society. Common conceptualizations such as "media environment" or "media landscape"—which are two oft-used concepts—in fact produce different approaches to the mediatization process. If we understand the "media environment"—or, for that matter, "media ecology"—as the entire body of available media at any given time (Hasebrink and Hölig 2014: 16; Jensen and Helles 2015: 292; Livingstone 2001: 307), we could theorize these qualitative and quantitative dimensions in terms of intricate webs of complex nature, kinds of "rhizomatic" and complex media structures. But we should also be careful regarding our use of metaphors. Given the natural scientific roots of the "environment" or the biological roots of "ecology" metaphors, complexity can indicate an organic change or development of the media. In some traditions, this might imply some sort of "technological determinism", where technology develops through an internal logic of its own, independent of human action.

Another possibility of reflecting on this complexity is offered by the term "media landscape". This concept puts emphasis on the constructedness of the media as a specific combination of technologies and contents, being formed, used and appropriated socially (Bolin 2006). The landscape metaphor rather points to the totality of media that is present at any one point in time in a society; the technological and symbolic media structure, the amount of technologies and contents (signs and messages) that an individual can react to, act against, or ignore. Some of these technologies and semiotic structures are more accessible than others, and, depending on the individual trajectory that people have through these landscapes and the experiences they have acquired, the landscape will privilege certain types of approaches and actions over others. Media landscape is a spatial metaphor that indicates a phenomenological "social world" perspective. And the core of this concept is to emphasize the "fabricated nature": landscapes are symbolic and material structures that are shaped by humans, for some purpose. Thus, the metaphor of landscape allows us to think about the media in ways that transgress the structure-agency dichotomy and make it possible to see actions structured by frameworks that were produced by previous social actions, by preceding others. However, this inclusiveness can in a less sophisticated use also result in a certain vagueness of "landscape", being much harder to operationalize in empirical research than the concept of media environment.

Irrespective of whether one uses the concept of "media environment" or "media landscape", when it comes to the complexities of mediatization, both hint at the same: the complexity which is caused by the variety and diversity of present technologically based media in their entirety *and* relatedness. In such a media environment or landscape, processes of communicative construction take place across these different media, which we thus have to understand in their interrelatedness. This is discussed by the help of various concepts in media and communication research: "re-mediation" (Bolter and Grusin 2000), "polymedia" (Madianou and Miller 2013), "media plenty" (Ellis 2000), "transmedia" (Jansson and Lindell 2014) or "media manifold" (Couldry and Hepp 2017). While these concepts differ in detail and their reference to complexity theory, the main argument is always the progressively deepening cross-media relatedness with respect to everyday practices of communication (see Hasebrink et al. 2015; Schrøder 2011). For example, when we seek information, maintain contact with others, build up networks, work in our organizations' offices, and so on, we do so across different media. As a result, certain functionalities can move from one medium to another, or one medium can carry the potential for various functionalities, depending on the ways it is used. Consequently, we can expect media-related transformations to be less attributable to the influence of a single dominating medium, as was the case in former times. This complexity results in many dynamics and is a major challenge for mediatization research.

Second, there is the *complexity of an entanglement of communication practices with digital media technology.* At this point, mediatization research can learn a lot from practice theory, which for a long time emphasized not only that practices are "embodied" but also the need to consider the nexus of practices with "artefacts, hybrids, and natural objects" (Schatzki 2001: 11). The argument to focus on the "entanglement" (Ezzamel and Willmott 2014) of practices with objects is of special interest because with mediatization communicative practice increasingly turns into a media- and therefore object-related practice. Here, practice theory itself puts emphasis on the media as a specific kind of object when it comes to the production of meaning: "writing, printing and electronic media mould social (here, above all, discursive) practices" (Reckwitz 2002: 253). This is the reason why many communicative practices are "media practice[s]" (Couldry 2004: 125); that is, they are undertaken in relation to media. And as recent digital media are no longer only means of communication but at the same time means of collecting and aggregating data, it is striking how much algorithms become part of the present complexities of mediatization.

One possibility might be to call this "algorithmic complexity". This term, however, has a very particular meaning, which refers to the computational representation of social life (and nature). Information theory defines "algorithmic complexity" as the "simplest computational algorithm that can reproduce system behavior" (Manson 2001: 406). But this is less the complexity we have in mind with reference to the entanglement of communication practices with digital media technology. Rather, the complexity comes from the process of "delegating" certain forms of (communicative) practice to software. There are very simple examples of this in the present stage of mediatization. Based on the digital traces a person has left when using the search engine Google, for example, news and advertising get specifically tailored for this person. Based on the network of friends a person already has on Facebook, he or she gets suggestions for further friends. Or based on the previous digital purchases or selections of users at Amazon, Apple Music or Spotify, the algorithms produce suggestions for further titles they might like.

In a certain way, there is an "algorithmic complexity" related to this: a complexity of how to program software in a way that such "recommendations" can become possible. But the more crucial point we want to make is a specific *social* complexity related with this: when software becomes part of processes of social construction, the "involved humans" but also the "observing researchers" are confronted with a lack of clarity of how to capture agency. One possibility to solve this problem is to extend the understanding of agency as it is done, for example, within actor network theory which also conceptualizes "things" and "technology" as having a certain form of agency (Latour 2007). However, the risk of this is to lose analytical sharpness and a critical position by mixing human agency (which is in principal controllable) and the *delegation* of this agency by the help of various technologies.

Within mediatization research, we can instead refer to a longer discussion about the "materiality of media" (Gumbrecht and Pfeiffer 1994), with concepts such as "affordances" (Hutchby 2001: 444), "modus operandi" (Hjarvard 2013: 17) or the "moulding forces" (Hepp 2013: 54) of media. As most media today are digital media and therefore software-based (Manovich 2013), the challenge is to extend such concepts to reflect the changing character of the materiality of the media. This is done, for example, with reference to the affordances of "mobile media" (Schrock 2015), of "blogs" (Hopkins 2015) or of "network sites" (boyd 2010). However, and in addition to this, having in mind the changing media environment or landscape and its fundamental cross-media character, the challenge is that within the present stage of mediatization, transformation can no longer be grasped by focusing on any one single medium in isolation but by understanding specific media in relation to others (Chadwick 2013: 207).

Third, all of this comes together in the *complexity of levels of analysis*. For a long time—and the chapters in this volume refer to the discussion (see the section before)—in early mediatization research, we were used to handling the complexity of levels of analysis by a clear distinction of micro, meso and macro (Hjarvard 2013: 27): The micro level is typically considered the level of "action", "practice" and "doing". The meso level is considered the level of "organisations" and "institutions". And the macro level is considered the level of a mediatized "society" as such. Analytically speaking, such a distinction is helpful and goes back to a long-lasting discussion in social sciences about the micro-macro link (Alexander et al. 1987; Coleman 1990).

When it comes to recent processes of mediatization, the challenge is that such distinctions are a bit too clear-cut to grasp the complexity of mediatization as a cross-level phenomenon. First of all, we cannot understand mediatization without reflecting media *also* as organizations and institutions. However, even these institutions are constructed by human practice, since structures are always produced and reproduced through micro processes and therefore are a cross-level phenomenon, as David Morley (1992) has pointed out. In addition, for a longer time, the (communicative) construction of society is based on mediated communication and therefore deeply linked to media which are the basis of this. Therefore, understanding mediatization in its present stage might rather mean putting emphasis on its interlinking character instead of pressing this into a clear-cut analysis of distinct levels. Complexity at this point refers to the problem of analysing the interrelatedness not just of media but also of different sub-processes of mediatization in and across the various domains of the social world.

This refers to what we can call the domain-specificity or mediatization. The term "social domain" is used by scholars of mediatization as a generic term to grasp the different "meaningful sections" of society (i.e. Ekström et al. 2016; Hjarvard 2013; Lunt and Livingstone 2016). The scaling of what is called social domain can vary from relationships, groups, communities and organizations up to whole social fields or systems. While this can be understood as a certain vagueness in terminology, the core issue of using the term "social domain" in mediatization research is to point to the fact that mediatization is not a homogeneous process across all parts of society resulting in a one-dimensional transformation of social construction.

The dynamics of mediatization in each social domain can be understood as a sub-process of mediatization. When it comes to the complexity of understanding the interrelatedness of such social domains of mediatization, the challenge is to find a proper terminology for this. Up to now, scholars of mediatization have used various terminological approaches to address this: for example, by using the concept of "social fields" as it was originally developed by Bourdieu (Couldry 2012: 144–153), the idea of "systems" in the sense of Luhmann (Kunelius and Reunanen 2016: 8–12) or the concept of "social worlds" as it comes from symbolic interactionism and social phenomenology (Hepp and Krotz 2014: 6–9). However, because of their origin in general sociology, all of these concepts are not centred on mediatization itself, and they remain vague when it comes to questions of media and communication and their role in social and cultural change.

As a consequence, any mediatization research that wants to address the complex interrelatedness of mediatization sub-processes needs a concept that is able to describe how media and communications vary in different social domains and at the same time reflecting human agency and practice. One idea for doing this might be the approach of analysing the different communicative figurations of these social domains: their actor constellation, frames of relevance as an overall orientation in practice, and the communication practices entangled with a certain media ensemble (Couldry and Hepp 2017: 66; Hepp and Communicative Figurations Research Network 2017: 27). Other approaches are, of course, possible. But irrespective of which detailed approach one takes, the challenge is to develop a better language for analysing the multi-level complexity of mediatization.

15.4 Perspectives of How to Research the Complexities of Mediatization

It is obvious that the challenges that are related to the complexities of mediatization cannot be addressed in one theoretical approach or one empirical study alone. However, the reflections discussed so far do offer the chance to formulate some perspectives for mediatization research.

First, when it comes to the media environment or landscape, an important task for mediatization research is to develop a better contextual understanding of how mediatization relates to more general changes in culture and society. While mediatization is a domain-specific process and we should indeed carefully address this process specifically, we also have to be aware that the environment or landscape of the media stretches across different domains. Hence, some of the media-related changes are more general, while the consequences of these changes remain highly domain-specific. One important perspective for mediatization research is to reflect more carefully on how the trends of the overall media environment or landscape change over time. At this point, highly general statements like "digitalization" seem to be less helpful, not because they are wrong but because they are not concrete enough for proper empirical mediatization research. The question is rather: considering digitalization as a matter of fact, or a point of departure, in which way does the overall human media environment change?

It is obvious that this question is an abstraction in the sense that there is not one media environment or one media landscape but that there are also variations of them—within as well as between different societies. And it is obvious that we cannot talk about these variations without also focusing on questions of political and economic power, since media environments or landscapes are not just given but are constructed by humans who act in specific cultural, political and social settings. This is something that has to be integrated into such an analysis. It remains an important perspective for mediatization research to reflect on questions of the overall interrelatedness of media and how this defines the practicalities of communicating with individual media. This is the point where historical studies are important, as historical perspectives allow for more detailed understandings of the present particularities.

A second perspective is to integrate questions of technology—including data and algorithms—much more deeply into mediatization research than has been the case so far. When communicative practices become entangled with *digital* media technologies, there is a special need to put emphasis on this. At present, the discussion about "metric power" (Beer 2016), "algorithmic power" (Mager 2012) and "datafication" (Schäfer and van Es 2017) mostly takes place in parallel to mediatization research. Sometimes, one has the impression that parts of mediatization research are much more closely related to questions of electronic mass media than to the most recent developments of digital media. At this point, an important task for mediatization research is to integrate discussions about data, software, metrics and algorithms—including the adoption of digital methods—into analytical approaches that can help us understand the most recent forms of mediatization. Arguably, the digitization of (almost) all media has introduced a range of qualitative shifts that have affected production and reception processes, market formations and social relations in ways that are as of yet clearly under-researched, and there is a strong need to rethink the consequences this has for mediatization theory. If Walter Benjamin (Benjamin 1977 [1936]) contemplated the fate of art and culture in "the age of mechanical reproduction", we should in a similar manner ask questions on the consequences for art, culture, sociality as well as the political and the economic in "the age of digital reproduction" (Bolin 2009: 348).

A third perspective for mediatization research is to extend its own terminological approach. As a general term, mediatization highlights a problem of what to research critically: that is, the interrelation between the changes of media and communication on the one hand and the wider changes within culture and society on the other. Taking this as a point of departure, we already learned a lot about different sub-processes of mediatization in the various domains of society. However, to have an overall picture of what is going on when it comes to mediatization, such different studies should speak in a better way to each other. There should be the possibility to link the outcome of their research in a better way. Thus, it is necessary to develop a discourse on possible concepts that is able to interrelate the different kinds of research in a better way.

This extension and clarification of terminology should also include a more detailed discussion of the relation between "mediation" and "mediatization". Terminologically spoken, both concepts are needed. Whereas "mediation" refers to the process of communication in general—that is, how communication has to be understood as involving the ongoing mediation of meaning construction (Martín-Barbero 1993; Silverstone 2005)—"mediatization" is a category designed to describe change. As it is argued in mediatization research (Couldry and Hepp 2013: 197), it then becomes possible to link the two concepts: "Mediatization" reflects how the overall consequences of multiple processes of "mediation" have changed over time with the emergence of different kinds of media. But how can we relate the two analytically? What does change of mediation mean in detail? And how does this take place in our present media manifold? Such questions indicate the amount of terminological as well as analytical and empirical work only when it comes to relating mediation and mediatization.

However, we should at the same time be careful that such a discourse does not become too homogenizing. Because of the complexity of mediatization across the different domains of society and because of the contextual character of each media environment or landscape, we need a variety of different terminological approaches within mediatization research. Therefore, the main perspective is to move forward in a joint discourse on what we might call *bridging* concepts: that is, analytical concepts that are sharp enough to link the research on the complex dynamics of mediatization in different social domains but at the same time are open enough to connect to the variety of further concepts that are needed for proper empirical mediatization research within the specific social domains.

For sure, there are still other important perspectives of mediatization research that could be worth exploring. In this volume, we have put an emphasis on the importance of analysing mediatization in relation to other meta-processes, such as globalization, individualization, commercialization and even modernization. Addressing these interrelations has meant reflecting on issues of the overall media environment or landscape, on issues of practices being entangled with digital media technology, and on issues of interlinking the levels of analysis. It is our hope that the perspectives outlined in the preceding chapters might be a starting point for furthering this analysis.

References

Alexander, Jeffrey C., Bernhard Giesen, Richard Münch, and Neil J. Smelser. 1987. *The micro-macro link.* Berkeley: University of California Press.

Baudrillard, Jean. 1971. Requiem pour les media. *Utopie* 4: 35–51.

Beer, David. 2016. *Metric power.* London: Palgrave.

Benjamin, Walter. 1977 [1936]. The work of art in the age of mechanical reproduction. In *Mass Communication and Society*, ed. James Curran, Michael Gurevitch, and Janet Woollacott, 384–408. London: Edward Arnold.

Bolin, Göran. 2006. Electronic geographies: Media landscapes as technological and symbolic environments. In *Geographies of communication. The spatial turn in media studies*, ed. Jesper Falkheimer, and André Jansson, 67–86. Göteborg: Nordicom.

Bolin, Göran. 2009. Symbolic production and value in media industries. *Journal of Cultural Economy* 2 (3): 345–361.

Bolin, Göran. 2011. *Value and the media. Cultural production and consumption in digital markets.* Farnham: Ashgate.

Bolin, Göran. 2014. Institution, technology, world: Relationships between the media, culture and society. In *Mediatization of communication*, ed. Knut Lundby, 175–197. Berlin: de Gruyter.

Bolin, Göran, and Jonas A. Schwarz. 2015. Heuristics of the algorithm. Big data, user interpretation and institutional translation. *Big Data & Society* 2 (2): 1–12.

Bolter, Jay D., and Richard Grusin. 2000. *Remediation: Understanding new media.* Cambridge: MIT Press.

Boyd, Danah. 2010. Social network sites as networked publics: Affordances, dynamics, and implications. In *networked self: Identity, community, and culture on social network sites*, ed. Zizi Papacharissi, 39–58. London: Routledge.

Chadwick, Andrew. 2013. *The hybrid media system: Politics and power.* Oxford: Oxford University Press.

Coleman, James S. 1990. *Foundations of social theory.* Cambridge: Belknap Press.

Couldry, Nick. 2004. Theorising media as practice. *Social Semiotics* 14 (2): 115–132.

Couldry, Nick. 2012. *Media, society, world: Social theory and digital media practice*. Cambridge: Polity Press.
Couldry, Nick, and Andreas Hepp. 2013. Conceptualising mediatization: Contexts, traditions, arguments. *Communication Theory* 23 (3): 191–202.
Couldry, Nick, and Andreas Hepp. 2017. *The mediated construction of reality*. Cambridge: Polity Press.
Curran, James. 2000. Introduction. In *Media organisations in society*, ed. James Curran, 9–16. London: Arnold.
Deacon, David, and James Stanyer. 2014. Mediatization: Key concept or conceptual bandwagon? *Media, Culture and Society* 36 (7): 1032–1044.
Ekström, Mats, Johan Fornäs, André Jansson, and Anne Jerslev. 2016. Three tasks for mediatization research: Contributions to an open agenda. *Media, Culture and Society* 38 (7): 1090–1108.
Ellis, John. 2000. Scheduling: The last creative act in television? *Media, Culture and Society* 22 (1): 25–38.
Ezzamel, Mahmoud, and Hugh Willmott. 2014. Registering 'the ethical' in organization theory formation: Towards the disclosure of an 'invisible force'. *Organization Studies* 35 (7): 1013–1039.
Gumbrecht, Hans U., and K. Ludwig Pfeiffer. 1994. *Materialities of communication*. Stanford, CA: Stanford UP.
Hasebrink, Uwe, and Sascha Hölig. 2014. Topografie der Öffentlichkeit. *APuZ* 22–23: 16–22.
Hasebrink, Uwe, Klaus B. Jensen, Hilde van den Bulck, Sascha Hölig, and Pieter Maeseele. 2015. Changing patterns of media use across cultures: A challenge for longitudinal research. *International Journal of Communication* 9: 23.
Hepp, Andreas. 2013. *Cultures of mediatization*. Cambridge: Polity Press.
Hepp, Andreas, and Friedrich Krotz. 2014. Mediatized worlds: Understanding everyday mediatization. In *Mediatized worlds: Culture and society in a media age*, ed. Andreas Hepp, and Friedrich Krotz, 1–15. London: Palgrave.
Hepp, Andreas, and Communicative Figurations Research Network. 2017. Transforming communications. Media-related changes in times of deep mediatization. *Communicative figurations working paper 16*. Bremen: Universität Bremen.
Hepp, Andreas, Stig Hjarvard, and Knut Lundby. 2015. Mediatization: Theorizing the interplay between media, culture and society. *Media, Culture and Society* 37 (2): 314–324.
Hjarvard, Stig. 2013. *The mediatization of culture and society*. London: Routledge.
Hopkins, Julian. 2015. Assembling blog affordances: Theorising affordances and agency in new media. *EASA Media Anthropology Network's 51st e-seminar*. http://www.media-anthropology.net/file/hopkins_assembling_affordances(2).pdf. Accessed 11 May 2017.

Hutchby, Ian. 2001. Technologies, texts and affordances. *Sociology* 35 (2): 441–456.

Jansson, André, and Johan Lindell. 2014. News media consumption in the transmedia age: Amalgamations, orientations and geo-social structuration. *Journalism Studies* 16 (1): 79–96.

Jensen, Klaus B., and Rasmus Helles. 2015. Audiences across media. A comparative agenda for future research on media audiences. *International Journal of Communication* 9: 291–298.

Krotz, Friedrich. 2007. The meta-process of mediatization as a conceptual frame. *Global Media and Communication* 3 (3): 256–260.

Kunelius, Risto, and Esa Reunanen. 2016. Changing power of journalism: The two phases of mediatization. *Communication Theory* 26: 369–388.

Latour, Bruno. 2007. *Reassembling the social: An introduction to actor-network-theory*. Oxford: Oxford University Press.

Livingstone, Sonia M. 2001. Children and their changing media environment. In *Children and their changing media environment. A European comparative study*, ed. Sonia M. Livingstone, and Moira Bovill, 307–333. London: Lawrence Erlbaum.

Loosen, Wiebke, and Armin Scholl. 2017. Die Komplexität der Komplexitätsforschung. Theoretische Herkunft und Anwendung in der Journalismusforschung. Paper presented at the annual conference of the DGPuK-Fachgruppe Journalistik/Journalismusforschung, February 16 2017, in Würzburg.

Lundby, Knut. 2014. Mediatization of communication. In *Mediatization of communication*, ed. Knut Lundby, 3–35. Berlin: de Gruyter.

Lunt, Peter, and Sonia M. Livingstone. 2016. Is 'mediatization' the new paradigm for our field? A commentary on Deacon and Stanyer (2014, 2015) and Hepp, Harvard and Lundby (2015). *Media, Culture and Society* 38 (3): 462–470.

Madianou, Mirca, and Daniel Miller. 2013. Polymedia: Towards a new theory of digital media in interpersonal communication. *International Journal of Cultural Studies* 16 (6): 169–187.

Mager, Astrid. 2012. Algorithmic ideology. *Information, Communication & Society* 15 (5): 769–787.

Manovich, Lev. 2013. *Software takes command*. New York: Bloomsbury.

Manson, Steven M. 2001. Simplifying complexity: A review of complexity theory. *Geoforum* 32 (3): 405–414.

Martín-Barbero, Jesús. 1993. *Communication, culture, and hegemony: From the media to mediations*. London: Sage.

Morley, David. 1992. *Television audiences and cultural studies*. London: Routledge.

Qvortrup, Lars. 2006. Understanding new digital media medium theory or complexity theory. *European Journal of Communication* 21 (3): 345–356.
Reckwitz, Andreas. 2002. Toward a theory of social practices. A development in culturalist theorizing. *European Journal of Social Theory* 5 (2): 245–265.
Schäfer, Mirko T., and Karin van Es. 2017. *The datafied society. Studying culture through data.*. Amsterdam: Amsterdam University Press.
Schatzki, Theodore R. 2001. Introduction: Practice theory. In *The practice turn in contemporary theory*, ed. Theodore R. Schatzki, Karin Knorr-Cetina, and Eike von Savigny, 10–23. New York: Routledge.
Schrock, Andrew R. 2015. Communicative affordances of mobile media: Portability, availability, locatability, and multimediality. *International Journal of Communication* 9: 1229–1246.
Schrøder, Kim C. 2011. Audiences are inherently cross-media: Audience studies and the cross-media challenge. *Communication Management Quarterly* 18 (6): 5–27.
Silverstone, Roger. 2005. The sociology of mediation and communication. In *Sage handbook of sociology*, ed. Craig Calhoun, Chris Rojek, and Bruce Turner, 188–207. London: Sage.
Thompson, John B. 1995. *The media and modernity. A social theory of the media.* Cambridge: Cambridge University Press.
Turow, Joseph. 2006. *Niche envy. Marketing discrimination in the digital age.* Cambridge, MA: MIT Press.
Turow, Joseph. 2011. *The daily you: How the new advertising industry is defining your identity and your worth.* New Haven: Yale UP.
van Dijck, José. 2014. Datafication, dataism and dataveillance: Big Data between scientific paradigm and ideology. *Surveillance & Society* 12 (2): 197–208.
Walby, Sylvia. 2007. Complexity theory, systems theory, and multiple intersecting social inequalities. *Philosophy of the Social Sciences* 37 (4): 449–470.

Index

O. Driessens et al. (eds.), *Dynamics Of Mediatization*,
Transforming Communications – Studies in Cross-Media Research,
DOI 10.1007/978-3-319-62983-4